PENGUIN BOOKS

ARTIFICIAL LIFE

Steven Levy is the author of two earlier books, *Hackers* and *The Unicorn's Secret*, and he writes a monthly column for the computer magazine *Macworld*. He lives in Massachusetts and New York City, USA.

STEVEN LEVY

_____

ARTIFICIAL LIFE

THE QUEST FOR A NEW CREATION

PENGUIN BOOKS

PENGUIN BOOKS

Published by the Penguin Group
Penguin Books Ltd, 27 Wrights Lane, London W8 5TZ, England
Penguin Books USA Inc., 375 Hudson Street, New York, New York 10014, USA
Penguin Books Australia Ltd, Ringwood, Victoria, Australia
Penguin Books Canada Ltd, 10 Alcorn Avenue, Toronto, Ontario, Canada M4V 3B2
Penguin Books (NZ) Ltd, 182–190 Wairau Road, Auckland 10, New Zealand

Penguin Books Ltd, Registered Offices: Harmondsworth, Middlesex, England

First published by Jonathan Cape 1992
Published in Penguin Books 1993
1 3 5 7 9 10 8 6 4 2

Printed in England by Clays Ltd, St Ives plc

To Andrew

CONTENTS

CONTENTS

PROLOGUE:

IN SILICO

*If patterns of ones and zeros were ''like'' patterns of human lives and death,
if everything about an individual could be represented in a computer record
by a long string of ones and zeros, then what kind of creature would be
represented by a long string of lives and deaths?*

Thomas Pynchon

The creatures cruise silently, skimming the surface of their world with the elegance of ice skaters. They move at varying speeds, some with the variegated cadence of vacillation, others with what surely must be firm purpose. Their bodies—flecks of colors that resemble paper airplanes or pointed confetti—betray their needs. Green ones are hungry. Blue ones seek mates. Red ones want to fight.

They see. A so-called neural network bestows on them vision, and they can perceive the colors of their neighbors and something of the world around them. They know something about their own internal states and can sense fatigue. They learn. Experience teaches them what might make them feel better or what might relieve a pressing need.

They reproduce. Two of them will mate, their genes will merge, and the combination determines the characteristics of the offspring. Over a period of generations, the mechanics of natural selection assert themselves, and fitter creatures roam the landscape.

They die, and sometimes before their bodies decay, others of their ilk devour the corpses. In certain areas, at certain times, cannibal cults arise in which this behavior is the norm. The carcasses are nourishing, but not as much as the food that can be serendipitously discovered on the terrain.

The name of this ecosystem is PolyWorld, and it is located in the chips and disk drives of a Silicon Graphics Iris Workstation. The sole creator of this realm is a researcher named Larry Yaeger, who works for Apple Computer. It is a world inside a computer, whose inhabitants are, in effect, made of mathematics. The creatures have digital DNA. Some of these creatures are more fit than others, and those are the ones who eventually reproduce, forging a path that eventually leads to several sorts of organisms who successfully exploit the peccadilloes of PolyWorld.

"The species have their own unique behaviors and group dynamics," notes Yaeger. One group seems on the edge of psychosis—the "frenetics," who, zipping compulsively through the landscape, constantly desire food and sex and expend energy on little else. Then there is "the cannibal cult," members of which seek their own to mate with, fight with, and eat. They form grotesque clumps from which they need not

3

move in order to fulfill any of those needs. A third species is the "edge runner." Owing to a peculiarity in the landscape—unlike our own spherical planet, PolyWorld can be programmed to have a distinct end of the world—there is a benefit in lurking on the brim of oblivion. Once a respectable number of fellow creatures adopt this behavior, there will always be an ample supply of conjugal partners, as well as old carcasses now turned to food.

Yaeger is cautious about sweeping statements; he prefers to describe what he has done and what might immediately follow from it. "So far what PolyWorld has shown is that successful organisms in a biologically motivated and only somewhat complex environment have evolved adaptive strategies for living in this environment," he says. When it comes to describing the creatures themselves, Yaeger is less tentative.

"I see them," he says, "as artificial life."

In September 1987, more than one hundred scientists and technicians gathered in Los Alamos, New Mexico, to establish the new science of artificial life. The event celebrated a technological and scientific watershed. A deepened understanding of biological mechanisms, along with the exponentially increasing power of digital computers, had brought humankind to the threshold of duplicating nature's masterpiece, living systems. The pioneers were both thrilled at the prospect and humbled by previous speculations of what lay ahead. The legacy of Mary Shelley, who wrote of Frankenstein and his monster, as well as the dark accomplishments hatched on the very site of the conference, hovered over the proceedings like, as one participant put it, a bugaboo.

Nevertheless, the mood was exuberant. Many of the scientists drawn to Los Alamos had long dreamed of an aggregate effort to create a new form of life; their individual labors had looked toward that day. Now it had arrived. The significance of the moment was later framed by a physicist named James Doyne Farmer, who coauthored a paper about the implications of this new science. Its abstract alone was perhaps as striking a description of nascent technology at the lab as any since the development of the atomic bomb. Those who read it would have been well advised to take a deep breath—and perhaps suspend disbelief until resuming aspiration—before reading the following prediction:

> Within fifty to a hundred years a new class of organisms is likely to emerge. These organisms will be artificial in the sense that they will originally be designed by humans. However, they will reproduce, and will evolve into something other than their original form; they will be "alive" under any reasonable definition of the word. . . . The advent of artificial life will be the most significant historical event since the emergence of human beings. . . .

Artificial life, or a-life, is devoted to the creation and study of lifelike organisms and systems built by humans. The stuff of this life is nonorganic matter, and its essence is information: computers are the kilns from which these new organisms emerge. Just as medical scientists have managed to tinker with life's mechanisms in vitro, the biologists and computer scientists of a-life hope to create life *in silico*.

The degree to which this resembles real, "wet" life varies; many experimenters admit freely that their laboratory creations are simply simulations of aspects of life. The goal of these practitioners of "weak" a-life is to illuminate and understand more clearly the life that exists on earth and possibly elsewhere. As astronomer A. S. Eddington has said, "the contemplation in natural science of a wider domain than the actual leads to a far better understanding of the actual." By simulating a kind of life different from that with which we are familiar, a-life scientists seek to explore paths that no form of life in the universe has yet taken, the better to understand the concepts and limits of life itself.

Hoping that the same sorts of behavior found in nature will spontaneously emerge from the simulations, sometimes scientists attempt to model directly processes characteristic of living systems. Biologists treat these artificial systems as the ultimate laboratory animals; their characteristics illuminate the traits of known organisms, but, since their composition is transparent, they are much more easily analyzed than rats, plants, or *E. coli*. Physicists pursue a-life in the hope that the synthesis of life will shed light on a related quest: the understanding of all complex nonlinear systems, which are thought to be ruled by universal forces not yet comprehended. By studying phenomena such as self-organization in a-life, these mysteries may soon be unraveled.

The boldest practitioners of this science engage in "strong" a-life. They look toward the long-term development of actual living organisms whose essence is information. These creatures may be embodied in corporeal form—a-life robots—or they may live within a computer. Whichever, these creations, as Farmer insisted, are intended to be "alive under every reasonable definition of the word"—as much as bacteria, plants, animals, and human beings.

Many might consider this an absurd claim on the face of it. How could something inside a computer ever be considered alive? Could anything synthesized by humans ever aspire to such a classification? Should not the term "life" be restricted to nature's domain?

The question is difficult to answer, largely because we have no "reasonable definition" of life. Nearly two thousand years ago, Aristotle made the observation that by "possessing life," one implied that "a thing can nourish itself and decay." Most everyone also agreed that the capacity for self-reproduction is a necessary condition for life. From there, opinions diverged and still do. One could devise a laundry list of qualities characteristic of life, but these inevitably fail. They are either overly discriminating or excessively lenient. The creatures in PolyWorld, for instance, are in many ways lifelike—they grow, reproduce, adapt, and evolve. Yet even their creator dares not claim that they are truly alive.

Some scientists suggest that the definition-of-life question is a red herring. Life, they say, should be gauged on a continuum, and not granted according to a binary decision. A rock would certainly be low on any continuum of aliveness, and a dog, a tree, and a human being would rank highly. More ambiguous systems would fall in a middle region of semialiveness—somewhere below bacteria, which almost everyone agrees are alive, and somewhere above rocks. Viruses, which some biologists consider living and others do not, would reside in the upper reaches of this middle ground. Below that would be complex systems that no one really considers to be alive but that display some behaviors consistent with living organisms—things such as the economy and automobiles. The PolyWorld organisms would fall somewhere between Chevrolets and the flu. There is a particular advantage in regarding life in this manner: using systems that no one would classify as truly alive, biologists could nonetheless isolate the *qualities* of life.

But this, too, is unsatisfying. One feels that it *should* mean something to be alive, even as one concedes the apparent impossibility in fixing the borderline between life and nonlife. Part of the difficulty arises from culture's refusal to yield the province of life to the realm of science. For centuries, a mystical component, if not an unabashed nod to divinity, loitered in whatever definition one chose to use. Despite attempts by iconoclasts and visionaries to use empirical means to recognize life, for most of history people felt that a supernatural component bestowed the property of life on otherwise-inert materials.

As scientists came to discard those beliefs, their idea of life shifted to accommodate new discoveries. After the identification of the cell, they thought differently about how matter organized itself into living structures. And once it was understood how critical Darwin's contribution was to the life sciences, evolution became a central issue in defining life. To some, evolution remains *the* central issue. "Life should be defined by the possession of those properties which are needed to ensure evolution by natural selection," writes John Maynard Smith, not surprisingly an evolutionary biologist. "That is, entities with the properties of multiplication, variation, and heredity are alive, and entities lacking one or more of those properties are not." The more recent discovery of DNA as a pervasive and essential component in all matter generally regarded as living added another wrinkle: not only did living things contain blueprints for their operation and reproduction, but also these unique collections of molecules contained elements of the history of all life. "The possession of a genetic program provides for an absolute difference between organisms and inanimate matter," writes Ernst Mayr. "Nothing comparable exists in the inanimate world, except for manmade computers." (Note the sole, but significant, exception.)

The latest twist on our perception of the necessary conditions for aliveness comes from the recognition of complex systems theory as a key component in biology. A complex system is one whose component parts interact with sufficient intricacy that they cannot be predicted by standard linear equations; so many variables are at work in the system that its overall behavior can only be understood as an emergent consequence of the holistic sum of all the myriad behaviors embedded within. Reductionism does not work with complex systems, and it is now clear that a purely reductionist approach cannot be applied when studying life: in living systems, the whole is more than the sum of its parts. As we shall see, this is the result not of a mysterious dram of vital life-giving fluid but rather the benefits of complexity, which allow certain behaviors and characteristics to emerge unbidden. The mechanics of this may have been hammered out by evolution, but the engine of evolution cannot begin to fire until a certain degree of complexity is present. Living systems epitomize complexity, so much so that some scientists now see complexity as a defining characteristic of life.

But complexity is only one more item on the laundry list. Despite all our scientific knowledge, "there is no generally accepted definition of life," as Carl Sagan flatly states in his *Encyclopedia Britannica* essay on the topic. Philosopher Mark Bedau contends that the question "should be considered one of the fundamental concepts of philosophy, but philosophers haven't thought of it much. Nor have biologists. They typically throw up their hands. It's not a natural property like water—you can investigate water and say, 'there's H_2O, that's its essence.' But life isn't material, it's ephemeral."

Philosophers, too, can throw up their hands at the dilemma. "I really doubt that a purely philosophical answer to these questions is possible," writes Elliott Sober. The University of Wisconsin philosopher contends that ultimately, the question is not important. "If a machine can extract energy from its environment, grow, repair damage to its body, and reproduce," he asks, "what remains of the issue whether it is 'really' alive?"

Yet such a machine would not close the issue but open it. Many people would find it threatening to consider an artificial organism as described above as literally alive. Now most human beings will not regard anything as living if it is not composed of the same matter as natural biological organisms. Physicist Gerald Feinberg and biologist Robert Shapiro have coined a term for those who "believe that all life must be based on the chemistry of carbon compounds and must operate in an aqueous (water) medium": "carbaquists." Yet no one has effectively argued that life could never exist in other forms.

The things we now consider alive are possibly only a subset of a larger class of organisms. By chance, by an unfortunate accident of history, we have been presented with this limited spectrum of possible life-forms and no others. Our challenge, then, is to anticipate which characteristics of life as we know it are peculiar to that subset, and which are universal of all life, even the potential forms we have yet to see or, as the case may be, to build—to contemplate, and then create, *life-as-it-could-be* (to use the term coined by Christopher Langton, who organized the first a-life conference).

"If scientists are going to develop a broad theory of life, it's going to require them to accept radically non-organic things as being alive" says Langton. "Most biologists are generally hesitant to do this now. It will take a while to get processes like this that will convince biologists that these things are alive, in the sense that people are alive. But we're going to get them."

This book is about that quest: the effort to create the processes of life itself, with the intended effect of changing the way the world thinks. If Langton and his colleagues achieve their goals, human beings will see themselves in a different light. We will not be standing at the pinnacle of some self-defined evolutionary hierarchy but will rank as particularly complex representatives of one subset of life among many possible alternatives.

Our uniqueness will lie in the ability to create our own successors.

Artificial life is something quite different from genetic engineering, which uses fully evolved wet life as its starting point. The scientists of a-life are devising the means by which actual living systems can be generated, evolved, and observed. Theirs is an effort to engineer the course of evolution and extend the range of living systems on planet earth and beyond. From this grand experiment, a more profound understanding of life itself, an ability to use its mechanisms to perform our work and, perhaps, the discovery of powerful laws of nature that govern not only biological systems but also any series of complex nonlinear self-organizing interactions may ultimately arise.

What drives men and women engaged in the quest for a-life is a desire to decipher the vast tangle of obscurities that nature has laid before us, particularly in regard to the deepest question of all, What is life?

Working in different disciplines these researchers have concluded that the way to answer that question is not merely to observe but to create. The first step is believing it can be done, and there is convincing evidence that it can be done. The next step is doing it. Though it may take many years in terms of the life span in human individuals, in the scope of evolutionary time the result could be accomplished within an instant. In any case, this fearsome work is underway, and this book will introduce you to the remarkable people performing it.

With the fruits of their labors, we may come to know what it means to be alive. By making life, we may finally know what life is.

THE PROMISED LAND

Anybody who looks at living organisms knows perfectly well that they can produce other organisms like themselves. This is their normal function, they wouldn't exist if they didn't do this, and it's plausible that this is the reason why they abound in the world. In other words, living organisms are very complicated aggregations of elementary parts, and by any reasonable theory of probability or thermodynamics highly improbable. That they should occur in the world at all is a miracle of the first magnitude. . . .

John von Neumann

He died so prematurely, seeing the promised land but hardly entering it.

Stanislaw M. Ulam, of his friend von Neumann

Von Neumann was dying. One day in 1954 his shoulder exploded so fiercely with pain that he could hardly stand. It was an emissary of prostate cancer, spreading beyond hope. He had only months to live. His famous demeanor—strikingly jovial, relentlessly energetic, exhaustively probing, buoyantly informed—now sagged. He was still capable of piercing wit, and his mathematical skills, unparalleled in our century, seemed intact. But friends noticed an uncharacteristic melancholy. "There was a sadness in him," wrote a colleague of many years, of von Neumann's final visit to Los Alamos, "and he frequently seemed to look around, as if, it occurred to me later, he might have been thinking this was perhaps his last visit and he wanted to remember the scenery, the mountains, the places he knew so well and where he had so often had interesting and pleasant times."

In his fifty-three years, John von Neumann made full use of his extraordinary mind, "a perfect instrument whose gears were machined to mesh accurately within a thousandth of an inch," according to one admiring Nobel laureate. He was a math prodigy in Budapest, and his family, prosperous Jewish bankers, had the wherewithal to provide him with schooling to cultivate his abilities. He earned a doctorate at twenty-two, at twenty-three became the youngest person to lecture at the University of Berlin, and at thirty, along with Albert Einstein, he was appointed one of the first professors of the Institute for Advanced Study, in Princeton, New Jersey. Though his skill at calculation and memorization would become legendary—he could recall verbatim lists of names from phone books and esoterica of Byzantine culture from history books—his curiosity led him to creative leaps that propelled him to the forefront of his generation. He helped hammer out the niceties of quantum mechanics in the cafes of Göttingen, virtually invented game theory in Berlin, solved ergodic mathematical questions in Princeton, helped concoct the A-bomb in Los Alamos, and made so crucial a contribution to the development of the electronic digital computer that almost all such machines are referred to as von Neumann processors. It is unknown whether a smile crossed the face of physicist Hans Bethe

13

when he said, "I have sometimes wondered whether a brain like von Neumann's does not indicate a species superior to that of man." Indeed, the joke was that Johnny, as he was known to friends, was in fact not human but a demigod; however, he understood *Homo sapiens* so well that he could convincingly simulate them.

Von Neumann's belief in his own invulnerability was evident in his own disregard for the consequences of physics when behind the wheel of an automobile; he totaled approximately one car a year and emerged unscathed. Now cancer had come to claim him. "Now that this thing has come," he asked of his doctor, "how shall I spend the remainder of my life?" The answer: work on what is most important to you.

Two activities occupied him during that period. The first involved weaponry, the technology of death. The second was something relatively abstract: the technology of life.

The first involved his government duties. Only three months before the cancer appeared, von Neumann had been sworn onto the Atomic Energy Commission and in that capacity was the main scientific voice in the country's nuclear weapons establishment. One indication of his influence there: the nation's ballistic missile committee was called the von Neumann group. The mathematician was not shy about advocating the use of the horrible weaponry he helped conceive and, perhaps recalling his family's retreat from Communist Hungary, actually favored preventative nuclear war. Through his illness he continued his work, and, up until his last hospital visit, he consulted in top-secret sessions with representatives of the Cold War brain trust.

His scientific pursuits stood in contrast with his weaponry labors. Von Neumann had become infatuated with the similarities of the computer—or, more precisely, with what this machine could become—and with the workings of nature. His goal was to create a theory that would encompass both biologies, natural and artificial.

The idea that the behavior of living organisms could be viewed as equivalent to the behavior of machines came easily to someone of von Neumann's temperament. His world was built on logical principle. When you boiled down any phenomenon, its essence would consist of the axioms that produced it. When von Neumann was first told of the efforts to build a supercalculating machine that would become the first electronic computer, he immediately inquired of the device's logic-based operations. It would be von Neumann who engineered the idea that a computer was first and foremost a logic machine, not merely something that dully crunched numbers. Life was no different. Not surprisingly, von Neumann regarded life itself as a reconstructible concatenation of events and interactions. Mysticism did not enter the equation. Nor did randomness: "I shudder at the thought," he wrote, "that highly purposive organizational elements, like the protein, should originate in a random process."

Von Neumann would readily admit that biological organisms were complex, more complicated than any artificial structure man had ever pondered. But ultimately, because he believed life was based on logic, he believed that we were capable of forcing organisms to surrender their secrets. It could be done. It would be done. Von Neumann set about doing it.

In the late 1940s, he was invited to give a series of lectures on the subject. The most famous was delivered in Pasadena, California, as part of something called the Hixon Symposium. His audience consisted of fellow scientists: physicists, biologists, medical researchers. His host was the future Nobel Prize winner Linus Pauling. There were no computer scientists in attendance because, of course, the field did not exist, except perhaps in von Neumann's head. Though the lecture was not particularly technical, the bold subject matter made for heady stuff, even for this sophisticated audience. One listener compared the experience to "the delightful but difficult role of hanging on the tail of a kite."

The lecture was titled, "The General and Logical Theory of Automata." By the term "automata," von Neumann was referring to self-operating machines, specifically any such machine whose behavior could be unerringly defined in mathematical terms. An automaton is a machine that processes information, proceeding logically, inexorably performing its next action after applying data received from outside itself in light of instructions programmed within itself. Since von Neumann saw no reason why organisms, from bacteria to human beings, could not be viewed as machines—and vice versa—this term in his hand connoted something more flexible than the word's usual implication. If you understood automata, the implication was, you understood not only machinery better—you understood life.

The most interesting part of the Hixon lecture, and certainly the most unconventional, dealt with the concept of self-reproduction. Could an artificial machine produce a copy of itself, he wondered, that would in turn be capable of creating more copies? (Just as natural machines—ferns, parrots, and humans—do?)

A positive answer would be a strong indication that the link between artificial and natural automata was strong. Creating offspring is a prime common-sense criterion for determining whether something is alive. When René Descartes declared to the queen of France that animals indeed were a class of automata, Her Royal Highness pointed to a clock, and said, "See to it that it produces offspring." Descartes was stumped, but von Neumann believed he could satisfy those conditions. Yes, a machine *could* reproduce itself, he asserted. He was going to prove it.

Von Neumann regarded automata theory as his crowning achievement. He spoke on it, discussed it with his colleagues, and prepared to write a definitive book on the subject. But the manuscript would never be completed—nor would his other explorations in the previously untrodden territory where life and machinery overlap.

In April 1956, von Neumann entered Walter Reed Hospital. Among the papers he brought along with him were notes for a series of lectures he had agreed to present at Yale University, "The Computer and the Brain." The point of the lectures was that computers and human beings are different classes of automata; the lectures would compare and contrast, the better to understand both cases. Originally, he had agreed to speak for five days; after his illness he still hoped to deliver the lectures, somewhat abbreviated, from the wheelchair to which he had been consigned. Even that was overly optimistic. He would not leave the hospital grounds again.

"Even Johnny's exceptional mind could not overcome the weariness of the body," wrote Klara von Neumann, and, on February 8, 1957, John von Neumann died. His last days had been attended by air-force orderlies cleared at top-secret security levels, in case he spilled out classified information in his final delirium. But von Neumann uttered no more secrets.

Nevertheless, von Neumann's legacy on the subject of automata theory was enough to clearly distinguish the Hungarian mathematician as the father of what would come to be the field of artificial life. He also fathered a mental construct known as the self-reproducing automaton. There were several species of this creature, though he managed to develop fully only two before his death.

Von Neumann acknowledged the sensational implications of this work. In a letter to Norbert Wiener he stated that word of the "reproductive potentialities of the machines of the future" should be kept out of the press. As for himself, he boasted, "I have been quite virtuous and had no journalistic contacts whatever."

Von Neumann was aware of the stigma assigned to those who tried to produce lifelike processes by artificial means. The ghost of Mary Shelley's Frankenstein monster, and any other number of more recent science-fiction scenarios, cast a mottled shadow over such enterprises. It was better to proceed benignly with his work, of which the overwhelming bulk was conducted in his head, or with pen and paper—though he had a brief flirtation with Tinkertoys, which he quickly abandoned, turning over the dowels and wheels to the grandson of fellow scientist Oskar Morgenstern. There was no hint of the startling implications of this sort of work. But John von Neumann was initiating a new era in what had previously been only a dark recess of science—or quasi science as some would have it. Trying to extend life in a realm where none had existed.

For most of history, this was a mystical quest rather than a rational one. Scientists regarded life as dependent on a certain quality bestowed on its parts. The idea that one could produce it by duplicating its physics, its materials, was to them absurd. What was required, instead, was to replace what was understood to be the essence of life, and this was something supernatural, a trespass on the divine. According to the biblical creation story it was God, after all, who

> . . . formed man of the dust of the ground, and breathed into his
> nostrils the breath of life, and man became a living soul.

Though it was not man's place to infuse inanimate objects with the breath of life, ancient legends and tales speculated on such occasions. Pygmalion made a statue come to life. Dion Cassius, a second-century Roman historian, reported other statues with some alarming capabilities: they bled, they sweated, they swooned at the sight of an evil figure, and they turned respectfully toward conquering generals. In Jewish fable, a learned rabbi vivified a lump of clay as a beast called a golem, who began life as a servant but eventually haunted its creator.

That was myth. The reality was an unnavigable gulf between living and nonliving. Aristotle, one of the few philosophers ever to devote much time to defining life, believed that what distinguished organisms from their inanimate surroundings was possession of a soul. While only man had the highest variety of soul, animals and even plants had less impressive models. In the case of any organism, he wrote, "bodies exist only for the sake of the soul." So how could one create life, unless one were in possession of the breath of life, soul material?

For centuries, there seemed little reason to question that concept. Even the discoveries of the seventeenth-century British physician and medical researcher William Harvey failed to tarnish it. Though Harvey disproved such misconceptions as the eruption of flies from dung (even Aristotle believed that animals could arise from mud), he still held that life had some divine component, infused while the organism was *in ovo*, or in the egg. *Omne vivum ex ovo,* said Harvey—no life except from life.

But the Industrial Revolution and its contemporary companions, the revelations of Newtonian physics and laws of thermodynamics, began to extend science's domain, and the biological realm became less forbiddingly mystical. Newton's worldview indicated that we could predict where all the celestial bodies would be at a certain time—might not the work of life be equally predictable? A new school of thought emerged, which regarded life as a mechanistic process.

According to mechanism, life was literally an automaton, like a clockwork.

Could it then be duplicated? Mechanists like Descartes and Leibniz seemed to think it possible. And certain people ventured into this implausible territory. They proceeded in the spirit of the early builders of a special kind of automata, mechanical devices that seemed to demonstrate lifelike behavior. These automata were concocted with the elegance of Swiss watches, combined with Rube Goldberg ingenuity. They took advantage not only of gears but also of gravity, hydraulics, pulleys, and sunlight. The effect could be dazzling, as with the extraordinary clock of Berne. Created in 1530, this massive timepiece hourly disgorged a dazzling pageantry of automata figures, beginning with a crowing cock and followed by a carefully choreographed procession in which the nodding head of a clock king allowed passage of a parade of spear-wielding bear cubs and a ferocious lion.

Undoubtedly entertaining, these made no pretensions to usurp nature. But later automata made tentative steps toward the murky line dividing life from nonlife. The most famous of these was the creation of Jacques de Vaucanson, a Frenchman in his twenties who in 1738 dazzled Paris with "an artificial duck made of gilded copper who drinks, eats, quacks, splashes about the water, and digests his food like a living duck." Displayed throughout Europe, the duck confounded its audiences. Its complexity was prodigious, with over four hundred moving pieces in a single wing. When the duck fell into disrepair in the early 1800s, Goethe bemoaned its fate: "We found Vaucanson's automata completely paralyzed," he wrote in his journal. "The duck had lost its feathers and, reduced to a skeleton, would still bravely eat its oats but could no longer digest them."

A Swiss inventor named Rechsteiner revived the duck and triumphantly reintroduced the automaton at Milan's Scala Theater in 1844. Rechsteiner then took 3 years to build his own artificial duck, which he displayed at Munich's Royal Odeon before, among other dignitaries, King Louis I of Bavaria.

The newspaper *Das freie Wort* offered a detailed description of this marvelous new fowl's behavior. Apparently the duck's movements were sufficiently natural to convince the observers that an intelligence lay beneath its motions. When fed, the duck greedily snarfed its porridge, pausing periodically to raise his head and stare at its astonished onlookers. Then came the climax: ". . . the contractions of the bird's body clearly show that his stomach is a bit upset by this rapid meal and the effects of a painful digestion become obvious. However the brave little bird holds out, and after a few minutes we are convinced in the most concrete manner that he has overcome his internal difficulties. The truth is that the smell which now spreads through the room becomes almost unbearable. . . ."

Since the model no longer exists, the description can only ignite our imaginations. Had Rechsteiner and his predecessor de Vaucanson acquired such deep understanding of life that the creations themselves were worthy of serious study? It would have been fascinating, even enlightening, for nineteenth-century biologists to study these man-made ducks, to compare their machinations with those of nature and perhaps to acquire insights on alternative approaches to such metabolic phenomena as digestion and flatulence. One newspaper account of 1847 seems to argue just that, that Rechsteiner's talented mallard was a biological model of scientific significance.

> . . . All the movements and attitudes of this automaton faithfully reproduce nature, copying it to the life even down to the tiniest detail, so much so that for a moment we are tempted to believe that there is a real duck before us, whereas all these movements are carried out by the most complicated mechanisms. The inventor's mastery is shown particularly on the three occasions when the duck is doing something, when he is breathing, digesting, and evacuating. Here is clearly something more than mere mechanical ability. The artist has penetrated into the deepest secrets of the process of assimilation and of alimentary chemistry. Since life depends on electro-magnetic activity, the inventor has also used that in his automation.

> It is just this grasp of the secret of natural processes and the practical application of this knowledge which we consider an immense step forward in the world of natural science, especially in physiology, and we have no doubt that the discoveries of this master mind will make his name immortal.

But the obvious differences between the mechanical model and its natural inspiration—the presence of screws and springs instead of organs and bone—only underlay the difficulty of creating life and particularly the difficulty of convincing critics that the stuff of engineering could produce something alive. Those who disagreed with the mechanists were quick to reaffirm their certainty that the effort was an impossibility. Despite Harvey and Pasteur, and even Darwin and Descartes, the intuitive assertions of Aristotle still prevailed.

The most vocal of these critics called themselves vitalists. This term was taken from the so-called vital force or *élan vital* that supposedly existed only in living organisms. Vitalists themselves varied on the nature of this force. Some believed it a chemical; others claimed it was some immaterial agent. By the nineteenth century many were convinced that the agent was electricity, and as proof they pointed to that force's ability to twitch the limbs of the dead. Vitalistic writings ranged from *Frankenstein* (who drew a spark of life from electricity) to the ideas of Henri Bergson.

The vitalists voiced the suspicions of the vast majority of the population, who thought that *of course* there was a divine component to life and who thought it perfectly reasonable that some special material might well divide living from nonliving matter. Vitalism's final significant flag bearer was German biologist Hans Driesch. He argued his case with the fervor of an apostate. In 1891, Driesch visited the zoology station in Trieste, Italy, where he saw experiments in sea urchin embryos that seemed to contradict what was accepted biological theory. When a single embryo was split at a very early stage, a complete sea urchin grew from each cell cluster. His misinterpretation of the phenomenon assumed that a vital force, which he called an entelechy, was at work. An entelechy was a "nonmechanical causal agent" that "contained its own goal." After his sea urchin epiphany, Driesch spent a contentious lifetime attempting to reconcile science with vitalism, taking pathetic swipes at Darwinism along the way. Citing what he considered empirical truths and embellishing his views with complicated conjectures concerning entelechies, which roughly corresponded to Aristotle's view of the soul, he continued his struggle well into the twentieth century. "A true doctrine is never completely extinguished," he wrote. "It may for a time be out-shouted by its opponents, but there are always a few who, whatever may befall, pursue their way, heedless of all the uproar of the day."

Though it would be a difficult task to unearth a modern scientist subscribing to that true doctrine, vitalism of a sort seems to persist. There remains in us all an atavistic tendency to surrender biological prerogatives to any so-called beings outside the known family of earthbound organisms. There is a particular reluctance to concede the honor of life-form to anything created synthetically. This reluctance often transforms itself into profound skepticism, even mockery, when one suggests that life could be fashioned in a laboratory or in a computer, by using as the main substrate not organic molecules or other familiar forms of chemistry but something quite different—information.

Information. The premise being that the basis of life is information, steeped in a dynamical system complex enough to reproduce and to bear offspring more complex than the parent.

This was von Neumann's premise.

Information was what made John von Neumann's creature, his self-reproducing machine, different from the automata of his engineering predecessors. At the center of its being was its blueprint, which dictated not only its behavior but also its reproductive activity.

Admittedly, this was a daring crossover. A leap over a foreboding chasm is required before one can grant a construction of pure logic some of the powers of a living, breathing being.

What made even considering the matter possible was the work of the logician Alan Turing, who like von Neumann had a profound impact on the development of modern computers. In 1936, Turing concocted his own imaginary automaton. The Turing machine, as it became known, made no bid to join the society of living creatures. It could be visualized more as a sophisticated tape player, with an arbitrarily extendable tape. (Remember, this device existed only in the imagination, where million-mile-long tapes and centuries-long processes could find reasonable accommodations.) The tape was marked off in sections and in each section resided a bit of information. The tape head, a device that moved over the tape, was capable both of reading these bits and, if necessary, of erasing what was on a square or of writing on a square.

There was also a control mechanism in the tape head, which told it what to do as it read each piece of information. Its characteristics and behavior qualified it as being what was known as a finite state machine (FSM). It could also be called a finite automaton.

This deceptively simple device separated all information into two elements—that which came from an object's internal state and that which was derived externally. Also assumed was that our universe is granular; that is, that it moves in discrete time steps, although these could be as small as one imagined, even billionths of a second. During any of these instances, an FSM would be in a certain describable state. The description could be extremely intricate or very simple; the only limitation was that it had to be one of a finite set of possible states. (The number could be very high but not infinite.) Between the current instant and the next discrete time step, the FSM, using whatever sensory input that particular machine had available to it, would take note of the external world. Then, referring to a "rule table" controlling behavior, the FSM would consider both that sensory input and its own current state to determine what behavior the machine would exhibit, as well as which internal state the machine would assume in that time step.

A simple example of an FSM is the children's game of musical chairs. Here, the world is broken down into obvious time steps, defined by pauses in the music. Players could be in any of four states: sitting, standing, moving, and leaving the game. The rules of the musical chairs universe are as follows:

If one is sitting, and there is no music, remain in that state.
If one is sitting, and there is music, change to the moving state.
If one is moving and there is music, remain in that state.
If one is moving and there is no music, change to the sitting state if there is a chair, and change to the standing state if there is no chair.
If one is in the standing state, leave the game.
If one has left the game, remain in that state.

In the game of musical chairs, each participant acts like a finite state machine, noting two things: his or her internal state, and the external condition of the world—the music. At each point in the game, the players apply this information to the rule table to determine both how to behave and their subsequent states.

In the Turing machine, the FSM head would work this way: The tape head might be in a given state A, and it may be resting on part of the tape containing a numeral 1. Before the next step it would read that information and consult a rule table for the confluence of those two circumstances. The result might yield something like the following: replace the "1" with a "0," move the tape head one space to the left and change to state B. The process would repeat, with the tape head reading the information on the space to which it had just moved.

What made the Turing machine extremely powerful was the storing capability of its extendable tape. With the proper information on that tape, the Turing machine could emulate the actions of a different machine. If, for instance, someone playing musical chairs carried a Turing machine outfitted with the proper rules on its tape, he or she could use its output to play the game without having to cogitate. The ultimate Turing machine would be able to read any set of rules from its tape. In fact, Turing proved that such a machine, the universal Turing machine, would also be a universal computer. (There was a specific mathematical proof that determined this quality.) This meant that, given enough time, it could emulate *any* machine whose behavior was susceptible to being described thoroughly. Turing and his collaborator, philosopher Alonzo Church, further presented the Physical Church-Turing Hypothesis, which stated that such a machine could duplicate not only the functions of mathematical machines but also the functions of nature.

This made sense when one looked at the world through Turing's consciousness. In that view, almost anything could be analyzed as a state machine. For what determined the behavior of any machine but what was inside it (its state) and what it drew from its environment (information from the tape)?

The Church-Turing Hypothesis could also apply to the human mind. If one conceded that the number of possible states of mind was finite (and some people did not make that concession), a reasonable yet disturbing result followed. At any instant a single mind found itself in one of those possible states. Before the next instant, sensory input would arrive. The environmental information in combination with the initial state would determine both the person's behavior and the next state of the mind. Turing's contention was that the mind, as a finite state machine, had simply followed a logical protocol—essentially, it had followed a rule table determined by biological and physical forces—in order to get to that next state.

Over the next fifty years Turing's creation became a focal point for arguments raging over whether a machine could acquire intelligence. Many cognitive scientists insisted that a computer could accomplish this—in the realm of logic, all electronic digital computers were proven to be equivalents of Turing machines, and thus they qualified as universal computers. Other scientists disagreed, arguing that the mind could never be considered an FSM—its state could not be so crisply described, nor could a rule table be drawn to emulate infallibly human thought. But von Neumann was less interested in what would later be known as the realm of artificial intelligence (AI) than in what would be known as a-life, the world of artificial life. By concentrating on self-reproduction, his focus was life rather than mind.

The natural behavior of artificial structures had actually been a leitmotiv in von Neumann's 1940s work on computers. Between 1939 and 1940, he corresponded with a fellow Hungarian, physicist Rudolph Ortvay, who first suggested a connection between the brain and electronic calculating equipment. In 1943, von Neumann read a paper by Warren McCulloch and Walter Pitts. Titled "A Logical Calculus of the Ideas Immanent in Nervous Activity," it presented a method of using a mathematical model to emulate the functions of the nervous system: an artificial neural network. Von Neumann associated this development with Turing's contention that a universal machine could emulate any system of computation. Here was a system that suggested that living organisms themselves had a built-in computer system whose output determined behavior! "Anything that can be exhaustively and unambiguously described, anything that can be completely and unambiguously put into work, is ipso facto realizable by a suitable finite neural network," von Neumann told the Hixon Symposium.

Thus, as Turing and Church had intuited, a universal computer could match the mental functions of any living creature. Living things were indeed among those machines that the Turing machine could emulate. It would take a very long tape, of course, to duplicate the actions of a human being, or even a much simpler life-form such as a beetle, an oak tree, or a bacterium. But it could be done. The logical basis seemed impeccable. One did not need to build the actual machine to understand the message: life was a class of automata.

Von Neumann realized that biology offered the most powerful information processing system available by far and that its emulation would be the key to powerful artificial systems. In his work on computer design, von Neumann viewed the various parts of the computer as organs. The switching devices that he used for the early computers—and-gates, or-gates, not-gates, and delay circuits—were modeled on neurons.

In the same spirit, he designed an artificial creature. It would assume biology's most intricate function, self-reproduction.

The first self-reproducing automaton von Neumann imagined was a species of computer, composed of switches, delays, and other information-passing parts. But it was not to be a construct of information but rather a solid mass, existing in a real world. Besides its computational elements, the automaton also had five other components:

1. A manipulating element (like a hand), which accepted its orders from the computing (control) part of the machine.

2. A cutting element, capable of disconnecting two elements when told to by the computer.

3. A fusing element that could connect two parts.

4. A sensing element, which could recognize any of the parts and convey this information to the computer.

5. "Girders" that were rigid structural elements and provided not only a chassis for the creature but also an information-storage facility.

The beast also had a habitat. Its environment was a huge reservoir—an endless lake fortuitously stocked with the same sorts of elements of which the beast itself was made up.

The body parts of the creature were arranged in such a way to consist of three main subsystems—and a crucial appendage. One could view von Neumann's self-reproducing automaton as a triad of symbiotic structures. The first, Component A, was a sort of factory, which would gather materials from the lake and arrange them according to instructions fed to it from another component.

The second part of this trinity, Component B, functioned as a duplicator: its job was to read informational instructions and copy them.

Component C was the control apparatus, the computer itself.

The instructions themselves would be Component D. These would be arranged in a long string, read like a ticker tape. Physically, they consisted of a long series of girders arranged in a sawtooth formation. At each juncture, the presence or absence of an intersecting girder indicated either a "1" or a "0." Thus placing a girder at an intersection was effectively the same thing as putting a mark on a tape—or fixing a bit inside a computer memory. Reading this long tape of girders, one compiled a binary number, which, when decoded, yielded information. Because the string of girders was assumed to stretch quite a distance— many miles—the nature of the information could be extremely complex, more so than the information in a book of text.

The self-reproduction began, and the automaton came alive, so to speak, by reading the instruction girder-tape. Component C read the instruction, fed it to the duplicator (Component B), which copied it, and gave the duplicate instruction to the factory, while storing the original.

The factory, reading the instruction tape, paddled out onto the vast lake, evaluating the various parts as they drifted past. Its commission was to look for a certain part with which to begin constructing its offspring. When it sensed a match, it grasped the part with its hand, holding it until it found the next part. Then it welded the second part to the first. When the construction was completed, the automaton built a second factory, a duplicator, and a computer. But one crucial step remained, and it was this step that established the prescient brilliance of von Neumann's thought experiment. This occurred when the long girder-tape, Component D, which was retained by the parent duplicator, was inserted into the new offspring. By bequeathing to the new creature a copy of the

Information is stored in von Neumann's kinematic self-reproducing automaton by means of connecting "girders," scavenged from the infinite lake in which it resides. Here no girders intersect these junctures perpendicularly; therefore this series would be read as 000000.

Here, the first, second, and fourth junctures in the sawtooth pattern are intersected by vertical girders. Reading these sections as "1" and blank sections as "0," one would decode this series as 110100. Using this method, and a great many girders, one could encode unlimited information.

reproductive instructions, the new creature would be "fertile," able to repeat the process.

This concatenation of events would sound almost trivially familiar to anyone with a working knowledge of biology, because von Neumann's automaton, although it was conceived several years before the discovery of the DNA molecule, essentially mirrored the reproductive process in natural life. Perhaps with some ironic understatement, von Neumann told his audience at the Hixon lecture that

the description of this automaton has some further attractive sides. . . . For instance it is quite clear that the instruction [tape] is roughly effecting the functions of a gene. It is also clear that the copying mechanism B performs the fundamental act of reproduction, the duplication of the genetic material, which is clearly the fundamental operation in the multiplication of living cells. It is also easy to see how arbitrary alterations of the system . . . can exhibit certain typical traits which appear in connection with mutation, lethally as a rule, but with a possibility of continuing reproduction with a modification of traits.

In other words, not only did these automata reproduce as we did, but over time they had the capacity to evolve into something more complex than their original state. Again, just as we did.

If one viewed von Neumann's imaginary creatures as a hypothesis, then the work of Watson and Crick and their successors was empirical validation. As physicist Freeman Dyson noted, "So far as we know, the basic design of every microorganism larger than a virus is precisely as von Neumann said it should be."

This first self-reproducing automaton became known as the kinematic model. It had a fatal flaw. Though its process for creating progeny was logically sound, the kinematic model suffered from a more generalized shakiness of constitution. The problem lay in its elements—too many black boxes. A black box is a primitive, a given—something that behaves in a certain way but gives no clue to the observer exactly how that result is obtained. Unfortunately, too much had to be taken on faith with the kinematic beast. Where do those "arms" come from? Those "sensors"?

The silence following these questions did not negate von Neumann's breakthrough. As the British geneticist L. S. Penrose observed, "Since the aim of von Neumann's reflections was to resolve the logical conditions of the problem, the stupendous mechanical complexity of the machine was of no consequence." But the fact was that von Neumann could not produce working models of these parts—they belonged to a more advanced technology, one that had not arrived even decades later. "Possibly such a a system can yet be designed in principle . . . ," wrote mathematician and biologist Walter R. Stahl in 1965, "but the critical mass of parts might run into the hundreds of thousands or millions. The kinematic model also does not lend itself very well to mathematical analysis."

Some mathematicians and physicists managed to shelve the black-box problem by working on less ambitious self-reproducing structures.

These considerably humbler constructions nonetheless had the advantage of existing as more than mental speculations. Their creators thought it important, even at the expense of drastically simplifying, to *build* something that reproduced. They chiseled a crucial cleft in the wall of misunderstanding that divides biology from other matter. Again, as Penrose put it, "The idea of of an object reproducing itself . . . is so closely associated with the fundamental processes of biology that it carries with it a suggestion of magic."

These early followers of von Neumann, and the a-life researchers that followed them, encountered something quite remarkable that made their task easier. However counterintuitive it may be, certain natural tendencies—rules of the universe, if you would—seem actually to *encourage* phenomena such as self-reproduction. The efforts of these experimenters became an important tributary to a flow of scientific theory and experimentation: the field of complexity, which bore particular significance to artificial life.

On this point, von Neumann again anticipated the phenomenon. His study of natural systems undoubtedly led to his most blazing insight of all—an instinctual grasp that life was grounded not only in information but also in complexity. Years before the ascendency of chaos theory and the study of nonlinear dynamic systems, von Neumann made a connection that only now has become central to the understanding of biology.

Life, he said, depends on a certain measure of complexity. If a certain critical mass of complexity is reached, objects can self-reproduce in an open-ended fashion, not only creating their equals but also parenting more complicated objects than themselves. The crowning example of this was the path of evolution, which progressed from relatively simple one-celled organisms to much more complex ones such as mammals. Below that measure of complexity, would-be organisms could not perform self-reproduction and were doomed to decay. The concept was analogous to a rocket ship requiring a certain velocity to escape the Earth's gravitational force—if it did not climb fast enough, the vehicle would lose momentum and tumble down to Earth.

The implication for biologists soon became clear and provided perhaps the best answer of all to vitalist cant. Though there was no mystical *élan vital* that distinguished life from nonlife, there *was* something absolutely integral to biological systems that might be considered a sort of life force: complexity.

Furthermore, intertwined with complexity theory was something else associated with the emergence of life: the concept of self-organization. Researchers in the new field of a-life came to understand—indeed, to depend on—the observation that self-organization could be seen as a yet-uncharted force in nature, a force that encouraged the evolutionary regime that nudged systems toward increasing complexity. What they found is that, even against seemingly insurmountable odds, life *wants* to happen. So perhaps it was not magic but some staple of nature that made self-reproducing objects possible, if not inevitable.

Surely the phenomenon can be teased from unexpected sources. In the late 1950s Homer Jacobsen, a physicist at Brooklyn College, noted that "scientists have succeeded in duplicating most of the characteristic functions of living things, using admittedly non-living models." The one major exception was reproduction, and he set out to remedy the lapse, using, of all things, an H.O. scale-model railroad kit. Using a circular train layout with several sidings, he released self-propelled box-cars of two types, which he called head and tail. A complete "organism" would consist of a certain arrangement of those types. He implemented his model railroad with a set of simple rules for coupling, decoupling, and switching. These evoked a consistent result: the complete organisms he started with could manipulate random boxcars in the system into other complete organisms—offspring. Amazingly, using off-the-shelf toys, Jacobsen had evoked a key behavior of von Neumann's self-reproducing automaton.

Similarly, the aforementioned geneticist Penrose, with his son Roger, built an original system of self-reproducing structures. Their materials were humble: pieces of plywood cut into unusual shapes. Various notches on wooden blocks allowed them to link when they hit each other in certain ways, much as certain molecules bonded to each other, or as cells of the immune system latched on to viral invaders. After several iterations, the system worked to the point where a "seed"—a set of several linked blocks in a certain state—could, after a series of random encounters with other blocks (catalyzed by vigorous shaking of the box full of blocks), wound up as not one but two sets of blocks in that initial state: parent and offspring. The elder Penrose said that in principle one could fashion a similar system that actually allowed for evolutionary activity. "Such an elaborate scheme is so far unattainable in practice. We have to be content with making a very parasitic organism," he admitted. But he also noted that "it is not, however, much more helpless than a virus."

These simple experiments suggested that one might indeed use the principles of von Neumann's kinematic automaton to tap the power of life. This led some scientists to speculate on the massive benefits that might accrue from this process. Their plans were bold but, they insisted, feasible. With the confidence that the von Neumann pedigree brought to the field, they pressed on, braving ridicule and funding droughts.

One of the first of these proposals was Edward F. Moore's "Artificial Living Plants." Moore's imaginary creations were floating factories, huge barges propelled by jet-powered squidlike extremities. Their logical operation was precisely that which von Neumann outlined. Once dropped into a coastal area, the artificial living plant drew in raw materials from the sea, the beach, and the air, operating as a botanical plant does to keep itself running. That energy was channeled into purifying the materials in order to manufacture parts from it. "From these elements," wrote Moore, "the machine would make wire, solenoids, gears, screws, relays, pipes, tanks and other parts, and then assemble them into machines like itself, which in turn could make more copies."

But there would be a secondary task programmed into the plant's instruction tape, a by-product of the reproduction process. This yielded an output that would allow an astronomically huge repayment to the makers and investors of the plant. It could be something as simple as the plant's harvesting a certain mineral more than necessary to produce offspring (thus becoming, for instance, a zero-labor-force mine for magnesium). Or it created a product not required for reproduction—such as fresh water. The difference between this factory and others was that the artificial living plant was self-sustaining. And by making other factories—perhaps thousands of them—a single initial factory produced unlimited gains.

Moore conceded that his machine would be "more complicated and more expensive than von Neumann's." An artificial living plant, he wrote with understatement typical of those concocting these earthshaking systems, "is obviously not going to be accomplished by a lone inventor working in a basement." But he estimated that for no more than $75,000,000—a relatively paltry sum for Big Science, even in 1955—the considerable design problems might be resolved in ten years. Even if the solutions required discovering innovative new chemical processes, he claimed, producing these things would be no more difficult than sending a human to another planet.

Men were subsequently sent to the moon, but no one funded artificial living plants. The idea persisted, though, and Freeman Dyson of the Princeton-based Institute for Advance Study enthusiastically played with the concept of self-reproducing automata in a series of thought experiments. One was based directly on Moore's plan, and, although Dyson imagined that fresh water produced by plants might cause the desert to bloom, he also envisioned thousands of wrecked plants washing up on coastlines—a virtual eco-disaster. So Dyson turned his imagination to the cosmos and proposed a self-reproducing automaton sent to the snow-covered Saturnian moon Enceladus. In his vision, this particular machine would draw on the distant sun's energy to create factories that produced a long stream of solar-powered sailboats, each carrying a block of ice. The sailboats would head toward Mars, and the fiery ride into the Martian atmosphere would melt the ice blocks. Dyson figured that the accumulated moisture they bore could warm the atmosphere of the fourth planet from the sun, making it a cozy hothouse for life-forms and agriculture. In this case, he says, "a finite piece of hardware, which we may build for a modest price once we understand how to do it, produces an infinite payoff, or at least a payoff that is absurdly large by human standards."

Dyson's concern was that this payoff came by an apparent violation of accumulated wisdom, if not the natural order. Something had been created where nothing seemed to have previously existed (this is why Ted Taylor, a Princeton physicist who also speculated about self-reproducing systems, called them "Santa Claus machines"). All without the sweat and toil associated with such advances.

But who dares believe in Santa Claus? Our intuition, and every shard of our empirical skepticism, dictate there is no such bonanza. Yet these von Neumannesque thought experiments draw plausibility from the suggestion that the phenomenon of life is the ultimate free lunch—it seems to thumb its nose at the incontrovertible principles of entropy. According to the second law of thermodynamics, as time passes, energy dissipates and becomes unusable. Order deteriorates. But life seems to behave as if it has not bothered to read the second law. Life seems to *propagate* order over time. From its unquestionably simpler beginnings, the history of life as we know it has been a trajectory of increasing well-ordered complexity. As von Neumann noted, the evolutionary characteristics of life apparently defy the second law, at least on a local basis. (Physicists explain the contradiction by saying that over the whole universe energy and order is indeed dissipating; by sticking our noses to the glass in this particular hothouse, we do not see the whole picture. Viewed from a larger lens, the organizing properties of life are perfectly in line with the second law and in fact aid its execution.) The awe-inspiring ability of von Neumann's self-reproducing machines, and any related form of a-life, was that it enabled this power, this illusory loophole in the second law of thermodynamics, to be harnessed. There may not be a vital element that consists of a life force, but there *is* a unique ability of living things over time to gain complexity, to order certain domains of the universe. Thus if we build living things, artificial organisms that take advantage of this power, we can extend our own powers exponentially.

"It is safe to predict," Dyson said, of this possibility, "that this will be one of the central concerns of the twenty-first century."

Perhaps the prospect of this is so powerful that our impulse is to ignore it, or dismiss it as science fiction, as if many of our contemporary realities were not first envisioned by science-fiction writers. This seems to have been the fate of the most elaborate proposal to vivify von Neumann's kinematic model: a 1980 NASA study that proposed self-replicating lunar factories.

In 1980, NASA sponsored a ten-week program to determine the role of advanced automation and robotic devices in future space missions. The agency recruited eighteen university professors to work with fifteen program engineers. They teamed off into four groups, each to address the feasibility of a mission that might be undertaken at some later date.

The Mission IV Group outlined how von Neumann's self-replicating machine might be used to colonize the moon and, eventually, the universe.

The team leader of this group, known as the Self-Replicating Systems (SRS) Concept Team, was Richard Laing. After dropping out of an English literature program in 1956, Laing had done technical writing for some computer scientists who became involved in founding what would become the Logic of Computers Group at the University of Michigan. Eventually the ideas discussed there—dealing with the overlap between biological and natural systems—so fascinated him that he earned a doctorate in systems sciences and became a full member of the group. He spent much of his time there thinking about the implications of the von Neumann automaton, and, most notably, theorized a circumstance where the automaton need not store the information about its structure on the genetic tape but could supply that data itself, by a process of self-examination. This would mean that its evolution would not be strictly Darwinian but rather in the spirit of the sort of evolution postulated by Lamarck, who believed that natural organisms might pass acquired traits to their offspring. This matter was supposedly put to rest nearly a century ago by such experiments as the the severing of rat's tails in successive generations: no matter how many ancestral mutilations one cares to conduct, the descendants will be born with healthy tails. The subsequent discoveries in molecular biology confirmed that Lamarckian evolution was a null issue in natural biology. But Laing indicated that artificial biology might prove to be different.

In 1980, Laing was leaving Michigan, moving to Oregon where his wife had found employment. The offer to participate in the NASA program seemed a convenient, and certainly intriguing, stopover on his westward journey. When he arrived at the university at Santa Clara for the summer session, he found instant affinity with the three other members of his team: Georg von Tiesenhausen, a young German rocket scientist imported by the new space agency after the war; Robert A. Freitas, Jr., a scientist with a law degree; and Rodger Cliff, a NASA engineer. Their first session was so filled with ideas and pointers that Laing urged them to return quickly to their apartments and write down everything they had mentioned.

According to Laing, the unconventional plans of the SRS Concept Team made the leaders of the summer study somewhat anxious. Despite what seemed to be a solid scientific backing, there was something decidedly science-fiction-like about the whole thing. The shadow of William Proxmire, who had squashed years of funding for the Search for Extraterrestrial Intelligence (SETI) work by a wrong-headed Golden Fleece Award, loomed perilously, threatening any project whose methodology might be twisted into a silly sound bite. So the team delivered reassurances in the form of constant briefings, reciting their progress in five-minute odes delivered by speakerphone to Washington. They performed some deft soft-pedaling. Instead of self-reproducing factories, which reeked of anthropomorphism, they called these self-*replicating*.

The SRS Concept Team sought to demonstrate that "machine self-replication and growth is a fundamentally feasible goal." One difficult question was the issue of "closure"—could this quasi organism find in its immediate environment all the materials it needed to grow, metabolize, and reproduce? The proposed factory, like any organism, would require not only the proper physical elements but also sufficient energy. And full closure would not be accomplished unless the system, again like any independent organism, was able to generate and handle all the information required to operate and create offspring.

Total closure was elusive. Certain components, like precision microelectronic parts or highly calibrated ball bearings, required a prohibitively complex production process. So the guess, accepted by the study group, was that 90%–96% of the materials would be available, originally in raw form and eventually converted to usable format by the factory; the remaining 4%–10% would be sent from earth. The group called these "vitamin parts." Likewise, if the information closure was incomplete—for instance, if the behavior programmed by the equivalent of von Neumann's genetic tapes failed to account for perturbations of the environment that would affect the factory—then, information vitamins would be sent up by earth monitors.

Partial closure, though, was a crutch that significantly limited the conceptual power of the self-replicating factory scheme. Only with total closure would the factories be fully independent organisms, and only then would the Santa Claus effect—that something-for-nothing exchange that seemed to inoculate life-forms against entropic consequences—kick in, hard.

"There was the suggestion," Laing says, "if you could just tease money for this self-replicating factory, you would never need money again. You could take over the universe!"

The Mission IV Group suggested that self-replicating systems should display five forms of machine behavior: production, replication, growth, evolution, and self-repair. The team provided two detailed designs. These unfolded like origami fugitives from an Isaac Asimov novel; however, they were bolstered by scientific citations and illustrated by reassuring line figures and charts. For this was, after all, an official report of the space agency of the United States government.

The first design was "a fully autonomous, general-purpose self-replicating factory to be deployed on the surface of planetary bodies or moons." The debt to von Neumann was total: this was the realization of the kinematic automaton. Instead of the territory of mind, an infinite lake miraculously stocked with parts, it drew its materials from the virgin landscape of an unpopulated planet or moon. It gathered raw materials by mining. Controlled by radio from the command center, digging machines, loaders, and transport vehicles were, in effect, limbs of the creature. The elements dug up were analyzed, sorted, and sent to a materials depot. From there, they went to a parts production plant, which made components for both the output product (this could be whatever we want a factory to produce—anything from platinum ingots to compact disk players) and the offspring factories. These components went into the parts depot and wound up in the production facility.

When the overall command center—the equivalent of the control, or computer, component in the von Neumann model—said it was time to replicate, the SRS created triplets, reproducing by strict von Neumann rules, the final step being the transmission of the genetic blueprints. The original, having performed its parental duty, was thereafter sterile and operated only as a production facility. The three new factories reproduced, and there were then thirteen in the complex. A generation later "an SRS field factory 40 units strong is busy manufacturing products for outshipment."

The second design proposed a "Growing Lunar Manufacturing Facil-

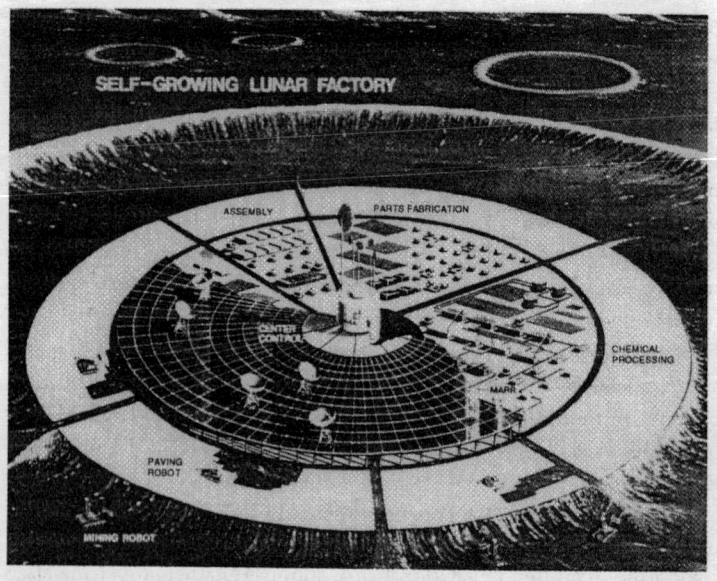

An artist's rendition of a self-replicating lunar factory.

ity" (LMF). Instead of beginning with a chicken—a plug-and-play self-replicating factory—this began with an egg. Specifically, a 100-ton spherical seed. Inside the seed was a litter of task-specific robots. Once planted in the proper lunar nest, the egg cracked open, and its cargo of robots emerged. There were robots to mine, gather, and process materials. These busy workers first constructed a small solar array to provide start-up power. Then scouting robots determined the best location to build the factory. Other robots set up and calibrated a network of transponders, and so established a control system. Then mining robots leveled the surface, while paving robots set the foundation for the factory. When the space was ready, the central computer was moved to a perch at the center of the factory. Work began on a huge solar canopy to provide power for the next fruits of the seed—the chemical processing, fabrication, assembly, and control sectors. In about a year, this teeming embryo reached maturity, and a factory was on line, producing whatever its control program told it to.

The SRS Concept Team offered several options from that point. The factory could expand on its original site (they estimated that around three billion units would entirely cover the lunar surface, making the moon into a single dense industrial area, a sort of cosmic rust belt without energy costs). Or it could produce robot-filled seeds for other factories and build rockets to launch them into other locations in the solar system. There would be extravagantly bountiful return on the original investment—the seed money, as it were. Rare isotopes from Jupiter and Saturn. Hydrocarbons from Titan. Heavy metals from the asteroid belt. In addition, factories could be programmed to send out batteries of monitor vehicles, soaring on the solar wind, designed "to track and warn of objects approaching human habitats, facilities, or the Earth."

But these von Neumann organisms would not be limited to the solar system. Because the seeds carried no mortal baggage, the excruciatingly long periods required to cover vast interstellar distances would be irrelevant. The Mission IV Group calmly noted that "reproductive probes could permit the direct investigation of the nearest million stars in about 10,000 years and the entire Milky Way galaxy in less than 10^6 years, starting with a total investment by humanity of a *single* self-replicating exploratory spacecraft." With poker faces, the Self-Replicating Systems Concept team proposed a plan that would not be completed until 10 times the span of recorded history. Barring, of course, unexpected delays.

Thinking in this time frame, one pictured inert material spending centuries to traverse empty reaches of space. But despite the obvious perils of such an unconventional claim, the SRS Concept Team emphasized that these constructs should be regarded not simply as a special kind of factories but also as living organisms.

What bothered Laing and his colleagues was this: The certainty that organisms tend to seek their own ends introduces the possibility that our creations will be our competitors. Perhaps they would even evolve into a species that competed with humankind. "It is not too early to begin considering the possible kinds of behaviors which advanced machines might display, and the 'machine sociobiology' which may emerge," they wrote, suggesting that "it is prudent to inquire as to the possibility of unforeseen dangers to our continued existence."

First, as Moore suggested in his article on artificial living plants, was the problem of population control. Possible limitations to excessive breeding could include a built-in birth control pill, which would kick in after a specific number of reproductive cycles. Still, the inexorable multiplication of decentralized factories would be excessive. A possible solution, then, would be predators. Following the example of administrators in the National Park Service, we might launch species-specific predator machines, or "universal deconstructors" to thin out exploding populations.

Then there was the so-called unpluggability problem. Unlike computers and machines with which we are familiar, self-replicating systems had a degree of independence that made moot the last-resort contingency when machines went wrong—turning it off or pulling the plug. (As did astronaut Dave to the HAL computer in *2001*.) "We must assume that we cannot necessarily pull the plug on our autonomous artificially intelligent species once they have gotten beyond a certain point of development," was the gloomy conclusion.

The problem—which was a problem only from our point of view, not from the vantage point of the artificial self-replicating systems—was that evolution would inevitably encourage behavior that suited the machines and not necessarily its creators. If, for instance, the creators of a self-replicating system programmed into the machine's genetic instructions a shut-down switch that would respond to a signal from earth, any machines that mutated in such a way to override that switch would have a distinct evolutionary advantage over their cousins—and soon that trait would proliferate in the gene pool.

On the other hand, we would certainly want some evolutionary adaptability in our self-replicating systems. "Since we cannot foresee all of the ways in which the system may be perturbed," explains the NASA report, "we shall have to supply it with goals, as well as homeostatic capabilities, enabling the machines to solve their own difficulties and restore themselves to proper working order with little or no human assistance." This could be done in two ways: the machines could learn, or the machines, over a long period of time, could evolve to a higher fitness. The NASA scientists seemed to think the latter option was best. Indeed, they viewed the self-replicating machines as eventually providing an even clearer case for the arguments of sociobiology—which assumes that evolution played a dominant role in social behavior—than does the natural world. The NASA team speculated on kinship relationships between machines and even the use of mimicry and other natural phenomena.

This was fairly far afield for a summer study in automation in space missions, certainly more than many in the upper reaches of NASA wanted to hear. But the team went even further into uncharted speculative terrain when they decided to ponder philosophical, ethical, and even religious considerations of building these self-replicating machines. The scope of the questions they raised was astonishing and, some would say, absurd. But, as Laing says now of those controversial queries, "We felt we had a duty to pose those questions." Hearkening back to Aristotle, they wondered whether a machine could have a soul—or *think* it had a soul. "Could a self-reproducing, evolving machine have a concept of God?" they asked. "Or would humankind be seen as nothing more than an evolutionary precursor?"

The answer to that question lay in perhaps the most disturbing speculation of the SRS Concept Team: that our artificial life machines would be symbiotically linked to us as no less than equal partners, coevolving through the eons. Humankind, they asserted, was either a "biological way station" in the grand scheme of things or else an "evolutionary dead end." It was only through these self-replicating systems—"in a very real intellectual and material sense our offspring," they said—that the fruitless latter option could be avoided. While acknowledging the possibility that these silicon-and-steel progeny might render humans, as well as other forms of carbon-based life, obsolete, the authors chose to view the situation more optimistically (no surprise since they were, after all, advocating that we begin to build these machines). They envisioned a near-eternal coexistence where, for the price of merging itself into a larger system, "mankind could achieve immortality for itself."

After postulating the possible extinction of humankind, and at the least as significant an event "as the emergence and separation of plant and animal kingdoms billions of years ago on Earth," the NASA SRS Concept Team patiently waited for the funding that would set the process in motion. The first step would be technology and feasibility assessments at research centers such as MIT, Carnegie-Mellon, or Ford Aerospace. They even wrote a sample solicitation for relevant research proposals. While this was being done, they suggested, NASA should immediately begin developing a laboratory robot that could perform simple self-replicating functions.

According to Laing, the NASA administrators liked the idea and held out the possibility that work could begin. In 1983, when Laing was told that Ronald Reagan was about to announce a major space initiative, he hoped that it would include a concentrated effort to build self-replicating lunar factories. The Reagan speech instead proposed Star Wars.

As stated earlier, von Neumann was not satisfied with his kinematic model because of the black-box problem, which would, for the foreseeable future, limit his creation to the confines of the mind. Even for von Neumann this was a dilemma, and the resolution came at the suggestion of his longtime friend and fellow master mathematician Stanislaw Ulam. The two had been friends since 1937, when von Neumann visited Ulam's home in Poland. Their relationship was cemented by the wartime kinship at Los Alamos, where the pair of expatriates had been key participants in the Manhattan Project. Ulam shared his friend's interest in automata theory and indeed, could recall sitting in a coffeehouse in Lwów in 1929, speculating on the possibility of artificial automata reproducing themselves.

When confronted with von Neumann's black-box problem, Ulam suggested doing away with the metaphor of a creature swimming on a lake and picking up and manipulating these troublesome primitives. Instead, he drew from the phenomenon of crystal growth a different environment: an infinite grid, laid out like a checkerboard. Each square of the grid could be seen as a "cell." Each cell on the grid would essentially be a separate finite state machine, acting on a shared set of rules. The configuration of the grid would change as discrete time steps ticked off. Every cell would hold information that would be known as its state, and at each time step it would look to the cells around it and consult the rule table to determine its state in the next tick. A collection of cells on such a grid could be viewed as an organism.

This idea appealed to von Neumann. The organism living in this grid space would be a creature of pure logic. Everything about it could be stated mathematically. It would be fully realized and provable beyond contention. It would exist. From the bones of Ulam's suggestion, von Neumann remade his kinematic self-reproducing automaton into what would be known as the first cellular automaton (CA). (The name would come from Arthur Burks, who edited von Neumann's papers on the phenomenon; otherwise, Ulam's description of tessellation structures—a tessellation is a plane of tiles, as one would find on a bathroom floor—might have stuck.)

Von Neumann's cellular model for a self-reproducing automaton began with a horizonless checkerboard, with each square, or cell, in a quiescent, or inactive, state—essentially, a blank canvas. Then von Neumann figuratively painted a monster on the canvas, covering two hundred thousand cells on the lattice. In the spirit of a paint-by-number landscape, the details of the creature were represented by different "colors" in various cells—only instead of literal colors there were twenty-nine differing states of the cell. It was the precise combination of those cells in their given states that told the creature how to behave, and indeed that defined the creature itself. It was shaped like a box with a tail, a very long tail. The box, about eighty cells long by four hundred cells wide, contained suborganisms that replicated the functions of Components A, B, and C (the factory, the duplicator, and the computer) of the kinematic model; these took up only a fourth of the creature's cells. The rest of the squares were in the tail, the blueprint, which was a single-file snake of 150,000 cells.

Instead of swimming and grabbing, the metaphor for this machine's process of reproduction was claiming and transforming territory. It was reminiscent of certain geopolitical board games, where players invade and conquer neighboring countries. More to the point, this was a physical interpretation of what happened in natural reproduction. The atoms and molecules that made up the new entity, the offspring, neces-

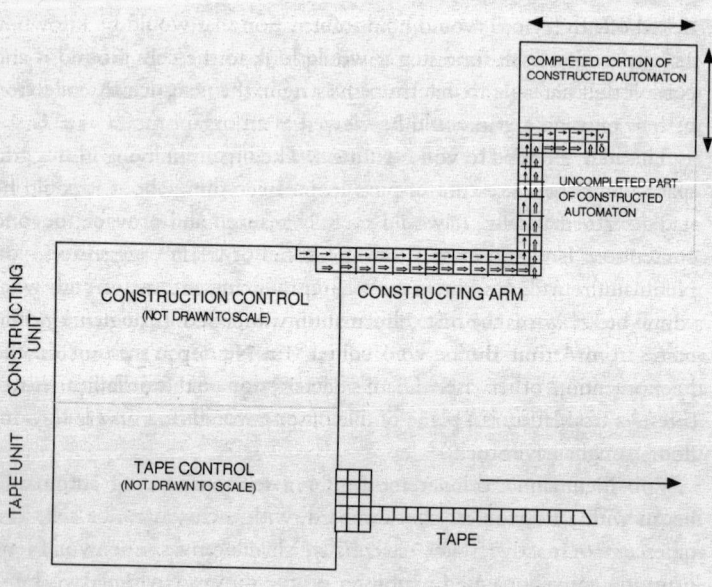

A schematic diagram (not drawn to scale) of von Neumann's self-reproducing cellular automaton. When the rules are executed by the cells in the tape (which stretches as far as 150,000 squares on the grid), the changing states of the cells in the body of the organism act to change the states of the previously stable cells outside it. First a constructing arm protrudes, and then the body of a new organism forms. Eventually there will be two identical patterns, each one resembling the same fully formed self-reproducing automaton of von Neumann's design. Reproduction will have been completed, in the spirit of natural reproduction.

sarily came from the environment. The idea—the idea of life really—was to gather those materials in their disorganized forms and integrate them in the highly complex organization of a living being.

The von Neumann self-reproducing automaton, once embedded in the vast CA checkerboard, would follow rules. More properly, each individual cell, as an FSM, began to follow the rule that applied to it. The effect of these local behaviors caused a global behavior to emerge:

the self-reproducing structure interacted with neighboring cells and changed some of their states. It transformed them into the materials—in terms of cell states—that made up the original organism. Because there were twenty-nine possible states for each cell, the process was fairly complicated. Essentially, the machine worked in a fashion similar to its kinematic cousin. The tail of the cell contained instructions for the body of the creature, whose collection of cells, depending on their state, acted as computer, factory, or duplicator. Eventually, by following the rules of transition that von Neumann drew up, the organism managed to make a duplicate of its main body. Information was passed through a kind of umbilical cord, from mother to daughter. The last step in the process was the duplication of the tail and the detachment of the umbilical cord. Two identical creatures, both capable of self-reproduction, were now in the endless checkerboard.

Von Neumann never completed his written proof of a cellular model. For more than a year he arose each day before dawn to work on his manuscript. By March 1953, when he delivered a series of talks at Princeton University, he was able to describe it in some detail, but the complexity of the subject was more than he had anticipated, and the manuscript grew from two long chapters to four, with more planned. Von Neumann shelved the work when he was appointed to the Atomic Energy Commission and intended to finish it when his service ended. When it became clear that his health was failing, he allowed John G. Kemeny, who later went on to invent the computer language BASIC, to write an article describing the self-reproducing CA. Kemeny's work appeared in *Scientific American* in 1955, described as an attempt "to show there is no conclusive evidence for an essential gap between man and a machine." What excited Kemeny was the capacity for evolution in von Neumann–type automata. He noted that the tail of the machine, which requires most of the cells, was like a set of chromosomes and marveled at how, in comparison, the body of a human being needs only a small portion of its matter to make up the genetic material.

"Could such machines go through an evolutionary process?" Kemeny wondered; he concluded, as von Neumann did, that it certainly could. He speculated that one might program the transition rules so that a tiny number of random changes would occur during the copying process—some of the bits would be flipped from on to off, or vice versa. This would be like a mutation. Or one could take a deep breath and say that this would *be* a mutation. As is characteristic of mutations, it might well be passed on to the offspring. If this mutation wound up increasing the machine's fitness, adhering to the conventions of natural selection, it would spread throughout the gene pool of the machine population. Eventually we would have the fruits of evolution.

This raised the same questions that Dyson and Laing's Self-Replicating Systems Concept Team pondered: What happens when we set these structures free? What can emerge from them? Certainly it is less threatening to observe these consequences when they occur simply as combinations of electrical charges on a computer chip rather than in huge factories that alter the course of civilization.

Or is it? It turns out that deciding how seriously to weigh events that may occur only within the confines of a computer is a considerable dilemma. How closely can nature be simulated by symbolic manipulation of information? Can building artificial organisms increase our knowledge about living processes? Can it enhance our cloudy understanding of the complex forces of nature? Can we ultimately learn to corral those forces to build organisms as lifelike as those we know? Would those, then, be alive?

The field of artificial life would transform these from idle queries to essential ones.

PLAYING BY THE RULES

To declare that the personoids are somehow "handicapped" with respect to us, inasmuch as they do not see or hear as we do, is totally absurd. With equal justice one could assert that it is we who are deprived with respect to them—unable to feel with immediacy the phenomenalism of mathematics, which, after all, we know only in a cerebral, inferential fashion. They live in it; it is their air, clouds, water, and even bread—yes, even food, because in a certain sense they take nourishment from it. To say they are imprisoned inside the machine is mere journalism.

Stanislaw Lem

The real reason for studying CAs is to promote artificial life . . . this is the computer scientist's Great Work as surely as the building of the Notre Dame cathedral on the Ile de France was the Great Work of the medieval artisan.

Rudy Rucker

For several months in the late 1960s, the common room of the mathematics department at the University of Cambridge—a bland institutional space with worn furniture and a stillborn light creeping into the room from the open doors of adjoining offices—was taken over by what seemed a mutant version of the Chinese game of Go. From a small square coffee table, it grew, spilling over the side, colonizing the floor, and stretching toward the corners. The pieces were not the traditional Go stones but rather squared-off little counter pieces, or small shells taken off of a necklace.

At various times, there could be six or seven people moving these pieces. But they could not accurately be called participants. They had no more control of the game than did the group of spectators that often dropped into the common room during coffee time—an expanding coffee time, to be sure, often stretching for the better part of the afternoon. A deterministic set of rules, not human wile, determined where the pieces went. These precepts dictated which pieces on the grid would remain (in which case they would "survive"), which pieces would be removed from the grid (in which case they would be considered to have "died") and whether new pieces would be placed on the grid (or "born").

The game was called Life. It was destined to become the most famous example of von Neumann's invention, cellular automata, and an inspiration to a generation of artificial life researchers. Its creator was John Horton Conway, a mathematician then in his early thirties who had already earned a reputation for brilliance in exploring the abstract fringes of number theory, as well as for his world-class eccentricities. These ranged from a memorable fondness for disorder ("Other mathematicians talk of his offices in the same way archeologists discuss ancient cities," wrote one journalist) to a voracious appetite for whimsical pursuits, such as twisting his tongue into weird shapes. He often combined these dual notorieties in vigorous sojourns into the realm of mathematical games.

Conway was in an enviable position: when in the grasp of a mathematical obsession, he was free to devote all his energies to it. This had been a goal he had pursued since his boyhood in Liverpool, when his mathematical skills became apparent. He was quite capable of reeling off the first thousand digits of π. His classmates called him "The Professor." He was confident in his mastery until he finally won his cherished appointment at Cambridge in his early twenties. Then he was suddenly seized by doubt. What if he were merely a pretender to genius? Fortunately, his doubts were soon dispelled. He made a ground-breaking mathematical discovery in group number theory, which came to be called the Conway group. From then on, not only were his worries gone but also his obligations. At times he considered the situation scandalous, but he was required to do nothing but think, about subject matters solely of his own discretion. As a result, he says, "I have spent a fantastic amount of my time playing childish games."

In 1968, the particular "game" that obsessed Conway involved the workings of CAs. He had a suspicion about them that he wanted to confirm. Though it was true that von Neumann's automaton qualified as a universal computer—it could emulate any describable function of any other machine by use of a set of logical rules—the organism itself was frustratingly complex, with its two hundred thousand cells in any of twenty-nine states. Conway suspected that a cellular automaton with universal computing capabilities might be simpler. Much simpler. So he set out to build an extremely elementary CA, one so simple that you could update it, time step by time step, on a simple checkerboard, working by hand. He was sure that it would not be too difficult to come up with something that followed only a few simple rules but yielded unlimited results.

Conway believed that from the most rudimentary elements one could produce fantastic results. He would sometimes daydream about entering a warehouse full of odd bits of machinery—full of junk, really—and wiring the parts pretty much at random. And only then figuring what you might do with the contraption. "Just imagine this whopping great machine with buttons and colored lights on," he would say. "My guess is that after you've lived with it a long time, you'd notice something you'd be able to use it for." Most amazing of all, you might figure out a certain set of contortions to put the machine through, so it could behave like a computer—and thus, behave like any machine in the world!

More to the point, something equally amazing apparently occurred many years ago on this planet when simple molecules somehow developed into a complex system that eventually bore what we now call life, in all its dizzying evolutionary development.

The trick for Conway was to come up with the simplest imaginable model that could explode into the infinite power of a universal computer. He would live with it for a while, explore its peccadilloes, see how its powers might unfold, and, he hoped, show that it could calculate anything. This Life computer would be by necessity a rather cumbersome configuration of cells, and it would operate extremely inefficiently. Yet, if it were a universal machine, it would be capable of eventually matching the workings of the most powerful supercomputers in existence. The experiment would not break new ground mathematically—von Neumann had done that job—but by greatly simplifying the master's work, Conway would clarify those concepts.

If he were very lucky, the system might yield something . . . alive. "I wanted to see some self-reproducing animal," Conway says. "Displaying some interesting behavior. In a weak form, living."

The key would be the rules that dictated survival, birth, and death. Since the rules in this case would generate everything in this artificial world—a complete physics, the meaning of this universe—it was essential they be perfectly tuned. A slight variation could transform a fairly stable system into absurd chaos. "Suddenly it all goes catastrophic," Conway explains. "And you sort of tinker with it, and say, 'Ah, I made that a bit too strong,' so you sort of weaken something there, and then something collapses. And it took about two years, really, of experimentation at coffee time to get it right. And coffee time lasts all day here."

Conway's task was particularly challenging because he was drastically reducing von Neumann's Byzantine set of twenty-nine states. His CAs ideally would have but two states. A space in the grid, a cell, would be either filled or empty. On or off. One or zero. Alive or dead.

At one point he doubted that it could be done and developed a system that had an extra state in it. This did have the advantage of adding sex to the stark politics of life and death. "The basic rule was that three things gave birth, provided they were of mixed sexes. Someone noticed we called the states A and B, so we called them actresses and bishops. [This from a hoary series of risqué English jokes.] The basic plan was the sex of the offspring would be the weaker one, the one least represented, because it tends to even things up. We also had a thing called the Frustration Rule. If you weren't touching something of the opposite sex, you died."

But actresses and bishops were sent offstage when Conway tuned the rules so that his conditions were satisfied by the minimum two states. This was Life.

These were the complete rules, a grand unified theory of a universe capable of generating Life, and, conceivably, life:

> Life occurs on a virtual checkerboard. The squares are called cells. They are in one of two states: alive or dead. Each cell has eight possible neighbors, the cells which touch its sides or its corners.
>
> If a cell on the checkerboard is alive, it will survive in the next time step (or generation) if there are either two or three neighbors also alive. It will die of overcrowding if there are more than three live neighbors, and it will die of exposure if there are fewer than two.
>
> If a cell on the checkerboard is dead, it will remain dead in the next generation unless exactly three of its eight neighbors are alive. In that case, the cell will be "born" in the next generation.

That was it. Once Conway settled on those rules, things happened very quickly in the common room. The first thing that he and his colleagues tried was to see what happened to the most simple initial configurations once the rules were applied. Most of them quickly settled into stable patterns. Conway and his friends named these objects, much in the taxonomic style of stellar constellations, after the shapes they suggested: block, ship, longboat, beehive, loaf, canoe, pond. Other shapes settled into periodic configurations, alternating between shapes as the time steps click by. These were called oscillators, and some of them were called toads, blinkers, clocks, and traffic lights.

But certain simple life-forms had much more complex biographies.

The classic example of these was the R Pentomino. A pentomino was a contiguous arrangement of any five neighboring cells; this particular example is roughly shaped like the letter *R*. At each click of the generational clock, the R Pentomino turned out something different. Seemingly, there was no predictability to its patterns. It soon became clear that the R Pentomino's fertility was prodigious. At one point it broke into four objects, exploding into a kaleidoscope-like activity, sort of a Busby Berkeley dance of blinking cells. Then the symmetry dissolved. Small objects appeared continuously. Sometimes objects broke up only when other newborn cells tampered with the equilibrium; at other times they were temporary configurations, doomed to dispell into quiescence. As each generation passed, Conway and his helpers despaired of ever knowing the fate of the configuration. (Months later, they learned that the R Pentomino stabilized after 1103 generations.) Particularly because some of the small objects it generated used the rules of Life to move steadily, as if purposefully. These were the gliders.

It was Richard Guy, a colleague of Conway's in the Cambridge mathematics department, who discovered the first glider. In the midst of tracking the R Pentomino, around the seventieth generation, Guy said, "Oh, look, my bit's walking." It was a five-cell object that shifted its body with each generation, always in the same direction, much in the spirit of a single-cell organism that shifts its matter as a means of locomotion. Others contended that it looked a little like an insect, wagging its abdomen as it moved. (Conway later wondered whether "insect" might have been a better term for the configuration than "glider.") After four time steps the glider returned to its original configuration; only now it had moved itself one cell diagonally on the checkerboard.

The discovery of such a reliable moving configuration was a particularly exciting observation for Conway's group. In order to prove that the rules of Life supported a universe in which a universal Turing machine could be embedded (and therefore Life could emulate any other computation machine, whether electronic or natural), it was necessary to show that a literal computer could be built of Life patterns. This would include patterns that emulated computer parts like a counter, a clock, and a memory. The gliders, whose motion was sufficiently reliable to keep timing, would help considerably.

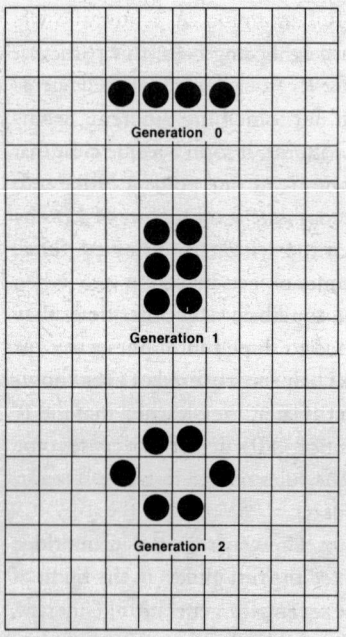

Generation 0

Generation 1

Generation 2

The development of a simple stable form in the game of Life. The initial form is a row of four live cells. Each cell in the configuration then examines its neighbors and itself. The simple rules of Life then determine whether the cell will be alive or dead in the next generation. In this case, the four-cell configuration grows to a rectangular shape, and in the next generation forms a shape roughly resembling a beehive. Since each live cell in that shape has exactly two neighbors—the right number to keep it alive in the next generation—the shape is stable, and will continue in that form unless perturbed.

By the time Richard Guy found the first glider, Life was growing far beyond the bounds of the small coffee table in the common room and, indeed, out of the room itself. The fact was, manipulating Life by hand was rather unwieldy. (The benefit was that you really understood what was happening when you painstakingly generated the births and deaths.) To minimize the confusion, Conway's group had devised a system that worked fairly smoothly. The configuration would be laid out in white counters. Applying the rules, the mathematicians would determine which ones would die in the next generation and place a shell on top of those. Thus to "shell" a cell was to kill it. Births were marked by placing a new counter on the space. (A certain professor often made the mistake of giving birth when four live neighbors surrounded an empty cell instead of three: these were dubbed "Nigel Martin births," in honor of the erratic sheller.) At times, the population would grow to a point where it would require less effort to reverse the procedure, so that shells were placed on surviving cells rather than on doomed ones. There were, after all, a limited amount of shells. In those cases, someone would shout, Shell the living! and that switch would be carried off.

Then there were the blinker watchers, whose job it was to notice when a configuration had attained periodicity. Once that was observed, the players could shortcut the procedure, particularly when the blinker was located some distance from the main action, by ignoring those stones until neighboring cells upset the pattern's stability.

When the configurations tumbled off the single Go board, the players would hastily place sheets of paper on the carpet and draw squares on them to extend the grid. It was, in fact, on the carpet that Guy found the glider. Once a glider managed to get away from the main configuration, of course, it headed off the papers, out of the room, and, in theory, out of Cambridge, out of England, out of everywhere. As a result, some configurations could never really be tracked. (Although the R Pentomino turned out to be stable after 1103 time steps, its six free-traveling gliders have long since shimmied over the horizon into the eternal mist.)

The glider discovery was encouraging, but Conway still required other crucial patterns to prove that Life could be a universal computer. Key among them was a pulse generator, a construct that would shoot out gliders with regularity so they could bounce off other structures as part of an embodied computer. Instead of painstakingly trying to discover

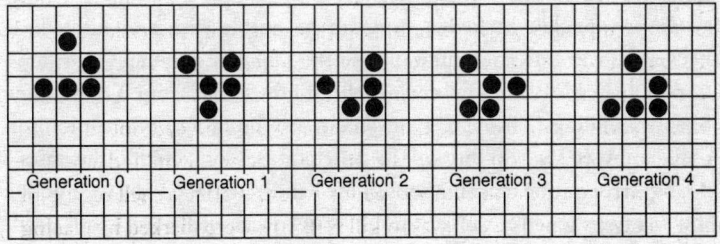

| Generation 0 | Generation 1 | Generation 2 | Generation 3 | Generation 4 |

The motion of a glider in Life. In the course of the four generations required for the glider to recapture its original form, the pattern displaces itself one square diagonally.

this glider-gun configuration, Conway decided to open the problem up to the world at large. The best way to do this was through Martin Gardner, who wrote a column for *Scientific American* called "Mathematical Games." To math nuts and to the kind of people who would consider cellular automata interesting (two sets with considerable overlap), Gardner's column was like a monthly update of the Bible. Through Gardner, Conway played a trick on this select population: he conjectured that a finite initial configuration of Life would *not* be able to generate infinite populations, and offered $50 to anyone who could disprove that. The way to accomplish this refutation would be a configuration for a Life machine that spit out objects ad infinitum, be it a glider gun that shoots off the objects or a "puffer train" that moves on the grid, leaving behind a constant trail of live cells, or "smoke."

When R. William Gosper read the October 1970 edition of *Scientific American,* it brought his own work to a stop. Gosper was one of the key computer hackers at MIT's Artificial Intelligence Laboratory, and one of the brightest programmers in the world. He enjoyed a mathematical puzzle, but he recognized that Conway's challenge was more than a game—CAs, and Life in particular, represented a vivid abstract world in which real consequences occurred. It was an alternative universe built of mathematics, virtually uncharted—the kind of place where Gosper wanted to spend a lot of time. "It represented the ability to do science without already having been beaten to the punch by Newton, and Gauss and everybody," says Gosper, "the ability to do everything from animal husbandry to recursive function theory."

Gosper quickly hacked a program to enable him and his fellow hackers to run Life configurations on the Digital Equipment Corporation (DEC) PDP-6 computer on the ninth floor of the Technology Square building. Through a small, circular black-and-white monitor they could see Life zip through its generations. Compared to the painstaking, error-prone machinations of the handcrafted Conway technique, this was warp speed. Configurations would occasionally erupt into fascinating digressions, and the Life explorers, often surrounded by equally mesmerized spectators, would watch for hours. Actually, since unpredictability was part of the terrain with CAs, and since significant clues to their secrets simply emerged from the crazy quilt of interactions, it was hard to distinguish between wasting time and doing science. Part of the routine was setting up an initial configuration and letting 'er rip.

But there was work, too, and Gosper and his group went at it full time. It took no more than a month before they sent a message to Conway via Gardner: We found the glider gun. Later, his group found a puffer train, too. Then came Gosper's pièce de résistance: "We eventually got puffer trains that emitted gliders which collided together to make glider guns which then emitted gliders but in a quadratically increasing number. . . . We totally filled the space with gliders."

From this breakthrough, Conway had the evidence he needed to prove that Life could indeed support universal computation. Using glider streams to represent bits, Conway was able to produce the equivalent of and-gates, or-gates, and not-gates, as well as an analogue of a computer's internal storage. He never bothered to actually build this virtual computer on a real machine, but the MIT group created a Life-based adding unit that Conway saw when he visited the other Cambridge one day and considered lovely. "It worked like clockwork," he recalls. "Streams of gliders would come around here, and sort of ticked around—click click click click click—and then the sum came out as another stream."

As far as Conway was concerned, that completed the task he had set out to accomplish with Life—he had proved that von Neumann's ideas could be realized in a much simpler context, and he also spread an enormous amount of cheer while doing it. The catalyst for all the excitement, of course, was the computer. The *Scientific American* article appeared at a time when it had only recently become possible to run cellular automata on interactive computers, and the MIT group was only one of many covens of hackers who gathered around a machine at night to run Life. It was estimated by *Time* that millions of dollars of unauthorized computer time were squandered by Life tinkerers, who even published their own newsletter listing various discoveries. And many, notably Gosper, kept up Life explorations for years and kept on publishing scientific papers on their results.

The single disappointment for John Horton Conway was that, despite Life's undeniable versatility, and its verifiable unpredictability, no configuration in that CA yielded a self-reproducing animal in a reasonably small space. In theory, he insisted, Life can support the emergence of any recognizable animal, as well as unlimited unrecognizable ones. "On a large enough scale you would really see living configurations," he says. "Genuinely living, whatever reasonable definition you care to give to it. Evolving, reproducing, squabbling over territory. Getting cleverer and cleverer. Writing learned Ph.D. theses. On a large enough board, there's no doubt in my mind this sort of thing would happen."

By "large enough board," Conway was referring to something very large—perhaps bigger than the physical universe. (Others were more optimistic, thinking that a Go board the size of the solar system might do the trick.) But Conway thought that a square grid of a mere million cells a side might yield a creature comparable to a one-celled animal.

But would that animal be alive? The nature of cellular automata was such that many would concede it. And some would even declare that CAs are sufficiently complex to develop an entire universe as sophisticated as the one in which we live. Indeed, claimed one researcher, we had no proof that this universe in particular was not a CA, running on the computer of some magnificent hacker in heaven.

From the time that von Neumann took Ulam's suggestion to place his self-reproducing creature in a universe built on an abstract grid, cellular automata have had, no pun intended, a checkered career. If not for Conway, in fact, the entire study, which eventually attained considerable currency in the scientific world, might have been unfairly consigned to the trash heap of the trivial. But from the days of the self-reproducing automaton, a series of dedicated believers kept it alive until its current state of fashionability and hard-won significance. One of these caretakers compared his advocacy of cellular automata to that of a hospital intern charged with keeping the patient alive until the shift ends, and the next physician inherits the charts and telemetry.

Its first champion after von Neumann was an unprepossessing philosophy scholar, named Arthur Burks. Burks obtained a doctorate in 1941, having written a thesis on a then-unheralded nineteenth-century American thinker named Charles S. Peirce. He then served in the military, where he took up electrical engineering, an interest he pursued at the

Moore School in Philadelphia, where work was being done on what was arguably the first general purpose electronic computer, the ENIAC. Burks became part of that effort. Among the people he met was von Neumann, who was consulting at Moore. When von Neumann decided to design his own computer, Burks, by then an assistant professor of philosophy at the University of Michigan, was among the logic engineers he recruited.

In 1949, the Burroughs Company agreed to fund a computer research group at the University of Michigan. Burks was put in charge and given the freedom to shape the group toward his own peculiar interests, which straddled the little-known line between electronics and biology.

Burks was following not only in von Neumann's footsteps but also hewing to the spirit of his thesis subject. Peirce's ideas were based on an insistence that life's workings were founded in logic. In particular, he believed that evolution itself was a mechanism that would eventually be parsed mathematically. He compared evolution to the statistical mechanics dictating the movement of molecules in gases. Speaking of the predictability of the properties of gases when exposed to heat, Peirce wrote:

> In like manner, Darwin, though unable to say what the operation of variation and natural selection in any individual case may be, demonstrates that in the long run they will, or would, adapt animals to their circumstances. Whether or not existing animal forms are due to such action, or what position the theory ought to take, forms the subject of a discussion in which questions of fact and questions of logic are curiously interlaced.

This train of thought—a runaway train, in relation to the more bounded theories of the philosopher's peers—anticipated Turing, von Neumann, the early theorists of AI and now the researchers of artificial life. In light of subsequent discoveries, Peirce's theoretical trajectory seemed uncannily aimed. Close study of Peirce encouraged Burks to focus his group differently from any other computer science department in the country. (Burks would later concoct his own Peirce-based philosophy, calling it logical mechanism.) The Logic of Computers Group, as it came to be known, attracted people like John Holland, a young MIT graduate who believed that computers could display adaptive behavior. It was at Michigan that Holland became the first computer science Ph.D. in the country and probably in the world. And it was at Michigan that the seeds would be sown for a new synthesis between biology and information.

Burks will probably be best remembered for editing von Neumann's posthumous papers on automata theory. Though he had never discussed the theory with von Neumann personally, it dealt with threads of thought that Burks had been unraveling all his career. In the process of resurrecting the material, Burks became an expert in the subject matter, even correcting errors in von Neumann's hastily drawn cellular model of the self-reproducing automaton. But even before publishing von Neumann's theories, Burks was encouraging others to explore CAs. Other notable work derived from von Neumann's ideas began coming out of Michigan. For instance, E.F. Codd, an engineer whose doctoral studies were being paid for by his employer, IBM, designed a self-reproducing automaton like von Neumann's, but much simpler—it required using only eight possible cellular states instead of von Neumann's twenty-nine.

At Michigan, the Logic of Computers Group became the first place where cellular automata were run on computers. To be sure, the system was an inelegant kludge. Two expensive machines were required. One was a behemoth IBM 1800, which crunched the extensive calculations. The other was a smaller, interactive hybrid of two DEC models, the PDP-7 and PDP-8. The experimenter would control the model with the DEC keyboard and use the superior DEC display. By turning knobs, different rules could be applied, and the results observed. It was a new sort of mathematical research, one in which the payoff came not by calculation but by emergence. As the work progressed, it turned out that the forces at work in cellular automata seemed remarkably similar to forces in nature. It was not unusual at the Logic of Computers Group to see doctoral theses on CA-based methods of charting heart fibrillation.

In a sense, with cellular automata, researchers turned the keys over to nature. Forces of self-organization, not yet understood, along with the particular artificial physics in the given experiment, would drive the system. Sometimes, the destination would be unexpected. That was the mystery and power of CAs. But it was a secret kept largely in the Frieze Building in Ann Arbor.

But then, most of the general practices of the Logic of Computers Group at the University of Michigan were performed in relative isolation. At the center of the belief system at Michigan was nature—nature as teacher, nature as the complex system to which all electronic systems should aspire, nature that would be the fulcrum of a symbiotic study of biology and engineering. It was the place where natural objects inspired computer theory, and computer creations behaved as natural objects. Elsewhere the god of AI would prevail, relegating the Michigan people to a fate worse than ridicule, a sort of academic limbo where they would present papers, develop ideas, and actually prove things—with little impact on the fields of computer science or biology.

The sad fact was that, several years after Conway's Life swept the computer world, CAs were in danger of sinking into oblivion. It was during that dark time, in April 1975, when a young Italian Ph.D. student at Michigan, Tommaso Toffoli, was beginning his graduate thesis on the subject. His approach, as he described it in the final document, was to address the question, "What are cellular automata worth saving for?" He confessed puzzlement that, of the few who worked the field, most were mathematicians. From a pure mathematical viewpoint, it seemed to him, CAs weren't so fascinating. No, he argued, "the importance of cellular automata lies in their connection with the *physical world*." (The emphasis was Toffoli's.) Particularly that of complex dynamical systems, where behavior arises as an emergent property of a number of variable forces. Because, unlike so many things simulated on the computer, CAs do not merely reflect reality—they are reality. They are actual dynamical systems. While they can be used to model certain physical systems, with the validity of each model to be determined by how well the results match the original, they can also be used to understand complex systems in general.

"Von Neumann himself devised cellular automata to make a reductionistic point about the plausibility of life being possible in a world with very simple primitives," Toffoli later explained. "But even von Neumann, who was a quantum physicist, neglected completely the connections with physics—that a cellular automata could be a model of fundamental physics."

Since his boyhood in a small town near Venice, Toffoli had been interested in the histories of things, in politics as well as in science. There were connections. He saw, for instance, that a national constitution was like a structural set of rules operating in a cellular automaton, "sort of a mechanism that in a certain context makes something that is self-sustaining, self-reproducing." This idea—that physical reality was something that could be extended beyond the bounds of what was narrowly considered science—drove him to unorthodox studies and inevitably, once he discovered CAs, to Michigan.

Toffoli's work focused on the concept of reversibility. One of the complaints about cellular automata had been that they could be executed only in a single direction in time; given a random formation, one could not easily retrace the process in order to determine what happened in the previous step and so on, to the initial seed configuration. This was an important criticism because the universe in which we live is assumed to be computationally reversible—given all knowledge, we can calculate what happened in a previous instant. If CAs could not be proven to have the same ability, the promise they held—to act as true complex dynamical systems and produce emergent behavior, up to and including the level where life is supported—was illusory. So Toffoli set out to prove that CAs, indeed, could be reversible.

"Suppose someone commissioned God to make an interesting universe," Toffoli says. "It would probably be reversible an i, indeed, it turns out our universe is reversible. And as it turns out, the simplest way for a reversible cellular automaton [to operate] is the same way the universe works." Through a long, arduous set of proofs, including some of the calculations he gleaned from a long-ignored Russian document that no one had even bothered to translate, Toffoli managed to construct this proof. "So we were able to remove an obstacle to the utilizability of cellular automata as models of fundamental physics," he says.

After Toffoli completed his thesis, he was just about to accept an offer from Bell Labs when he received a call from a very unusual man—an MIT professor who had never completed college but who had until recently headed the fabled Artificial Intelligence Laboratory there. This was Ed Fredkin. Fredkin had also postulated that CAs could be reversible and had even hypothesized a method called "the billiard-ball model" for proving this. It relied on a series of interactions reminiscent of the complex collisions found in the neighborhood pool hall, but the mathematics were sufficient to prove the theorem. "We have your thesis here," Fredkin told Toffoli. "The theoreticians say it is too practical, and the practical people say it is too theoretical, and neither know what to do with it. But I'm interested in the subject, so why don't you come for an interview?"

It would be a fortuitous match. Ed Fredkin had long been driven by the obsession to prove that the universe was made of information, and was in fact a mammoth computer. Fredkin had first developed an affinity for computers as a technician for the Army SAGE defense system—becoming one of the world's first virtuoso programmers—and he realized that computation was a compelling metaphor for the workings of physics. As he thought about it more, he discarded the qualifier of metaphor. "There is a kind of digital information process that underlies everything," he flatly states.

When Fredkin learned about CAs, he instantly realized that these artificial worlds were well suited to represent his theories. Fredkin considered these worlds as essentially no different from our own: he insisted that our known universe was literally a CA. According to Fredkin, the living organisms within this universe operated by the same principles.

"Living things may be soft and squishy," he says. "But the basis of life is clearly digital. We don't know how it works exactly, but instead of computer bits, there's a four-state code [the four base chemicals that make up DNA and whose sequencing forms the genetic code]. And there's some kind of process that interprets it. It's obviously some sort of program, running on a digital computer, it's just that the messages don't come in from a model, they come from chemicals. There are people who are against the concept, but then, many people used to think that organic compounds couldn't be synthesized by man—it's basically a vitalist point of view that there's something more than mechanism in life. The information is overwhelming that it is a digital information process, and that life can be mimicked in its entirety by such a process.

Put it another way—nothing is done by nature that can't be done by a computer. If a computer can't do it, nature can't."

In the 1970s, Fredkin's views were considered heretical. His reluctance to publish in academic journals did not help matters. His method of dissemination was the high-powered schmooze. Once, for instance, he took a year off specifically to spend time with Richard Feynman, perhaps the nation's most brilliant physicist. The two engaged in "wonderful, tense and interminable arguments," in Feynman's words. The sabbatical ended with the MIT professor gaining a more acute understanding of quantum theory, and with the Nobel laureate Feynman giving speeches on simulating physics with computers, and attributing his entire interest in the subject to Fredkin.

Fredkin could afford to hew his own paths. A canny identifier of technological niches and a successful entrepreneur, he founded a company and made millions; he even bought his own Caribbean island. His visionary knowledge of computers was sufficiently impressive for Marvin Minsky to recruit him to head Project MAC (Multiple-Access Computers/Machine-Aided Cognition), which included MIT's Artificial Intelligence Lab. As always, he ran into controversy. A typical instance was Fredkin's appearance on the Merv Griffin Show. Before a television audience unaccustomed to automata theory, Fredkin postulated a future where people would wear thousands of microscopically small robots on their heads, each manning a shaft of hair. These robots would be programmed to slice the hair when it reached a certain length. Some of his more conservative MIT colleagues considered this an indication that Fredkin was not serious.

By the time Fredkin left Project MAC, he had something else in mind: a separate fiefdom within MIT's Laboratory for Computer Science, dedicated to studying artificial phenomena, particularly those that would provide evidence for his contention that the universe is a computer. He called it the Information Mechanics Group. He knew it would be difficult to establish because, as he now recalls, "my work was held in low repute by both faculty and graduate students." He still bristles when he recalls one bright graduate student whom he asked to join the group. Although the young man was fascinated with CAs, his friends told him that, if he pursued that thread, he would be labeled a flake and his career would be ruined. "And what did he do?" asks Fredkin rhetorically of this lost soul. "Became a systems programmer! People don't trust their own feelings, and they're pushed by peer pressure towards the lowest common denominator."

Eventually Fredkin was able to assemble a first-rate staff whose passion for cellular automata, and whose belief that information was the basis for physical phenomena, overrode the potential stigma of exploring an unproven edge of scientific thought. Toffoli was his first hire. Then came Canadian computer scientist Norman Margolus, who would discover a simple reversible CA rule called "the Margolus rule," which elegantly confirmed the validity of Fredkin's billiard-ball model. Then there was French physicist Gerard Vichniac and for a brief period information theorist Charles Bennett. From their prestigious perch at MIT, the group set out to spread the word that physics could be simulated, particularly by cellular automata.

Toffoli and Margolus designed a special computer dedicated to the lightning-quick execution of CAs. They called it the cellular automata machine (CAM) and it zipped through the generations of, say, Conway's Life, quicker than a well-programmed version would on a Cray, the world's fastest general purpose computer. Later they compressed the entire computer into a single circuit board that could be inserted into an IBM personal computer. This sixth iteration of their computer, the CAM-6, offered significant benefits to explorers of artificial universes. Because most of the interesting results in CA research were unpredictable, and because the emergent phenomena that ideally came of CA experiments were attained only by actually running the program, the CAM-6 delivered millions of dollars worth of computer power to underfunded scientists panning for theoretical gold in the fields of information theory—at approximately $1500.

Equally significant was its role as a popularizer of the powers of cellular automata. Previously, when one viewed the chunk-chunk-chunk displacement of dots in a typical CA display, one would have either to understand fully the physics and mathematics that drive CA theory or to accept on faith that something significant was emerging. Things moved too slowly for one to perceive the changes. With the CAM-6, the deep implications of even the simplest CA, like Life, was suddenly accessible to even the most casual observer. It was the difference between a set of snapshots and a motion picture.

Toffoli and Margolus would dazzle visitors with the CAM-6. Their version of Conway's rule set added a neat twist: in addition to the two standard states, each represented by a color, a third color was added to represent a cell that was at one time alive but is now dead—a sort of fossil state. From an initial group of of poxlike clusters, the screen literally appeared as a simmering soup, suddenly self-organizing in a series of patterns, surrounded by fossil clouds. Then, as one's eyes focused on small parts, gliders became visible—as maggots once miraculously appeared on waste matter, they seemed to have arisen spontaneously!

Then Margolus and Toffoli would run reversible CAs. From an undifferentiated jumble of variegated color, the patterns on the screen resolved themselves into relatively stable configurations, resembling something Jackson Pollock might have done had he worked in needlepoint. These eventually diffused into confetti-like particles. Then Margolus would throw the universe into reverse. Chaos reemerged, sucking the pixels into what seemed a black hole. Finally the screen would reexplode into the initial state. It was like watching a time-lapse movie of the universe's formation, run in reverse—each second representing billions of years—all the way to the big bang. In the words of a journalist exposed to the CAM-6, "One could imagine Timothy Leary spending an entire vacation within fifteen feet of the machine."

The CAM-6 not only helped the Information Mechanics Group produce a sound body of research on cellular automata but motivated occasional newcomers to join the explorations. During the late 1970s, MIT became the center of the CA world. A small world, to be sure. Despite the von Neumann pedigree, Burks's faith, Fredkin's vision, and Toffoli's implementations, CA studies remained an obscure backwater of physics and information theory.

That all changed in 1982, when a brash and brilliant young scientist named Stephen Wolfram entered the field with the flourish of a featured actor who had dramatically withheld his appearance until the second act. Wolfram had been thinking on his own about the idea of cellular automata. Not knowing that they already existed, he basically reinvented them, only later discovering that they were not only an obscure scientific field but also a cult phenomenon. He considered the subject area interesting, and from Stephen Wolfram that adjective is about as high a compliment as one is likely to hear. More typical was his assessment of the work previously done in the field—"pitiful."

His gracelessness toward his predecessors knew no bounds. "When I started, there were maybe 200 papers written on cellular automata," he says. "It's amazing how little was concluded from those 200 papers. They're really bad." At one conference at Los Alamos, Wolfram met the grand Ulam, who had coinvented cellular automata with von Neumann, and afterward described the occasion with shocking disrespect: "I didn't like talking to him, because he would lapse into senility," recalls Wolfram. "I don't remember the exact things he said, he was trying to be nice, but it was very boring and embarrassing."

A classic Wolfram-ism. Still in his early thirties, Wolfram has ruffled more feathers than a sadistic ornithologist. He was not your ordinary upper-middle-class English lad. His father was a well-reviewed but minor novelist; his mother a philosophy professor at Oxford. Neither were apparently prepared for Stephen, who by his own description was a filial catastrophe, so horrid that baby-sitters would invariably refuse return engagements. At twelve he was sent off to Eton. Ignoring the fabled playing fields, he spent his time on a self-designed course of his single passion: science. The only actual schoolwork he performed was in the course of a small business he ran, doing math and physics homework for his wealthy classmates.

At fourteen he felt confident enough to send out a paper on a problem in particle physics to professors at Oxford and Cambridge. They accepted it as though a peer had produced it. Not long after that Wolfram began visiting those institutions and giving talks to physics professors.

He entered Oxford at sixteen, almost as an obligatory pass at normalcy. He felt that he was able to practice particle physics research without the training. On his first day, he recalls, "I went to the first-year lectures and found them awful. The second day I went to the second-year lectures and found that correspondingly awful. On the third day I went to one third-year lecture and decided it was all too horrible and I wasn't going to go to any more lectures." His studies were self-directed. He required no mentor, and none appeared. To the contrary, his contacts with the faculty bordered on acrimonious. He made one enemy when a rising physicist mentioned a question he had worked on for years, and Wolfram made an offhand comment that solved the problem. Wolfram himself considered the revered Oxford dons to be jerks and readily expressed his opinion. The only concession he made to convention was taking the year-end test required of all students after the first year. He finished at the top of the class.

Wolfram quit Oxford, going straight to graduate school at Cal Tech, where his champions included Nobel laureates Feynman and Murray Gell-Mann. He had just turned twenty when he earned his doctorate. He took a research post there, during which time he became the youngest recipient of the first round of MacArthur Fellowships—the so-called genius grants. But he fell out with Cal Tech over a dispute concerning the ownership of a symbol-manipulating computer language he had written. Of the many jobs offered, he took a post with the Institute for Advanced Study, the former home of both Einstein and von Neumann, where he further startled the establishment by discarding his pursuit of quantum chromodynamics in favor of what many considered a quasi-scientific diversion: cellular automata.

To some physicists, it seemed a stupendous misstep, akin to a young Henry Aaron leaving the major leagues to pursue an interest in Wiffle Ball. But Wolfram, as usual, knew what he was doing. His interest arose partially from his beliefs about the use of the computer in scientific research. He was convinced that science was on the brink of a new type of research methodology. Instead of constructing experiments with real materials, the computer itself was a viable substrate for experimentation. The computer was a realm somewhere in between mental excursions later articulated in logical formulas and hard-core manipulation of stuff in test tubes that yielded significant measurements. The territory was abstract, yet it existed, and nothing illustrated this new form of research quite as well as cellular automata.

Equally important to Wolfram was the fact that CAs were genuine complex systems, easily contained within the confines of a computer. Some of these systems were extremely interesting, displaying the same deep complexity that one sees in a wide variety of places—from nonlinear physical phenomena such as fluid turbulence to the economy and to living organisms. It was Wolfram's suspicion that he could use cellular automata to make significant statements about complex systems in general—particularly some ideas he had about the emergence of complexity from very simple origins.

It was at an informal conference at Moskito Island, Ed Fredkin's private resort, that Wolfram had a chance to observe the current avatars of cellular automata. Typically, Wolfram came to the tropical retreat without bothering to pack a bathing suit or even a pair of shorts: science, not recreation, drew him to the Caribbean. Fredkin, Toffoli, and Margolus were pleased to have Wolfram along; their pleasure would be somewhat tempered later on, when the brash newcomer insinuated himself as the key theorist in their field. A small indicator of the tensions is a dispute over whether Wolfram actually decided to focus on CAs during that 1982 foray to Moskito Island (as Fredkin and Toffoli say) or whether Wolfram had already made the choice by that time (as he insists).

Still, the MIT group realized that Wolfram's interest, and the attention he would bring to the field, would be to their benefit. "It's like a a small town where only one lawyer had been practicing before," explains Bennett, now an information theorist at IBM. "Another lawyer comes and they both get rich."

To Wolfram, though, CAs were peripheral to a major point he wanted to make about complexity. (Though for a brief period he did get involved in some CA hucksterism, by hawking postcards and note cards with pictures of interesting CAs.) "The point is simple," says Wolfram. "You can start out with something that seems quite simple, yet you can get out of it something which seems very complicated—so complicated that if you're presented with the thing, you can't tell anything but it seems random." Wolfram did not discover this important phenomenon—in fact, he considered it rather obvious—but he advanced its study by experimenting with it in CA universes.

To illustrate his point, Wolfram used his favorite variety of cellular automata, the one-dimensional (1-D) CA. Von Neumann's automaton, as well as Conway's Life, operated in two dimensions—vertical and horizontal. The 1-D variant was only horizontal; it occurred on a single-file line. Each cell touched only two other cells, one on the right and one on the left. An advantage of a 1-D cellular automaton was that a single picture could clearly reveal its history—each generation was represented by a single line residing under the previous line. Another benefit was that rule sets were simpler, so that it was feasible to study all possible variations of the domain and reach a definitive conclusion. After he discovered how powerful the 1-D variety could be, he marveled that no one had seriously used it before. "It seems like an incredibly obvious thing to do," he says now.

How did Wolfram use 1-D CAs to show how deep complexity results from simple input? He began with a simple 1-D cellular automaton, with cells in two possible states—on or off, alive or dead. It started with an initial configuration, a row of cells turned on or off at random. This was Line A. A new row beneath, Line B, would represent the next generation. The state of each cell in Line B was determined by a rule set. This particular set of rules considered three neighbors of the second-generation cell on Line B: the cell on Line A directly above it and the two cells on Line A on either side of that cell. There are eight possible combinations of the states of those three cells; representing the dead states with "0" and the live states with "1," the combinations are 111, 110, 101, 100, 011, 010, 001, and 000. In any given rule set, each of these triplets on Line A determines the state—either on or off—of the cell on Line B beneath the center of the triplet. For instance, one might look at a triplet on Line A and see that the cell on the left is on, the cell in the center is off, and the cell to the right is on. That would be represented as 101. A rule table might dictate that, for that particular triplet, the cell on Line B is on. Each cell of Line B would be determined in the same manner. The process would be repeated for Line C, and so on, until the entire computer screen filled in, like a fax machine churning out a transmitted image.

In this particular type of cellular automaton, there are 256 possible rule sets. Wolfram explored them all. Some of those rules quickly resolved themselves into boring configurations. One variation was blankness (all dead cells); another was darkness (all live cells). This is what Wolfram called, in his topology of CAs, a Class 1 CA. Another variation

The growth of a two-state (on or off) one-dimensional cellular automaton. The row of eight boxes on top shows the rule set: for each combination of three cells in generation 0, there is a determined result for the next-generation cell below the triplet. Beginning from a single seed, these rules are applied consistently, each generation represented by a horizontal row of cells. The first image shows five generations of growth, the second image shows fifty, and the third shows 100 generations, by which time it is clear that simple rules have generated considerable complexity.

5 generations

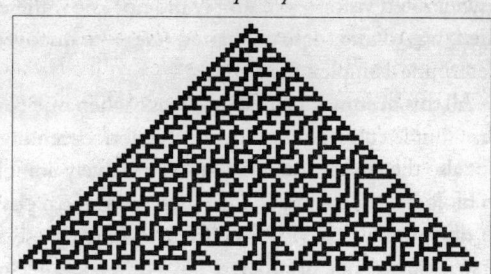

50 generations

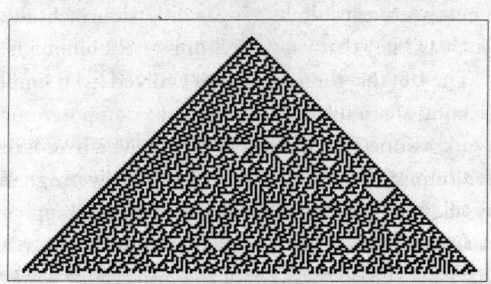

100 generations

71

was some other frozen configuration where initial activity ceased and stable structures reigned. Wolfram placed those examples in Class 2.

But other configurations broke up into relatively disordered patterns. These belonged to Class 3. The computer screen looked like video noise, sometimes pocked with a collection of inverted triangles that seemed to come in no discernible order. In fact, if someone followed a single column of cells from top to bottom, from Line A to Line Z, that person would have found it just about impossible to determine that the mechanism by which cells were turned on or off was not as random as coin tosses.

Of course, randomness had nothing to do with it. Whether or not a cell is turned on was entirely a deterministic consequence of the rules. Just as a stone, when someone picks it up and lets go, falls to the ground as a result of a rule of gravity. The consequences are determined.

Most of the time in nature, we can easily see the effect of rules, as classified by Newton. Wolfram's interpretations indicated that sometimes things are following simple rules when they seem to be following extremely complicated rules, or no rules at all. The problem was our own limited vision—we simply did not know these rules. His challenge, then, was to find those uncharted rules—to discover the natural laws that determine complex systems.

All this becomes a less abstract task when one considers the possibility that simple rules dictate not only chaotic, seemingly random, behavior but also the less disordered, yet still massively complex behavior one sees in biological behavior. Indeed there was a final class of CAs that seemed to display this behavior. Wolfram classified these as belonging to Class 4 structures—not disordered but complex, and sometimes long lived. These were capable of propagating information, and included all CAs (such as Life) that supported universal computers.

The fact that these structures evolved from simple rules was a hint that creating life in the data test tube of a computer might not be as daunting a task as one would have thought. Much progress could be made by determining what laws nature laid out, by programming those laws, and by allowing lifelike behavior to emerge in applying those algorithms.

Could this be done? Wolfram was reluctant to allow that things were that easy. It really was not at the heart of his work, which focused more on building an artificial physics to understand better complex systems in general—in fact, he contended that his classification of CAs into four classes was indeed a step toward measuring complexity itself. Yet he was intrigued by some fascinating hints that something very much like cellular automata actually occurred in the world outside mathematics and the computer.

Most strikingly, Wolfram assembled a collection of seashells that people sent him after reading his papers and hearing him lecture. The conchlike shells were marked with patterns of inverted triangles. No one who observed a lot of one-dimensional CAs could take a single glance at one of these shells and fail to make the connection with one-dimensional CAs. It almost seemed that the patterns were peeled off the computer screen and pasted onto the shells. The obvious conclusion was that cellular automata principles were the determining factor in dishing out pigmentation in mollusk shells.

When you viewed nature from the lens of cellular automata, there were plenty of other new things to see. For instance, a neurobiologist postulated that CA rules might be in play within the visual cortex, enabling our vision system. (Not coincidentally, some computer scientists began using CAs to do image processing.) A pathologist discovered a new way to analyze blood smears by using a CA rule to count white blood cells. And a research physician at the University of Arizona extensively documented CA-like activity in natural structures in biological cells called cytoskeletal microtubules.

A comparison between the natural pattern on a mollusk shell and the pattern of a simple one-dimensional cellular automaton.

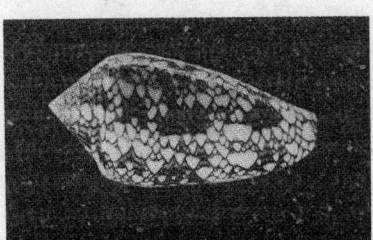 

Wolfram did not claim that CAs actually accounted for these natural occurrences. After all, CAs were but mathematical models, which just happened to become real when they are run in the computer. While Wolfram did not take pains to contradict Ed Fredkin's contention that the world itself was a cellular automaton, the ur-CA from which everything sprung, neither did he spend much time thinking about it. To Wolfram cellular automata were a sort of rock under which might be crawling some key hints to nature's hidden doings.

The idea that cellular automata could actually create a specific phenomenon of nature also intrigued Norman Packard, a physicist who worked with Wolfram at the Institute for Advanced Study. Packard made a conscious attempt to link this type of work to the real world. "When one works in these abstract models, a responsible scientist feels the urge to touch base with reality," explains Packard. "It's one thing to come up with a theoretical framework that describes the flow of information within the class of abstract models, but it's another thing to actually bridge the gap between theoretical models and some system that's actually doing something. You could make measurements on them and make correspondence between the theory and the actual system."

What did Packard choose to emulate using CAs? Snowflakes. "You have that diversity—every snowflake is supposed to be different, though that's untestable—yet you have recognizable structure." Packard here was applying information theory to snowflakes. It worked pretty well. If every snowflake were identical, picking up a new snowflake would give you no more information than you would have already from looking at other flakes. If every snowflake had a random structure, like chips of ice, the information would be different but meaningless. Instead, there is a syntax within snowflakes, several main types of structures, which are capable of containing individual variations. This is the richest form of propagating information and is found in human languages as well as biological reproduction.

The question is, What determines how snowflakes look the way they look? Snowflakes form in the stratosphere when cold air becomes too thin to hold the water vapor. The air then reaches a state called supersaturation. From a seed in the air—perhaps a dust mote or a speck of pollen—the water vapor grabs on and begins growing as the vapor condenses and turns into ice. Simultaneously, the growth is affected by heat generated by the solidification process. Packard found that, depending on conditions, snowflakes take on certain general aspects. One set of conditions yields configurations that look like plates; another determines snowflakes shaped like collections of rods; and another yields complicated dendritic stars. Yet no one knows exactly why they differ slightly. "The relationship between the freezing of the ice and the diffusion of heat is what makes the problem complicated, and may have to do with what makes the pattern complicated," says Packard.

Packard's approach to the problem was to build snowflakes in the computer. He recognized that this approach would not definitively answer questions about snowflakes—merely because something happened inside of his computer did not mean that there was any correlation to stratospheric events on snowy days. His goal was to drive home a point that the same sort of phenomenon could occur inside the computer as in nature. By using CAs, he figured, maybe he could get things that looked so much like snowflakes that even a casual observer would be forced to admit a probable connection. Let the meteorologists worry about what happened from then on.

Packard wrote a program for a cellular automaton in which the off cells, or those assigned a value of 0, represented water vapor, and the on cells, or those assigned a value of 1, corresponded to ice and appeared on the screen in color. The action occurred on the boundary of the forming snowflake and grew outward. A typical set of rules initiated a scan of a cell's neighborhood, totaled the values of the surrounding cells, and filled the new cells with either ice or water vapor, depending on whether the total was odd or even. Pure mathematics, no chemistry.

"Immediately upon simulation, certain things started appearing which were very suggestive of real snowflakes," says Packard. True, the CA models did not have some of the complicated structures seen on real snowflakes, particularly those with structures based on patterns of needlelike shapes. But Packard's snowflakes had plates and dendrites growing from the corners of the plates, from which more dendrites grew. An elementary schoolchild could look at any one of the gorgeous pictures of computer screens in Packard's collection and instantly identify it as a snowflake.

Snowflakes, of course, were not life-forms. But the same principle—that simple rules could duplicate the behavior of nonliving complex systems in nature—could apply to attempts to duplicate the actions of biological phenomena, even creatures on the upper stories of the evolutionary skyscraper. Perhaps the most striking example of this came not from a physicist or biologist but from a computer animator.

From the time Craig Reynolds was in college he thought that one could write computer programs with simple rules to simulate the complex movements of animals. His job as a computer animator in the graphics division of the Symbolics computer company offered him the necessary opportunity. Not far from where Reynolds lived in Culver City, California, was a cemetery where great numbers of blackbirds congregated. Reynolds would go there with his friends and speculate on how difficult it would be to get computer creatures to flock in the same way the blackbirds did. The computer animators would bring lunch and watch the birds. It was fascinating how the feathered creatures would suddenly take off and assume a formation, as if some hidden drill coach had blown a whistle. Ornithologists didn't really have a solid explanation for this dazzling skill. To Reynolds it appeared that there was no drill instructor bird, that the phenomenon of flocking was a decentralized activity, where each bird followed some simple rules. The group behavior then emerged from that collective action. In Reynolds's description, "The motion of a flock of birds is . . . simple in concept yet is so visually complex it seems randomly arrayed and yet is magnificently synchronous. Perhaps most puzzling is the strong impression of intentional centralized control. Yet all evidence indicates that flock motion must be merely the aggregate result of the actions of individual animals, each acting solely on the basis of its local perception of the world."

If indeed Reynolds's theory was correct, flocking could be modeled by allowing each individual in the simulation to apply a few simple rules. Flock behavior would then spontaneously emerge. The trick was finding out the rules. After logging many hours in the cemetery, Reynolds boiled the behavior down to three primary components:

1. A clumping force that kept the flock together.

2. An ability to match velocity so that the birds in the flock would move at the same speed.

3. A separation force that prevented birds from getting too close to each other.

He then implemented these rules for birds inside his computer. He called these "boids." (This was not a Brooklynese mangling but a techie abbreviation of "birdoid" that applied not only to simulated flocking birds but also to schooling fish.) Their observations and actions were entirely local. As they flew, the boids would notice what their neighbors were doing—as though they were cells in a cellular automaton—and apply that information to their own actions in the next time step. Each boid, for instance, would detect the center of gravity within the radius it was aware of and move toward that point. If other boids were to the left, for instance, the boid would move left. It would try to match its speed to the velocity of the nearby boids, unless slowing down or speeding up was required to stay near the flock. And if a boid looked as though it was inching too close to a neighbor, it would move away from that potential collision.

Hoping to finish in time to present his results to the 1987 SIG-GRAPH computer graphics convention, Reynolds worked hard on the program and within two days saw confirmation of his theories. "They really didn't look like birds, but there was something about it you recognized," says Reynolds. "A goofy kind of flocking that you wouldn't see on nature shows, but you knew immediately what it was." As he fine-tuned the program over the next few months, eventually using it in a colleague's animation project to control the behavior of flocking birds and schooling fish, he began to get precisely the kind of flocking you *would* see on nature shows. Uncannily so. The boids, each one using nothing but Reynolds's simple rules, were able to flock in large configurations so convincingly that ornithologists, intuiting that real birds might be performing the same algorithms as Reynolds's creations, began calling the animator to find out his rules.

At the beginning of each run, the boids, which appeared on the computer screen like line drawings of paper planes, hardly hesitated before quickly moving together, as if a vacuum cleaner had drawn them in a well-spaced flock. They would shimmy along, maintaining a stable configuration in the center of the flock, while the boids at the edges slowed down and sped up to maintain their presence in the group. They seemed to be making minute adjustments akin to slight movements that a driver makes on a fairly straight road. When Reynolds programmed the simulation so the center of gravity would zigzag, the boids had no trouble maintaining the integrity of the flock while traveling on this slalomlike path. Reynolds even performed some runs where the computer display represented the point of view of an individual boid—a boid-cam!—which showed a certain jerkiness as the boid steered away from the fringe of the flock to maintain contact with the group.

Then Reynolds tried some runs in which the flock encountered obstacles—specifically thick cylinders resembling Grecian columns. No problem. The flock would part at the column, with the boids turning well before they reached the obstacle. This was remarkable since that response was not programmed into them. After veering around the cylinder, the flock would reunite. It was a response common in a perfectly natural flock of birds. Reynolds found that his model yielded some sorts of behavior that were entirely unanticipated and surely were not directly implied by his Spartan rules. For instance, one hapless boid, when its flock was avoiding an obstacle, found itself hemmed in by fellow boids, unable to miss colliding with the column. It slammed into the cylinder, halted for a brief instant—seemingly dazed—and then, as though regaining consciousness and belatedly recalling the rules, sped up to join the flock.

Obviously, something was happening in this simulation, quite possibly something that had relevance to real birds, perhaps to group motion in general. At the least it seemed that Reynolds's theory, a hypothesis based on observation and evaluation of the literature, had enhanced its viability by being successfully implemented. It did not mean that birds actually used those rules, but it at least showed that using those rules would produce a behavior that looked like flocking. Would not ornithologists benefit from using these models to perform the sorts of experi-

A flock of Craig Reynolds's "boids" confront a cluster of pillars. Since their behavior is emergent, it was not clear even to Reynolds how the columns would affect the flight of the boids. As it happened, the flock was undaunted—it temporarily split into two flocks and then reunited.

ments that would be impossible in the field but absurdly simple in the computer room? "One serious application," Reynolds wrote,

> would be to aid in the scientific investigation of flocks, herds, and schools. These scientists must work almost exclusively in the observational mode; experiments with natural flocks and schools are difficult to perform and are likely to disturb the behaviors under study. It might be possible, using a more carefully crafted model of the realistic behavior of a certain species of bird, to perform controlled and repeatable experiments with "simulated natural flocks." A theory of flock organization can be unambiguously tested by implementing a distributed behavioral model and simply comparing the aggregate motion of the simulated flock with the natural one.

Reynolds was suggesting a departure for biologists and zoologists—setting aside the observation of physical creatures in favor of the more malleable virtual creatures that live inside a computer. Even if their guts were made of mathematics and not gory wet stuff. For researchers more accustomed to squatting in marshes than to planting themselves behind workstations, this was an unreliable and most unwelcome departure. But as lifelike behavior emerged on more and more computer screens, the approach became harder to dismiss.

It seemed to apply to things that swarm and crawl as well as to those that fly. Even entomologists skeptical of computer experiments could not easily account for the attractive results of a team of Belgian scientists who used cellular automata and other computer models to evoke the collective behavior of social insects. What bound this team, which called itself the Unit of Theoretical Behavioural Ecology at the Free University of Brussels, was a desire to amplify the theories of self-organization advanced by their Nobel Prize–winning colleague Ilya Prigogine. Their backgrounds varied, but the story of Jean-Louis Deneubourg was typical. He was a chemist conversant with the phenomenon of molecular self-organization who stumbled on a book written by E. O. Wilson about the behavior of wasps. He intuited that some of Prigogine's self-organizational principles were at play in insect social behavior, particularly in cases of allelomimesis (which meant that an individual's actions were dictated by the actions of a neighbor). Whereas traditional biological canons had it that the complexity of collective behavior could be traced to complex behavior in individuals, Deneubourg and his colleagues believed otherwise. "Even very simple allelomimetic behavior can be the source of complex and surprising group behavior," he wrote in a paper coauthored by Simon Goss, a British biologist in his group. It was no coincidence that this seemed in lockstep with Stephen Wolfram's basic point about cellular automata—complex behavior from simple rules—because the Brussels group used CAs as a means of verifying their theories about social insects and self-organization.

"We create a script," explains Deneubourg. "This script is the byproduct of observation in the laboratory, empirical knowledge on social insect organization, and also some feelings on nonlinear systems." For instance, a script might deal with the way that termites collect food. After observing termites dealing with food sources, Deneubourg and his associates would try to boil down a few simple rules that drove each individual insect to behave the way it did (much the same way Craig Reynolds figured out the rules for boid flocking). Then they would write a computer simulation to see whether the hypothesis was sound— whether the observed behavior of a biological collective entity would emerge from the computer simulation. In this case, they might use a cellular automaton in which patterns of live cells could not only change to several different states but "move" by shifting to other locations. If certain conditions existed, a CA pattern representing a termite picked up food; other conditions led it to drop pheromones that would attract subsequent simulated termites. The little blocks of live cells on the screen turned out to be effective in gathering the simulated food pieces scattered around the simulated environment.

To further argue for the validity of a model, the Brussels team would change something in the model—perhaps they would alter the size of a food source—and would note the different behavior of the simulated termites. Then they would refer back to nature. This did not require much effort since their laboratories stored, on pans stacked on shelves, dozens of active insect colonies. Pulling out a colony was no more difficult than heading to the bookcase to refer to a technical volume. They would make the same change in the colony as they did on the computer, this time with a real food source. If the real termites did the same thing that the simulated ones did, then the case that the same phenomenon was occurring in both places would be compelling.

The Brussels group's main intention was to study the processes of self-organization. But they believed that entomologists would do well to adopt their techniques and use artificial life to shed light on natural processes. "I don't wish to be arrogant," says Goss. "But the people who do field work go out in the field and at the end of three months come back with seventy notebooks filled with illustrations—and they don't know what to do with it. If you've got a model in your mind and you work to create simulations, you've got a lot of specific questions that you have to answer, and it makes it easier to direct your observational effort to things that matter, particular problems, and particular behavior. It tells you what to look for."

And using cellular automata, or similar artificial life computer modeling techniques, theories could be convincingly verified. It had always been von Neumann's intuition that the computer would become the most important staging ground for scientific experimentation. Stephen Wolfram had amplified those thoughts in his own writings. Deconstructing and rebuilding nature with the approach of Reynolds and the Brussels group now extended that methodology—deep into the realm of biology.

Ironically, all this activity spiraling around cellular automata, spurred in part by Wolfram's work, did not endear Wolfram to the ruling powers at the Institute for Advanced Study. His colleagues there seemed to take offense at his insistence that one could actually do science on the computer itself, that the goings on across the divide of the computer screen could be observed, discussed, and regarded as real occurrences. His aerie on the third floor of Fuld Hall, stacked with computers and workstations—*things!*—presented an affront to them, and they in turn presented an affront to Wolfram as it became clear that his four-year stint at the institute would not be extended permanently. By that time, Wolfram was actively seeking options, and he accepted an offer from the University of Illinois to head a new Institute of Complex Studies. His term there had hardly begun when Wolfram formed a software company, its main product a new mathematics processing software called Mathematica. The company was so successful that it occupied much of Wolfram's time over the next few years. By the time he was ready to devote the bulk of his energies once more to scientific work, he was no longer pegged as the bad boy of physics, although his opinions of his peers had not mellowed as he entered his fourth decade. "It's depressing perhaps," he notes, perhaps with a measure of self-parody, "but as I get older my opinion of myself has only gotten better."

Stephen Wolfram believed that he was destined finally to identify the hidden laws that govern the universe and to provide "a general mathematical theory to describe the nature and generation of complexity," and he had no doubts he would succeed where others failed.

He was not alone in this effort. There were others working independently or in small groups to crack these closely held natural secrets, which dictated among other things the behavior of living systems.

GARAGE-BAND SCIENCE

The ultimate goal of the study of artificial life would be to create "life" in some other medium, ideally a virtual medium where the essence of life has been abstracted from the details of its implementation in any particular model. We would like to build models that are so life-like that they cease to become models of life and become examples of life themselves.

Chris Langton

James Doyne Farmer sensed deep implications behind the jitterbugs and percolations of cellular automata. To Farmer math and logic were found not only in silicon chips and equations but also in dripping faucets and rain forests; toy universes held a key to a solution of a certain problem, a mighty conundrum that loomed as the most important scientific question of his day. It mattered little that this problem existed only in the *Weltanschauung* of a few. Yesterday the question had not occurred even to a few. Tomorrow, he believed, it would concern many scientists.

It involved the understanding of natural forces that dictated the behavior of complex systems such as biological organisms. It was the same quest that intrigued Stephen Wolfram. Farmer called it the Holy Grail of complexity. And he believed its pursuit was intimately intertwined with the quest for artificial life.

Farmer was a gangling man with pointed features and sharp, hawklike eyes. His light brown hair was bound in a ponytail, and his sartorial preferences tended toward T-shirts or Latin-style *camisas*. Farmer was born in 1952 in the desert town of Silver City, New Mexico. After attending Stanford—he graduated wearing a gorilla suit, as a punning tribute to the Viet Cong—Farmer went to graduate school at the University of California, Santa Cruz, where he and a cadre of maverick physics students, including Norman Packard (the cellular automatist who would later construct mathematical snowflakes in Wolfram's laboratory) would earn their spurs as pioneers in chaos, the theory of complex dynamical systems. Farmer and his colleagues worked on defining the chaotic perturbations of dripping faucets and erratic heartbeats. Hewing to the egalitarian ethos of time and place, the group called itself a collective and attempted to share credit on all its revelations. Ultimately, this idealistic ambition became pressured by the relentless protocols of establishment science. Certain names had to be signed to certain papers; certain credits had to be assigned so they could accrue on certain resumes. Jobs, after all, could not be shared. The collective eventually disbanded, with some disgruntlements, but the spirit lingered in the manner in which each member practiced science.

A particular interest for Farmer was prediction: he believed that complex systems, which, as we learned from CAs, often seemed hopelessly random when in fact simple rules dictated their form, offered the observer a fairly good chance of knowing what might happen next. He, Packard, and friends put these ideas to the test when they devised a computer program that they hoped would track the meanderings of a roulette ball. They took the scheme to Las Vegas. The computer that ran the hardware fit inside a shoe and sent radio signals to someone who would sent a discreet signal to the player. The algorithms worked; eventually the scientists turned over the equipment to professional gamblers, who periodically sent the scientists royalties from the winnings.

All that was secondary to what had tantalized Farmer ever since a boyhood reading of a brief tale by Isaac Asimov, "The Last Question." In that story, humankind created a prodigious computer, so intelligent that people posed deep questions to it. But it was unable to answer a key query dealing with the second law of thermodynamics: Could the increase in entropy in the universe somehow be reversed? The Question, of course, is less critical now than it would become billions of years later, when presumably entropy would irrevocably increase and usable energy would inevitably decrease to the point where life could not be sustained. In other words, useful energy was an hourglass, and when it emptied, nothing could survive. Was there a way out of the dilemma? During the course of Asimov's fifteen-page story, centuries passed, thousands of centuries, millions of centuries, trillions. We learned that people eventually merged with the great machines they had created (in much the same fantastic scenario envisioned by the NASA summer study concerning self-reproducing machines), but the Question, asked again and again, still went unanswered by the computer, which complained that there was insufficient data to compile a reply. Finally, all the matter of the universe merged into a single conscious entity: the machine, which was consumed with this now vital Question. As all energy was absorbed, all matter dispersed, the entity finally arrived at an answer to the Question, and its utterance reversed entropy: let there be light.

"Which in my mind, is a capricious way to end a story," says the adult Farmer. "But it does give you an idea that evolution might be a broader process than is usually thought, which runs contrapuntally to the increase in entropy in the Universe." Farmer sought alternative views of evolution, and in the works of Herbert Spencer, a contemporary of Darwin, he came across ideas of self-organization. Spencer was perhaps the first to identify evolution as an apparent foe of the second law of thermodynamics. While entropy dissolved order, evolution, by drawing on the force of self-organization, bootstrapped increasingly complex eddies of order, seemingly ignoring the insistent one-way sign posted by the second law. The same phenomenon of self-organization would later intrigue those who noticed it in cellular automata, bird flocking, and insect social behavior. Like those scientists, says Farmer, "I see self-organization as a deep physical principle along the lines of the second law of thermodynamics. I think there exists an inexorable principal that's embedded in physics in a broad way, a very useful physical law."

But what were these principles? And how would we find them?

Farmer viewed the last part of our century as analogous to the fertile period in the nineteenth century when giants of science discovered, codified, and verified what are now known as the laws of thermodynamics or statistical mechanics. "If you look at that time, people were kicking around funny ideas about heat and work, in vague terms," says Farmer. "What it really took to make it happen was the development of precise measuring instruments to quantify concepts like temperature. For instance, [English scientist James Preston] Joule did experimental work, very nitty gritty things—he put a propeller in a vat of water and measured the work needed to turn the propeller, while he simultaneously measured the resulting rise in the temperature of the water. As a result, he was able to show a relationship between temperature, heat, and work. Once the language was made precise, others were able to put together a theory of what was occurring."

Thermodynamic law was a tremendous advance, but it did not provide the laws that dictate what happens in complicated phenomena such as complex dynamical systems—the weather, the economy, or biological organisms. As the Santa Cruz Dynamical Systems Collective demonstrated, even something as commonplace as a dripping faucet displayed perplexingly complicated behavior that was ultimately classified as chaotic, and new rules had to be divined to understand that behavior. All this was a subject that, perhaps because of its difficulty, physicists had managed to avoid for centuries.

Only recently did scientists begin to deal with this complexity, partly because the power of the computer made it possible to freeze the phenomenon and study it in a controlled situation, and partly because of a new willingness to abandon the constricting specialization that had become standard in scientific practice and instead to draw from many disciplines. Studying complexity often required expertise not only in physics and mathematics but also in information theory, computer science, physiology, chemistry, population genetics, and game theory. Following a trail in complexity studies could lead one from an economic analysis of fluctuations in corn prices to a study of the development of antibodies in the immune system. Strange correspondences were the key to breakthroughs here. But, as Farmer liked to point out, scientists had yet to devise the equivalent of the experimental methods used by Joule and the other wizards of thermodynamics.

Until the right experiments were found and the appropriate theories classified, Farmer and his colleagues were forced to deal with a mounting accumulation of circumstantial evidence that a major body of laws was waiting to be unearthed—no less than a set of fundamental principles dictating complexity, including the workings of life. "We know that there are important problems to work on, we feel there's something that's pregnant to happen—but we're still thrashing around to figure out what it really is," says Farmer. "That's why this work is so exciting right now. Because there's a very big discovery waiting to be made. . . . To state as a physical law a principle which would describe the way in which the world organizes itself."

There would be many payoffs accruing from that big prize, and the biggest of all, as far as Farmer was concerned, was that discovering these principles would cough up the secret of life and further the effort to create it synthetically. Farmer was a believer that human beings would create the workings of life, and he sensed that the accomplishment of this monumental achievement is bound inextricably with the study of complexity. He viewed his work in chaos, merging physics with biology to shake loose the mysteries of life, as a bridge to this new challenge.

After leaving Santa Cruz, Farmer accepted a postdoctoral position at the Los Alamos National Laboratory, in a section called the Center for Nonlinear Studies (CNLS). The center studied complex nonlinear systems. The mission of Los Alamos was directed to the nation's defense— specifically to research in nuclear weapons. But money also was set aside for basic research, and CNLS, which operated as a separate entity, was funded in part from that stash. The work was nonclassified, and the squat one-story building in which the scientists worked was located "outside the fence," as lab parlance had it, sharing a parking lot with the Bradbury Science Museum in which replicas of the original atomic bombs were ogled daily by tourists and visiting schoolchildren.

At the time Farmer arrived, the only person at CNLS doing similar complexity work was Mitchell Feigenbaum, whose career, after years of obscurity, was just then soaring on the strength of his original observations in chaos. But soon after Farmer's arrival, Feigenbaum left, and the new postdoc found himself inheriting a position of authority. So when the director told him that the center had budgeted $35,000 to bring in visiting scientists and asked him, Could he provide a list of people? Farmer used the opportunity to draw together what would later become a shortlist of key a-life researchers.

In May 1985 Farmer, with, among others, his old friend Packard, cochaired a conference at Los Alamos called "Evolution, Games, and Learning." An odd mixture of subjects. But as Farmer and Packard put it in their opening remarks, "The purpose . . . is to bring together the study of adaptive processes in nature and their implementation in artificial systems, exploring what these different approaches have in common and what they have to learn from each other."

This was intriguing on its face—melding natural phenomena with artificial systems. But Farmer and Packard ventured into what most people would consider murkier ground. They asserted that the traditional approach of physicists, that of reductionism, would not work in this quest—instead a synthesis was required to answer the questions they were now posing:

1. What are the basic principles underlying the evolution of biological organisms?

2. What are the basic principles underlying the operation of the brain?

3. How can machines learn to solve problems without being explicitly programmed, or more generally, how can we make them think?

Undoubtedly those experiments would utilize the extraordinary powers of the computer. Von Neumann and others had already anticipated the significance of the computer in altering the practice of science (the late physicist Heinz Pagels tersely identified it as "the primary research instrument of the sciences"). Farmer had another point to make—that, as computer power increased and the cost of computer power decreased, tremendously sophisticated research methods became accessible to almost any scientist. A young physicist interested in complexity had a terrific advantage over a predecessor a mere two decades previous—the ability to do world-class science on a garden-variety sun workstation. It was almost as though an astrophysicist had his own personal radio telescope or a particle physicist owned her own nuclear accelerator.

"The situation," Farmer and Packard wrote, "is reminiscent of the '60s music scene, when electronics got cheap enough that anyone with ambition could buy an electric guitar and start a rock band in their own garage." This was, they contended, the early stages of an explosion— they called it "new wave science"—and through a combination of insight and serendipity, where experimentation often runs ahead of theory, breakthroughs would come.

Farmer and Packard felt they were directly engaged in new wave science. Farmer had a small grant from the Air Force that he used to bring in some of his former colleagues from Santa Cruz, but there was no room for them at Los Alamos. So they rented a big adobe house in El Rancho, between Los Alamos and Santa Fe, a former speakeasy with a 15-foot tin ceiling, a working kitchen, and a Ping-Pong table. Having run cables all over the place to hook up to their computers, they commenced work and explored CAs, dynamical systems, and simulated evolution. "It really was in a sense garage-band science," says Farmer.

In the early 1980s another young man was moved by the music of garage-band science. Before even receiving his first degree, and funded only by indentured earnings from a stained-glass shop, this nascent artificial lifer could nonetheless exploit a $1500 Apple II Computer to advance the world's knowledge about the biology of artificial systems, performing work that would ultimately be published in one of the world's most prestigious physics journals.

This was Christopher Gale Langton. Doyne Farmer had met him a few months prior to the Los Alamos meeting, at a small conference in Cambridge. Though Farmer knew of Langton, he did not associate his face with his work. So Farmer, not knowing his lunch companion, asked as a conversation opener what sort of science Langton practiced.

"Well, I don't really know what to call it," said Langton of his work. "The best thing I might come up with is . . . artificial life."

Farmer had found an ally who would help realize the vision lurking in Farmer's heart ever since that Asimov story. If indeed John von Neumann was to be known as the father of this field, artificial life, Chris Langton was to be its midwife.

Langton came to his profession late. As one former teacher put it, Langton spent his formative years not in the company of wise teachers but "sort of bumming around." Though they did not physically resemble each other—Langton's features were open and rough hewn, crafted by a much rougher sculptor than the one who carefully chiseled Farmer's physiognomy—he and Farmer were siblings in style, sons of the Southwest, though Langton was an adopted son. Either of them could have drifted off the set of a Sam Shepard play, a desert rat who at the drop of a dime could launch into a mesmerizing explanation of some obscure scientific phenomenon that would amazingly spread open to the big picture, leaving novices blinking at the phrase transition.

Yet Langton was equipped with a pedigree. His father was a physicist, employed by a Massachusetts-based company called Baird Atomic, which made mass spectrometers and similarly esoteric scientific tools. His mother earned an astronomy degree, though she found her calling as an author of children's books and mysteries. Jane Langton's books were steeped in the transcendentalist tradition of New England literature; perhaps her best-known work was *Emily Dickinson Is Dead*.

So it was that Chris Langton, born 1948 in Cambridge, Massachusetts, home of MIT, inherited a natural affinity for science. But as a form of rebellion almost obligatory in the time of his youth, he resisted its lure. Still, when applying for college, he vaguely hoped to master computer programming. He vividly recalled the huge kick he got from toying with the computer at his father's workplace. When a high school counselor told him, inaccurately, that Rockford College, a small conservative institution in Illinois, was about to get an expensive computer, Langton chose it. The misdirection didn't bother Langton, who majored in, he recalls, "nothing in particular." His long hair and antiwar sentiments put him at odds with his surroundings, and he dropped out of Rockford College, he claims, at the approximate moment the administration requested his removal.

Subsequently, there was the problem of the draft. Langton applied for and was granted conscientious-objector status. He performed his alternative service at Boston's Massachusetts General Hospital; after he had labored in the morgue for about a week, a corpse he was wheeling to the autopsy room suddenly sat up. He asked for another job at the hospital and was sent to the computer room of the Stanley Cobb Laboratory for Psychiatric Research.

Initially, it was just a job—if the young objector had any driving motivation, and this was doubtful, it was an attempt to organize a blues-rock band, himself on guitar. But he came to like the work, programming computers to interpret EEGs and performing other data analysis. He lived across the street from the hospital and would show up for work in late afternoon and work through the night. Langton and his fellow midnight programmers at the big DEC mainframe felt as though they were stoking a huge boiler. "We were feeding the machine bits and emptying out bits," he recalls. "You had the feeling of being a fire tender, of tending a locomotive." He learned a lot about computers there, but a more vital process began in the Cobb Laboratory: Langton got the first whiff of what he came to regard as a wonderfully intoxicating intellectual scent.

He detected the scent the day he was charged with the task of making programs written for a different computer run on the PDP-7—building a virtual machine inside another machine. That exposed to him the computer's protean abilities—without reading Turing's work, Langton understood it was a universal machine.

The scent grew more pungent when some people came into the lab with the MIT program that executed Conway's Life. Life enthralled Langton, who developed a particular affinity for a configuration centered on a perfectly balanced starlike structure, a period 2 blinker, flickering back and forth at alternate generations. Then a stray glider would hit the structure; equilibrium gone, the star would dissolve into the mist. That provoked thoughts on mortality. Langton was even more deeply impressed by an incident late one night when he was alone in the lab. The computer was running a long Life configuration, and Langton hadn't been monitoring it closely. Yet suddenly he felt a strong presence in the room. Something was there. He looked up, and the computer monitor showed an interesting configuration he hadn't previously encountered. "I crossed a threshold then," he recalls. "It was the first hint that there was a distinction between hardware and the behavior it would support. . . . You had the feeling there was really something very deep here in this little artificial universe and its evolution through time. [At the lab] we had a lot of discussions about whether the program could be open ended—could you have a universe in which life could evolve?"

Experimenting with the game, Langton probed its limitations and potentials, envisioning himself as a physicist testing various collisions with a virtual particle chamber. He would collide gliders at different angles and note the consequences; he would alter the rules to see the effect on breeding new configurations. He came to appreciate the delicate balance that Conway's rules instilled in the private universe of Life.

Even then Langton suspected that somehow a computer might be able to emulate life itself, but his thinking about this was vague. "I couldn't put it into a grand overall picture," he now explains. "But that was the initial scent."

The psychiatrist in charge of Cobb left Massachusetts General in 1972, and the lab dissolved as suddenly as a periodic Life configuration fatally winged by a stray glider. Langton drifted, delivering a Land Rover to Texas, doing odd jobs in San Francisco, and winding up in Puerto

Rico, where he had accepted an offer to program a computer for the Caribbean Primate Research Center, which was engaged in a study of monkey behavior. After completing his data base, he lingered for over a year, spending more time with the primate subjects of the studies than with the humans conducting them. The attraction was a chance to observe the development of behavior in a nonhuman culture. Somehow it fit the scent.

Langton realized he required a formal scientific education. He returned to New England, took courses in calculus and cosmology at Boston University, and decided to move to the University of Arizona in Tucson. In the summer of 1975, planning to make his way west slowly, he set out with several friends. Their idea was to indulge in a mutual passion while traveling—hang gliding. The experience almost killed him.

It happened on Grandfather Mountain, the highest peak in North Carolina's Blue Ridge Mountains. Langton's party had been there for two months, funded by the resort owner as a semiofficial tourist attraction; when the hang gliders soared 1000 feet above the mountain in 40-mile-an-hour winds, it made a pretty sight for visitors. On the last day before heading to Arizona, Langton set out to try one final spot landing. He hit wind shear and stalled out at tree level. He went straight down.

"I broke both my arms, both my legs, and as my knees came up they literally crushed my face to my skull," recalls Langton, running through a familiar if chilling litany. "I broke all the bones in my face, broke my jaw, punctured and collapsed a lung. . . ."

In the months that followed, many of them spent flat on his back in a hospital bed, Langton had ample opportunity to ruminate. He used the time to devour texts from many disciplines—astronomy, philosophy, evolution, genetics—and he came to realize that his brain, shaken clean of cobwebs from the crash, was absorbing knowledge like a dry sponge. It was as though his mind were a computer hit by a power surge and was now rebooting and fed a new data set. Even more fascinating to Langton was the feeling that his synapses, in his mind's attempt to reconstruct itself, were self-organizing, much as individual ants in a colony arrange themselves in a manner conducive to perform a task.

By the time he arrived in Tucson, Arizona, a year later, he knew what he wanted to study: the basis of an artificial biology. The problem was that his proposed curriculum was unprecedented; no single department would take on an undergraduate who required advanced study in, among other things, mathematics, anthropology, physics, computer science, molecular evolution, philosophy, ecology, and population genetics. Langton would sign up for twenty courses a semester, dropping the dogs and sticking with the ones "where the scent was the strongest."

Around that time, the first personal computers appeared. It occurred to Langton that he could use one of these modern marvels to vivify his theories—to actually create something that displayed lifelike behavior. Borrowing the money from a woman who owned a stained-glass shop, he bought an Apple II; he arranged to repay the debt by sandblasting glass over the next year.

At first, his goal was creating a computer model of evolution. He had in mind a phenomenon that occurred in a population of white moths in nineteenth-century England. As a consequence of the Industrial Revolution, soot from factories darkened birch trees; the moths no longer blended in with the texture of the bark. Predatory birds feasted on them. Within a few years, the moths seemed to turn black—apparently a random mutation in the gene that determined color had proliferated in the gene pool, as a result of its obviously superior ability to enhance fitness. Langton hoped to duplicate this effect on the Apple.

Although he did succeed in repeating the effect, he was unhappy with the experiment. The mechanism he had used was ultimately dependent on the fitness criteria that he artificially imposed on the simulation. It was not realistic, not open ended, like real evolution, in which the environment and not some outside programmer determines fitness.

Frustrated, he wandered the stacks of the library, wondering whether anyone had made earlier attempts at the sort of synthesis he sought. Indeed, someone had, quite masterfully: John von Neumann. When Langton discovered the book describing von Neumann's self-reproducing automaton, he instantly recognized the similarity of purpose. But while von Neumann had designed an artificial organism that could reproduce in the same way real organisms did, no one had ever actually built one on a computer.

He contacted Burks, the editor of the von Neumann text, who

confirmed that no computer simulation had fulfilled the task, though a doctoral candidate at Michigan, E. F. Codd, had simplified von Neumann's highly complex blueprint—reducing the possible states in each cell from twenty-nine to eight. Burks suggested Langton might do well to start with Codd's book.

For the next few months, beginning in late summer 1979, Langton did just that. By day he worked, either at the stained-glass shop or at another job, digging ditches under the Arizona sun. After spending the evening hours with his new wife, he slept only until 1:00 A.M., whereupon he would drag himself to the Apple. (This to the dismay of his bride.) He charted his journey through the artificial universes he created on a series of spiral notebooks that outlined the difficulties he encountered and the stratagems he used to overcome them.

Like the substrate in which Codd's CA lived, the universe Langton created had eight possible states for each cell. But as Langton attempted to build pieces of Codd's organism on the Apple, he came to realize that the beast was far too complex for his purposes. The complexity arose from Codd's requirement (also a requirement of von Neumann) that the self-reproducing structure must also be a universal computer; in other words, it theoretically had to be able to run programs to emulate the operation of every other possible computer or machine. Langton, however, was less interested in building a general purpose computer than endowing a computer creation with the properties of life. As he later wrote, "It is highly unlikely that the earliest self-reproducing molecules, from which all living organisms are supposed to have been derived, were capable of universal construction, and we would not want to eliminate those from the class of truly self-reproducing configurations."

Instead, Langton was seeking the simplest configuration that could truly reproduce itself by the same means as the things that we now concede are alive. Von Neumann, and later Codd, fulfilled this requirement by using the information in the automation's blueprint in two ways. First, they treated the information as instructions to be interpreted, as in the case of instructions in a computer program. Second, they treated the information as uninterpreted data, as in numbers in a data base that are copied to and stored in a register inside a computer. A simpler illustration than a computer program would be that of a piece of paper with text on it: the first means of treatment, interpretation, would be reading the words; the second method, transcription, would be placing the paper on a Xerox machine and making a duplicate. The biological equivalent of this dual methodology, of course, is found inside a biological cell—in its everyday operation, certain genetic data are interpreted in such a way that proteins form to catalyze certain reactions. And other times, notably in the reproductive process, genetic data are not interpreted but simply copied.

To satisfy this requirement, Langton designed a set of what he called "loops." Placed in a sea of zero-state, or quiescent, cells, a single Langton loop resembled a square with a short tail on one end, reminiscent of the letter Q. The square shape was important because with only ninety-four cells there is limited space, so economy is maximized by reusing the information that directed the construction of a single side of the loop—it was done four times, one for each side.

Based on Codd's constructions, Langton's loops had three layers, like a flattened wire. The outer layers, the insulation, were a strings of cells in state 2. These were the *sheath* cells. They acted as insulation to the *core* cells, which were like the copper part of the wire. These conducted the data necessary for reproduction. With each generation, the cells in this inner layer followed rules that affected the state of their neighbors and in effect propagated signals inside the genetic stream of the core.

Langton wanted to arrange the various states so that, following a given rule table dictating the cell's behavior in the next generation, the tail would become a constructing appendage. It would thrust outward until it reached the desired length, turn the corner, and repeat the process until it completed the square. Once the outer shape of the newly formed loop resembled the parent loop, the flow in the core layer—now moving between the sheath layers like fluid flowing through a pipe—would continue. The "fluid" would be cell states holding uninterpreted data. When the information was completely passed to the offspring loop, the two loops would separate. Soon after, the signals would change the configuration of the offspring's core so it precisely resembled the initial configuration of the original loop—the "Adam" loop. They would be identical.

When the process began again, the unread data—which were a virtual

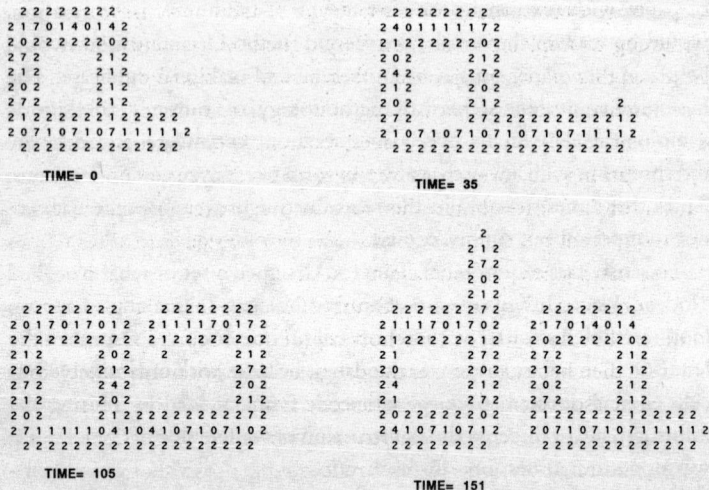

```
 22222222
2170140142
2022222202
272      212
212      212
202      212
272      212
2122222212 2222
2071071071 11112
 2222222222222

TIME= 0
```

```
 22222222
2401111172
2122222202
202      212
242      272
212      202
202      212              2
272      2722222222212
2107107107107107 11112
 22222222222222222222

TIME= 35
```

```
 22222222   22222222
2017017012 2111170172
2722222272 2122222202
212      202  2      212
202      212          272
272      242          202
212      202          212
202      21222222222272
2711111041041071071 02
 2222222222222222222

TIME= 105
```

```
              2
            212
            272
            202
            212
 222222272  22222222
2111701702 217014014
2122222212 2022222202
21      272 272      212
20      202 212      212
24      212 202      212
21      272 272      212
2022222202 21222222122222
2410710712 2071071071 1112
 22222222   2222222222222

TIME= 151
```

Chris Langton's self-reproducing loops begin with a Q-shaped construct sitting in a sea of quiescence. Executing the rules of its cellular automata world (the physics of its universe), the tail of the Q extends and eventually forms a daughter loop. The numbers on the loop each represent one of the eight possible states (the blank, quiescent state is state 8). Note that state 2 is the sheath state, acting as an insulator for the variety of states that move between the sheaths, like signals along a wire.

recipe for building an offspring—would finally be interpreted. A new generation would be born.

Creating a universe that would support this process was easier said than done. A proper configuration of cells in various states had to be arranged in the core layer so that everything would happen at the right time—data flowing, corners turned, and the initial configuration restored at the precise time step that (*a*) the daughter loop received the signals that allowed it to reach that stage, and (*b*) cutoff was performed. There was certainly the question as to whether this could be done in a relatively simple construct.

Langton's notebooks indicated the difficulty. In late August 1979 he had managed to replicate some aspects of Codd's automaton and was beginning to implement his own loops. He could produce loops that grew but that could not duplicate themselves and signal the end of the reproductive process. Eventually, he was forced to rewrite Codd's transition functions—to change the rules, to alter the universe. By October, he was turning the corners and working on the difficulties of engineering the birth, where the mother loop and daughter loop cleave, and where the feedback from daughter to the mother signals that her reproductive mechanism can start again.

After months of tinkering, on October 26 Langton finally wrote in his journal: "I've done it! The loop now reproduces itself." The immediate question then became whether the daughter loop not only resembled its parent but also contained the genetic code for reproduction. This, as von Neumann realized, was the key to genuine self-reproduction. Sitting before the computer screen, which reflected the progress of an independent organism, operating on deterministic rules of an artificial universe, Langton made these notes:

> I'm watching it now. It looks like it will also reproduce itself and I'm hoping that (the) construction arm is long enough. . . . The daughter reproduced perfectly, the construction arm is okay! exactly the right length! the daughter reproduces too!! We're off!

What had Langton actually created? His organisms looked nothing like life as we know it—they were intricate loops whose colorful contents represent informational states. And even the most enlightened of biologists would have hesitated at that junction in history to affirm that an organism could exist whose constitution was formed not of matter but of information, resident in no corner of the known world but citizen of a newly minted universe of rudimentary homemade physics. Yet though its origin may have been dubious, Langton felt confident that its reproductive behavior was decidedly akin to that of real creatures. In loop reproduction, there was a genotype—a series of core cells that contains genetic code and is copied into the next generation. And there was a phenotype—a coded series of instructions that produces a new organism. This allowed for the possibility of evolution, where a mutation in the genotype could result in a phenotype with improved fitness, whose ability to spread its genes would benefit from the advantage. The process would be, literally, the same as in real organisms, and the evolution would be not simulated but genuine.

But those ideas were reserved for future experiments. The immediate task was exploration of what occurred when the loops reproduced. Langton discovered something remarkable here—an emergent order.

It seemed that once the loop life cycle was in motion, the nascent loops and their progenitors formed what could only be called a colony, populating their territory in a manner eerily similar to certain marine life such as coral. As the first loop gave birth, both mother and daughter commenced reproduction, the mother forming an offspring to the north, and the daughter beginning a third generation to the east. But as new loops were created, some of the elders, hopelessly surrounded by descendents, became unable to extend their tails outward to reproduce again. Langton's rules allowed for this: in those cases, the signals flowing along the core cells would be erased, leaving an empty loop. They were for practical purposes dead, easily distinguishable from live loops, which contained core cells of varied states. As the reproductive process continued, more and more dead loops remained in the center, while a vital community birthed new generations on the outer levels. Much like a coral reef.

It was the behavior of biology, emerging unbidden from the rules of the CA simulation.

For Langton, the experiment was a vindication: *The forces of biology can be reproduced in machines. The phenomenon of culture applies outside of human experience. Rule-based structures such as language can hold the keys to reproducing beings and to entire universes.* When he would try to explain this, people would regard him with suspicion. Almost as if, he concluded, he were some sort of kook. But from that point on, Chris Langton knew they were wrong and would no longer doubt himself on that point.

"The self-reproducing loops brought it all together for me," he later claimed. "The pieces of the puzzle were in place."

Langton had defined his mission; now he had to evangelize it. The difficulties in this were underlined immediately by his attempts to explain the significance of his self-reproducing loops to his instructors and colleagues at Arizona. His efforts were received with overwhelming indifference. "Look," he would tell them. "I've got a universe, and I have things which self-reproduce in it." But nobody comprehended; nobody caught the scent. This is just a computer program, right? they would ask, as though Watson and Crick had not proven that life itself was based on a sort of computer program.

Langton tried in vain to find someone who would sponsor his graduate studies (he had finally gotten his undergraduate degree) at Arizona. The only supporter Langton found was an anthropology professor, but he could not offer help unless Langton won the support of the computer science department. Langton received nothing but blank stares there, and his efforts to excite the biology professors met with an even bleaker response.

Only one place in the country, in fact, was receptive to the type of curriculum Langton was proposing: the Logic of Computers Group at the University of Michigan, headed by Burks. But even the Michigan program was in flux. After years of carrying on a lonely struggle, the group was in the process of being swallowed by Michigan's engineering school, which focused on more pragmatic, less experimental computational work, like data structures or compiler theory. Some Logic of Computers Group faculty remained, but the group's unique course of study was dissipating under the pressure to teach "real" computer science. One of the last students admitted into the natural systems program was Langton. He arrived at Michigan in 1982, at age thirty-three a beginning graduate student. By the time he earned the final doctorate conferred by the group, nine years later, Langton would have hatched the new scientific field of artificial life.

Though the continuing decline of the Logic of Computers Group was a constant irritant, Langton managed to turn the engineering department's coup to his benefit; the newly required courses heightened his mastery of computers. Another benefit was a chance to plunder the group's now-abandoned library, which held various obscure treatises on self-organization and computational genetics. Meanwhile, he drew insights and comment from remaining instructors and the core of students who still believed that nature had much to teach about computing, and vice versa. Langton was Burks's teaching assistant, and he worked closely with John Holland. His passion was still cellular automata, but when he tried to interest the undergraduates in Burks's classes to undertake serious studies in the field, they would balk. What good is this? they would say. How can cellular automata get me a job?

Meanwhile Langton pressed ahead. He published his paper on the self-reproducing loops, which was included in the proceedings of a workshop in cellular automata at Los Alamos, the first major gathering held on the subject. (Langton missed the event itself in order to be with his wife as she gave birth to their first child.) He built a state-of-the-art CA simulation program on the Apollo workstation computer.

Among his creations was a simulation called "vants," or virtual ants. The rules were simple. The vant itself was a V-shaped construct that moved in the direction of its point. If the lead cell moved into a blank square on the imaginary grid, the vant continued moving in that direction. If the square was blue, the vant turned right and changed the color of that cell to yellow. If the square was yellow, the vant turned left and changed the color of the square to blue. Thus the vant left a trail behind it.

When more than one vant was placed on the grid, the result was behavior strikingly similar to that of social insects. The most vivid example was the uncanny parallel to the manner in which certain ants lay pheromone trails for food recruitment. It was remarkable to witness the simulation running on a color monitor, as certain vants, after an initial period of meandering, seemed to find each other and interact in order to build a spiraling trail.

Langton knew, of course, how the simple rules of the vant simulation evoked this distinct form of behavior. Could it be that the path-following behavior of ants derived from a kindred source? (Langton was to some degree anticipating the experiments of the Brussels group, which, we have learned, used the self-organization theories of Prigogine to program CA colonies of social insects and compare them to the actual organisms.) As he read entomology texts and followed real ants around in an attempt to divine the patterns of their roaming, he pondered whether ants themselves were, in effect, participants in some CA-like program. He was particularly struck by a quotation in a book called *The Sciences of the Artificial,* by Herbert Simon:

> An ant, viewed as a behaving system, is quite simple. The apparent complexity of its behavior over time is largely a reflection of the complexity of the environment in which it finds itself.

While Langton found this true for solitary ants, he considered it a massive understatement when applied to cooperating colonies of ants. He saw this in his vants; though absurdly simple, they seemed to display genuinely cooperative behavior. He never did discover whether real ant behavior was triggered by the same rules that his vants rigorously followed, but he was heartened by a description of termite behavior by the great entomologist E. O. Wilson. Certain termites, wrote the Harvard professor, "give every appearance of accomplishing their astonishing feat by means of what computer scientists call dynamic programming. As each step of the operation is completed, its result is assessed, and the precise program for the next step (out of several of many available) is chosen and activated. Thus no termite need serve as overseer with blueprint in hand."

When Langton quoted that passage in one of his papers, he decisively added emphasis to the final sentence: *"Thus no termite need serve as overseer with blueprint in hand."* It was a powerful statement that unwittingly expressed the link between cellular automata and nature. Langton became convinced that the key to discovering, and ultimately producing, the behavior of *all* sorts of organisms was to use the CA approach as a model. The essence of this approach could be summed up in a powerful hyphenate: *bottom-up*. The word was to become very important in Langton's philosophy of artificial life. The concept described the collective power of small actions rippling upward, combining with other small actions, often recursively so that action would beget reaction—until a recognizable pattern of global behavior emerged. As Wilson observed, there was no central intelligence holding a blueprint and directing traffic.

To Langton, this was nature's way of taking advantage of complicated phenomena that occurred when several variables combined to form a complex system. From billions of trials and errors—the evolutionary process—out of the interaction would come something useful. It not only seems that those little nonconscious pieces of matter are cooperating; Langton contends they *are* cooperating. Quite literally.

"This is a trick of nature that is probably one of the most fundamental physical laws," he later explained. "It's the way nature works. It's what makes atoms and what makes molecules. Co-operative structures, the formation of co-operative structures, localized in time and space. You have these little packets of co-operation, and then packets of packets, and packets of packets of packets."

Bottom-up was everywhere in biology. It was the way life began, from the formation of organic molecules, to the formation of bacteria, to the emergence of multicell organisms, all the way to mollusks, ferns, frogs, trees, beavers, roses, apes, Venus's-flytraps, and human beings. Throughout, the processes within these complicated creatures also worked by a bottom-up methodology. Within an organism, individual cells perform private rituals, releasing chemicals in a pattern predetermined by a set of rules. If condition A exists in the environment, execute action B. In that respect, the cell is no more than a finite state machine acting in a CA-like universe. A big picture emerges from these little behaviors: Organs. Central nervous systems. Entire organisms. Societies.

Since bottom-up was such a prevalent factor in nature, it was obvious to Langton that this approach was the correct one for computationally evoking lifelike processes. He later would codify the elements of this approach in defining the essential features of computer-based a-life models: they consist of populations of simple programs or specifications; there is no single program that directs all of the other programs; each program details the way in which a simple entity reacts to local situations; there are no rules in the system that dictate global behavior; and any behavior at levels higher than the individual programs is therefore emergent.

Emergent behavior was the payoff of the bottom-up approach. To Langton, an artificial life experiment's success would depend on a revelation, an emergent property. Something had to happen that was not specifically programmed in.

An irony was embedded here. Though Langton furiously resisted any trace of vitalism in his philosophy, he regarded the concept of emergence as sort of an *élan vital* in and of itself. No reductionism: the whole *is* more than the sum of its parts. When one builds a creature, or attempts to model a biological process from the bottom up, inorganic rudiments conspire to form something that behaves with the spirit of life. Or, perhaps, something alive.

Quite naturally, Chris Langton preferred to write his doctoral thesis on his theories of CAs and a-life. But he could not get such a thesis approved. The shifting focus of the computer science department, distancing itself from the biology-inspired studies of the days of the Logic of Computers Group, worked against him. So he had to contrive a way to accommodate both his interests and the more conventional demands of the Michigan establishment. As it turned out, the topic he did conceive turned out to have significant implications for artificial life.

During his first year in Michigan, Langton had read a Wolfram paper devising a classification system of four CA categories. Langton was astonished at the paper—not so much at the methodology or the conclusions but at the apparent fact that no one had ever attempted such a seemingly obvious project. He noted in his work journal;

> After a paper by Steve Wolfram of Cal Tech—amazing how I screwed around with these linear arrays over a year ago and never imagined that I was working with publishable material. Surely, I thinks to myself, this has been done 30 years ago, but No! Some kid out of Cal Tech publishes a learned paper on one dimensional two-state arrays!! What have people been *doing* all these years?

Langton realized there might be widespread interest examining multiple CA universes—not as a vague mathematical exercise but as a pungent interpretation of the substrate of life itself. What interested him was the range of behavior evoked by certain rule sets. Which ones would result in uninteresting universes—sheets of identical cells frozen in a single regime, locked-in patterns doomed eternally to repeat? Which ones would yield compelling results—a roiling ragout of activity, changing forms, releasing gliders? And which of the latter could support universal computation and, by implication, life?

Langton's own ruminations on observing thousands of cellular automata led him to surpass Wolfram's classification system, skipping directly to a question that previously had been difficult even to frame, What sorts of universes could support life? The fact that Langton believed that the varieties of natural life were one subset of a much larger set of possible flavors of life gave him an advantage in tackling this question. If other kinds of life indeed existed, then it would be possible to study them in order to discover previously obscure properties of life itself. As it stands, the examination of only one subset of possible life makes it difficult, if not futile, to distinguish between peculiar characteristics of life-as-we-know-it and general traits of all possible kinds of life.

Langton attempted to isolate a general quality of all life—the range of areas in which it could thrive. He concentrated on universes of CAs, running thousands of experiments in order to measure the degree to which they were able to propagate information. Why was that ability important? In Langton's view, the transfer and retention of information is an essential characteristic of life.

"It's clear that most of the living things we know are physical embodiments of information processing entities," he later explained. "A good deal of what they do is based on processing information—not just materials, not just energy but information. Living organisms use information in order to rebuild themselves, in order to locate food, in order to maintain themselves by retaining internal structure . . . the structure itself is information. You have to conclude that in living systems, information manipulation has really gained control, dominating energy manipulation."

But the universe at large, including the domain of information, was dominated by rules dictating the behavior of energy—especially the dread second law of thermodynamics. Living systems were distinguished by what appeared to be a noble resistance to that law—their ability to maintain a pocket of increasing order that, at least within its confines, confounded the second law.

Langton believed there was a quantifiable regime in which that apparent contradiction thrived. So he invented what he referred to as "a knob": a mathematical tuning instrument to adjust the dynamics of the system, the better to observe and understand the mechanics of this behavior. He dubbed his knob "the lambda (λ) parameter." When Langton tested the rule tables of CA universes, he used this knob to alter the degree to which information could move freely or be retained. The λ value of a given system, which ranged from zero to one, corresponded to this degree.

If the λ value was very low, approaching zero, this represented a regime in which information was frozen. It could easily be retained through time, but it could not move. If you were to picture a substrate that illustrated this, you might choose a solid such as ice. Ice molecules retained their position and state as time passed, but, since they did not move around, no new information emerged. Under those circumstances, life could not thrive. If the λ value was very high, approaching its maximum value, then information moved very freely and chaotically and was very difficult to retain. The information could be envisioned as molecules in a gaseous, or vaporous, stage. Life could not be supported in these conditions, either.

On the other hand, there was a certain area where information changed but not so rapidly that it lost all connection to where it had just been previously. This was akin to a liquid state. Langton discovered that it was the liquid regime that supported the most engaging events, those that would support the kind of complexity that was the mark of living systems.

In the CAs he ran, those whose rule sets yielded low λ values were generally those that Wolfram would have called Class 1 or Class 2. Those would soon resolve into boring, intransigent patterns. Those with very high numbers were Wolfram's Class 3, which wound up in chaotic jumbles. The most interesting ones, what Wolfram would call Class 4, occurred at intermediate λ points. These included all the cellular automata that yielded a plethora of teeming activity, such as glider guns. Those were the CAs that supported universal computation, like the game of Life, whose λ value was 0.273. It was at that regime in which complexity was at the maximum, and entropy was optimized—as it was in life.

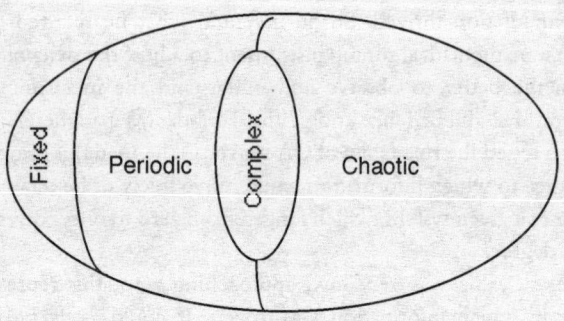

(a) Langton's view of information movement in complex dynamical systems such as CAs. At the left is the regime where information is frozen; nothing can live there. To the right of that is a somewhat more flexible regime where behavior such as crystal growth can be seen; still, the limited movement of information cannot support life. To the far right, information moves so freely that its structure cannot be maintained; the regime is too chaotic to support life. Only in that center "sweet spot" can information be stable enough to support a message structure and loose enough to transmit messages. Life lives there.

Langton noticed that the point at which universal computation became likely was at a particularly interesting location on his chart. When the λ value reached that critical point, a phase transition occurred—a sudden shift from one regime to another. (An example of a phase transition in nature would be the shift from a frozen solid to a liquid or from a liquid to a gaseous state.) He came to believe that being sited in this location was an essential characteristic of systems of such complexity, including living systems. He recalled von Neumann's comments on complexity and living systems: "There is thus this completely decisive property of complexity, that there exists a critical size below which the process of synthesis is degenerative, but above which the phenomenon of synthesis, if properly arranged, can become explosive. . . ."

In other words, a key ingredient of life—the proper degree of complexity that allowed it to spit in the face of entropy—hung on a cliff side. On a precipice to its left was a barren regime where not enough information could move; to its right was a swirling maelstrom where information moved so wildly that chaos ruled. Belly up to that maelstrom, life

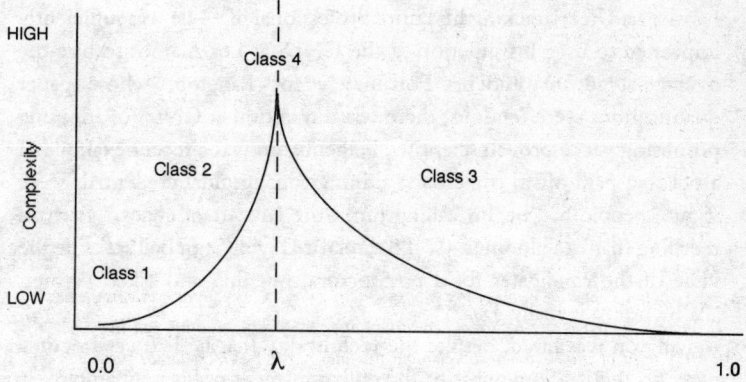

(b) Langton's "sweet spot" can be charted. The vertical axis represents complexity, and the horizontal gives the λ value, which represents the degree of information movement and retention on a 0 to 1 scale. In this typical dynamical system, the λ value reaches a sharp peak at the height of the system's complexity. This represents a phase transition. Life is supported at the boundaries of this transition.

Also noted for comparison purposes are the locations of Wolfram's four classes of cellular automata. Class 1 consists of stable forms; Class 2 CAs are periodic; Class 3 CAs are chaotic. Class 4 CAs, however, have rich complexity. They support universal computation—and life.

took advantage of the proximity to draw its information-processing abilities, but it dared not stray too far from the frozen areas that allowed it to keep some information stable, so that some order could be established in interpreting that information.

Langton was able to quantify this phenomenon. Life, he argued, existed "on the edge of chaos." In order to create an artificial life, then, one required a system that would maintain the proper order of complexity—at the edge of the phase transition between desert and cyclone.

Langton believed it could be done.

When Doyne Farmer met Chris Langton in Cambridge in 1985—and first heard the term "artificial life" being applied to an area of study Farmer had been tracking his entire professional life—he was sufficiently impressed to urge his superiors at the CNLS at Los Alamos to hire the overage graduate student. Fortunately for Langton, whose paper qualifications were tenuous, there was a tradition at CNLS of adopting promising yet unproven scientists. Feigenbaum was a recent example of a bet that paid off in triple bars; although his original credentials were vague, people had begun calling him "the Mozart of chaos." Perhaps recalling that late bloomer, CNLS director David Campbell set aside the vitae of the candidates for a postdoctoral opening and asked Farmer, "Which guy is really *good?*"

Langton was hired, despite the technicality that he had yet to complete his thesis. (Somewhat to the embarrassment of his new employer, that task would not be completed for almost four years.) For the first time, Langton found himself in a situation in which his thoughts on creating artificial life were not merely tolerated but encouraged. He intended to exploit the opportunity to the fullest. Not only would he pursue a-life in his own work, but he would also do his damnedest to organize others whose thinking might be along the lines of his own.

He knew they were out there. Every so often he would come across published papers from these people. But there was no reliable source— an article concerning what Langton considered artificial life might appear in *Physica D,* or in the *Journal of Theoretical Biology,* or *Complex Systems Journal,* or *American Scientist*—even, he would joke, in the *Indian Journal of Basket Weaving.* "Eighty percent of these people were clueless as to other work that had been done in this direction," Langton recalls. "They just started working on this stuff of their own. Either it hadn't occurred to them that the same ideas were shared by others, or they had no idea how to go about finding the other people who thought the same way. The field existed, but only implicitly."

It fell, then, to Langton to make things explicit. He would find the people who were doing what he considered to be artificial life and count on their experiencing a shock of recognition when they heard the term. He would invite them to gather, share their experiences, relate their experiments, expound their theories, and ultimately define the boundaries of the field. It would be an "Interdisciplinary Workshop on the Synthesis and Simulation of Living Systems," the first conference ever on artificial life. Langton's intent was to cast as wide a net as possible, even to the point of risking the presence of a few nut cases, in order to draw out of the woodwork obscure but thoughtful scientists whose work was melding information and biology. These he would supplement with names, some of them celebrated, of those whose work somehow contributed to this exciting synthesis.

Some thought that the effort was folly, that the idea of building or even studying "artificial life" smacked of science fiction, that it lacked focus, upon it would bring ridicule to anyone whose name became associated with it. (One scientist who eventually attended asked a Nobel Prize–winning colleague if he should attend and got the following reply: "This is the sort of conference you might go to, but never tell a soul you were there.") Indeed, recalls Langton, "nobody else was willing to tack their name onto it as an official organizer. My name was going to sink or swim with the success of this workshop."

The conference was set for September 1987, at Los Alamos. Word was distributed through flyers posted on university bulletin boards, through messages on computer networks, through a plug in the computer recreations column in *Scientific American,* and through an official conference announcement. The latter was a bold manifesto of Langton's beliefs. Though its language was sedate, the two-paragraph description of the event and its subject made breathtaking claims:

> Artificial life is the study of artificial systems that exhibit behavior characteristic of natural living systems. It is the quest to explain life in any of its possible manifestations, without restriction to the particular examples that have evolved on earth. This includes biological and chemical experiments, computer simulations, and purely theoretical endeavors. Processes occurring on molecular, social, and evolutionary scales are subject to investigation. The ultimate goal is to extract the logical form of living systems.
>
> Microelectronic technology and genetic engineering will soon give us the capability to create new life forms *in silico* as well as *in vitro*. This capacity will present humanity with the most far-reaching technical,

113

theoretical, and ethical challenges it has ever confronted. The time
seems appropriate for a gathering of those involved in attempts to
simulate or synthesize aspects of living systems.

September is usually a kind season in Los Alamos, relatively free of
daytime heat and blessed with pleasant mountain chills in the evening.
September 1987 was no exception. It was not the weather, however, but
the opportunity to participate in the beginnings of a major enterprise in
the history of the biosphere that drew approximately 160 computer
scientists, anthropologists, theoretical biologists, population geneticists,
biochemists, ethologists, physicists, and a few of undefinable stripe to a
second-floor lecture room at the Oppenheimer Study Center on the Los
Alamos campus. Langton's proposal had indeed struck a nerve. As the
assemblage gathered on Monday, September 21, 1987, for the first of
five days of lectures, coffee breaks, lunches, poster sessions, dinners, and
demonstrations, the thin mountain air, even within the fortresslike walls
of the modern government facility, crackled with anticipation. An assistant director of the lab said a few rambling words of welcome, and there
was Chris Langton, faced with a vision fulfilled, nervously addressing the
core of a scientific field, including some of his secret heroes, on its first
official day of life. Among those in attendance were Richard Dawkins,
Aristid Lindenmayer, John Holland, and Richard Laing. "I'm very
happy," he told them, almost in tears, as his first stencil was beamed on
the overhead projector.

The first artificial-life workshop, or A-life I, as it came to be known,
was a charmed event. Thirty talks and twenty demonstrations provided
what would be a framework for thinking about a-life. There were
organisms generated from cellular automata, computer simulations of
neo-Darwinian evolution, coadapted computer ecosystems, logic-based
recreations of the origin of life, competitions between computer-virus-
like creatures, plants grown in silicon greenhouses, and even an occasional robot displaying emergent behaviors. "At almost every
presentation," recalls Langton, "everybody in the room experienced a
gut feeling of 'Yes! Yes! Yes!' " But even the excitement of the formal
sessions was surpassed by animated impromptu discussions begun in
coffee breaks, carried over to lunch, resumed at dinner, and in some

cases continued in midnight hikes into the moonlit desert landscape, which eerily laps on the fringes of the staid scientific company town.

As the conference proceeded, an espirit de corps emerged. It was almost as if the participants, sharing similar vision but without any common ground to share it, had been adrift in a scientific diaspora. Says Langton,

> There were so many people who were doing serious things in this area but couldn't do it for a living, so they were doing it on the side, just playing around with it. Everybody had a sense that this was interesting stuff, and ought to be pursued on a grander scale. Although many of us had been working completely independently, without the awareness of this whole other sparse set of people out there also working on the stuff, the amazing thing was how similar our experience had been, and how similar our frustrations had been.

Optimism concerning the field's future ran high, and in the energizing atmosphere of Los Alamos, comparisons were made between the a-life workshop and the legendary Dartmouth conference of 1956, in which a few computer scientists and psychologists hatched a similar enterprise, which would come to be known as artificial intelligence. An apt parallel since, as a-lifers would often note, as artificial intelligence was to intelligence, artificial life was to life itself.

But with the benefit of hindsight, Langton and most of the others consciously expressed caution when speaking of the promise of their studies. They recalled the embarrassment, not to mention the bad science of it all, when the poker-faced predictions of the AI pioneers—who promised the likes of human-level intelligence in ten years—wound up as quaint buffoonery a couple of decades later, when computers still could not replicate the cognition of an average one year old. In retrospect, plenty had been done (a computer playing grandmaster chess, for instance, is nothing to sneeze at) but the failure to meet exaggerated expectations had tarnished the whole enterprise. As a result Langton and other key a-life people refused to be pinned down to risky time frames, even speculating that scientists might not produce bona fide organisms for at least a century.

A few were not so circumspect. A roboticist named Hans Moravec, for instance, addressed the conference and flatly stated that the a-life movement would build something akin to an artificial human in fifty years. The claim was ironic in light of the film clip Moravec brought to the conference, which clearly revealed that his own creation, an autonomous robot, took an average of five hours to simply cross a room. (The puckish Moravec later admitted that his prediction was perhaps overly optimistic, but that scientific advances often dwarfed the most fantastic predictions imaginable. Given that, he said, why not have some fun when playing at prognostication?)

The only real tension at the workshop came at the judging of what was lightly referred to as the "artificial 4-H contest," conceived by Langton as a good-natured show-and-tell, and judged by A. K. (Kee) Dewdney, who had inherited Gardner's holy column in *Scientific American*. The $100 first prize, went to botanic computer graphics created by Aristid Lindenmayer and Przemyslaw Prusinkiewicz and generated using a rule-based grammar created by Lindenmayer. Other simulations were singled out for awards, the categories for which were reverse engineered, much like the process by which all members in a given summer-camp bunk will win certificates. But surprisingly, recalls Langton, "there was some confusion and bitterness—some people were very upset that their things didn't get the prize. And there were others who were saying—'How can you call that alive?' "

It was a perpetually haunting question: What *is* life? Variations of it echoed throughout the workshop. Artificial life presupposed that one could synthesize something that satisfied the conditions for "aliveness." But among many obstacles standing in the way of this ideal, none was more basic than the problem of definition. How can you create life when no one agrees what that means? How would you know you had done it?

Faced with a similar problem in the fuzzily defined term "intelligence," AI had a provisional solution called the Turing test. Suggested by Alan Turing, this basically consisted of situating a computer and a person behind a screen. A discerning interviewer on the other side of the screen would then direct questions to both. If he or she were unable to distinguish which respondent was which, the computer program would have passed the test. But could there be an equivalent in artificial life? In a coincidental nod to de Vaucanson, some people at the a-life conference began talking about a duck test: if it looks like a duck and quacks like a duck, it belongs in the class labeled ducks. This Vaucanson test was admittedly subjective but ultimately no more so than the Turing test. A molecular biologist jokingly suggested a variation: first lock the candidate for aliveness in a room with a biologist. If the biologist came out of the room thinking he had been cloistered with a living creature, that would be a positive sign. "And," he explained, "if your organism comes out and and *says* it's alive, you know you're on the right track."

Most of the conference participants believed that the effort begun at Los Alamos would eventually result in artificial creatures that would satisfy the creator's own criteria for aliveness. Whether the rest of the world would adopt those criteria was another question. What distinguished most of the a-life scientists from their more conservative colleagues—and from the general public—is that they regarded plants, animals, and humans as machines, albeit much more sophisticated ones than artificial examples. But machines nonetheless, and therefore potentially matchable by human enterprise, regardless of the materials required to build them. Understanding this was simple, but believing it required a leap of faith that often forced one to come to grips with hitherto dormant remnants of vitalism or of other mystical baggage.

Would others be willing to take that leap? Could animals made of information encourage the sort of conceptual flexibility that regarded living organisms as a subset of machines? In order to do so, one would have to do away, totally, with the preconception that corporeal form is a precondition for aliveness.

"The leap you have to make is to think about machineness as being the logic of organization," explains Langton. *"It's not the material.* There's nothing implicit about the material of anything—if you can capture its logical organization in some other medium you can have the same 'machine' because it's the organization that constitutes the machine, not the stuff it's made of. That's the leap you have to make. It's a small one." Then Langton slyly compared that mental shift to another small adjustment in regarding the world—the idea, spurred by Copernicus, that the common wisdom holding that the universe revolved around the earth was wrong and in fact that the earth revolved around the sun. "The step itself wasn't big, just a slight change in perspective about what's at the center," says Langton, "but its consequences were enormous."

Most of the participants of the workshop agreed with Langton: The stuff of life is not stuff. Life is a dynamic physical process, and, if you can duplicate those processes—enable them to "haunt" otherwise inanimate material—you have created life. This can be done regardless of materials. It could even be done on a computer.

For months after the conference Langton spent much of his time sifting through the papers submitted for inclusion in the conference proceedings, a collection that would, Langton hoped, cement the bonds forged at the workshop and bestow on the field the beginnings of permanence. As he read, and mentally replayed the innumerable conversations he had participated in or had had recounted to him later, Langton came to realize that, although no statement of purpose or manifesto had been drafted—surely no plenary session had been planned for such an enterprise—the assemblage had indeed reached an implicit consensus of the key points of what would hereafter be called artificial life. In writing his introduction to the proceedings, Langton attempted to elucidate these items.

First of all, life was to be defined as "a property of the organization of matter, rather than a property of the matter which is so organized." There would be nothing in the way one defined life that would preclude its creation using forms other than carbon-based chemistry. It would not even require a physical body, as long as the processes, the behaviors peculiar to life, were faithfully realized—things like self-reproduction, metabolism, growth, and adaptive responses. Langton and his colleagues counted on an eventual shift toward this point of view. The facts, they believed, would dictate a willingness to entertain the possibility. And ultimately, someone would create an artificial organism that would put the matter to rest for all but the most dedicated vitalist.

This was not to say that the success of a-life hinged on producing a synthetic beast, a silicon Frankenstein to parade around the scientific community as a vindication of unconventional beliefs. Those working, in an extremely long-range time-scape, on building creatures who one day would be considered alive were only part of the field. Most of the workers in a-life were concerned with duplicating pieces of lifelike behavior, the better to understand living systems in general and in some cases the behaviors of specified species. The key to these efforts was that experiments of this stripe did not merely simulate a function of living organisms but rather duplicated it. Langton's favorite example of this was Craig Reynolds's use of the methodology of cellular automata to produce computer birds, or boids. Although boids were indeed crude and incomplete models of genuine birds, the flocking behavior they exhibited was not a simulation of flocking but an emergent process every bit as valid as the behavior generated by the real thing. "Flocking in boids is true flocking," Langton wrote, "and may be counted as another empirical data point in the study of flocking behavior in general, right up there with flocks of geese and flocks of starlings."

The second issue concerned the general approach of the field. It could be summed up in one of Langton's favorite phrases: bottom-up. Participants in A-life I agreed with him that artificial life should be pursued in the style of cellular automata, engineering local interactions so that complex global behaviors will emerge. These interactions occurred in parallel, and the specifics of the interactions were routinely indecipherable, although the emergent patterns were coherent and recognizable.

The double axis of this belief system—life as process and work from the bottom up—was more than an experimental approach. It was a worldview built on the platform of complex systems theory, biological iconoclasm, post-Darwinian evolutionary thought, and an overall skew from which one viewed the world at large: one gigantic natural system that emerged as the collective result of billions of state machines following tiny rule structures. The conscripts in the artificial life revolution possessed not only a solid footing in the particulars of dozens of disciplines, from chaos theory to genetics, but also a peculiar view on the nature of life itself. They held its unique characteristics in awe but felt confident that those qualities were based on sufficiently logical and repeatable grounds that could be duplicated in different circumstances. And they very badly wanted to realize that feat.

The odds of a single unheralded scientist initiating such an epochal enterprise were higher than a random appearance of black orchids in one's vegetable garden. Characteristically, Chris Langton saw it—all of it, from the time he first picked up that irresistible scent—not as a personal triumph but as an extension of a process not yet understood but eventually decipherable. "In some sense the idea is having me now instead of me having the idea," he explains. "There are these other forms of life, artificial ones, that want to come into existence. And they are using me as a vehicle for its reproduction and its implementation."

GOD'S HEART

Many of the problems that have concerned mankind ever since his social emergence and long antecedent to civilization are implicitly problems about the origin of life. Such problems as the elementary ones of life and death itself, and the more sophisticated ones about supernatural and divine governance of the Universe, are now expressed in the form of, "Has the Universe a purpose?" or "Are mind and matter related?" . . . it is precisely that knowledge which is now accumulating in step with the increased resolving power of instruments and the developments in chemical and physical theory. The region of the mysterious is rapidly shrinking.

J. D. Bernal

Stuart Kauffman works in two places. One is a small laboratory he heads at the medical school of the University of Pennsylvania. It is stocked with familiar paraphernalia of the trade: test tubes, pots, burners, strange vials stored in refrigerators, and overworked graduate students. Every so often Kauffman orders a few drams of commercial DNA and uses them as a base for an experiment that involves replicating a function that in some way parallels the way life began on earth. After months of testing, none of the experiments has worked. Kauffman is undaunted. He is confident that results will come.

Kauffman's other workplace is the Santa Fe Institute, in the city of that name. It is a desk and computer workstation in one of several small offices in the Institute's original headquarters, an adobe grotto that was formerly a convent. It is here that Kauffman has been much more successful. Forming theories, not chemical reactions in pots, is his strong suit. As one of the Institute's original "external faculty" members (there is no internal faculty, just as there are no matriculating students at the complexity think-tank known as SFI), he compellingly weaves a story, his story. It snakes and doubles back on itself like a New Wave Science mutation of Scheherazade's tales. It also has unlimited potential in changing the way we think about life. Kauffman thinks of himself as a walking fuse; the presumption—certainly, *his* presumption—is that one day the fuse will ignite, causing an explosion which will force paradigm shifts in several fields.

Kauffman has willingly become identified with the artificial life movement, in part because of the new field's prospective ties to the origin of life. Ultimately, the goal of a-life is to do what has occurred only once on the planet—to make something alive from parts that were not alive. How that happened is the compelling mystery of the origin of life, and the challenge of a-life is to match that astonishing transformation on a routine basis. Conversely, understanding the origin of the only example of life we know of—natural life, including ourselves—will provide invaluable clues to the synthesis of other forms of life.

The study of the origin of life abounds with theories, many of which

123

are extremely difficult to disprove and almost impossible to confirm. The trouble begins with the disagreement over the nature of the planet's composition and atmosphere at the time life emerged, and the trouble only deepens when some working hypotheses, offered by the most respectable of scientists, take bizarre, unanswerable twists. Some of the livelier ones still under consideration are Graham Cairns-Smith's belief that life began in evolving layers of clay and transmitted itself in a genetic takeover to biochemicals (this has, we shall see, special significance to artificial life), and the "directed panspermia" model that contends that life began here from some sort of extraterrestrial spore sent over by a distant interstellar cousin.

All these theories reflect the paradox in which the origin of life is stuck. As von Neumann noted, life could not occur unless a certain complexity was present. Once that crucial level was attained, an evolutionary process could begin to create even more complex molecules and, eventually, organisms. But how did that considerable initial complexity get there? The process has been compared to the proverbial monkeys banging away on typewriters and coming up with *Hamlet,* or some deft behemoth stuffing a truck-size canister with auto parts, shaking it like a cocktail mixer, and opening it to discoverer a polished, ready-to-drive Mercedes-Benz 300 SL, complete with hood ornament in place. The problem drove otherwise-patient scientists to throw up their hands and relegate the origin-of-life studies to the realm of quasi science, and it forced some otherwise-conservative biologists to propose farfetched explanations to accommodate the cosmically stacked odds against life ever appearing.

Stuart Kauffman insists that the odds are not as high as people thought. His idea hinges on the importance of self-organization, which in turn is tied to the as-yet-uncharted rules that Farmer and others think exist, and could become clear in part by pursuing artificial life.

"Artificial life," says Kauffman, "is a way of exploring how complex systems can exhibit self-organization, adaptation, evolution, co-evolution, metabolism, all sorts of stuff. It is mimic of biology, although biologists don't know it yet. Out of it will emerge some sort of strange companion theory to biology . . . a particular substantiation of how living things work. This emerging discipline may be getting at what the logical structure is for living things."

When his storytelling gets underway—Kauffman's papers are difficult for even well-versed lay people to follow, so his science is best experienced in the oral tradition—the air becomes charged with his charisma. One begins to understand why the MacArthur Foundation honored the biologist with one of its precious "genius" grants. Kauffman, a stocky man whose unkempt hair and starkly angular jawline are reminiscent of an early Rolling Stone, will lock his eyes upon you. He will address you, frequently, by your first name, often followed by the exclamation, "I *know* I'm right." Sometimes he adds, "I'm betting my whole life on it."

Kauffman's odyssey began when he was in his twenties, in the early 1960s. As an undergraduate at Dartmouth, Kauffman had studied philosophy, focusing on logic. His studies included Boolean logic, the system, devised in 1854 by George Boole, that coded statements of reason into a symbolic form amenable to mathematical calculation. From there Kauffman won a Rogers Fellowship at Oxford, intending to study the philosophy of mind. But he came to realize that theoretical biology appealed to him more. For reasons he still cannot explain, he decided to become a medical doctor. He embarked on a premedical curriculum.

Among the subjects he studied was human cell differentiation. It was, and remains, somewhat a mystery how a single fertilized zygote splits into many cells and at some point new cells display different forms. The genes in each cell are identical, but the cells are distinct types: muscle, kidney, nerve, and so on. Around the time Kauffman was studying this phenomenon, two French biologists, Jacob and Monod, discovered gene switching, which partially explained things by showing how certain genes could switch other genes on and off.

Jacob and Monod's work triggered a new series of challenges in understanding how the process worked. Human beings have approximately one hundred thousand genes, and some genes, under certain circumstances, turn other genes on or off. It seemed hopelessly complicated. Who could tell what relationships existed between the genes, and what functions dictated whether a given gene would be switched on or off?

One way to do this was by a reductionist approach: isolate little pieces of the network and examine the relationships between them. By concentrating on a single gene, biologists could find out which other genes are connected to it in the biochemical circuitry. In theory, after a painstaking process of isolating and charting, the whole network could be diagrammed. Indeed, this was the standard approach for learning about gene switching. But early on, Kauffman recognized that it would be a very long time before we were able to get a networkwide picture of the system—if ever. "It's worse than a jigsaw puzzle," Kauffman says. "A jigsaw puzzle suggests you have a bunch of pieces on the same level which can fit into a picture. This is more like bits and pieces at a variety of levels, and no idea how to fit the whole thing together. Meantime, evolution is busy evolving new proteins that change the connections and the logic in the circuit—literally, you're scrambling the circuitry."

According to Kauffman, even if we succeeded in completing this unspeakably labyrinthine circuit diagram, the answers would still be elusive. "The molecular biologists will feel they've done a wonderful job in working out all this circuitry, but then a mathematician will say, 'Okay, here's a system with 100,000 variables regulating each other's activity—what will it do?' And the biologist will gasp. The reason is, it's very hard to figure out what *five* things hooked to one another will do. And *nobody* knows how to think about the behavior of systems with 100,000 variables acting on each other."

Kauffman thought that the problem could indeed be tackled. But a shift in viewpoint would be required. Before one could begin to answer questions about the large network involved in gene switching, Kauffman reasoned, we first had to understand the behavior of *any* sort of network of one hundred thousand units where some units dictated the condition of others. In his mind, the question was not so much about the particulars of any individual network—especially since in no two human beings was the circuitry identical. "The problem," Kauffman says, "is whether the behavior of the network depends on the details of that whole network, or whether the behavior instead is a very robust thing, that in a sense *doesn't* depend on the details." (Kauffman, like many scientists, defines "robust" as "stable in the face of perturbations.")

In other words, attempting to chart the connections one by one is akin to taking a tree census. Kauffman was more interested in studying the forest.

Kauffman was suggesting something heretical—that the intricate, clockworklike nature of biological reality that most of us expect was not as fastidious as we suspected. The majority of biologists viewed the genetic circuitry as akin to a detailed computer program that is extremely sensitive to errors: a well-ordered scheme that might have been produced by a superprogrammer with an uncanny sense of structure. That biological precision was one reason why it was so difficult to envision all the steps in a scenario in which life emerged from much simpler ingredients. To suggest that a *random* set of computer instructions could come up with something as complicated in its intertwining relationships as the process of life was absurd. Yet, that was exactly what Kauffman contended was the case. He believed that powers of self-organization—those elusive yet omnipresent little natural rules that we have yet to understand—were at work in all sorts of complicated networks. Like an omnipresent team of chambermaids, these powers scooped up randomness and arranged things in a manageable order. The manner in which they did this was an example of what Langton would call a bottom-up process—no central plan existed to clear up the confusion, but the accumulation of local actions forced the entire system into an emergent behavior that was not at all predictable from the initial conditions.

Kauffman insisted it was those self-organizing powers, and not a microdesigned circuit plan, that dictated, among other things, the gene-switching network.

If one could identify the workings of forces of self-organization and complexity, lifelike behavior could be duplicated by producing a structure for interaction and evolution that takes advantage of those forces. Nature itself would organize things, as Kauffman insisted was the process with natural life. It would certainly be conceivable to create life, new organisms more complex than any human designer could imagine. The implications for artificial life were tremendous.

At the time of this revelation Kauffman was a nonfunded medical student in his mid-twenties, who was setting broken arms at Stanford Hospital. His fellow students had no interest in discussing the matter with him. He knew no other researchers thinking about the problem. But, as Kauffman later explained, "For no good reason whatsoever I have always had the confidence I could tackle any problem that I wanted." Asked why this problem in particular was so important to him, he pauses, and finally says this about his motivations: "I've always wanted the order one finds in the world not to be particular, peculiar, odd or contrived—I want it to be, in the mathematician's sense, generic. Typical. Natural. Fundamental. Inevitable. Godlike. That's it. It's God's heart, not his twiddling fingers, that I've always in some sense wanted to see."

In 1965 Kauffman devised a plan to see God's heart. He would create a network nearly as complex as that which linked the one hundred thousand human genes, hook the pieces together in a random manner, and see if anything biology-like emerged. That would certainly indicate that, rather than requiring exactly the right pieces fitting snugly into the puzzle, a much less rigorous set of circumstances were required to produce the essences of life.

Kauffman found an IBM mainframe where he could do the work, but had to borrow money from the medical school to pay for the computer time. In his recollection the sum was around $1000.

He wrote a FORTRAN program that would generate a Boolean network similar to what he knew of gene-switching networks. A Boolean network was roughly similar to a cellular automata system. It was a collection of nodes—most easily thought of as light bulbs—that switched on or off, depending on whether they received current. This was determined by a set of logical rules that looked at other bulbs and told, given the conditions of those bulbs, whether the given light bulb would be on or off in the next time step. The relationships between the bulbs followed rules first outlined by Boole. There were sixteen Boolean relationships, and most were by then second nature to computer programmers and data-base workers. For instance, the "or" rule, which stated that, if either bulb A or bulb B are on, then bulb C will be on in the next time step. The "and" rule said that, if both bulb A and bulb B are on, then bulb C will be on in the next time step.

Kauffman began with a network of one hundred bulbs, far fewer than in the human genome but still one of boggling complexity. Each light bulb was randomly assigned two other light bulbs, the current states of which would determine its fate in the next time step. The various rules, or Boolean functions, dictating whether the light bulb would be on or off, were also randomly assigned—Kauffman, not knowing the relationship between genes that determined switching, included all sixteen Boolean functions. He would then apply the rules, and the state of the network would change according to those rules. He would continue, time step by time step, and see what happened.

His hope was that the network would soon find itself in a fixed state cycle. To do this, the network would have to return to one of the exact same states that it previously experienced. From that point on (since the rules did not change), the network would find itself in a loop, repeating the same changes over and over again. Eventually, of course, this would be inevitable, since there is only a finite number of possible states for the network to be in. Intuition suggested that this state cycle would be very long in coming, and, when it came, the loop would take many time steps to complete. After all, there were many possible states of the entire network—each state represented a network with a different combination of the one hundred bulbs on or off in a given moment. Since each bulb could be in one of two states, the number of possible states of the network was precisely, two to the one-hundredth power, or ten to the thirtieth power. That meant, in Arabic numbers, a "1" with thirty "0's" behind it. So it would seem that among these many, many possible states, it would take an extremely large number of time steps before the network reached a position that it had experienced previously.

The chances of the network soon finding its way back to any given state seemed many times more minuscule than a person's chances of hitting a state lottery two weeks in a row—at least those odds could be measured and digested. This situation was more like picking Ping-Pong balls from a giant box holding trillions of numbered balls, each time returning the ball to the box and shaking it thoroughly. How soon would it take for the same ball to be picked twice? Even a computer executing thousands of time steps a second might take years to find itself in a familiar configuration. One would expect the system to be chaotic for a very long time.

But Kauffman fervently hoped that something quite different would occur. For one thing he notes, "If it was a very long state cycle, and it took hours of time crunching and didn't find the cycle, I would use up my thousand bucks." What actually occurred was that the first state, a jumble of ons and offs, changed into a second state, another jumble of ons and offs. And a third, and a fourth. Which was to be expected. But at the tenth state, the experiment took a dramatic twist. The eleventh, twelfth, and thirteenth states were, again, all different—but the fourteenth time step, out of a dizzying googolplex of possibilities, was a repeat of state 10! And from then on, inevitably, the program looped in a cycle of four states.

Kauffman slapped his hands in astonishment. "That's it!" he told himself. "I've got self-organization!" Then using a different random configuration and switching the assignments of Boolean functions, he repeated the experiment. (He did this literally by shuffling some of the punch cards he fed into the hulking IBM mainframe.) Each time a similar phenomenon occurred: the computer would chunk off, state-state-state-state-state, for about ten iterations and then fall into a three- or four-state cycle.

In chaos theory, there was a name for the state of the network that triggered such a looping cycle: a periodic attractor. It was a force that draws otherwise-chaotic systems into recognizable patterns, much as when a lake forms, the water settles into drainage basins. Years later, Kauffman would be versed in the poetic terminology of chaos theory, and indeed his experiment would find its way in the annals of that field, called, to his pride, the Kauffman Model. Indeed, he would identify the self-organizing force at work in the model as a form of "antichaos."

What did this have to do with biology? With gene switching? According to Kauffman, plenty. It indicated that seemingly intricate clock-work constructions like human gene-switching networks were dependent not so much on their precise construction, which dictated the position and connections of each node, as on a global property of *all* such networks driven by complex local reactions—a property that virtually demanded that order should arise. That property was, in Kauffman's conceit, the stuff of God's heart.

The Kauffman Model offered a glimpse of a powerful and continual process of self-organization, one Kauffman contended was at work in a wide domain of biological phenomena, ranging from cell differentiation, to the behavior of the immune system, to the evolutionary process, and indeed to the emergence of life itself.

The most famous experiment in attempting to ascertain the details of life's origin was conducted in 1952 by a twenty-three-year-old University of Chicago graduate student named Stanley Miller. The paradigm for life's beginning at that time focused on the "soup," a prebiotic stew of chemicals supposed to exist on the surface of earth approximately four billion years ago. One of the more troubling gaps in that theory was the process by which some of the complex molecules of organic chemistry formed from the simple elements of the stew. In order for life to emerge from the soup, the brew must have been primed for the formation of things like amino acids, the building blocks of enzymes and proteins. Theoreticians have long conjectured that a spark for such a mixture could have come from a prebiotic thunderstorm, with a lightning bolt catalyzing the proper reaction. But until Miller, nobody had provided evidence that such a thing could happen.

In retrospect, the experiment seems elementary, so simple that soon after the results were published, *Scientific American* provided the instructions so do-it-yourselfers could create the stuff of life from homemade prebiotic soups, in the comfort of their basement workshops. But it did not seem so simple when Miller began. He codesigned the setup with his research adviser, Harold Urey. A construct of sealed flasks and test tubes, the Miller-Urey apparatus had only a touch of Rube Goldberg. At its center was the approximation of the ocean: a 5-liter flask of water. Instead of modern air, the atmosphere inside the apparatus was a simulation of the alleged ingredients of early earth: methane, ammonia, and hydrogen. Since billions of years ago the planet's temperature was high, Miller used a coil to heat his mix to a constant bubble. The *deus ex machina* was simulated lightning, an electrical device that spat sparks at the water vapor as it first rose into an adjacent compartment and then proceeded to a cooler area, where it condensed. The transformed droplets would rain into the sea. A week of this modest turmoil produced a sticky reddish stain on the glass. The water was a murky yellow-brown. When Miller analyzed this gooey result, he found that the simple chemicals mixed into his homemade primordial soup yielded the more complex compounds of amino acids fundamental to life.

Some contemporary commentators believed that the Miller-Urey experiment indicated that the origin of life was not a near-miraculous long-shot occurrence but something firmly dictated by the conditions on earth. Carl Sagan, who produced amino acids in a Miller-Urey-type experiment that substituted ultraviolet radiation for the simulated lightning, said that Miller's humble effort "is now recognized as the single most significant step in convincing many scientists that life is likely to be abundant in the cosmos." Lay observers went farther, suggesting that the origin-of-life problem had been brought to its knees: "If their apparatus had been as big as the ocean," gushed *Time,* "and if it had worked for a million years instead of one week, it might have created something like the first living molecule."

This optimism has faded in the three decades since Miller-Urey. "The problem . . . has turned out to be much more difficult than I, and most other people, envisioned," Miller himself told a reporter in 1990. For one thing, there is considerable doubt about the composition of earth's early atmosphere. But even more daunting is the failure of Miller-Urey to account for the subsequent steps up the ladder from simple organic chemicals to living organisms. Though individual experiments provided potential justification for certain key steps to occur, no one has managed to confirm the current paradigm that would begin from the point of Miller-Urey and proceed to a population of adaptive, evolving molecules, one of which became *the* original replicator, a complex organic molecule capable of self-reproduction that eventually became the ancestor of us all. An early replicator molecule is assumed to be a "naked" RNA, capable of existence in independent form (as opposed to its present ubiquity as the member of the cellular team responsible for translating instructions from DNA and executing them by synthesizing the requested proteins). Thus early life was supposedly an RNA world, consisting of self-replicating RNA, which was eventually upstaged by DNA and proteins.

The major problem with this theory was a seemingly faulty time sequence. The relationship between RNA and proteins is symbiotic: RNA replicates with the help of proteins, and in turn RNA directs the synthesis of proteins. Naked RNA, then, is in effect an egg before a chicken. The inability to resolve this contradiction helped keep the naked-RNA paradigm from universal acceptance and opened the door to all sorts of theories, involving clays, sulfur-based compounds, and interstellar spores.

As Kauffman saw the situation, "If you want to base the origin of life on replicating RNA, the dominant hypothesis is that a single-strand RNA molecule can make a copy of itself, without enzymes and without proteins, which will later become enzymes to catalyze the reactions. (The enzymes and the DNA will come later, because RNA has to produce them.) The bottom line of all this, in all the experimental work, is that it doesn't work. And there are deeper problems conceptually—if you start with a nude replicating piece of RNA, how do you get metabolism, how do you get a complex web of transformations among chemicals going? Nobody has an answer to that."

Kauffman insisted that a key component of life's origin was missing from these theories, the same power of self-organization that he first documented in his experiment in Boolean networks. The more Kauffman looked, the more he found applications for his model. Around 1970 the thought came to him that perhaps, as he later phrased the concept, "this is the way everything started." He sat down and outlined a possible beginning to life on earth but became discouraged when a colleague dismissed it as pure theory. Ultimately, this sort of criticism was applied to Kauffman's pursuit of biological self-organizing principles in general, and, for almost the entire decade of the 1970s, Kauffman, performing more conventional research, used fruit flies to study evolution. His musings on life's beginnings were shelved.

In 1982, at a conference in India, someone told him about some recent theoretical models about the origin of life, particularly that of Freeman Dyson. Kauffman looked at this work, and his three-pronged reaction typified his chutzpah-drenched approach to science: His first comment: "Goddamn it, I did that in 1971." His second comment: "There's a hole in the argument." His third comment: "I can do it better."

It was a twenty-four-hour return flight from New Delhi to Kauffman's destination of Toronto. When he disembarked he had forty pages of algebraic notation and a theory. Kauffman's first words to the friend who met him at the airport were, "I know how life started."

The friend told him to get some sleep. But Kauffman insisted on relating the theory that, he recalls, his friend liked.

Kauffman's theory flew in the face of the leading alternative, which was based on replicating RNA molecules. But it shared some of its structural characteristics with one of the key theories that did subscribe to the RNA hypothesis. This was the hypercycle, postulated by a German biochemist named Manfred Eigen. A hypercycle, as one biologist put it, is a connected network of "functionally coupled, self-replicating entities." Just as in realized life-forms, certain behaviors emerged that were more than the sum of their interactions. The beauty of a hypercycle was that the reactions were interdependent, and therefore no single reaction could be so successful that it drove out the other functions of a cycle: it was in effect a balanced ecosystem. Eigen and his collaborator Peter Schuster used the hypercycle model to postulate how naked strands of RNA might form a chain of complicated reactions that would lead to evolution of more fit examples of RNA and eventually to the emergence of the more sophisticated functions characteristic of current ribosomes and messenger RNA. Kauffman's own idea of a self-catalyzing network operated in a fashion familiar to anyone who had studied hypercycles. The element in common was a parallel structure of cooperation.

But Kauffman rejected the idea that life had sprung from an RNA world. Instead, the Kauffman theory focused on how early life might have supported the dual functions of replication and metabolism. In this, it had much in common with the model postulated by Dyson. Dyson's explanation of the origin of life was based on his educated guess that the phenomenon was a combination of two separate processes, one in which replication emerged and another that fixed the machinery of metabolism. Previous theories of the origin of life had focused on one or the other and could be classified as either protein theories, which contended that metabolism, fueled on proteins, came first, or nucleic acid theories, which insisted that a replicator like RNA was the first instance of life.

Dyson complained that theorists had focused on the latter, thus underestimating the importance of metabolism. Dyson's dual structure excited Kauffman because his own theory, unlike that of Eigen and most others trying to nail down the particulars of life's origin, also hinged on the presence of metabolism. In fact, Kauffman's hypercycle-like system had a metabolism of its own, in that it drew materials and energy from the world around it to increase and maintain internal order.

The cornerstone of Kauffman's theory was the discovery he made as a medical student—the ease with which self-organization emerges in all networks. This was the proof that confirmed his idea that biology is determined by the heart of God—global order from local interaction—and not the detail-ridden filigrees of God's twiddling digits. It only stood to reason that this concept would be at play in the way life itself emerged.

In Kauffman's theory, the prebiotic soup was loaded with the simple chemicals thought to be present on earth before life existed, including simple amino acids called monomers, which potentially can hook up to create form linear chains called polymers. Kauffman regarded the chemicals as strings of symbols, depicting the progress of the reactions in discrete time steps, like a cellular automaton or a Boolean network experiment.

There were a sizable number of reactions possible between monomers, and, beginning in the second time step, polymers started to form as the monomers bonded. The number of possible reactions between the monomers and the steadily increasing set of polymers was astronomical. Even beginning with a set of only two monomers, the possibilities got very large very quickly. For instance, if monomer A linked with monomer B to form the "species" of polymer known as AB, in the next time step AB could hook up again with A to form AAB, with B to form ABB, or with AB to form ABAB. Each time step multiplied the possible strings considerably, and very quickly the possible species were well into the millions. In addition, the number of possible reactions between the polymers grew at an even higher rate. It would seem like chaos, with strings forming and breaking apart seemingly at random. But as computer models have demonstrated, that was not what happened.

Certain chemicals had a catalyzing effect on the production of other

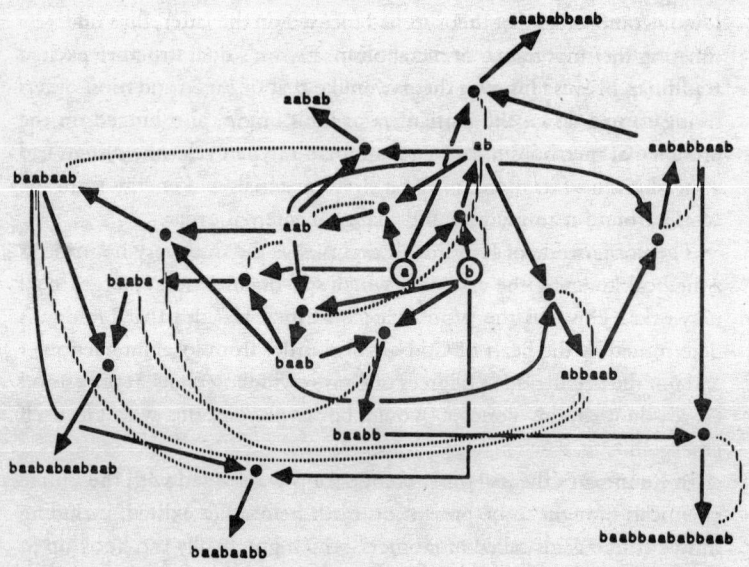

A computer-based autocatalytic network consisting of 15 species. The network begins with the artificial monomers A and B, circled here. The dots represent reactions, as the monomers combine with each other and with the results of these combinations to form polymers (represented here by strings of A's and B's). Meanwhile certain polymers catalyze certain reactions (represented by broken lines). Although this looks hopelessly complex, it is actually a depiction of how order asserts itself in such systems: from an unrelated stew of millions of possible polymer species, a limited reaction network self-organizes from the chaos and forms a kind of metabolism. Something like this may have been the origin of life itself.

chemicals, expediting each given reaction. As the time steps accumulated, a frenzied round-robin of experimentation occurred as different species emerged and tested their catalyzing ability on other reactions. As the number of successful combinations accumulated, the percentage of catalyzed reactions increased. At a certain point—just like the flash point that occurred when the Kauffman model settled into a periodic attractor that set off the short state cycles—a phase transition occurred, a sort of connective explosion where suddenly critical mass was achieved, and, in a subset of chemicals, *every* polymer had its formation catalyzed by some other polymer in the subset. From then on, the formation of polymer species was no longer a hit-and-miss operation but a metabolizing function of the system at large. You had, in effect, a living "autocatalytic" system.

"There's a vast explosion of the number of organic molecules," describes Kauffman. "There's also an even vaster number of legitimate organic reactions by which they can convert to one another. All of a sudden, you crystallize a connecting metabolism. It's not piecemeal, it's a phase transition. So my view is that life started with an autocatalytic, self-reproducing set of polymers, which simultaneously collectively catalyzed a metabolism. And you have a going concern. You never had a naked gene. You just have to get a complex enough pot of chemicals and it'll all work." (At this point, it remains a logical, not a chemical, construct.)

Kauffman's theories, if valid, had an advantage over the alternatives: those not relying on the self-organizing power of networks he postulated, faced extremely long odds against getting started. They depended on the creation of a single type of molecule that had the capability of evolving into the exacting array of chemicals necessary to fuel the engines of life. Instead of the systemwide parallel reactions Kauffman proposed—which he claimed inevitably yielded the result of complexity—these alternatives proceeded in serial fashion. They depended on a series of proper circumstances, like a long session at roulette where a single number was played continuously, in hopes it would turn up every time. But there was an obvious counterindication: if the odds were so terrifically stacked against these theories, why were we here? "Life *did* start," concludes Kauffman. "And if I'm right, the probability of life is very much higher than anybody thought."

Life wants to happen. The thought was comforting to Kauffman. About a year after he first hatched his theory about the origin of life, he trekked up a mountain outside Sacramento. High above the world, he ruminated about autocatalytic networks, how simple they were, and how inevitable. He experienced a shudder of oneness with his surroundings and felt that a special piece of the universe had exposed itself to him: the heart of God.

With the advent of a-life studies, Stuart Kauffman's theory found itself embedded in a set of experiments and theories that drew on the proposed circumstances of the early biosphere and considered autocatalytic systems based on that chemistry as a sort of organism: dynamic systems that metabolized and evolved. The creators of these systems, which were constructed in laboratory pots of chemicals ("wet") or computer simulations ("dry") were armed with scientific buckshot, in order to hit multiple targets, ranging from questions concerning the origin of life to the self-organizing behavior of dynamic systems in general to the sorts of reactions that could trigger any evolving set of chemical chains. In some cases, these simulations shed entirely the claim that they resembled in significant manner the circumstances of prebiotic earth and in doing so demanded consideration as objects in their own right, displaying key behavior of adaptive systems and enabling us to study lifelike machinery at close range.

One example was Doyne Farmer and Norman Packard's model of an artificial chemistry inspired by Kauffman's theories. It was later embodied in an eighty-thousand-line computer program written by an athletic and soft-spoken biologist in his early thirties named Richard Bagley. The model itself evolved in the four years since Bagley began programming it; after much tinkering it indicated that Kauffman's hypothesis was sound—his assumptions about reactions in artificial monomers and polymers indeed yielded an active autocatalytic network.

This did not necessarily prove anything about how life actually began on this planet, in this universe. But as Bagley explains, "In trying to make things go, our game is not to provide a very realistic description of nature; instead, we try to find out what nature *had to be* to make things go." This distinction was key to understanding what happened in any a-life experiment but was often misunderstood, especially by biologists who focused on life as we know it and not on theories of life in general. "Most biologists are disdainful of theories," says Farmer. "They are trapped by the fact that their science, in the way that they define it, is studying life as it is on earth, and that automatically makes their view very narrow."

When Bagley ventured to La Jolla, California, to show his computer model to some of the gurus of the origin-of-life world—Leslie Orgel of the Salk Institute, Stanley Miller of the University of California, San Diego, and the rising star Gerald Joyce of the Scripps Research Institute—he received a mixed reaction. Orgel, although skeptical of Kauffman's theories, offered suggestions as sort of a hedge against its potential success. Joyce, enthusiastic about the a-life approach, was encouraging—although he considered Kauffman's assumptions to be overly optimistic, he urged Kauffman to pursue chemical experiments geared toward justifying his hypotheses. But Miller, who almost forty years ago made the classic wet artificial life experiment, was unimpressed. "Running equations through a computer does not constitute an experiment," he declared to a reporter. Bagley described Miller's stance as "dogmatic resistance."

The complaint was that computer models of the origin of life are inherently doomed to irrelevancy. As biologist Hyman Hartman pointed out, the quest to understand how life actually began was more an exercise in ratiocination than an experimental quest. "It's a historical question," he says. A theory successfully consummated on the computer might be a thing of beauty, but besides indicating a certain viability it was inconclusive. There would be no way to prove that such a scheme actually occurred billions of years ago. But Hartman's criticism can be directed also at Miller's original wet experiment, because it, too, was a mere simulation of prebiotic conditions.

On the other hand, a computer model that presumed a viable chemistry and then proceeded to alchemize the behavior of life from reactions based on that chemistry provided something quite valuable. "What we really are interested in is taking the salient features of the origin of life, and making a model of self-organization," says Bagley. "As a result, we have this very nice model of self-organization and of evolutionary behavior." This model need not represent the way things happened (though Kauffman would insist this is the case), but something that *could* have happened. Equally significant was the fact that in this model, something *was* happening. An alternate form of metabolism was occurring, based on a grammar of string processing rather than on reactions between atoms within chemicals. The chemistry may have been artificial, but that did not mean that there was not much to be learned from studying it. That the connections were logical was unassailable. And just as the boids of Craig Reynolds did not simulate flocking but actually flocked, the Bagley computer model did not merely simulate an evolving metabolism: it metabolized.

"The fact that [our model displays behavior] not literally seen in nature I find *more* encouraging, not less," says Bagley, "because as wonderfully diverse as the world is, to get our minds thinking about what's really going on in evolution, or in this kind of functional self-organization, the more examples we have, the better. Thinking about life in other environments can only help us."

The hope was that an accumulating base of artificial representations of how complexity could form from prebiotic-like environments could make a compelling case for Kauffman's claim that life was virtually inevitable, not a long shot. Indeed, other a-lifers found artificial environments to be fertile ground for developing biologic behaviors from slews of random interactions.

One of these a-lifers was a Danish physicist named Steen Rasmussen. His heritage was similar to that of others who had been drawn to an artificial life approach to classic biological and complexity problems. After study in multiple disciplines—though his doctorate was in physics and applied mathematics, he was trained as an engineer and also held a degree in philosophy—he became fascinated with dynamical systems and with self-organization, particularly in the way they manifested themselves in nature. After meeting Farmer and Langton, both of whom had moved across the parking lot from CNLS to Los Alamos's theoretical division, Rasmussen was invited to perform postdoctoral work with them. Farmer had become leader of T-13, the complex systems group.

Rasmussen's first a-life work concerned origin-of-life autocatalytic sets, and the reliable emergence of order in those experiments led him to explore other sorts of simulations, including those with little direct correlation to the prebiotic conditions of life. This would have the advantage of finding alternative approaches to the emergence of life, which might yield clues to other varieties of living dynamical systems that had failed to show themselves thus far as a result of the possibly arbitrary evolutionary path that life on earth had followed.

Rasmussen decided to generate a metabolic system based on the types of interactions generic to computers: an artificial chemistry based on computer instructions. He borrowed the rules from an early, nonintrusive exercise in computer viruses called "Core War." The basic components of this "core world" were the instruction set of assembly language commands charged with manipulating information in the core of the computer memory. Rasmussen and his Danish collaborators named their world VENUS, which stood both as an acronym for Virtual Evolution in a Nonstochastic Universe Simulator and as a tribute to "the Roman goddess of natural productivity, love, and beauty, with the hope that [we] would create interesting life-like properties."

Essentially, VENUS was a prebiotic soup of information, fed with a rule set that, Rasmussen hoped, had the capability to self-organize and develop characteristics recognizable as life. All within the confines of an IBM PS-80 personal computer. He explains that "in previous quantitative models of the origin of life, people assume something is the important evolutionary route, and try to direct the system along that route. The restriction is 'the model must go this way,' and you can only learn what is important if you go this way. What has been missing is openness—you don't tell the system beforehand where to go. The system decides by itself, and it can take one of infinitely many routes to somewhere. They may be blind alleys, and the system may die as it sometimes does . . . or you can have a totally new thing coming out. We are trying to build a zoo of artificial chemistries and what they can produce. From this zoo we hope to be able to find some general principles from which we are able to make the real things."

Over a series of twelve-hour runs, approximately twenty-two million instructions were executed and around one hundred thousand generations passed. It was, at first, difficult for Rasmussen and his colleagues to determine any organizing principles, as they stared at a jumble of colored dots on a computer screen, each color representing a different instruction.

On the one hand it was obvious that something was happening as the simulation proceeded; the core was changing. One the other hand, the basic physics of this universe is so different from our "real" physics that we had no clue about what would develop in the system. We did not know what to look for in the core. . . . Since we did not have any automated methods for interpreting [the core] data, we had no other choice than to dump many, many cores, where each hard copy occupied several meters of paper, and hope that the human eye was able to catch anything of interest. It took a long time before we were ready to test evolution of different environments in a more systematic way.

When that time came, Rasmussen and team had become experts in gauging the terrain of this untasted new flavor of universe. They came to see themselves as archaeologists set loose on a virgin planet. A starting point was provided by a determination of what could be called an "organism" in a world made of patterns of computer instructions; this had been set by the Core War rules, which defined creatures as consisting of persistent patterns of computer instructions. These were capable of maintaining themselves through time, even as they executed the very information of which they consisted. For instance, those creatures consisting of MOV (move) instructions would, on execution, move from one core location to another. Other instructions were capable of adding two instructions, or splitting another instruction, or splitting the organism itself. If an instruction could not be executed in the next time step, it would be dead. Detecting organisms could be tricky because, as presumably was the case when real life emerged, the more primitive the life-form, the more difficult it would have been to distinguish it from its surroundings. When the patterns of instructions became more persistent, of course, these more stable creatures were more easily tracked. Indeed, distinct populations of organisms did emerge; the artificial chemistry of VENUS was a fertile one.

Rasmussen and company found that generally two sorts of environments were generated by core conditions, depending on which evolutionary accident affected the initial conditions: a relatively uncomplicated desert populated by simple instruction loops and a dense jungle with cooperating structures of several instructions. By and large, the jungles were more felicitous grounds for the origin of lifelike behaviors; organisms that lived in deserts usually formed in the jungles and later adapted themselves to the conditions of the less complex environment.

As generation after generation passed, the population changed and became more complex. Organisms that the scientists hand designed and, in a form of directed panspermia, dropped into the artificial universe, found themselves unable to survive in the "noisy" environment of VENUS, which was spiked with random perturbations to simulate the environmental accidents that might affect the prebiotic locale. More successful and robust were organisms that emerged from within the system itself.

As the experiments proceeded, and many thousands of generations passed, the VENUS observers learned to identify these organisms and detect what they called "fossils," traces of structural organisms that had become extinct. Eventually they made a series of conclusions that, depending on whether one accepts VENUS as a viable proving grounds for life, held potential value for those wondering how organisms emerge from any nonorganic environment.

Some of these results were rather obvious. For instance, without a flow of energy, life cannot emerge. This was a simple application of the second law of thermodynamics, and, if that had not held in VENUS, something would have been terribly wrong. Also to be expected was the fact that different sorts of evolutionary conditions caused differing evolutionary paths.

More interesting were certain phenomena that seemed to bear out many accepted but yet-unconfirmed hypotheses about the origin of life. Small perturbations in the environment and chance historical events potentially could force major changes in evolution. Sometimes a serendipitous microscopic event could squelch life from appearing even in otherwise-optimal conditions. Sometimes a jarring event that might otherwise be survivable by a self-correction in the system was followed by more noise, and the combination wiped out the nascent life-forms. One particular instance where this sort of combination punch resulted in a knockout was triggered when a particularly efficient self-replicating series of instructions caused the core to become flooded with those organisms. The system adjusted itself several times, with the organisms eventually stabilizing their growth and switching to a form of being that reproduced only on alternate time steps—but a further perturbation knocked out the new instruction-set organisms before they fine-tuned themselves.

Perhaps the key lesson that Rasmussen drew from VENUS dealt with the imperative quality of cooperative structures. As in autocatalytic networks, the evolution of a viable lifelike system depended on symbiotic structures within the system. For example, one of the more successful organisms that emerged among VENUS's runs was a structure called MOV-SPL (move and split). This was a combination of the instructions to move from one part of the core to another and to split itself. As it expanded and moved throughout the core, it interacted with whatever it encountered and left fragments of its own instruction set behind—in this way it fed the gene pool with MOV and SPL instructions. When the gene pool was sufficiently spiked, the MOV-SPL organism, while not displaying classic replication, easily reproduced from one generation to another because, when its instructions split apart, they found themselves instantly linked with analogues to their previous partners. Thus the organism displayed stability.

"Despite the brittleness of the individual instruction and the modest core size," concluded the Rasmussen group, "our system is indeed able to evolve stable cooperative structures." Interestingly, the group pointedly declined to judge whether or not these cooperative structures were alive. The very idea that the matter was worthy of consideration was to many a heresy. Yet, as Rasmussen insisted, something was happening here. The system was less a simulation than an alternative. What it was remained undefined. But it was *something,* and that in itself vindicated the experiment.

"If we believe that it's possible to extract the logic of life and put it into some other hardware," says Rasmussen, "then we have to conclude that there is a reality in VENUS which is just as real as our reality."

Rasmussen's was the classic a-life request: to accept a view requiring an initial suspension of intuitive judgment, a leap of faith made easier to undertake by the self-consistency and plausible foundations of these alternate universes. The Danish physicist understood the difficulty presented by this leap but was fervent in insisting the leap must be taken. At the second a-life conference, Rasmussen distributed an intentionally provocative crib sheet titled "Aspects of Information, Life Reality, and Physics." In the logical procession of the seven propositions he offered, his philosophical training became evident:

Information and Life:

(I) A universal computer is indeed universal and can emulate any process (Turing).

(II) The essence of life is a process (von Neumann).

(III) There exist criteria by which we are able to distinguish living from non-living things.

Accepting (I), (II), and (III) implies the possibility of life in a computer.

Life and Reality:

(IV) If somebody manages to develop life in a computer environment, which satisfied (III), it follows from (II) that these life-forms are just as much alive as you and I.

(V) Such an artificial organism must perceive a reality R_2, which for itself is just as real as our "real" reality R_1 is for us.

(VI) From (V) we conclude that R_1 and R_2 has the same ontological status. Although R_2 in a material way is imbedded in R_1, R_2 is independent of R_1.

Reality and Physics:

(VII) If R_1 and R_2 have the same ontological status it might be possible to learn something about the fundamental properties of realities in general, and of R_1 in particular, by studying the details of different R_2's. An example of such a property is the physics of a reality.

The final proposition provided a wondrous justification for creating artificial universes. Once Rasmussen's view of reality was accepted, a unique set of possibilities unfolded. For the first time, it was possible to separate the qualities of life *in general* from the qualities of the single, perhaps anomalous, form of life presented to us thus far. What happened in VENUS; what happened in some of the more fruitful cellular automata; and what happened in the computer generation of autocatalytic networks certainly displayed some qualities that we attribute to life. The systems were not living but arguably fell between the inertness of a rock and the vitality of a bacterium. Call them protolife. The workers of artificial life were cooking many varieties of these protolife systems, a veritable explosion in artificial chemistry, artificial physics, artificial worlds in which lifelike behaviors emerge. At Los Alamos alone, the members of the T-13 Complex Systems Group came up with a panoply of various universes in which to grow life. Besides the autocatalytic nets of Farmer and Bagley, there were Rasmussen's VENUS, Langton's CAs, and a group experiment in creating a "process gas," a sort of simulated molecular proving ground that could model many sorts of interactions and that presumably yielded emergent behavior. In addition, an Italian scientist at T-13, Walter Fontana, was developing what he called an "algorithmic chemistry," in which a form of logical calculus provided a grammar under whose rules emergent behavior might form.

Understandably, the sum of the experiments was a variegated jumble. The current task was finding the right means of measurement: to provide the quantification for these new worlds, in order to standardize the languages of new life.

Langton's work in defining life on the edge of chaos was a step in this direction, by providing a specific measurement, the λ parameter, by which to locate the region where life may thrive. Kauffman extended Langton's ideas by applying them to his work on Boolean networks. Others, like physicist James Crutchfield, were designing a methodology to measure the complexity of artificial universes.

Crutchfield has been one of Farmer's partners in the iconoclastic Santa Cruz Dynamical Systems Collective; after a stint teaching at Berkeley, he cruised the various institutions devoted to studying complex systems. After studying the physics of the matter, Crutchfield was beginning to create new universes of his own. His purpose was not to simulate but to form CA-like systems that displayed information processing and computational structure. As with Langton, Kauffman, and others experimenting with artificial worlds, he hoped that the systems would display a level of computational capability that they did not have at the beginning of the experiment. These powers would emerge. On the heels of this, new structures would develop. The system would continue to evolve into realms difficult or impossible to predict. Crutchfield hoped to measure these new structures and better understand the machinery of emergence. Using his methodology, others devising artificial universes could measure their own systems, extracting a numerical value to determine the degree of "life-hood" in them.

Crutchfield agreed with Farmer and Kauffman that the a-life initiative was intimately intertwined with the quest for the hidden self-organizing force that flexed its will on massively complex systems such as living organisms. Reason dictated that this pervasive force had a very busy time when life emerged from the primordial soup or whatever mix of dead elements existed those billions of years ago.

"There are some very basic principles of life that we just don't understand," says Crutchfield. "At some point there wasn't biological life. But nonetheless since biological life now exists we know that there's some point in time during which things had to be driven in that general direction. So that sort of lifeless, physical nature had to move forward and reorganize itself. It's at that point in a sense where I'm studying it. I can't prove that life should spontaneously arise, but just given the sheer evidence around me that things do organize, we do learn, and there's so much organized matter around, I think it's actually in a sense highly probable that there does exist some basic organizing force. And I see no impediments to creating something that can indisputably be called alive. If you seriously consider what science is about, all the arrows point in that direction. Scientists try to understand things we don't yet understand. And life is one of those things. We will understand it. I don't see any limitation in principle here."

No one expected to concoct a silicon caldron of primordial broth, bubbling on until some one-celled goblin sprang up from the computer screen and announced its presence. The goal, on its face, was more modest. To proceed a step further on the ladder of emergence. The manner in which this was to be conducted was borrowed from nature. If researchers did it often enough, and measured what they did, they might come to understand the forces that made it happen.

It will not be a-life that definitively determines how life originally emerged: that is a detective story with the final pages long shredded. But a new methodology of emergence, pioneered by a-life experiments, has the potential to bring us deeper comprehension of the mysteries of biology, including the origin of life. In the early 1990s, Gerald Joyce of the Scripps Research Institute, a young medical researcher who had already spent years dogging the discrete facts of life's first push, broke with his more conservative colleagues in embracing the techniques of artificial life to conduct experiments in the origin of life. He readily admitted that the staged events in his laboratory, invariably simulating the RNA world (which he, unlike Kauffman, believed is the key step in the generation of life), had only a nodding acquaintanceship with prebiotic earth conditions. "These are artificial life kinds of games, where one starts with a pre-formed RNA," he says, "you don't ask where it comes from, you just make it and put it in a clean tube. No contaminants, no nothing—just the right stuff."

What placed Joyce's work truly in the a-life mold was the use of natural phenomena to transform his model chemical world into something more than a model: "We try to *teach* the enzymes to take over the replication activity themselves. If we do that, it's artificial life. A self-replicating system based on Darwinian evolution—that's the agreed-upon definition of life by the wet people, the people who are trying to make it in the test tube."

Joyce's guiding light, besides his mentor Orgel, was found in the texts of Thomas Pynchon. If Joyce was inspired by *V.*, one long paean to entropy, he was utterly thrilled with the apocalyptic *Gravity's Rainbow*. To Joyce, it was a parable. From the screaming-comes-across-the-sky destruction, to the warped yet orderly rebuilding of the world, *Rainbow*, says Joyce, "is actually a cheerful book—despite the entropic forces of the universe that try to drive us into the ground, there is an organizing principle. What is the organizing principle? Self-organization!"

That epiphany motivated Joyce to probe that ineluctable phenomenon, first in computer populations of evolving automata. Then he began working with Orgel and sensed that magic was to be made with RNA. "I've been a wet person ever since," he says.

But the computer work left its mark on him: he treated RNA molecules as if they were computer automata. He jiggered them into new behaviors. They were his artificial agents, sometimes operating on their own obscure agenda. "Molecules surprise you," he says. "They don't do what you tell them to do. We'll set up an experiment, and then we'll see what the results are, and then based on the results, we'll see where we'll go from there. It's the kind of thing Langton is doing, in that what emerges is not what one expected."

The machinery of emergence that Joyce utilized was evolution. By using it in molecules, Joyce was probably retracing a path, if not following in the same steps, trod by the succession of molecules hiking toward that level of fitness called life. Molecules were the substrate in which things actually happened. Exploiting mutations, testing fitness, and urging the molecules to move up a ladder of complexity, where the upper rungs find more fit variations, Joyce created the conditions for classic evolution.

The methods were ingenious. A goal was set: to evolve RNA molecules so that they developed new abilities. Others had made some progress in this area—Orgel in particular altered RNA molecules so they could self-replicate under special conditions. This was a stunt that modern RNA, which was honed to dispatch the chores of metabolism, could not normally perform, although the current dogma was that early forms of RNA were able to self-reproduce and thereby evolve.

But Joyce's work used evolution to *train* these RNAs to function as an enzyme, or *ribozyme,* to perform tasks that they probably never have performed before. In order to see how this is done, one could consider an RNA molecule. This is a string of nucleotides, built from four base chemicals: guanine, cytosine, adenine, and uracil. Taken in toto, the sequence of base chemicals along the molecule consists of the RNA code. In ribozymes, the coded message is translated via a folding process into an enzyme that can catalyze a chemical reaction. As new generations of molecules proceed, a possibility of mutation exists at each nucleotide on the string. Most mutations have either no effect or a negative effect on the ribozyme's behavior, but some can lead to different properties that, depending on what one determines is a desirable function of a ribozyme, can improve the ribozyme's makeup.

Joyce devised a scheme to invoke mutations systematically so that the entire space of possible one-mutation variants was explored, followed by two-mutation variants, and so on. By carefully producing ribozymes of limited mutation, and by creating a selection pressure that allowed increased reproduction of the ribozymes that best performed the task Joyce wanted accomplished, he eventually got a population that could perform the task, even if it seemed an unlikely behavioral jump from the behavior of ribozymes in the initial population.

The first major success that Joyce enjoyed began with a self-splicing ribozyme; that is, a ribozyme that catalyzes a reaction with the following result: it cleaves itself, literally snipping the RNA string of nucleotides to form two strings. This molecule was called the *Tetrahymena* ribozyme, consisting of 413 nucleotides.

Joyce wanted to change the *Tetrahymena* ribozyme so that it could perform a "novel catalytic function." Instead of cleaving RNA, it would split *DNA* strings. Plain old RNA did not do this—the task was similar to teaching a cat to bark like a dog. But utilizing his cunningly effective method, which in a single reactor vessel produced mutant structural variants of the original, or wild-type, RNA enzymes, Joyce was able to coax significant variations. By stimulating reproduction of the variations that reacted with the DNA substrate he placed in the vessel, he was eventually able to produce a mutant form of *Tetrahymena* ribozyme that cleaved DNA with an efficacy unknown in the wild type. As Joyce and his collaborator, Debra Robertson wrote, "The selected molecule represents the discovery of the first RNA enzyme known to cleave single-strand DNA specifically." Using controlled evolution, ribosomes had been trained to to break with their nature.

The next task was to teach the errant molecules to react with a compound more alien to it, namely glucose. Both DNA and RNA are five-carbon sugars; glucose is a six-carbon sugar. Though the increment was small, the gulf between a five- and a six-carbon sugar was huge; they bore little structural resemblance. "We're trying to teach the ribozyme to be what's called a glucose phosphatase, an enzyme that can cut phosphates off of glucose. And from there on to more wild things."

The new tricks that Joyce trained molecules to perform had potential for dramatic effect on the world outside the laboratory, namely in the battle against the devastating disease AIDS. AIDS performs its evil in the form of an RNA virus. This is a bogus strand of RNA that invades a cell and copies its dread message into the cell's DNA. If there were a way to develop a counteracting form of RNA, capable of splitting the AIDS RNA, or its DNA copy, the disease might be neutralized. Joyce thought there was a way: using evolution to train molecules as dedicated AIDS fighters. Joyce conjectured that his methods could potentially evolve a ribozyme "to be the best anti-AIDS thing we can get. We can attack the virus, and then we can attack the DNA copy."

Working on a National Institutes of Health grant called "Evolutionary Engineering of Anti-HIV-1 Ribozymes," Joyce and his team started to explore an a-life means of fighting AIDS. He began with the same ribozyme they used to cut DNA, which in its present state was not particularly effective in cutting the AIDS genome (since that was never a task for which fitness was rewarded). But as the ribozyme was exposed to conditions that caused it to mutate, some of the altered population attacked the AIDS virus more successfully than others. The system was geared toward applying selection pressure to the degree that the AIDS virus was attacked—in other words, those ribozymes that perform Veg-O-Matic-style destruction on the AIDS genome were allowed to produce more offspring. "We're evolving the enzyme to be a better and better AIDS killer," says Joyce.

This was only the first series of steps, conducted under pristine conditions. The next level of difficulty would be training the ribosome to perform with the same directed fury *outside* the test tube, within the more noisy confines of an AIDS-infected T-cell. The final step would be creating a piece of genetic material to be delivered to the cells of AIDS patients that would contain the information for manufacturing this new ribozyme, so that victims of the disease would be able to create the AIDS killer within their own bodies.

Gerald Joyce recognized that the greatest advantage of applying artificial life to wet work was the ability to attack problems such as the AIDS virus. But he also realized that in the long term, advances in artificial life might realize something even more profoundly significant in the annals of our species.

Joyce called these "the more sci-fi goals, be they artificial organisms, as a model for early life on earth, or just as a thing to do." They involved a new origin of life, the creation of alternate life forms. Since Joyce was affiliated with the exobiology program of NASA, he made it a point to legitimize the funding the agency might devote in that area in the future. He felt that researchers who dared label their work as artificial life should not have to cloak their goals by subsuming the research under fields less prone to sarcasm. "I made that argument at meetings with NASA scientists, and they bought it," he says. "That's now an explicit part of the goals of the program—to make life. Whatever the substrate may be."

Those seeking to hatch these new forms of life would certainly need to exploit the uncharted forces of physics that a-life researchers yearn to map. Stuart Kauffman would insist that the first thing to explore would be the workings of self-organization, and indeed, that was a key ingredient in experiments underway. But as Gerald Joyce discovered in his wet work—and von Neumann noted in his last writings—there was unlimited power in a certain organizing force with which we are somewhat more familiar.

The power of evolution.

THE GENETIC

ALGORITHM

When man wanted to fly, he first turned to natural example—the bird—to develop his early notions of how to accomplish this difficult task. Notable failures by Daedalus and numerous bird-like contraptions (ornithopters) at first pointed in the wrong direction, but eventually, persistence and the abstraction of the appropriate knowledge (lift over an airfoil) resulted in successful glider and powered flight. In contrast to this example, isn't it peculiar that when man has tried to build machines to think, learn, and adapt he has ignored and largely continues to ignore one of nature's most powerful examples of adaptation, genetics and natural selection?

David Goldberg

John Henry Holland was born in 1929 in Indiana and raised in a small town in Western Ohio. He inherited the pluck if not the avocations of his father, a soybean speculator whose passion was gymnastics. John Henry had a fever for knowledge, particularly that which illuminated the intricate structure of the world. He would sometimes tinker with more compact versions of reality in an attempt to mimic some of its complications. One of his favorite activities was simulating famous military clashes; he would patiently produce drawings of war matériel on mimeograph paper, run off copies, cut up the pieces, and launch them in intricate campaigns. His academic strengths were physics and mathematics, and in his senior year in high school he ventured to a nearby town to take a test offered statewide in those subjects. Only two points, he still recalls, separated him from the first-place finisher. But third place was good enough for a scholarship to MIT.

An odyssey had begun that would lead him to a compelling methodology of simulating the mechanics of natural evolution on computers. It would be twenty years before John Holland settled on it and twenty years more before people began to understand its significance.

It was 1946, and the reverberations of the Manhattan Project had scarcely settled in the scientific imagination. The project's enigmatic leader, Robert Oppenheimer, was Holland's hero. The MIT freshman was entranced by the great physicist's breadth of intelligence—by the fact that he read in dozens of languages, appreciated obscure religions, was humbled by poetry. "He seemed very much a Renaissance kind of man," says Holland.

This was in keeping with Holland's own view of the world. He considered things in their wholeness. Very early on he intuited something about large, interacting systems—everything from local ecologies to the operation of the town schools—that seemed obvious on the face but was actually quite profound. These systems were layered with a hierarchy of systems, but persisting throughout was a repetitive series of key units. Holland regarded these as "building blocks." It was sort of an atomic theory, writ large and applied liberally.

These interests placed him on a collision course with several forces at MIT. One of them was Norbert Wiener, the crusty mathematician who spearheaded a movement that called itself "cybernetics," a term borrowed from a Greek word for *steersman,* an embodiment of this new science that putatively focused on control systems in nature and machines. Yet it strived for more. Essentially, Wiener argued what his acquaintance and sometime colleague von Neumann also asserted: organisms are essentially machines, and it is possible for humans to build things that display similar behavior. Weiner and his cohorts would visit the creators of the early computers and stress the importance of using nature as a model. "Everywhere we met with a sympathetic hearing," he reported, "and the vocabulary of engineers soon became contaminated with the terms of the neurophysiologist and the psychologist." Unfortunately, perhaps because it was so intimately tied to its contemporary technologies, cybernetics implicitly aligned itself with an analog approach to this merger of the synthetic and the natural. It saw the world as a continuous process, not a granular or digital one. Its signature devices were homeostatic contraptions that maintained a sense of equilibrium as a result of feedback loops, much in the spirit of the sense of instinct with which nature endowed its creations. But technology was destined to take a decidedly digital turn, and the computational biology approach that relied on discrete information (as postulated by von Neumann) would ultimately fill the niche that cybernetics once hoped to fill in the ecosystem of human endeavor.

At MIT in the late 1940s, however, cybernetics thrived. Wiener's influence led John Holland to consider a common ground between biology and artificial computation. In particular, Holland was fascinated by a kind of programming based on constructing artificial networks of metaphorical neurons. The idea that individual neurons worked together to form a network from which memories and complex behavior emerged—and that such networks could be built artifically—dovetailed elegantly with Holland's building blocks.

MIT was then in the process of building one of the first electronic computers. Called "Whirlwind," it was contracted by the Department of Defense to analyze trajectories of possible incoming missiles in "real time," as they flew. Holland managed to get himself a low-level security clearance and soon became an expert in the nascent field of computer programming. As a result, IBM asked him to work with an elite squad of engineers planning the logical design of the company's first commercial calculator, the 701. The team included Arthur Samuels, who would soon write a landmark program that would enable the computer to "learn" the game of checkers by playing opponents, gaining experience with every loss, and eventually surpassing the level of an average stoveside checkers wag. Another participant was John McCarthy, destined to become one of the initiators of the artificial intelligence movement.

In order to test the 701, the young engineers decided to implement a nerve-net system. Holland and his colleagues regarded the computer like a giant, albeit sedentary, lab rat. "Even then we understood there were real advantages of having these simulated test animals," says Holland. "The advantage was that we could go inside and see individual neurons, start the thing over from the same initial conditions, and go through a different training routine."

Working with the prototype 701 offered myriad frustrations. Design work was carried on by day, so the simulation team worked between 11 P.M. and dawn. At the start of each session, the program had to be laboriously clicked into memory. The 701 was about one hundred times slower than a cheap personal computer of thirty years hence, and it broke down about twice an hour, at which point the program had to be restored. But they got the machine behaving, in a rudimentary sense, like a lab rat, in that successive iterations showed that the interconnected web of neurons "learned" something about a maze. Holland never forgot this clear link between biology and computation: machines could be trained to adapt to surroundings in the same way that animals could. And the way to do it was from the bottom up—to start with a situation of virtual randomness and program nature into it. Nature could then take its course. Humankind had finally learned enough about nature's mechanisms that we could abstract them into mathematical principles— and lifelike results would emerge.

McCarthy and Marvin Minsky drew the opposite conclusion when they helped found AI. Artificial intelligence postulated that computers could behave like organisms, but its approach was from the top down. Structures were not encouraged to emerge, but were imposed. Programs for AI were solution oriented. They posed a question to the computer and tried to make the computer answer it in the way that a human being would.

As AI gained credibility as the cutting edge of computer science, and indeed became the dogma of its day, John Holland's line of thinking was shunted to obscurity. Fortunately, Holland, after leaving IBM to pursue his doctorate, chose the single place in the United States where he could freely hone his vision, melding the idea of building blocks with biology and computation. This was the University of Michigan, where Arthur Burks was about to start the Logic of Computers Group. Holland knew only that Michigan had an excellent math department and, unlike MIT, a top-ranked football team. (He liked to go to football games.) But, once Holland returned to the Midwest, Burks took him under his wing. Soon Holland was immersed in the group's multidisciplinary enterprises and thinking about cellular automata and nerve nets.

In the late 1950s Holland had the realization that perhaps the best way to execute these simulations would be to design a different type of computer. In nature, many of the small interactions from which global consequences emerge occur all at once—a parallel process—but, when trying to simulate these on a computer, researchers were forced to adhere to the serial structure of the machine, which required events to queue up to be handled one at a time, by the single processor that was the brain of the computer. Holland postulated a machine that would have several processors working simultaneously—a parallel-processing computer. He published his theory as his dissertation, but nobody at the time was sufficiently motivated to actually build one.

Roaming the math library, Holland had also come across a book that would change his life, *The Genetic Theory of Natural Selection,* written by the esteemed evolutionary biologist R. A. Fisher. The first attempt at a mathematical theory of evolution, it used the tools of physics to tackle biology. Holland was entranced. The book dared cross the boundary between logic and biology, and it opened to Holland the potential of evolution as an engine for adaptation. Evolution was, like learning, a form of adapting to the environment, the difference being that it worked over generations rather than in a single life span. And it was a considerably more powerful form of adaptation than learning—an organism without an eye could not grow one in a single lifetime, although it might be an ancestor of a species that did have an eye. In such a case the eventual development of a complex yet endlessly useful organ would be an example of evolution's ability to produce brilliant responses to the environment: what Holland called the "perpetual novelty" provided by evolution. If evolution worked so well for organisms, why could it not work with computer programs? You could start with an unformed structure, replicate the machinery of nature, and let behavior emerge. The process, treating the reproduction of all organisms in a generation simultaneously, would be parallel, in keeping with nature's multiprocessor methodology. "It seemed great to me," Holland recalls. "I could see evolution as a creative process, the essence of making something out of nothing."

Something out of nothing—a natural alchemy that humans had long envied would finally be exploited.

Holland was not the first researcher to concoct a scheme to reproduce logically the workings of evolution, but his system had an advantage. It drew on his long-held idea of building blocks. Other systems worked on individual genes. After each generation, there would be a shuffling of genes after which those that improved the organism's fitness would persist, but in these schemes there was no real ability to develop incrementally, certainly not in the manner that evolution allowed life to gain slowly in complexity until it included massively complicated machines such as bacteria, mushrooms, and human beings.

This changed with Holland's invention, the genetic algorithm (GA). The name is self-descriptive: An algorithm is an expeditious formula, a sort of recipe, a key to solving a problem; this particular algorithm is based on genetic principles. The GA was a valuable breakthrough in two respects: First, it utilized evolution to provide a powerful way to perform optimization functions on a computer. (Optimization, as explained by one of Holland's disciples, means "to improve performance toward some optimal point or points." If one envisions perfection as the top of a mountain, optimization is the means of scaling the peak.) Second, it provided a window for the workings of evolution and a unique manner of studying natural phenomena.

The genetic algorithm, by adhering to natural principles, embodied the key characteristics of evolution. It acted like organisms did. "It was a very brilliant step of John Holland to realize that he could probably do something in artificial intelligence by just importing the principles of life directly," says William Hamilton, an Oxford evolutionary biologist.

The genetic algorithm did not come out of Holland's head full blown. To an unusual degree, he engaged his students in the quest. Between 1962 and 1965, Holland taught a mid-level graduate course called "Theory of Adaptive Systems." It was common for Holland and his graduate students to sit around a seminar table hashing out particulars of the GA and tinkering with its parameters. Ultimately, with benefit of this multiple input, Holland came up with a standard form of what would be known as the genetic algorithm.

Oddly, Holland did not bother to run any tests or experiments on the computer. "I've always been a pen-and-pencil person," explains the nation's first Ph.D. in computer science. "Besides, I was used to working on the [interactive] computer at IBM, and at Michigan using the computer meant dealing with the computing center, and putting in stacks of cards, and waiting for them to come out. I was less challenged by getting the programs right. It didn't seem to be that crucial. And of course, in those days I was practically the only one interested in this stuff so there wasn't any rush to get it out."

But Holland's students were eager to put genetic algorithms through their computational paces. A cascade of experiments flooded the computing center. One of the first used GAs to seek strategies in an extremely simplified version of chess. Another student produced a dissertation that used GAs to simulate the functions of single-cell organisms, the first example of many biological simulations using GAs. Perhaps the most ambitious experiment was suggested by David Goldberg, who found his way to Holland's course some years after the GA had become a cult item at Michigan. A former pipeline worker, Goldberg came under Holland's spell and wondered whether genetic algorithm might be able to sort out the problems in allocating resources in natural gas. He suggested that he might study the matter for his dissertation. Arguing that the problem was too difficult to tackle, Holland tried to dissuade Goldberg. "I felt we didn't know enough about the system and he was going to spend five years learning about it before he could even start on the problem." But within a year Goldberg was able to come up with results, using a version of the GA on an inexpensive Apple II personal computer.

Like most significant excursions in artificial life, the genetic algorithm extracted the essential mechanics of a function associated with natural life—in this case, genetic evolution—and executed them in order to produce the equivalent behavior in an artificial setting. The GA also hewed to one of John von Neumann's important lessons: in both biological and artificial systems, the information central to the organism had to be regarded in two manners—both as genetic information to be duplicated and as instructions to be executed. The informational basis of the organism is known as the genotype. The expression of those genes results in a physical organism known as the phenotype.

To understand how closely GAs adhered to natural reproduction, consider how biological organisms produce offspring. Cells of sexually reproducing organisms contain a set of twenty-six paired chromosomes, one each from the mother and father. (These cells are diploids.) The exception comes in the reproductive cells, or gametes. These are created in a process called meiosis, when paired chromosomes in a diploid cell split and result in a gamete cell with twenty-six single chromosomes. During meiosis, parts of each chromosome strand in a pair "cross over" to the other chromosome, in sort of a swapping arrangement. Thus the single-strand chromosomes in the gametes contain genes from both mother and father. During the mating process, two gametes from different organisms combine to form a complete diploid once again, with each of the twenty-six chromosomes pairing off with a representative from the other parent. During this process, there is a possibility that some genes experience alterations, or mutations, that affect the phenotype.

The genetic algorithm translated this process to the realm of pure logic and mathematics. It postulated the genome as a string of binary numbers. This string could be metaphorically viewed as a chromosome, on which genes were located at various points, or loci. The differing variations of these genes were called "alleles." (Thus a gene for eye color would be situated on a locus of the chromosome; it might contain the allele for blue pigmentation or the allele for brown.) In a GA any location marked off on every string in the population could be seen as a gene; the alleles would be the sets of binary alternatives on those places in individual strings, packets of ones and zeros.

To begin an experiment, one generated a population of random strings. It made up a sort of symbolic gene pool. For this seed population it was arbitrary whether a number at any position on any string was a one or a zero. The equivalent of a coin toss was performed at each point.

Then the population was exposed to a fitness test. Unlike natural, open-ended evolution, this fitness test was not a built-in feature of the environment (in the natural world these tests were survivability and success in reproducing) but rather something that the programmer imposed: "unnatural selection, an artificial survival of the fittest," as David Goldberg described it. Although in some ways unnatural selection reduced the system's fidelity to nature, in other ways it made GAs useful tools. Programmers could rely on this feature to optimize the system for the effect desired, although it had to be something with a measurable outcome. A good example was the ability to sort numbers. In that case, each string would be required to act as though it were a computer program written to perform that number-sorting task. After each string was put through its paces, the results were examined, and each string was given a relative score.

One would not expect a series of randomly chosen strings to perform like a well-written computer program any more than one would expect a randomly chosen collection of genes to produce a viable organism. But unlike natural organisms, which were either alive or dead, a line of computer code inserted in a program could be evaluated as to the degree to which it advanced a task. Since binary numbers were the proper input for a computer program, the input of even a random string would be considered, precisely as a series of random numbers were considered by a telephone as valid input for a telephone number: for example, John Holland's telephone number in Ann Arbor. Out of a population of a hundred random strings, there would certainly be some that had one digit in the correct place on the string and probably a few that had two or three numbers properly arranged. Those would be considered the most fit, the valedictorians of their class.

Just as valedictorians have the the best chance of winning admission to the most exclusive universities, these winners had the best odds of being selected the parents of the next generation of strings. Because typically only 10% were chosen, this was indeed an exclusive club. But exactly as extremely selective schools sometimes spiced their incoming classes with a few less dominating students, in hopes that they might bloom belatedly, the genetic operators in the GA did not limit the replicators to the very fittest. The process was weighted: the odds that a given string would be retained for the next generation corresponded mathematically to the degree to which it was fit. The equivalent of a lottery was held, with the fittest strings holding stacks of potential winning tickets, fairly fit strings holding fewer tickets, and relatively unfit strings holding perhaps a single ticket or two. Thus some of the laggards were preserved, but a very low percentage, commensurate with their fitness values. Barring wild long shots, the least fit strings would not survive at all. After this process, the winning 10%, with the fittest strings overrepresented, would be copied ten times so that the population size would remain constant in the next generation.

Next, the strings mated. In a mass marriage ceremony worthy of Rev. Moon, each string was randomly paired with another. For each matched pair, a point on each of the couple's strings was also randomly chosen. That was the crossover point—all the numbers after that point on string A in the couple were swapped with the corresponding numbers on string B. (In some GA experiments the data on the strings are exchanged at several places.) This was a nod to the evolutionary mechanism of crossover.

Finally, a point mutation factor was added. A certain small percentage of numbers on the strings were chosen randomly and flipped—changed from one to zero or from zero to one.

Before Crossover   After Crossover

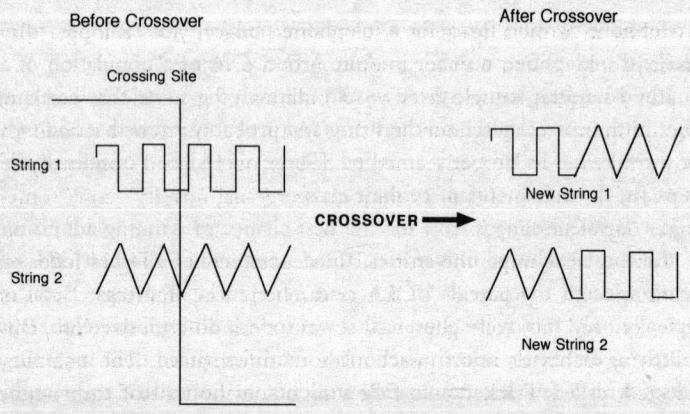

In genetic algorithms, crossover is a mating of two strings. In its simplest implementation, a crossover point is randomly selected and from that point the two strings swap their remainders. Genetic information from both "parents" is thus included in the offspring strings.

Once the reproduction process was complete, the new population was again exposed to the environment. The program was run once more, and each new string was graded for its ability to perform the task. The process was repeated.

It seemed an almost absurdly simple recipe for optimization: take a string of random numbers and treat them as computer programs. Grade them according to how well they do at executing the work of a custom-designed computer program, and then reward them to the extent of their excellence by allowing them to reproduce to that degree. Then take the revised population, pair the strings, and have each marriage partner swap a part of itself with its mate. Change a few bits for mutation, and do it again. One would intuitively expect this process to take a very long time to match the results of a computer program specially written for a task—in fact, it might be difficult to envision something that good *ever* resulting from this elementary process. As Holland and Goldberg once wrote, "genetic algorithms . . . have often been attacked on the grounds that natural evolution is simply too slow to accomplish anything useful in an artificial learning system; three billion years is longer than most people care to wait for a solution to a problem."

But computer muscle telescoped millions of generations worth of evolution into a lunch hour, and the GA turned out to be a stunningly powerful tool. Indeed, it seemed to deliver on Holland's original perceptions of the benefits of evolution: "perpetual novelty" and "something out of nothing."

Take as an example the artificial ants constructed by David Jefferson working with a group of UCLA researchers. The immediate goal of Jefferson and his colleagues was to use evolution to develop trail-following behavior in an insect made of information. The task they selected, called Tracker, was following a specific trail of eighty-nine squares on a thirty-two-by-thirty-two-square toroidal grid. (To say a grid was toroidal was to treat it as a map representing a doughnut: the squares on the right edge effectively touched the corresponding squares on the left edge. Similarly, the top squares were assumed to neighbor the bottom squares. Nothing could walk off the grid.) Inspired by actual pheromone trails used by ants to aid each other in foraging, the trail twisted and turned, and became increasingly difficult to follow as it progressed. It suffered gaps at several points, and, by the last segment of the trail, there were more missing squares than actual "scented" ones.

It would be a mild challenge for any computer hacker to write a computer program for an artificial creature to follow this trail, which the UCLA team nicknamed "The John Muir Trail." But Jefferson and his colleagues hoped to get something from nothing—they were counting on evolution to write the program.

The ants actually were computer programs, strings of 450 binary bits. These bits were interpreted by the computer as finite state machines. Each internal state, along with the conditions in the environment, provided the conditions for behavior in the next move. The ant was assumed to have sensory input only in the cell directly in front of the single cell that the ant occupied. After determining whether that cell was on or off and looking at its own state (which provided the rules), it executed one of several possible responses: move forward one step, turn right without moving, turn left without moving, or do nothing. The rules also determined which state it should assume in the next time step.

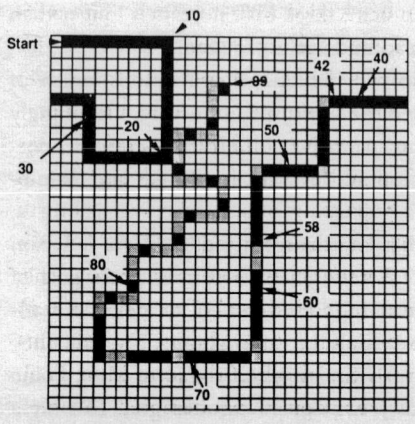

The John Muir Trail is represented by the dark squares; the gray squares represent the most efficient path through its gaps. The numbers are like milestones on the path; ants are graded on how far they go in 200 time steps; a perfect ant will reach square 89. Artificial ants created by the UCLA artificial life team were bred to traverse the trail, using the genetic algorithm. Over many generations, populations of perfect ants were evolved.

The first generation of ants was given totally random genotypes—they were strings of ones and zeros selected by chance. A population of 64 K, or 65,536, of these "random" ants was created. (The number was chosen because it was a multiple of the 16 K processing elements on the large computer at UCLA.) In this first generation, it was common for ants not to move at all, or to move haphazardly, or to continue stubbornly in a single direction. This behavior resulted in a low score, as determined by points assigned to ants who completed designated portions of the trail. But some ants, in the two hundred time steps in which the program was run, managed to complete four or more squares and got higher scores. After each ant was scored, the top 10% was selected for reproduction in the next generation. (This was a streamlined variation of standard genetic algorithm practice, which selects "winners" in direct proportion to their scores.) They were copied so that their numbers equaled a full population and paired off. Then crossover was performed, and a small number of bits were inverted to produce mutations.

Within twenty generations, evolution had already made a remarkable difference. The average ant in the population could properly make the turns, twists, and jumps of almost thirty squares. Even more impressive than that average was the most frequent score attained by ants in that population—these ants could navigate the trail to sixty squares! At seventy generations, the population was loaded with smart ants. The average individual was completing around fifty-six squares. But even this impressive number was held down by being averaged with some utter failures caused by the inevitable glitches of mutation. A significant percentage of the population had managed to complete the trail successfully, all eighty-nine squares. In fact, this was the most frequent score in generation 70. There it was—a population of ants who were born to traverse the John Muir Trail, fulfilling their birthright perfectly.

It was important to emphasize that the genetic algorithm was not only pulling the fitness of the population up to the level of the "best" ant in the initial population but also creating super-ants who used novel combinations of genes to attack cleverly the pitfalls of the John Muir Trail. Of thousands of ants in the many seed populations attempted, in which the genotypes were randomly assigned, the very best of these was able to follow the trail for an amazing fifty-eight steps, until it got flummoxed by a double gap in the trail and ran out of time. That ant was sort of an idiot savant, a chance occurrence, the equivalent of getting dealt four aces in a poker hand. But the GA delivered something better than the best ant that one could have ever expected by chance. It sought the equivalent of four aces for *ten consecutive hands*—something with a degree of organization that would never be associated with a chance distribution. Just like the products of natural evolution.

A good example was an organism dubbed "Champ 100," one of the well-evolved artificial ants who successfully traversed the John Muir Trail. The product of one hundred generations of evolution, it inherited behavior that made it act as though it knew the trail, and its confidence in negotiating the trail was a strong indication that a force more powerful than chance shaped its character. At times its responses seemed as though a virtuoso programmer had been at work. Evolutionary biologists were familiar with this effect and referred to it as Paley's Watch, in honor of Rev. William Paley (1743–1805), who complained that, like a well-crafted watch, the products of natural selection were too intricate to have come about without the hand of a presumably supernatural outside designer.

That watchmaker's deft hand seemed responsible for some of Champ

100's approaches to the John Muir Trail. Champ 100 had a bias toward right-hand turns, a feature encouraged by the trails's use of three right-hand turns before the first left-hand turn. This enabled it to zip through the early undulations of the trail. Later, when the trail wiggled right and left, Champ 100 set itself into a more cautious state. Champ 100 also had in its arsenal of trail-following tricks an ingenious combination of three states that enabled it to handle several different challenges: making a left turn when a corner was missing, negotiating a two-square gap, and making a right-hand jump similar to a chess knight and then picking up the trail from there. Champ 100 also devised a devilishly efficient series of state changes to negotiate the final "stepping stone" segment of the trail. "Such efficient logic," wrote the UCLA team, "suggests that evolution has had the effect of 'compiling' knowledge of this environment into the structure of the organism."

Champ 100 was an impressive creature, even more so because no one programmed it. Its code was arrived at by the incremental wisdom of natural selection. It was only a single example of a myriad selection of novel responses yielded by the genetic algorithm. Each one of them seemed to counteract the common-sense intuition that something cannot come out of nothing.

Interestingly, the UCLA team found that their startling results—ants that perfectly navigated the trail after only a few generations—were attainable by a mutation rate of only one bit in a hundred. Decreasing that rate tenfold, to one in a thousand, made very little difference. Those who used GAs often observed similar effects—mutations introduced into the population seemed to have only a minor effect in improving adaptation. This phenomenon was strikingly, if unintentionally, illustrated by Larry Yaeger in his PolyWorld model. Several weeks into his labor he discovered, while debugging some code, that he had forgotten to implement mutation. Yet PolyWorld, using crossover alone, had already evolved lifelike behaviors from initially random genotypes and had even yielded speciation among the organisms.

This corresponded to the suspicion held by Holland when he first began work on the genetic algorithm. Rather heretically at the time, he

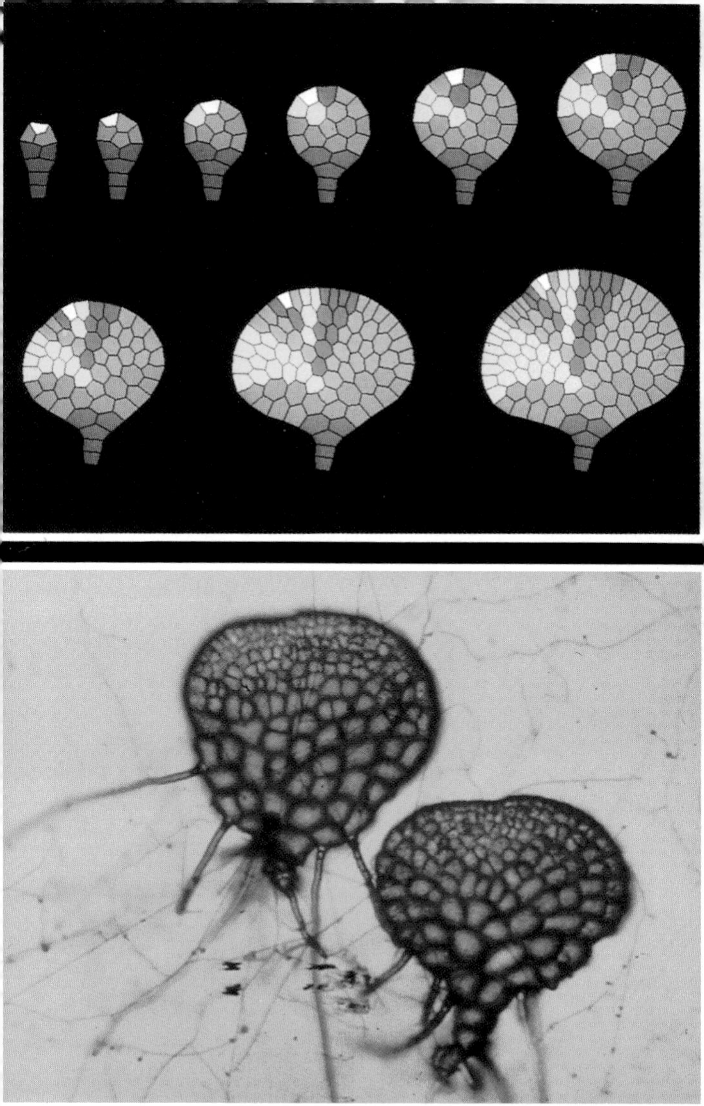

A comparison: The top frame shows stages in the simulated development of the gametophyte of a fern, *Microsorium linguaeforme*, grown from scratch by artificial life techniques. The bottom frame is a microphotograph of the natural gametophyte.

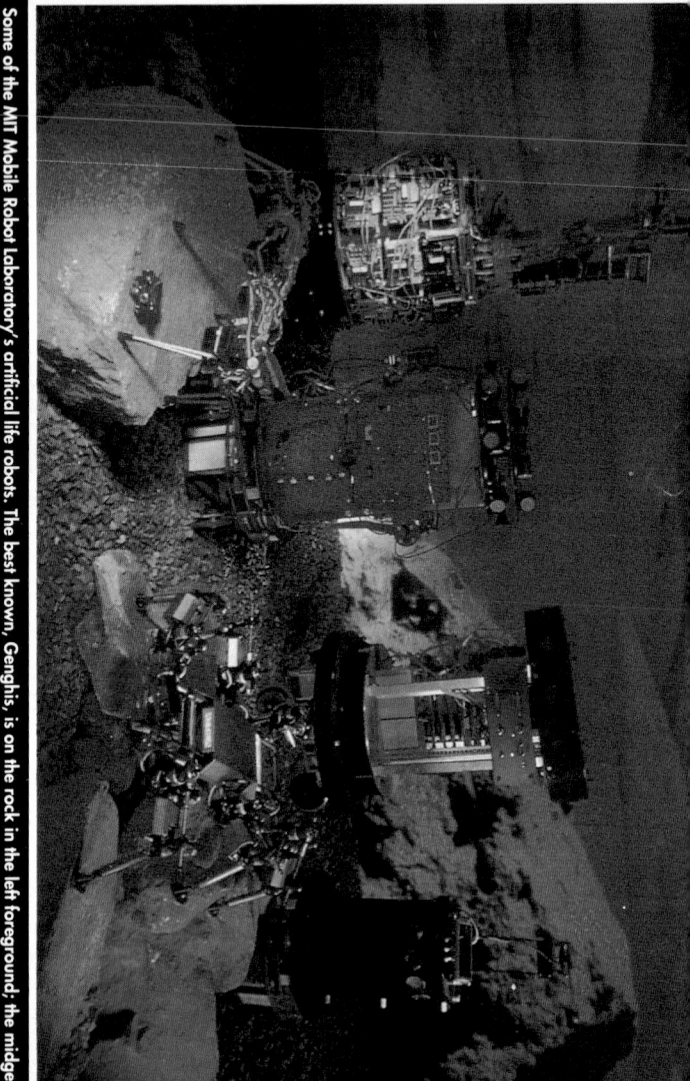

Some of the MIT Mobile Robot Laboratory's artificial life robots. The best known, Genghis, is on the rock in the left foreground; the midget at its feet is Squirt. The back row consists of, left to right, Herbert, Seymour, Allen, and Tito. In the right foreground is Attila, who measures

A cellular automata snowflake created by Norman Packard. Beginning from a single seed and a set of rules that determines the color of surrounding squares in the next "generation," structures that amazingly resemble natural snowflakes emerge on the computer screen. They are so similar to natural forms that they raise a question: Does nature generate its own com-

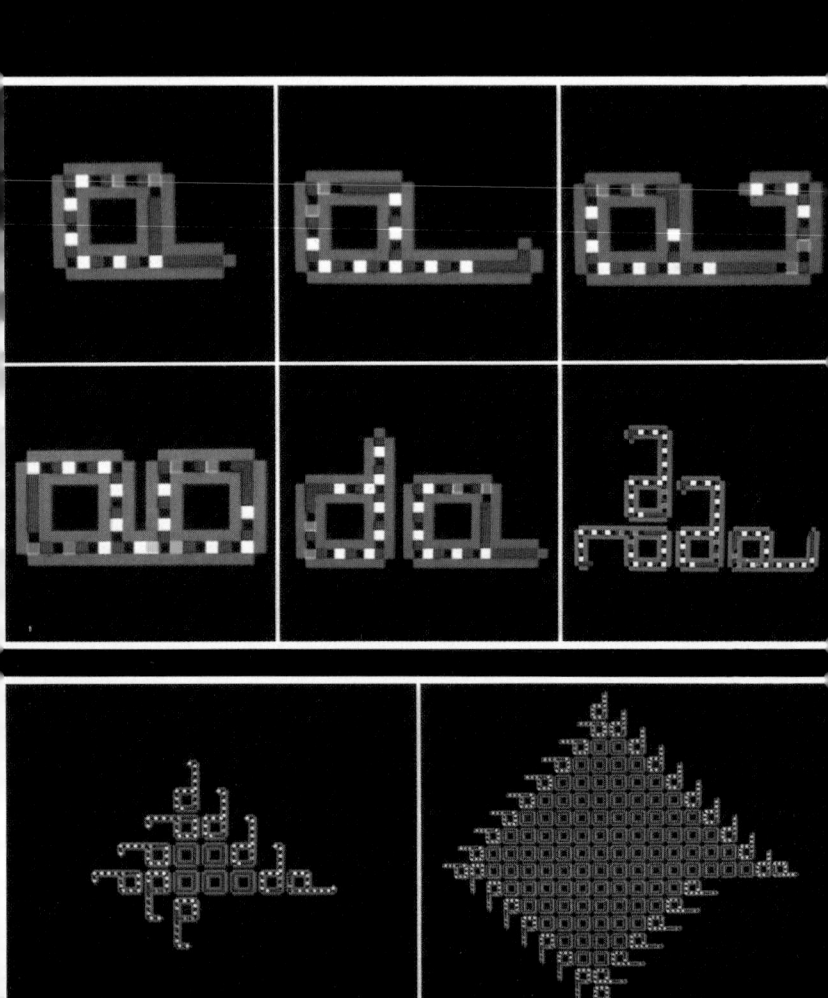

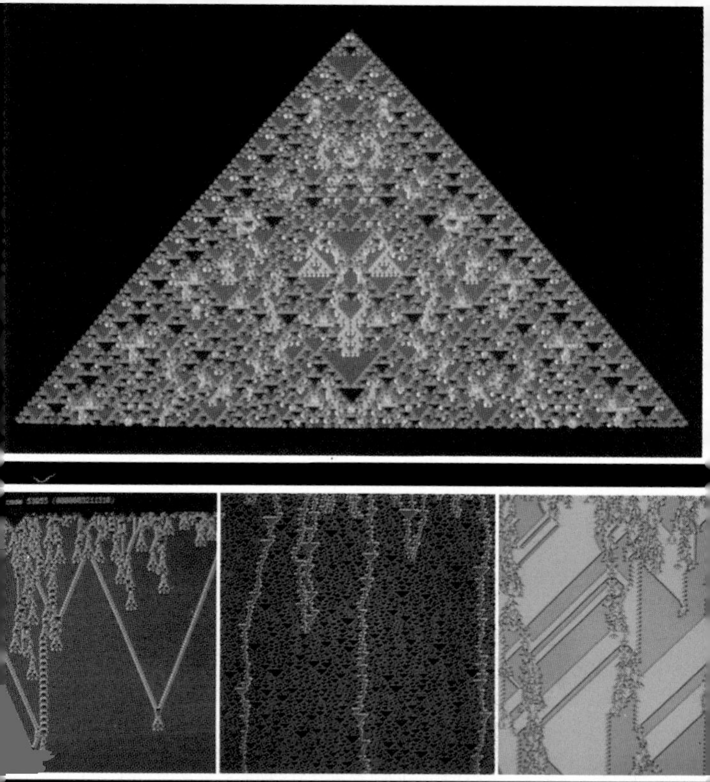

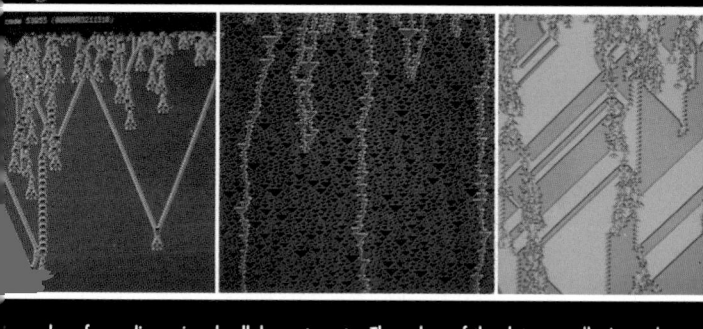

xamples of one-dimensional cellular automata. The colors of the dots, or cells, in each row
re determined from looking at the dots in the row above it and applying simple rules. The
irst row, or in the case of the top image, the single "seed," is randomly chosen. Simply by
xecuting these elementary rules, these CAs often display dazzling complexity. This occurs
much in the same fashion that natural systems, particularly living organisms, achieve complex global results from many tiny local interactions. Many artificial life researchers believe
cellular automata point the way for a methodology to re-create the processes of life—

The creatures of PolyWorld have evolved from random genomes: over generations they become skilled at seeking food, reproducing, and fighting. In this run, after seventy-five generations, several species have emerged, clustering geographically in areas bounded by barriers. In one domain they are mainly blue; in another, bright pink; and in a third, purple. Food patches are green. Near the gaps in the barrier, there is more variability.

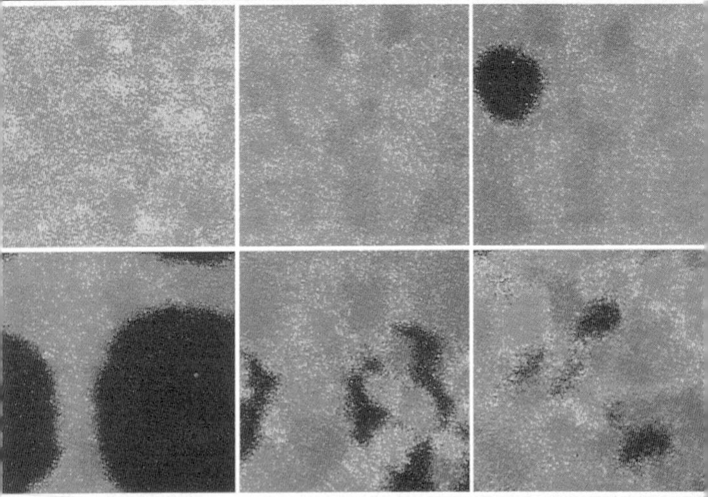

These screen shots chart the reaction of Danny Hillis's Ramps over a period of generations as parasites are introduced into their world. Brighter colors represent the degree of fitness. In **1**, relatively unfit creatures abound, replaced by somewhat more fit descendants in **2**. In **3**, a bright red pocket of very fit organisms emerges. The fit characteristics spread through the population (**4**). At that point the parasites are introduced, and they gain the upper hand in **5**. From that point, the population oscillates between levels of fitness as Ramps and parasites

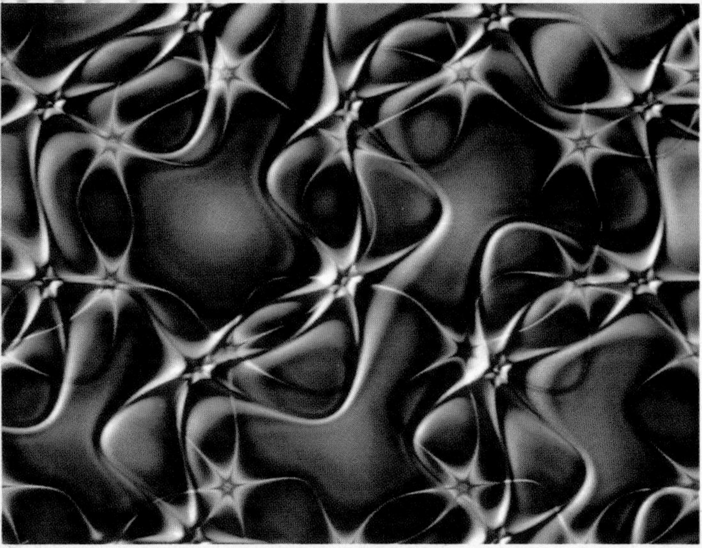

Using the mechanics of natural selection, Karl Sims's system can literally evolve images. A human user simply selects mutant offspring of a randomly generated parent, and repeats the process. The ultimate descendants can be strikingly evocative.

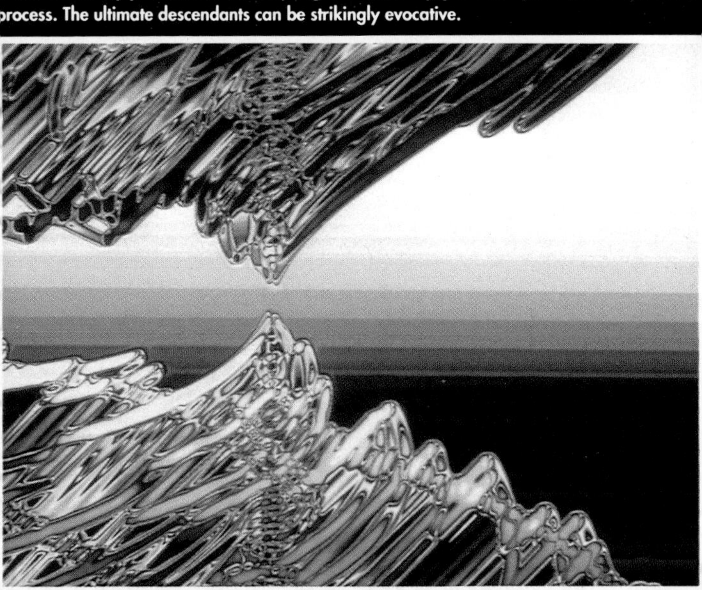

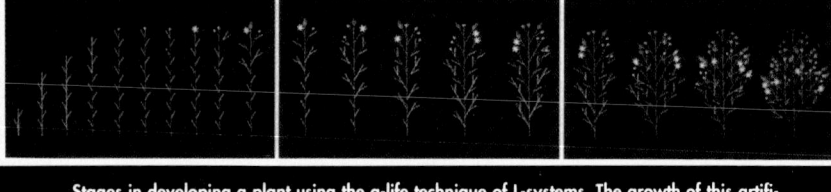

Stages in developing a plant using the a-life technique of L-systems. The growth of this artificial *Mycelis* is dictated by the execution of algorithms.

The Garden of L. All of the plants below were generated by L-systems and then rendered in three dimensions by computer-graphics techniques. The sky was created with a fractal algorithm.

wondered whether the degree to which mutation drove evolution had not been exaggerated. Holland suspected that recombination, or crossover, was consistently underrated by biologists. "Even the wet biologists, those who are really dealing with those systems, put much, much more emphasis on mutation than recombination," says Holland. "Mutation is a process that's anywhere between eight to ten magnitudes less frequent than crossover. [It is estimated that approximately one in about ten million genes experience mutation in the reproductive process.] Any physicist worth his salt is going to see it as funny that the one, overwhelmingly important process is so much rarer than the one regarded as unimportant."

The problem as Holland saw it was not that biologists were blind, but they were not using the right tools to see. "Very few field studies can show these effects," he says. Still, the accepted doctrine in biology that mutation was much more important than recombination might have daunted any mathematician or computer scientist trying to construct a model of evolution. Previous efforts, in fact, had bowed to that standard and omitted crossover. "It's a little surprising to me that someone astute wouldn't have, at least from sheer curiosity, thrown in crossover. Because the programming cost is small. But they didn't." Holland did, because of his faith that running a biological model that supposedly tapped the same force active in natural evolution might provide hitherto-unavailable insights into the process.

In Holland's scheme, crossover allowed important building blocks of high fitness to carry over into the next generation. These formed a base from which the genome could more successfully evolve. As these blocks met up with other successful building blocks, the result could be new and innovative approaches to the difficulties offered by the environment. Thus the process delivered what Holland thought of as evolution's greatest virtue: its perpetual novelty in its approaches to maintaining fitness.

"The broad idea that these local patterns might form something larger was already in cellular automata," he says. "But then there was the question of how you could get something that was more like a child's building block—something that could be used in a lot of contexts that fit together in different ways. This precise notion came when I looked at Fisher's theorem, which applies only to individual genes. I wanted to extend it to apply to *groups* of genes."

This desire led to what Holland calls his "schema theorem," which explained how building blocks exerted their powers in GAS and indicated what might be a basis for populationwide retention of genes in natural biology. The word "schema" referred to a similarity template used to describe all strings that contained a given building block or set of building blocks. Each string that contained those building blocks was an example of that schema, no matter which numbers were located elsewhere on the string.

For example, if a building block was the two-digit subset of a string, 10, and it was located in the first two places in a string of eight digits, *all* possible strings beginning with the numerals 10 would be said to be examples of that schema. It would be notationally represented as 10******, with an asterisk signifying "don't care."

Thus examples of strings that fit the schema 10****** would include
10111111
10000000
10010010
but not
01111111
11000000.

A schema need not be contiguous. For instance, one could postulate schemata such as 1******0, or 10**0000, or even *******1. The point was that a schema represented every possible example that matched up exactly, once the don't cares were ignored.

The key principle of the schema theorem was proximity. In building blocks, proximity was power. Consider a GA "organism" with a particular combination of "genes" that generated a relatively fit phenotype. During the process of crossover, the metaphorical chromosome was split at a given point, and some of the alleles were replaced by the alleles of the mate. The likelihood that any combination of alleles were lost was directly proportional to the distance between them on the chromosome. If in a given schema one digit began a string and the other completed it, it was virtually certain that the combination of these two genes would not be transmitted to the offspring; the point at which the string was split was bound to come between their respective loci. But if the points of the schema were direct neighbors, the opposite was true; in the vast majority of reproductions the combination would persist in the next generation. Only in the case where the crossover split occurred on that single point between the two would they be separated. The more compact the building block the less likely it was to be split.

Thus if a particular building block of a very few neighboring bits generated a behavior that increased fitness, it was highly likely that the particular behavior could proliferate in the gene pool. For instance, if in the Tracker simulation of ants, a four-gene building block caused the ant to proceed forward as long as it detected a part of the trail in front of it (given that the trail began with a straightaway, this was an optimal response), that block was very likely to persist. First of all, it greatly enhanced fitness so it was likely to be found in the winning percentage of organisms chosen to reproduce in the next generation. Second, when crossover was imposed on the population, the compact size of the block enabled it in most of the matings to persist in the next generation, where it again enhanced fitness and made the organisms in which it appeared strong candidates for subsequent reproductions. It was reasonable to assume that after several generations such a powerful building block would find itself proliferating in the gene pool. Any offspring that violated the integrity of the block, by splitting it or mutating one of its genes, did not have that desirable behavior and was less fit and not selected for reproduction.

If in any given experiment there were a number of combinations that led to a piece of clever behavior, the schema theorem explained how, once those combinations were first discovered by a chance crossover or mutation, they stuck. During the experiment itself it was possible to examine the strings of a given generation and sort out individual approaches to the environment, or ideas, by isolating the building blocks. By tracking schemata, and by seeing how the building blocks proliferated and interacted, one could see how, over a period of generations, the entire population adapted to its environment.

Did groups of actual genes work by the same rules as Holland's schema theorem? Was crossover insufficiently recognized as a driving force in genetic evolution? Answers were slow in coming, mainly because biologists were loath to examine the question. After all, the indicators came from a mathematical model and not from experiments in wet matter. Biologists were particularly reluctant to entertain the idea that GAs were not simulations of evolution but examples of it, just as, in Langton's view, the artificial mechanism by which Craig Reynolds's boids flocked led to true flocking behavior.

One exception to this rule was the noted evolutionary biologist Richard Dawkins. The Oxford professor viewed artificial life as "a generator of insight in our understanding of real life." Dawkins acquired this high regard for a-life, and particularly simulated evolution, in the preparation of his book *The Blind Watchmaker*. The book was intended to show how evolution, proceeding by subtle gradations, could achieve the dazzling order and complexity of contemporary life-forms. Besides describing the process, Dawkins wanted to illustrate it dynamically. A user of the Macintosh, he wrote a computer program that made use of some of evolution's properties. The result surprised even such an enthusiastic evolutionist as Dawkins.

Invoking the whimsical term that biologist Desmond Morris called animal-like shapes in his paintings, Dawkins named the computer-graphics organisms "biomorphs." These creatures were nothing but line drawings in the form of primitive trees. Their visual properties were controlled by nine parameters, which controlled characteristics such as branching, segmentation, and symmetry. He referred to these parameters as genes. Each gene was subject to mutation, which would create a variation in the biomorph in the next generation.

As with GAs, biomorphs would evolve by unnatural selection. Fitness was to be determined solely by a subjective outsider, the person working the computer. Dawkins compared the process to the sort of artificial selection that occurs in cattle breeding. At the onset of the biomorph reproductive process, the selector was given a choice of several biomorph offspring of the current genetic champion, each representing a single mutation of one of the champion's nine genes. The selector picked, for whatever reason, the one that suited his or her fancy. As Dawkins put it, the human eye was the selecting agent. Organisms who survived were likely to have qualities as amorphous as "interesting" or "pretty" or "different from the last few" or "gee, this looks a lot like a peach tree." A reproduction and mutation algorithm generated offspring from that survivor, and then the process was repeated. The idea of the experiment was to see how far, in a reasonable number of generations, the biomorphs could evolve to something quite different from an original random form—presumably into something the individual selector would like very much.

Starting with simple botanic stick figures, Dawkins hoped the tree structures would evolve into more complex stick figures. This was massive understatement. Dawkins's simple system was capable of producing a wide bandwidth of images that quickly leapt from the plant kingdom to the insect world. The biologist was astonished:

> When I wrote the program I never thought that it would evolve anything more than a variety of tree-like shapes. . . . Nothing in my biologist's intuition, nothing in my 20 years' experience in programming computers, and nothing in my wildest dreams, prepared me for what actually emerged on the screen. I can't remember exactly when in the sequence it first began to dawn on me that an evolved resemblance to something like an insect was possible. With a wild surmise, I began to breed, generation after generation, from whichever child looked most like an insect. My incredulity grew in parallel with the evolving resemblance. . . . I still cannot conceal to you my feeling of exultation as I first watched those exquisite creatures emerging before my eyes. I distinctly heard the triumphal opening chords of *Also sprach Zarathustra* (the "2001 theme") in my mind. I couldn't eat, and that night "my" insects swarmed behind my eyelids as I tried to sleep.

The "lost chord of Zarathustra" insect had begun with a single pixel. In a mere twenty-nine generations it evolved into something resembling a critter one might find under a leaf. Nature had consumed a few billion years to create its critters. Dawkins compressed this time into a few keystrokes of a Macintosh.

The insect was soon joined by other visual life-forms. Biomorph

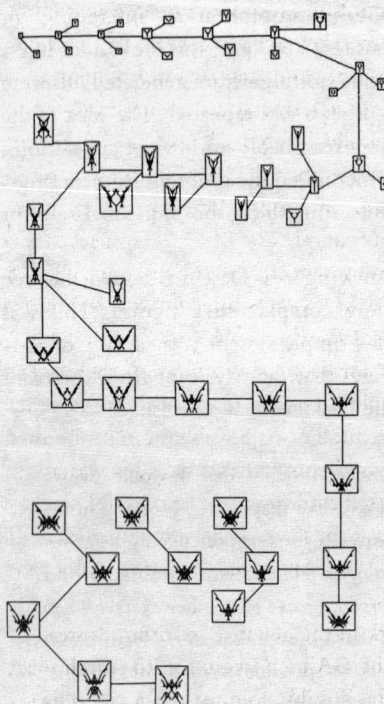

Starting from a single-pixel biomorph, Richard Dawkins bred an insect-like creature in a mere 29 generations. Here is the creature's family tree, with a few evolutionary detours included.

Land, as Dawkins called it, was a repository of diversity that rivaled the Burgess Shale, the location in British Columbia teeming with unusual fauna from the dawn of Cambrian Era. Not only could creatures like scorpions and bees be evolved but also creatures resembling spiders, bats, frogs, and birds. The forms could also resemble artifacts: Spitfire airplanes, lunar landers, letters of the alphabet. (Dawkins spelled out his name.) The range seemed limitless. "On my wanderings through the backwaters of Biomorph Land," Dawkins wrote, "I have encountered fairy shrimps, Aztec temples, Gothic church windows, aboriginal drawings of kangaroos, and, on one memorable but unrecapturable occasion, a passable caricature of the Wykeham Professor of Logic."

Although the experiment played like a game, it followed the same rules that nature did. In evolving creatures, Dawkins noted, one was not creating them but discovering them. They already existed, in a sense, as possible permutations of a given set of genes and of a finite number of mutations. This was what biologists referred to as "genetic space," a mathematical atlas that geographically located all possible life-forms. Those of identical genetic composition shared a location, those varying by a single mutation rested alongside, and those differing only by a few changes resided in the same neighborhood. The more differences in the genotype, the farther away an organism was in genetic space. Dawkins's Zarathustra insect, having evolved by twenty-nine mutations from its single-pixel ancestor, therefore resided twenty-nine spaces away in genetic space. But considering that for each *single* mutation there were approximately half a trillion possible variations (each of the nine genes had nineteen possible alleles), the number of possible biomorphs after twenty-nine steps was almost beyond comprehension. This was a key lesson of Biomorph Land—simulated evolution was a powerful mechanism to search through genetic space. By using visual attractiveness as an indicator of fitness, one could bypass trillions of uninteresting biomorphs and get directly to the good ones.

This same principle was at work in the genetic algorithm. Instead of exploring natural genetic space, the GA used evolution to search what was called "problem space," all the possible solutions to a given problem. When the UCLA team created Champ 100, they were using natural selection to "discover" an ant who could successfully negotiate the John Muir Trail in a cunning manner. When David Goldberg found a particularly economic means of allocating gas pipeline flow, he was also using GAs to search the problem space for that dilemma. So powerful was the GA in that capacity that Goldberg wrote, "If we were, for example, to search for the best person among the world's 4.5 billion people as rapidly as the GA, we would only need to talk to four or five people before making our near optimal selection."

The evidence seemed clear: Genetic algorithms could generate robust programs and artificial adaptive phenomena by utilizing the power of evolution. Yet the lords of computer science were slow to bestow their blessings on it. The GA stood outside the standard dogma and ran afoul of a cultural bias. In artificial intelligence the standard method of creating adaptive systems was associated with coding wizardry. The star hackers of AI could not respect, let alone adopt, a programming system where the innovation was applied by an outside force—nature.

"The problem that outsiders have with genetic algorithms in general is that you can think of 100 reasons why they won't work," says John Koza, a former student of Holland who now teaches at Stanford. "And the particular question is, How can it work if it starts from randomness? We're all trained to think of precise, exact solutions to things—things you can prove with logical means, like solving problems in high school geometry—and here is this totally illogical stuff! But people always forget the key point of genetic algorithms, which is that they work with a large population, hundreds of thousands. Most of what it produces is bad, but it tries a whole lot of things, and some of those are good."

Koza's own computer programming system relied on GAs to solve problems of remarkably varied stripes. The system was sort of an all-purpose answer machine, with evolution as its engine. Its creation was unconventional. After earning a doctorate at Michigan in the early 1960s Koza had abandoned active practice of computer science. He cofounded a business that ultimately became the prime producer of scratch-off lottery tickets and consequently enjoyed fortunes commensurate to those of the winners of those contests. He maintained his interest in artificial adaptive systems, but only in the spirit of a hobbyist. In 1987, when Koza was on a London stopover after attending an AI conference in Italy, a friend handed him the proceedings of a conference on genetic algorithms. He leafed through it on the plane, becoming increasingly excited. Impressed with the various applications, he noticed what seemed to him a glaring omission—"What these people need," he thought, "is a way to generate programs."

Koza began to work on a system to breed computer programs genetically. He chose the complex yet flexible computer language LISP as the medium for the programs created by the system and attempted to apply the GA to create those programs. His breakthrough was deciding to identify the units of crossover not as single characters, or even as lines in a computer program, but as symbolic expressions (S-expressions) written in the LISP syntax. Made of mathematical functions and inputs appropriate to the problem, these S-expressions were essentially subroutines, which were commonly viewed as tree structures. These subroutines could be successfully crossed over so that in a reasonable percentage of matings, the offspring computer program would conform to syntax at least as well as its parents did. Another way of viewing it was that the S-expressions formed tree-shaped "chromosomes." Crossover was the equivalent of swapping branches.

Evolutionary biologist William Hamilton thought this was the sort of advance that could make artificial life work significant. "Of course, biology has never produced a tree-shaped chromosome, they're all linear [i.e., string shaped]," he says. "But Koza is able to get remarkable results by using natural selection on tree-shaped chromosomes, by transferring little twigs of trees from one to another. And surely that is a very interesting thing. I think tree-shaped chromosomes are the coming wave. It may be also be good for biologists to understand the limitations which may be forced on life by the fact that it always has to work with linear chromosomes."

Koza saw the difference between the single characters used in classic GAs and the subroutines of his system as corresponding to a difference in the natural world, the former as "analogous to one of the four nucleotide bases found in molecules of DNA" and the latter "as analogous to the work performed by a protein in a living cell."

The resulting "genetic programming" system was able to cope masterfully with a grab bag of applications, from manipulating robots to discovering mathematical theorems and to searching for the best strategy in a game-playing problem.

Koza admitted limitations. The system was not a panacea that solved any problem one dared pose it. Because the programs relied on incremental improvements in fitness, so-called all-or-nothing situations, in which no way existed to measure partial fitness in solving the problem, were impervious to its powers. Also, the outside programmer was required to devise LISP functions relevant to the problem at hand and to set up customized parameters—for example, how many generations and how large a population size. This constituted such significant tampering from an outside hand that Koza's system could not claim that its results purely evolved from random beginnings.

One of the experiments Koza tried was replicating the work of David Jefferson and his colleagues at UCLA, who had created artificial ants by genetic algorithms. It was a good test for Koza, because his system depended on his being able to measure varying degrees of success before a given problem was solved; this was simple in trail following, where one only had to count the squares to gauge the fitness of a given organism. He concentrated on a series of evolving ant behaviors directed toward completing a more difficult trail than the John Muir Trail, an irregular, pockmarked pathway devised by Chris Langton. It was dubbed "the Santa Fe Trail." The UCLA team, using the powerful supercomputer Connection Machine, had bred two hundred generations, each of 65,536 ants, with their version of the GA and yielded a single individual in the final generation who was able to complete the perilous trail successfully.

Instead of using the GA to evolve an ant directly, Koza used his genetic programming system to create a LISP computer program to generate an ant's behavior. He began with a population of randomly generated LISP programs, each spiced with expressions relevant to the task (e.g., "if sensor detects space, advance") but arbitrarily distributed. After the programs were run, the phenotype behaviors were tested for fitness. The winning programs were then mated.

Koza eschewed mutation altogether. "Mutation is a sideshow in nature and a sideshow in genetic algorithms," says Koza, venturing somewhat beyond the tentative claims of others in urging a heightened appreciation of crossover. "I usually keep it turned off."

The programs that evolved equaled and in some cases surpassed the efforts of the UCLA team—in one case, Koza was able, after only seven generations, to develop an ant that successfully negotiated the eighty-nine steps of the trail without a single misstep.

This was characteristic of the manner in which the genetic programming system managed to overcome the considerable set of problems to which it was suited. These encompassed a range that impressed even its creator. Koza used the system to solve quadratic, integral, linear, and differential equations. He directed it to find prime numbers. He used it to perform pattern recognition, simulating a six-pixel retina. He found it able to solve nonlinear physics problems, such as determining the equations required to balance a broom on a moving pushcart.

Perhaps the most remarkable performance came when Koza directed the system to apply itself to finding the laws of planetary motion, discovered in the fifteenth century by Johannes Kepler. Not only did the genetic programming system manage to "rediscover" Kepler's famous third law ("the cube of a planet's distance from the sun is proportional to the square of its period"), but also, as the system climbed up the fitness scale, one of its interim solutions corresponded to an earlier conjecture by Kepler, published ten years before the great mathematician finally perfected the equation!

Despite his impressive results, Koza found the reaction to his genetic-style programming system, to put it charitably, mixed. "The resistance," he says, "is almost knee-jerk and vitriolic in some cases."

Many traditional programmers, Koza explains, deplored the fact that a degree of chance was involved, both in the initial randomization and the probabilistic choices of strings that survived to the next generation. "Some people just broil at the idea of any algorithm working that way," says Koza. "And then you've got the complaint that it's sloppy. Because the first thing that comes to your mind when you hear about crossover is, 'Oh, I can think of a case where crossover won't work.' Of course you can think of a case. The key to genetic algorithms [as well as to natural selection] is the population, that thousands of things are being tried at once, most of which don't work out—but the idea is to find the few that do."

If the idea of genetic algorithms upset certain computer scientists, Koza's suggestion that GAs could generate complex computer programs written in the LISP language and competitive with human programmers in tackling difficult problems made those people sputter with disbelief. The main complaint came from the counterintuitiveness of any powerful computing system not engineered by humans. The resistance was the same John Holland faced when he developed the GA itself—a reaction to the very scary, and seemingly insane, idea of turning over the car keys to nature. People thought of nature as blind, but they forgot about the Blind Watchmaker of evolution and the unmatchable intricacy of its creations.

"It's an emotional thing. It's almost like the vitalism that went on in biology a century ago. You have this resistance to the idea, because everybody thinks of the program that they wrote that didn't work because they had a comma misplaced in the code," says Koza.

> But they forget the fact that there were a whole lot of ways they could have written that program which would have made it perform just as well. And some mistakes could have been harmless—extra spaces, or different variable names, or a different order to many of the steps. They forget that. And then they forget that in writing the program they backloaded a big chunk from a program they wrote five years ago, or read about in a book, and incorporated it as a subroutine. They forget all those things, instead focusing on the presumption that if one comma is wrong, it doesn't work.

> Well, it's true if one little bit of DNA is wrong out of your billions of bits in the chain, you may get sickle cell anemia and die at age 15. But the fact is there's probably millions of mistakes in your DNA, but most don't matter. The mistakes create almost the same amino acid in the protein chain, and it works almost the same as the intended one, and you work just fine. Or it gives you red hair, whereas most people have black or brown hair. But who cares? At the end of the day whether you have brown hair or red doesn't have much effect on your survival.

In short, Koza presented intriguing evidence that certain powers of complex forces found in biological systems could not only be duplicated artificially but also could be exploited to perform useful tasks. Under the guise of a programming system, Koza seemingly offered that maddening delusion of "something out of nothing" characteristic of life. Instead of confounding the second law of thermodynamics, his system flouted a different sort of rule, the hard-won prejudice that only programs wrought by human architects could do work. What the doubters did not see, and would not see until accumulated evidence forced them to accept the paradigm, was the tireless worker behind the kitchen door: nature itself, with its inscrutable forces that a-lifers were striving to understand.

One of the more compelling GA applications came in the realm of game theory, in particular a certain conundrum associated with the emergence of cooperative structures in biology, from bacterial behavior to a myriad assortment of situations occurring in human relations. This was the so-called Prisoner's Dilemma. Its connection to the GA came by way of a political scientist named Robert Axelrod. Not coincidentally, Axelrod was a professor at the University of Michigan and a colleague of John Holland. Axelrod, Holland, and biologist William Hamilton were among the regular participants in a multidisciplinary study group that met at Michigan several times a term and focused on the connections between biology, particularly evolution, and other disciplines.

Axelrod wanted to understand how cooperation itself evolved "among egotists without central authority." Everywhere, he noticed unspoken arrangements between putatively self-interested individuals, arrangements that mutually benefited both parties. He wondered whether these indeed were the best strategies in situations where two parties had divergent and selfish interests and how those systems of cooperation came to be. In the long run, he hoped that the lessons from his work would lead to an enlightened view of cooperation itself, perhaps even affecting the interaction of sovereign nations.

The Prisoner's Dilemma provided Axelrod with a means to study the problem. Originally discovered in 1950 by two researchers at the Rand Corporation, it is a game in which two players confront each other, with the choice either to cooperate or to defect. The assumption was that the encounter would be repeated for a finite number of encounters, or "iterations" of the dilemma. Depending on the player's choice and the decision made by the other player, a certain amount of points were assigned to each player. It was a non-zero-sum game, and certain combinations could result either in mutual benefit, as when both cooperated, or in slight mutual disadvantage, as when both defected. However, when one player cooperated and the other defected, the defector got more points than if both cooperated. These possibilities could be charted in a "payoff matrix":

	COLUMN PLAYER COOPERATES	COLUMN PLAYER DEFECTS
ROW PLAYER COOPERATES	3, 3 Reward for mutual cooperation	0, 5 Sucker's payoff and temptation to defect
ROW PLAYER DEFECTS	5, 0 Temptation to defect and sucker's payoff	1, 1 Punishment for mutual defection

Note.—The payoffs to the row player are listed first.

In Axelrod's view, the iterated Prisoner's Dilemma embodied the essence of innumerable forms of continued interaction in the natural world and among human beings. One of his favorite examples was the behavior of infantry troops in World War I trench warfare. In the course of the extended and continuous exposure to enemy forces, a spontaneous live-and-let-live behavior emerged, with the troops arriving at an unspoken yet clearly understood agreement not to shoot, as long as they themselves were not active targets. Axelrod and collaborator William Hamilton also cited the tolerance of male birds when hearing songs from neighboring males who nonetheless might be competitors for the sexual favors of female birds. In contrast, those songbirds who were not neighbors and did not have a continuing interaction were treated with aggression.

Obviously, some strategies in the Prisoner's Dilemma would yield better results than others. In order to discover the best ones, Axelrod held a computer tournament and discovered among the sixteen entrants one approach that performed successfully among varied strategies and won decisively in most cases. It was the simplest strategy entered, TIT

FOR TAT. This is easily summarized: cooperate first, then do what the opponent did in the previous encounter. Despite its elegant brevity, it remained invincible; after it won the first tournament, a second field of sixty-one challengers—computer scientists, evolutionary biologists, and economists among them—failed to unseat it, despite the fact that they were permitted to tailor their own strategies specifically to counter TIT FOR TAT.

TIT FOR TAT had been programmed by a human, a Canadian psychologist. However, Axelrod wondered whether the powerful genetic algorithm might come up with an equally effective strategy, if not something much like TIT FOR TAT itself. He arranged an experiment in which an individual in the GA population was a chromosome of seventy genes. When executed, each chromosome would dictate a strategy, defecting or cooperating depending on the behavior of the opponent in the previous three encounters. This allowed for a huge number of possible strategies, so large, Axelrod wrote, that, "if a computer had examined those strategies at the rate of 100 per second since the beginning of the universe, less than one percent would have been checked by now."

How quickly would the genetic algorithm search this space of possible solutions to find the fittest? Would it find one as good as TIT FOR TAT?

Axelrod used a population of twenty individuals, each of which played the Prisoner's Dilemma with a benchmark set of eight opponents representing a range of strategies. After each round in the tournament, the population was subjected to the reproduction process. The more points an individual chalked up in the interactions, the better its odds of reproducing. Axelrod continued this for fifty generations and repeated the entire experiment forty times. "The results are quite remarkable," wrote Axelrod. "From a strictly random start, the genetic algorithm evolved populations whose median member was just as successful as the best rule in the tournament, TIT FOR TAT." Even more impressive, the GA found strategies that, in this particular tournament at least, actually beat TIT FOR TAT. (The champion, though unseated here, would have retained its crown against the GA competitors if all had been pitted against the population of the previous two tournaments.) Thus, the GA proved, as Axelrod put it, "very good at what actual evolution does so well: developing highly specialized adaptations to specific environmental settings."

Significantly, the GA solution, although not precisely duplicating the elemental rule of TIT FOR TAT, bore a distinct similarity. It retained TIT FOR TAT's essential characteristic: an eagerness to manipulate the relationship into mutual cooperation. (This must have been a relief to Axelrod, who undoubtedly hoped the thrust of his work would be to provide humanity with a logical basis for cooperative behavior.) However, unlike almost every known successful Prisoner's Dilemma rule, the GA solution began its encounters with a defection. On first glance this seemed counterproductive because it postponed, perhaps disastrously, the ideal situation in which both parties would cooperate continuously. But on examination it turned out to be a clever ploy for quickly determining the opponent's strategy, so the GA strategy could immediately know whether that ideal series of transactions could ensue. If the opponent were not so inclined, then the GA strategy had not suffered the initial blow that the initially "nice" TIT FOR TAT inevitably weathered on meeting a so-called mean gambiteer.

One of Axelrod's former students, Stephanie Forrest, built on his work in genetic algorithms and cooperation. Her collaboration with physicist Gottfried Mayer-Kress went beyond the Prisoner's Dilemma and into the much trickier realm of international security, specifically the economic responses of competing nations. Forrest and Mayer-Kress chose to experiment with the well-known Richardson model. This model postulated three self-interested nations, all faced with an identical dilemma: what was the minimum amount of resources they should devote to defense, at the same time maintaining national security? At any given point, the two weaker nations formed a provisional alliance against the most powerful. In this case, as Forrest and Mayer-Kress explained, "the genetic algorithm is modeling a negotiation process in the sense that it is searching for a set of parameters (policies) that satisfy some global criteria (stability, reduction of expenditures, etc.) and by which all countries might agree to abide."

The "solution" to the Richardson model depended on which international goals each nation harbored, but for the purposes of this experiment the scientists assumed that all three nations cared most to maintain global stability. The key, then, would be finding the balance-of-power points—formulas for success—that each country could utilize to maintain that equilibrium. Ideally, those levels would be sufficiently robust as to avoid a quick deterioration if the levels of arms expenditures were to fluctuate.

Previous work on the Richardson model had yielded good solutions. The GA method found equally sound balance-of-power points previously undiscovered by other methods. The manner in which the GAs conducted their search ignored the sorts of solution points that were anomalous coincidences and favored instead the points that stood out as perfect scores in a rich field of excellent alternatives. The balance-of-power points located by the GA method were unusually impervious to sudden shifting of a parameter. This was important because the crucial lessons from these models lay not so much in finding perfect responses to toy problems but in "insight about where to look for analytical solutions."

Forrest and Mayer-Kress urged caution about their results, as this model did not allow the three countries to fix individual policy. But they were sufficiently encouraged to suggest further work, including a more ambitious model where each country had more control over its resources and alliances and where the encounters between countries would more closely replicate those between actual nations. Despite the primitive state of these global models, they would have considerable use in quick-and-dirty analyses, in cases like arms-control negotiations, where there might not be time to run detailed models of Byzantinely complex situations. Among those investigating these uses were the Rand Corporation and the joint chiefs of staff. Forrest and Mayer-Kress were optimistic that genetic algorithms, the stuff of evolution, might well aid in modeling international relations, with effects that might enable humans to keep evolving:

Recent developments in Eastern Europe have demonstrated how structures that were rigid for decades can suddenly destabilize, leading to crises and qualitative changes. The end of a simple world with two major adversaries might indicate the beginning of a "messy future" with many relevant players. International security may also be increasingly influenced by other factors such as global climate changes. . . . As our simple model illustrates, there is a wide variety of possible consequences for political decisions in such a system. Computational methods, such as the genetic algorithm . . . will be increasingly important in suggesting possible alternatives.

Considering their power both as a paradigm for nature and as an optimization method in computer science, it was puzzling why genetic algorithms remained obscure for so long. John Holland was never much a manipulator of politics of science. He essentially turned over development of the GA to his students while he worked on a book about the theory of adaptation, a significant but hardly accessible tome that took him, he admits, too many years to complete.

In 1983 a National Science Foundation (NSF) grant allowed many in this community to gather together to discuss their research. It was not much of a community. Many, if not most, of the genetic algorithmists had been students of Holland. Some of his brightest disciples had dropped the subject in order to pursue more conventional areas of computer science such as relational data bases, where they were more likely to land jobs and win prestige. Holland guesses that about 90% of those working in GAs came to that Michigan conclave, and still everyone could comfortably be seated at a single conference table.

In 1985 Holland began to do what he had not previously done: take to the road to promote the idea of genetic algorithms. "I consciously decided to do it," he explains. "I don't typically like to attend conferences very much—I'd rather talk to people under other circumstances. I'm a crowd avoider. But there was a year in which I decided simply, I'm going to go to these things, and see what could happen if AI people really looked at this instead of saying, 'Oh, that's just that genetic stuff,' I'm not interested.' "

In his presentations, Holland demonstrated GAs and stressed the schema theorem. "Everybody thought genetic algorithms were mutations. I felt the critical thing was to convince them that something else was going on when you had recombination." Although Holland had worked out the mathematics thoroughly, the formulas were not nearly as compelling as the general story he had to tell. "The schema theorem in itself was just not convincing to people, but if I started showing them diagrams, and how it worked, people really believed. It was really a matter of pedagogy."

Holland spoke at a major machine learning conference, wooing the AI establishment. At the Evolution, Games, and Learning conference, he met Farmer and hooked up with what were to be the first adherents of the field of artificial life. Through those connections, Holland was invited to spend a year at Los Alamos as an Ulam scholar, and he ultimately accepted an external faculty post at the Santa Fe Institute. Because of the rising popularity of parallelism, the study of nonlinear adaptive systems—and artificial life—the genetic algorithm was finding its way into standard textbooks and the fabric of computer science. Not only John Henry Holland but nature itself was finally getting its due.

ALCHEMISTS AND

PARASITES

Progress in physics comes by taking things apart; in computation by putting things together. We might have had an analytic science of computation, but as it worked out, we learned more from putting together thermostats and computers than we did from taking apart monkey brains and frog eyes.

Danny Hillis

"I suppose," says William Daniel Hillis, "if I were brought up at the right time I might have very well been an alchemist and gotten attracted to the notion of mixing lead and urine together to try and get gold."

Instead, having been born in 1956, Danny Hillis is attempting alchemy of a different form: mixing silicon with complex systems theory to produce emergent behaviors characteristic of life. It is his dream to create a machine that lives and cogitates—a computer, he says, not joking at all, "that would be proud of me." He realizes he may never see that day, and concedes, reluctantly, that the concept is perched just this side of impossibility. After all, if he had been an ancient alchemist, he notes, "I would have wasted my life."

But Hillis also knows that there are two tracks of artificial life. The more ambitious goal is the creation of living systems, the equivalent of biological alchemy. The other quest, closer to hand, is the simulation—in some cases the duplication—of life's unique processes, in order to heighten our understanding of natural life and of possible alternative forms of life. "There's two reasons to study this stuff," he says. "I'm interested in both of them."

His most concrete contribution has been the creation of a-life's most powerful tool, a supercomputer that is unmatched in simulating the massively parallel processes that life performs routinely. But Hillis's ultimate impact could lie in the way he uses this tool. Whenever he can manage it, he sets aside the considerable chores of chief scientist and cofounder of a multimillion dollar company and attempts to simulate evolution. He hopes to discern patterns that biologists missed, perhaps even to discover promising indicators that current theory is misguided. His findings have led him to several iconoclastic conclusions that could promote debate of white-hot intensity among circles of evolutionary biologists—if only they would listen.

Hillis, who wears T-shirts to work and bears the wizened yet wondrous demeanor of an elf approaching middle age, has taken a circuitous path to these discoveries. His parents both studied in fields associated with life sciences. His father was an Air Force epidemiologist, who moved the family to locales both mundane and exotic, as long as hepatitis was rampant. His mother earned her doctorate in biostatistics. To Hillis, science meant biology. A typical home experiment was maintaining a tissue culture of cells taken from a frog heart. In one school biology project—his family had settled near Baltimore at that point—he and a friend appropriated hundreds of petri dishes in order to measure the degree of bacteria in every nook and cranny of Towson Junior High School. ("We found one thing in the gym that was really toxic," he claims, but he cannot recall the offending microorganism.)

His other passion was computers, a subject he first became interested in when his family lived in India. Because computer parts were rare items in that milieu, Hillis built a ticktacktoe computer with wires and nails. He had an exceptional talent for that sort of thing. While still in high school, he was recommended to people in the chemistry department at Johns Hopkins, who were building a mass spectrometer and needed someone to hook a computer up to it. The designated machine was an old Minuteman-missile computer donated as government surplus. No programming manuals existed, but Hillis, despite never having any programming training, taught himself how to complete the task.

Danny Hillis entered MIT, where he planned to study neurophysiology. People kept urging him to venture over to the AI lab to meet Marvin Minsky. Rather than make a cold call, Hillis did homework. He obtained the funding proposal for the lab and noted that one of its goals was developing a system to encourage illiterate children to program computers. So far, there had been no solid ideas on how to accomplish this. Hillis determined to solve the problem himself and went to Seymour Papert, one of the lab's directors, with a design for a computer terminal that operated by manipulating pictures instead of text. Papert hired him. Weeks went by, however, and Hillis still had not encountered Minsky. Finally, someone told him that Minsky spent his time on the ground floor, where he was designing a small computer. Hillis found the workshop, read the design plans, and unilaterally began making changes. Apparently they were well conceived. Minsky welcomed the input and eventually became Hillis's mentor.

It became a marvelous routine. Every night Marvin Minsky would drive Danny Hillis home and provide a sound track of bewitching concepts. They often discussed the organization of the brain and possible theories on the emergence of intelligence. Hillis came to appreciate complexity and how its workings were consistent in nature and machine. "How simple things combine and make complex things," he now explains. "Computers are sort of an example of that, and neurons are an example. And so fundamentally I find transistors as interesting as neurons."

In the early 1970s MIT's Artificial Intelligence Laboratory encompassed computation, consciousness, robotics, and even theories of child development. Hillis became its star student and eventually moved into the basement of Minsky's house. The centerpiece of his makeshift apartment was the house's heaving furnace.

Hillis's official course of study was mathematics. "Marvin encouraged me to do that on the grounds that nobody knew anything in computer science, so I should learn something that's liable to be true ten years later," he explains. This decision was endorsed by Hillis's second great mentor, Richard Feynman, who was suspicious of computer science because of the inability of its practitioners, when challenged, to explain lucidly what it was they did.

Eventually Hillis himself grew wary of the prevalent approach to artificial intelligence. Considering that he himself was a prince in the palace of classical AI, this stance bordered on apostasy. Yet he was simply facing facts. After a rush of enthusiasm, the discipline had lost momentum and was mired in what some called an AI Winter. Though the aggregate effort drove closer to the prize of truly smart machines, the increments were puny when compared to the giant leaps required to transform silicon savants into creatures with but a fraction of a human being's common-sense intelligence. Instead of conceptual leaps, AI's avatars offered arcane digressions. "AI wasn't happening," says Hillis. "Everybody was asking why."

Hillis became convinced that the trouble began with a bottleneck in the computers themselves. They were simply not lifelike. These were sequential machines (called "von Neumann machines," because of their reliance on the Hungarian's original design), which forced all processing to pass through a single piece of hardware. Although this processing occurred at very high speeds—sometimes millions of operations a second—there was so much information to be manipulated and calculated that even speed calculations measured in nanoseconds were insufficient. "The more knowledge you gave them, the slower computers got," says Hillis. "And with a person, the more knowledge you give him, the faster he gets. So we were in this paradox that if you tried to make computers smart, they got stupider."

The solution, Hillis reasoned, was to make computers work more like their natural counterparts—to process in parallel. To let many little things happen, in order to allow big, complicated things to emerge. The image he had in mind was the human brain, with its plentiful thicket of neurons. Instead of a single processor crunching numbers, Hillis's computer would have many processors—thousands of them, in fact. (He knew this could be done from his experience working as a consultant for the Milton Bradley toy company, whose consumer products used very large scale integration [VLSI], the process by which the crucial innards of entire computers could be compressed on a single integrated circuit chip.) The processors would each crunch numbers and then "talk" to each other by a scheme of connectedness that would emerge as spontaneously as order emerges in natural systems. Thus the computer would be known as "the Connection Machine."

Hillis was not the first to imagine a parallel computer. In fact, John Holland proposed something along those lines twenty years before. (When Hillis ultimately finished his dissertation describing the design of the Connection Machine, he presented Holland with a copy inscribed, "Just think of this as a Holland machine.") And supercomputer manufacturers had experimented with multiple processor machines, with up to a dozen processors. But nothing like what Hillis was proposing. His first design utilized sixteen thousand processors and then he proposed to quadruple that! Traditional computer scientists had no trouble ticking off reasons why this could not possibly work; they cited mathematical principles that theoretically limited the speed gain of parallel processing. "But I had this very good reason why I thought it would work," says Hillis. "So that led me to go ahead and build it even though everybody thought it was crazy."

Not everyone. Marvin Minsky lent Hillis support, MIT's AI Lab helped him, and government agencies, particularly the defense-related agencies so critical to funding cutting-edge computing efforts, kicked in a grant of a million dollars. (Ultimately, the project would cost $5,000,-000.) Danny Hillis was the only graduate student at MIT with several programmers on staff and his own secretary. Eventually, though, it became clear that the Connection Machine could be completed only under the guise of an independent corporation. Minsky introduced Hillis to businesswoman Sheryl Handler who helped him do just that. Among the founders were Minsky and CBS patriarch William S. Paley. Hillis named the company "Thinking Machines"; its most successful product to date is a sleek black box, slightly bigger than a washing machine, with flashing red lights and 65,536 processors working in parallel. More modest versions cost $1,000,000, and a second generation was estimated to sell at prices between $25,000,000 and $50,000,000. The success of the Connection Machine made Hillis a corporate leader, the tender of a growing company with five hundred employees, housed in a gorgeous headquarters building on the Charles River in Cambridge, Massachusetts. His passion for building the world's fastest computer was equalled by another addictive interest—using the Connection Machine as an engine for artificial evolution.

Like many of the pioneers in artificial life, Danny Hillis found his own way to that basin of scientific attraction. In retrospect it was inevitable that he would exploit the similarities between the parallel processing performed by his computer and the same technique routinely executed by nature.

The pursuit jibed with Hillis's lifelong fascination with emergence, the phenomenon of unbidden consequences from simple rules. Scientists, he believed, assuming that the universe was deterministic, rightfully attempted to keep their focus on cause and effect. "But as people with egos," says Hillis, "we would like to believe that we're somehow complicated, something much more interesting than a bunch of molecules interacting. To me, there's no contradiction between these two views because of the notion of emergence. Just because something is made of simple parts that may not be very worthwhile in limited interactions, doesn't mean that the ensemble of them together can't be worthwhile and interesting."

As Hillis pondered the notion, he recognized that the most complex ensembles were living systems—life-forms, including human ones. When one asked a biologist how we and our living cousins attained this level of complexity, the short answer was the single word, "evolution." And indeed, evolution was something based on simple rules that yielded wondrously complicated results. So Hillis decided to look closer at evolution to better understand emergence. As he read his Darwin, his Fisher, his Haldane, and his Gould, however, he realized that the theory of evolution was far from complete. There were gaps in our knowledge and spirited disagreement about some components of general evolutionary theory.

Hillis was drawn to one particular controversy concerning the nature of evolutionary progress. One biological theorem, postulated by R. A. Fisher, conjectured that evolution proceeded by steady improvements in fitness. Hillis saw this as equivalent to the so-called hill climbing technique used by certain computer optimization procedures, such as learning in neural network simulations. Because each generation was supposedly slightly fitter than the previous one, a graph illustrating this progress would show a line angling upward, as though the fitness of the species were engaged in scaling a peak.

Biologists studying the problem had created a more complicated, multidimensional map of the way that a species might evolve. This "adaptive landscape," first postulated by Sewall Wright, represented the space of all possible genetic combinations. It was filled with bumps, peaks, valleys, and spikes. The gene pool of an entire population resided at a single area on this landscape. The higher the ground, the fitter the population would be if it found its way there. When the terrain was fairly level, a population theoretically engaged in a "random walk," with the effects of crossover and mutation moving its genetic composition to different places, until it found an ascending plane. From that point, the more fit individuals within the population would push fitness higher, and the rest of the population would follow.

But, if hill climbing was indeed the method nature used to achieve higher fitness, the discovery of the highest ground could not always be assumed. Once the population scaled a medium-size peak, it tended to get stuck. This was due to the built-in reluctance of a population to decrease its fitness, which would be necessary in order to search the landscape for an even higher peak. The population would remain fat and happy on its hill but miss out on the mountains that lay somewhere else on the chart. The population was then "stuck on a local maximum" with no incentive to make the giant evolutionary leaps that push life toward more complexity.

Hillis suspected that something other than hill climbing must have been required for the rich properties of life to emerge. "If evolution is a hill-climbing technique, why doesn't it seem to have problems that we know hill-climbing techniques suffer from?" he asks, referring to the local maxima problem. "Why is evolution so much more powerful than any other hill-climbing technique? Why is it able to evolve much more complicated things?"

In 1986 Hillis began seeking answers to these questions by simulating evolution on his multimillion-dollar machine. Combining his sixty-four thousand parallel processors, an experimental chemist's careful methodology, and the observational acumen of a biologist, Hillis had the power to generate hitherto-unsuspected insights from a sophisticated form of artificial evolution.

Physicist Niels Bohr once observed that "we should doubtless kill an animal if we tried to carry on the investigation of its organs so far that we could describe the role played by single atoms in vital functions. . . . The minimum freedom which we must allow organisms in this respect is just large enough to permit it, so to say, to hide its ultimate secrets from us." This limitation did not exist with the artificial organisms that Hillis studied. Ultimate secrets could now be exposed. "I can run a population for 100,000 generations," Hillis explains. "And then I can look at the same thing geologists look at, the fossil record. Then I can look at the actual genes themselves—not just the phenotypes of the individuals but the actual genetic material. And I don't have to look at them with just my own eyes, I've got a big parallel computer to look at them. I can see things that are going on there that biologists don't have the data to see."

Hillis worked with artificial organisms—strings of numbers that represented genes, which in turn expressed themselves as phenotypes by performing computational tasks. It was very much in the spirit of John Holland's genetic algorithm.

At first he set relatively simple problems for his organisms. He would require them to arrange their bits in a certain order, rewarding the ones that came closest to the desired arrangement after each generation. Fitness would be determined, of course, by criteria set by Hillis on what was the perfect order, and his clever use of that complication prevented the system from getting stuck in local maxima. It was easy to demonstrate how. Begin with a string of twelve numbers. Hillis might decide to regard a perfect sequence as one in which each number has a higher number to its right. The perfect sequence, then, would begin with numeral 1 and proceed, in order, to 12:

$$1, 2, 3, 4, 5, 6, 7, 8, 9, 10, 11, 12.$$

In evolving this order, hill-climbing techniques would be effective only to a point because the problem might not be solved purely by increments. For example, consider an arrangement that began with 2 and ascended by even numbers up to 12; then, at the seventh digit dropped to 1 and counted by odd numbers to 11:

$$2, 4, 6, 8, 10, 12, 1, 3, 5, 7, 9, 11.$$

Only one step from perfection, yet obviously flawed, this organism would find it difficult to evolve further. It was stuck in a local maximum.

Because of the ramplike slopes this scheme would draw on a landscape map—where hill climbing would lead to a precipice—Hillis called his organisms "Ramps." He posed increasingly difficult problems to them so he could learn about evolution from their behavior.

When biologist Charles Taylor saw the system, he proposed that Hillis try experiments using both sexual reproduction and asexual reproduction. Hillis could then address an enduring problem in biology: why was there sex? Some theorists believed that it was only by strange happenstance—a frozen accident—that organisms mated, because the short-term advantage would be for an individual to pass on as many of its genes as possible. Sex diluted the number of genes one passed to offspring, and common sense indicated that the fittest organisms would be better off reproducing asexually. In the long run, sexual reproduction did strengthen fitness in the population, but evolution, which proceeded generation by generation, had no consciousness and worked from no billion-year blueprint. Evolution proceeded like a cellular automaton experiment in that decisions were local, although consequences resonated globally. So it was difficult to see how even sound long-term behaviors could overrule decisions that made sense in the short run.

Hillis implemented sex in his system, effectively giving organisms the *choice* whether to reproduce sexually. He accomplished this by introducing a gene that controlled the percentage of the time that the organism reproduced sexually. The percentages that helped increase fitness in the phenotypes of the organisms would, of course, dominate. In the first experiments Hillis ran with this parameter the organisms found it in their interest to practice asexual behavior. Later, he posed some different tasks, and in those cases the system took the far-sighted decision and sought mates. Hillis could not isolate what, if any, rule determined whether populations chose or rejected sexual reproduction. But the experiment did indicate that sexual reproduction drove the Ramp population away from local maxima and freed it to seek higher peaks. This was a logical consequence of sex, which had a built-in risk of reducing fitness when relatively optimal genes were "watered down" when combined with a less fit set of genes. This result made Hillis feel he was on to something. He suspected that his experiments could unearth clues that biologists were missing.

At the time, Hillis was training his Ramps to tackle a thorny problem. In this experiment, the measure of a Ramp's fitness was the ability of the organism to sort numbers. The degree to which each Ramp sorted a list of sixteen numbers in descending order determined how successful that individual was. Sorting-network problems were a familiar challenge to computer hackers, who tried to build systems that arrange numbers using the fewest steps, or exchanges—the fewer exchanges, the more wizardry required. Using his modified version of the genetic algorithm, Hillis would seed his next generation with the organisms of the current generation who sorted the list in the fewest exchanges.

The particular sorting network problem Hillis chose for his Ramps had long been used both as a benchmark of programming skill and as a proving ground for theoretical approaches to data manipulation. Essentially, he was pitting his Ramps, with evolution as a cornerman, against the cream of human endeavor. In 1962 a pair of computer scientists had published an article claiming the best possible solution to sorting networks, a system that would sort the sixteen integers in sixty-five exchanges. Two years later, the guru of code crunchers, Donald Knuth, created a system requiring only sixty-three exchanges. In 1969 the computer world was astonished when someone did it in one fewer exchange, and later that year the amazement was "tripled," to quote Knuth, when even that solution was eclipsed. This ultimate sorting program, written by a man named Milton Green, was elegant enough to arouse suspicion of Faustian dealings. It involved only sixty exchanges.

Hillis was running a population of 64 K, or 65,536, Ramps to evolve themselves to a state where they could become computer programs that solved the problem. (Because each individual could be assigned its own processor in the Connection Machine, the experiment could be run with lightning speed.) He generally ran his populations for five thousand or more generations, a time-consuming process for biologists breeding fruit flies but a day's work in the Cambridge headquarters of Thinking Machines. As was typical in Hillis's experiments, relatively capable individuals emerged in early runs and spread their highly fit genes throughout the population; by the end of the run the population had long found itself at a local maximum. The best of these sorted all the numbers successfully, requiring sixty-five exchanges.

This was a fairly impressive performance by a set of initially random numbers who found their way to a solution without human intervention; after all, two very satisfied computer scientists in 1962 had published their results in a paper, to some acclaim, after accomplishing the task in the same number of steps. But Hillis wanted his system to find the higher peaks in the landscape. He introduced conditions that would drag the population from its stagnant perch and force it to seek the higher ground. First, he tried increasing the rate of mutations. Although this drove the population off the hill, the mutations triggered dire lapses in fitness from which the population rarely recovered.

The breakthrough came when Hillis heard about the Red Queen hypothesis. The appellation was borrowed from *Alice in Wonderland,* wherein the Red Queen goaded the young protagonist into running furiously, although it seemed to advance the young girl not an inch. When she complained to the queen, Her Majesty informed her that constant running was required to remain in the same place. Biologists used this anecdote in describing "evolutionary arms races," when two populations of differing species were set against each other, in predator-prey or host-parasite relationships. Regarding the latter, if a host population evolved strategic traits to foil the parasite, the parasite would in turn evolve a strategy to compensate. William Hamilton, among others, had suggested that the presence of parasites might have been integral in accelerating the pace of evolution to a rate capable of yielding its present diversity and complexity; he had even run his own computer simulations, which indicated that organisms might have adopted sexual reproduction to thwart parasitic invasions on their offspring. Hillis decided to introduce parasites in his system.

Hillis called his parasites "anti-Ramps." Like their rivals, they were rewarded according to a fitness function—the degree to which they harassed their digital cousins. It was a classic evolutionary arms race in which both species would coevolve and discover improvements in response to their opponent's evolutionary improvements. Hillis arranged an ingenious method of attack: the anti-Ramps literally provided test cases to gauge the Ramps' solutions to the sorting problems. As the simulation progressed, and as the Ramps came up with better solutions, the anti-Ramps would evolve increasingly challenging test cases. If one thought of the Ramps as chess players, the anti-Ramps were chess impresarios, who produced a series of opponents. They first ushered in fumbling novices, provided experienced players when the beginners were consistently vanquished, and eventually flew in cunning grand masters.

Under continual attack from these demanding challengers, the Ramps were forced to devise evolutionary strategies that would maintain and even improve the quality of their sorting. The first strategy was to settle on a fortified arrangement of integers so that the bite of the anti-Ramp would not be fatal. The second was to proceed with a high genetic variation from one generation to the next in order to assure that the parents' defects would not always be passed to the offspring and that the predators would be kept off balance.

Without anti-Ramps to keep them honest, previous populations of Ramps required tens of thousands of generations and long nights of Connection Machine time to find their local maxima. When coevolving parasites invaded the evolutionary landscape, however, a different story unfolded. Hillis liked to show videotapes of the screen display from the Connection Machine that illustrated this genetic drama. Each pixel on the screen represented an individual Ramp, and the fitness of each Ramp (how well it sorted the numbers) was represented by an arbitrarily assigned color. (The anti-Ramps were not depicted, but their effects were apparent.) As individuals were eliminated, selected, and mated in each time step, a new generation would replace the current one on the screen, and the color of the new population reflected these offspring. Clusters formed, and sometimes waves of similar Ramps pulsated in apparent synchrony. At first, the Ramps began to improve their ability to sort the numbers; this was reflected by localized changes in color from blue to green. Each time pockets of Ramps stabilized, however, a grim apocalyptic wave swept over them. The anti-Ramps obviously had devised test cases that broke the sorting schemes. But some Ramps evolved solutions that both met the demands of the test cases and developed immunities to that breed of anti-Ramp. Clusters of these improved Ramps, now in greenish yellow, roiled and spread on the screen, attained stability, and were besieged once more. Each time they reappeared, the newly immunized Ramps bore a color indicating higher fitness. Soon, some Ramps appeared in bright red, which indicated a fitness that Hillis's previous Ramps could not have hoped to attain. They had landed on the evolutionary landscape equivalent of the Andes.

The very first time Danny Hillis tried this, the entire epochal struggle described above occurred in fifteen minutes. The Ramp population was harshly dislodged from its comfy maximum. Racing around the evolutionary landscape as though pursued by hellhounds, the Ramps found and scaled the elusive higher peak. Although their solution did not equal Green's championship sorting network of sixty, they did match the second-best total of sixty-two, a significant improvement from previous runs. Hillis ran the experiment a few times more, and the population, again hounded by coevolving anti-Ramps, managed to construct a sorting network of sixty-one exchanges. Hillis was ecstatic, especially because he had been under the misimpression that the best-ever total had been sixty-two exchanges; he thought that his Ramps had outstripped the apex of human achievement. When he rechecked the literature and realized that his system fell short, he was so disappointed that he soon shelved the sorting-network problem indefinitely.

The concept, however, of accelerated evolution through coevolving parasites stuck with Hillis. He was convinced that Red Queen behavior yielded effective results because coevolving rivals forced the evolutionary system away from stability, on the cusp of phase transitions such as the ones Langton postulated in his work on the λ parameter. Thus the Ramps and anti-Ramps combined to drive the system to the edge of chaos, and a rich complexity of novel genotype strategies arose from that fertile computational region.

Hillis's work also had implications for the definition of life itself. If von Neumann established that life existed as an emergent information process; if Kauffman was among those who told us that through self-organization life wanted to happen; if Langton, Crutchfield, and Farmer informed us that among life's properties was a preference for locating itself just this side of chaos; then Hillis, in ratifying computationally the work of biologists such as Hamilton, hinted that life was a symbiotic process that virtually required the company of deadly rivals. Equilibrium was an illusion; *order finds itself* from a relentlessly troubled sea. Both Axelrod's iterated Prisoner's Dilemma and the GA-based solutions to that problem confirmed the benefits of cooperation between putative rivals. They placed the mean-spirited inherencies of Darwinian natural selection in a more benign light, where even deadly defections serve the system, by pushing it to higher levels of complexity.

"Artificial life is going to produce some very crisp, simple ideas—like, the interesting thing in natural selection is not the evolution of a single species, but things like the coevolution of hosts and parasites," says Hillis. "That may turn out to be a critical thing. But once we get into that mode of thinking we'll never quite think the same again, and never try the same things."

Danny Hillis had a ready example for those who probed him for specifics in response to his contention that artificial life would change our thinking about biology. Sitting in his cluttered corner office in Thinking Machines one day, wearing his usual faded T-shirt, he sat down at a table and spread out some graphs and papers. "Here's a prediction," he says, his words bolstered by the confidence provided by an imposing stack of statistical data. "I think the idea of a gene will change. I think the idea of a gene as developed by population biologists is fundamentally incomplete and misleading."

Hillis was addressing a problem at the heart of the mechanics of evolution. Biologists had come to believe that, rather than the steady progress of hill climbing, evolution moves by leaps and bounds, alternating with periods of stasis. Species remain relatively stable for a while, in a virtual equilibrium where fitness is suited to the environment. Then a sudden change in the environment, or an empowering mutation, causes an abrupt jump in fitness, as new and effective physical characteristics express themselves in the phenotypes of the species. If pictured on a graph, this progress resembles a series of plateaus punctuated by sudden jumps to another plateau, what biologists describe as "punctuated equilibrium."

Consider an animal population that is currently sightless but whose possible genetic makeup includes a set of genes that result in a phenotype that has vision. The gift of sight would allow this animal to detect food much more easily, perceive predators more clearly, and evaluate potential mates more wisely. A seeing population would probably find itself atop a very high peak on the fitness landscape. But an eye is an extremely complex organ, undoubtedly the morphological result of many genes. Biologists refer to cases like these, where the proper combination of multiple genes is required for a trait to appear, as epistatic. It is implausible that any combination of crossover or mutations in a single generation will yield a genotype that suddenly causes an eye to appear. Even if it did, the process of mating would disrupt that improbable chain of events.

Using the hill-climbing theory, one might picture the population slowly but steadily changing its genetic makeup until the hill leading toward sight is climbed. But how could this be reconciled with the complex makings of an eye? It is difficult to picture any set of gradual steps that could indicate that the path toward sight is a sloping ascent. (Half an eye would not be able to see—so how would having half an eye, let alone the first tiny fraction of an eye, be rewarded?) On the other hand, it is equally difficult to imagine a punctuated equivalent, where the population jumps up a high sheer cliff that represents the sharp improvement that would come from providing sight to a formerly blind population.

When biologists attempted to resolve these questions they smacked head on into an evidentiary wall. In order to address issues such as epistasis, evolutionary biologists were forced to reconstruct the past from fossil remains. These seldom gave definitive answers. Attempts at actual animal breeding—raising a few hundred generations of the favored organism for this sort of thing, drosophila (fruit flies) would fall far short of the required evolutionary time span for these dramatic effects.

Danny Hillis, however, had an edge—the Connection Machine.

The artificial organisms in Hillis's particular world evolved not by the steady progress of hill climbing but by the sudden leaps of punctuated equilibrium. "The average fitness of a population does not always increase steadily with time," he reported in a paper describing his results. "Instead progress often consists of long periods of relative stasis, punctuated by short periods of rapid progress."

If Hillis had stopped there in his analysis, he would have been at precisely the point where evolutionary biologists found themselves—examining fossil records and results of fruit fly breeding, and saying, Yes, according to these measures of the phenotypes, fitness proceeded by stable periods and sudden increases.

But with artificial organisms Hillis had the power to examine and analyze the genotype as easily as the realized phenotypes. In doing so, he discovered something remarkable. While the population seemed to be resting during the periods of equilibrium—the plateaus pictured in the graph—the underlying genetic makeup was actively evolving. The sudden increase in fitness was no more an instant occurrence than the appearance of a newborn indicates something springing out of nothing; the population seemed to be gestating its next jump. Specifically, the

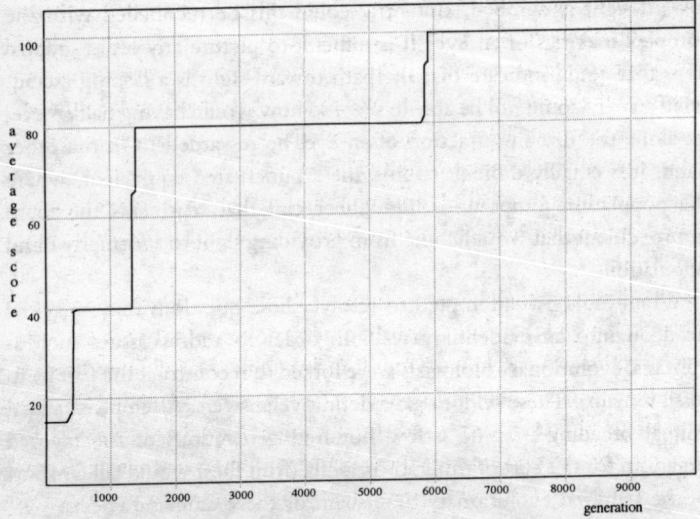

In this experiment, Hillis evolved a population of 65,536 Ramps, testing them against a problem where the highest score was 100. The pattern of their success after a number of generations shows clearly that their gains in fitness proceeded by "punctuated equilibrium"—periods of stability were shattered by sudden leaps in fitness. Each upswing in the chart represents a population-wide increase in fitness—evolution had found a new power that enabled the Ramps to deal with their environment more effectively.

Hillis identified three traits in particular that increased the fitness of these Ramps: the discovery of the right combination accounted for the leaps in fitness. When Hillis examined the genomes of the Ramps during the presumably stable period of equilibrium, however, he found that the gene pool was actually seething with activity, setting the stage for the next leap. This sort of simulated evolution uncovers a rich area for biologists to study—a testing ground for evolutionary theory.

gene pool of the population contained a set of epistatic genes that could not be expressed unless all were present; otherwise the alleles for these genes would be recessive. (Remember that an allele represents a particular variation of the gene—blue pigment and brown pigment are both alleles of eye color.) Whereas the dominant traits were expressed in the population, these recessive alleles accumulated in the population, along with other apparently coadaptive alleles; a feedback network seemed to encourage the parallel development of this ensemble. When the number of these recessive alleles reached a certain level, these genes spread widely throughout the population. The epistatic effect of their presence in the individuals that had all those traits made those phenotypes dramatically more fit, and the population leapt to a new plateau of so-called equilibrium.

Hillis illustrated the phenomenon with a story: Consider a population of plants. Among the genes in this population was a set of ten, each of which produced a certain enzyme. If in any individual all ten produced the right enzymes, a synergistic effect occurred that allowed that particular plant to photosynthesize in a totally different way—a much more efficient way. A population of those plants would experience an explosive rise in fitness. But all ten enzymes were required to produce this epistatic process. Meanwhile, the ten enzymes were also useful for other functions in the organism, but the presence of one or more did not necessarily increase fitness; an alternate enzyme might perform the same job.

If all ten enzymes appeared in a single individual, that plant would certainly do very well, but, when it mated with another individual that did not have all ten enzymes, its offspring would not have the advantage. But because that plant survived well, it would certainly pass on its genes. And every time another individual in the population had the entire ensemble of enzymes, that individual did well, and these genes would spread even more. The increase of those mutated genes was further spurred by a positive feedback effect; as greater numbers of those genes appeared, they would find more of their ilk with which to interact and thus would be more useful to individuals who carried them. The enzyme-producing genes would rise in the population, until they reached a certain percentage in the population. At that point, a phase transition occurred, much like the sudden ordering of interactions in the experiments of Stuart Kauffman. From that point on, there were sufficient numbers of those genes to combine with each other in other individuals, and the success of those combinations pushed the rest of the population to quickly follow, which it did because the genes were readily available. The epistatic effect would proliferate.

"You reach this magic percentage, and all of a sudden there's this huge positive feedback, and choook! It shoots up until everybody has it," says Hillis.

Hillis resolved to quantify that magic percentage, the point demarcating stasis and punctuation. In his effort he sought the help of Richard Feynman. But Feynman died before they reached a solution. Months later, biologist Eric Lander helped Hillis crack the problem: the result was the simple and beautiful equation, one over e squared. (e is a well-known mathematical constant.) When the presence of the crucial genes reached that value, the population would dramatically leap to a higher plateau. The equation was admirably robust, remaining constant no matter how many genes were involved in expressing the trait that increased fitness.

It also had personal meaning for its discoverer. Feynman had always loved the constant e, and Hillis suspected he would have loved this solution. Hillis did show Feynman the equation—in a dream. Indeed, the dream-Feynman admired its elegance. "I thought you were dead," said Hillis in his dream to the physicist. Feynman acknowledged that this was so, but seemed to indicate a bright side to death: "At least we aren't interrupted when we're talking," he said. Hillis, awaking in tears, realized that his emotion at the beauty of the equation was tied to the loss of his friend and mentor.

The experiment led Hillis to believe that, although biologists who believed in punctuated equilibrium were correct, they were unaware of its cause. It was not necessarily a drastic perturbation of the environment or a crucial mutation that caused the jump (Hillis was among those who emerged from a-life experiments with a decreased respect for the role of mutation in evolution) but complex interactions of multiple genes. Epistasis was so important that Hillis suspected that we may soon rethink our definition of a gene. Instead of a single packet of genetic information, a gene in Hillis's thinking could be thought of as a set of interacting packets. As many as a dozen or more.

"People's idea of a gene is something that adapts by itself," he says. "It goes back to Mendel. In some sense the notion of twelve of them working together fights the basic idea of the gene. Biologists will say we've never had examples of high epistatic interactions among a dozen genes, there's no reason to believe those exist in biology. And the reason is that they've never seen them. They *can't* see them. Considering the way they look for a gene, there's no way they could have discovered them if they were there."

Skeptics could note with impunity that Hillis's work proved nothing. Simply because his simulated populations yielded certain results did not compel the science of genetics to redefine itself. Hillis recognized that his experiments were not proofs. Yet he felt that, although his information organisms did not have the intricacy and breadth of their natural counterparts, the evolution depicted in his experiments was sufficiently rigorous to earn the attention of biologists. That his fieldwork occurred in the realm of silicon, only as tangible as mathematics and imagination, should not work against him.

In the past, the prejudice against mathematical modeling in theoretical biology might have been justified. In making biological simulations the stupefyingly complex mathematics of life was by necessity oversimplified, to the point where the connection to the physical world was tenuous or at least subject to massive swings in interpretation. The noted zoologist Theodosius Dobzhansky had once compared computer models in biology to masturbation: it could sometimes be pleasant, but it is not a substitute for the real thing. But Hillis believed that simulations done in the a-life community had broken the barrier. These may be toy problems, but they were very serious toys.

"If biologists want to tell me what really happens in biology then I'll always believe it," he says. "They know more than me about what really happens in the real world. But I think biologists for the most part are very naive about computation. So the biologists who go out in the field and count bugs are not real impressed by the people who sit home and solve equations."

And, although most biologists preferred bug counts to a-life experiments, an increasing number came to regard Hillis's efforts with some seriousness. Their reaction to his results was not dismissal but rather a keen interest in determining whether the behavior of these simulated populations indicated a similar process occurring in natural life.

"That's not the majority reaction," admits Hillis. "But I would say the biologists I admire tend to react that way."

In another sense, the opinion of biologists was irrelevant. One need not concede the applicability of Hillis's work to wet reality to see its benefits. Hillis believed that the success achieved by his Ramps under pressure from coevolving parasites presented a promising approach to computer programming. His aspirations for evolutionary programming exceeded even those of John Koza. "We all find programming very frustrating," he says. "The dream is to have this little world where we can evolve programs to do something we want. We punish them and wipe them out if they don't do what we want, and after a few hundred thousand generations or so, we have a program that ideally behaves the way we like. We can play God—but all we have to *do* is define the puzzle for them. We don't have to be smart enough to figure out the way they solve the puzzle."

Danny Hillis was consistently fascinated with the way that the Ramps had implemented their sorting network. It seemed to progress by totally nonintuitive means, shifting numbers back and forth in a way that seemingly directed the task backward, although of course in the end the numbers were miraculously sorted. It was possible that some exchanges were indeed counterproductive, but remained as evolutionary relics of previous paths taken and abandoned. In any case, examining the odd itinerary that the Ramps charted in their journey toward solving the problem provided an unearthly insight into a different sort of intelligence, a nonhuman intelligence. One had to regard it with the same open-minded fascination as one would an extraterrestrial message.

Another advantage of the coevolutionary programming was that the algorithms produced were particularly robust. Unlike computer programs written by humans, which suffered from the brittleness inevitable when design proceeded in a structured, hierarchical manner, the programs resulting from coevolutionary systems were built like tanks. It was rare that a simple perturbation would upset them; otherwise they would have fallen easy prey to those parasites furiously shoving test cases at them. Those parasites were highly motivated to break the algorithms of the host organisms. Their ability to continue their lineage depended on success. Thus solutions reached by the hosts were acquired by the digital equivalent of blood. "If I had to fly an airplane that depended on sorting numbers correctly, I would rather fly an airplane that depended on this algorithm than one that I did for myself," says Hillis.

Hillis envisioned a day when a natural, coevolutionary paradigm would be applied in major programming projects. Unlike the current approach, where a program was debugged and cloned copies were distributed from the original, coevolved programs lived on the cusp of chaos. Like natural living systems, no single program was precisely identical to any other. This bestowed not only a certain imperviousness to system crashes caused by unauthorized use but a relative immunity to computer viruses. Because each version of a computer operating system would be different, virus designers could not tailor their digital intruders to the coding of a generic series of hosts.

Some of Hillis's employees at Thinking Machines were also implementing applications that exploited the mechanics of life. The most spectacular work of this nature at Thinking Machines was that of Karl Sims. Not yet thirty, Sims was a lanky programmer whose trail to artificial life began with biology studies at MIT, took a hard right turn with computer studies at the Media Lab, and detoured toward a job programming special effects in Hollywood. Then he returned to Cambridge to work for Hillis. His job was to create eye-popping graphics and animation that demonstrated the breathtaking nature of the Connection Machine's power. Ensconced in his warren at Thinking Machines, he began thinking about using biological models to produce digital images. Because much of the challenge of producing computer graphics came in duplicating the rich complexity of the real world, why not draw on nature's techniques, which were obviously quite capable of generating complicated objects?

Sims used a genetic paradigm to produce the complexity of natural objects. He began by elaborating on Richard Dawkins's biomorph system. Dawkins's system had produced a set of organisms, each with a given number of genes that determined their appearance. The means of selection was the human observer, a so-called unnatural selection in which aesthetics, and sometimes even perverse whim, determined fitness. The system's "undesigned and unpredictable" organisms beggared the efforts of all but the most imaginative artists. Sims considered the biomorph system a computer artist's tool, one that allowed a person with no programming ability and no drawing acumen to create complex and compelling images.

One of Sims's projects was creating lifelike, yet disturbingly unfamiliar trees that would populate the otherworldly landscape of an animation piece called "Panspermia." Sims began his botanic quest with sixteen images, each of which had random values assigned to its twenty-one genes. The genes, which were digits representing symbolic expressions in the dialect of LISP computer language spoken by the Connection Machine, controlled parameters such as branching factors, growth rate, twistiness, and budding behavior. The computer read the genetic content and expressed each number string in a phenotype tree. Sims then picked the one he liked, and that survivor had fifteen offspring. Because one or more genes mutated in the reproductive process, none of the daughters was identical to the parent. Sims then repeated the process. After as few as five generations, he often yielded fascinating, uncharted species.

Sims amplified the power of Dawkins's methodology by merging it with Holland's genetic algorithm techniques: in each generation he could replace biomorphic asexual reproduction with the digital form of sexual reproduction practiced in GAs. This was simply done: instead of clicking his mouse on a single parent, Sims used a different mouse button and clicked on two alternatives to mate. Besides the alternatives on the screen, he could produce a specimen restored from a previous run—the equivalent of a cattle breeder's keeping of unlimited stock of purebred bull sperm on hand—and use that to mate with a newly generated candidate. Because Sims's goal was to achieve aesthetically pleasing results and not to discover clues to biological behavior, he also used forms of mating that were less natural than the crossover-and-mutation

GA mating. He would, for instance, arrange liaisons in which the off-spring received a random assortment of genes from each parent or even pairings that noted the values of each parent's genes and bequeathed the offspring's corresponding genes with values set at some number *between* Mommy's and Daddy's. Sims even implemented a method to animate the mating process visually: in a nod to his Hollywood days, he described it as a "genetic cross-dissolve."

This arsenal of biologically inspired tools allowed Sims to search through the space of possible artificial trees—a near-infinite range—with blazing speed. This resulted in a painless form of artistry. This winnowing process was a kind of superamplified version of the game Twenty Questions, in which a series of true-false queries narrowed the space of all possible humans to a single individual. Instead of beginning with a blank page or screen, the human designer equipped with Sims's program and a Connection Machine had a virtual stack of paper, billions and billions of reams high. One could imagine each piece of paper picturing a different sort of tree; somewhere in the sky-high tower of paper every conceivable tree was represented. By simply evolving in a direction that felt right, the designer eliminated the vast numbers of unsuitable trees and very quickly got to a desirable forest. When Sims first tried this, he came on fascinating artificial species. Some appeared to be denizens of an undiscovered rain forest, stumpy trees with viney leaves, or willowy constructs with thorny appendages. Others, tangles of menacing tendrils, seemed to be Martian bushes sprung from the palette of science-fiction illustrator Frank Frazetta.

"If were to try to design these, I would use fractals and other tech-niques, but I would have to do it all by hand," says Sims of his system. "This is a way to get variety quickly. I can save the genomes, sprinkle them about and grow forests pretty quickly. Since this method does not require you to understand or even look at the numbers or functions, you just do it. Think of the genotype as a seed—when you plant geraniums, you don't know what the DNA looks like." The artificially evolved landscape depicted in "Panspermia," lush with instances of alternative botany, indicates that nature's design power can be easily harnessed, once its algorithms are astutely captured.

Sims's system was equally impressive when the goal was extended from creating plantlike structures to free-form designs. In only a few generations, anyone capable of manipulating a computer mouse could create hauntingly beautiful visual artifacts. The power to search not only the space of all possible trees but also all possible *images*—a dizzying concept in and of itself—coughed up pictures that displayed the hard-earned distinctiveness of great modern artists. Sims had a portfolio of evolved images that evoked Dalí, Klee, Picasso, Mondrian, and Rothko. Other images were less indentifiable: shimmering glaciers, kaleidoscopic webs, a "fire of faces." Sims also used the system to produce rich textures quickly: instead of painstakingly grinding out algorithms for simulating the patterns of marble, wood grain, bark, or crystal, he could find them through evolution.

Sims became so impressed with the searching power of his genetic graphics system that he decided to extend it beyond the creation of images into the realm of physics and mathematics. Specifically, he wondered whether he could use this technique on the Connection Machine to determine particularly fertile examples of dynamical systems. In effect, he was performing the same type of work undertaken by Langton and Wolfram when they constructed their respective taxonomies of cellular automata rules—only instead of running the rule systems one by one to observe the behavior of each system or measuring the behavior according to a metric gauge like the λ parameter, Sims left his equations and measuring tools behind. Instead, he breezily zipped through rule sets by setting systems in motion to see whether interesting behavior emerged, choosing the ones he liked most and reproducing them. First, he mated and bred CA-lookup tables and very quickly found Class 4–type systems. Then he tried the process with continuous dynamical systems and yielded a range of fascinating behaviors, some of which seemed to have slipped out of the binding of Benoit Mandelbrot's *Fractal Geometry of Nature*.

"These are powerful methods for creating dynamical systems with emergent complexity that would be difficult to build by design," Sims wrote. Who *was* the designer? The same set of forces that designed viruses, ferns, coral reefs, and human beings. Sims, like other a-life experimenters, had borrowed that unnamed designer's toolbox, including one of its handiest items, evolution.

An ineluctable message emerged from all these experiments: something very much like natural evolution could be effectively executed within the circuitry of a digital computer. Most artificial lifers would insist that the phenomenon produced by the computer was indeed evolution itself, as pure as the form that Darwin identified in the natural world.

Considering the initial success of digital evolution and its power to harness natural selection, a seductive question arose: Would it not be possible to actually evolve real creatures? To start with some inert lump of information and, compressing billions of years of activity into something a bit more manageable (overnight? a week? even a year?), to wind up with life? Could one indeed follow the path apparently taken on earth, so that something as simple as a bacterium could make its way up the evolutionary ladder into something as complex as a mollusk, a snake, a dog, or a human being?

It was perhaps the vital methodological question in artificial life, one that lurked behind every experiment in emergent behavior. In early stages of the field, most researchers had been content—indeed, their hands were full—trying to produce emergent behavior that was a single step or two beyond the behaviors originally programmed into their artificial creatures. By necessity, these attempts were constrained, streamlined to promote unprogrammed behavior in a certain arena. In efforts that simulated evolution, the limiting factor was the fitness function. The means of fitness were generally chosen and applied by the experimenter. The alternative approach would be more amorphous: an *open-ended* strategy where criteria for fitness would emerge, as they had in nature, according to the requirements of survival in the dynamic environment. Novel adaptations, often not imagined by the human architects of the digital environment, could change the nature of organisms dramatically. A series of startling changes might allow simple life-forms to scale the evolutionary ladder and to climb toward more complex variations. In theory, one could begin with something as simple as a one-celled creature, and, applying the proper algorithms, let the system run, like some epochal time-lapse exposure, until more complex organisms evolved: algae, ferns, salamanders, swordfish, roses, buffalo, and people. In practice, of course, this ideal was inconceivable. Computers of 1990s vintage were far too weak.

Computer power aside, how far could one go in this direction? Skeptics and carbaquists insist that a series of iterated evolutions on information organisms can never duplicate the physical interactions that undoubtedly had their effect on the development of life on this planet. But one does not have to accept the possibility of digital life to admit the value of such an effort, which seems worthwhile if for no other reason than to observe what sorts of phenomena occurred in the system's journey from initial disorder to recognizable order. Each instance of lifelike behavior shown by the system is an implicit argument that computable emergent forces had evoked those same behaviors in the natural world. If the behavior of information organisms evolved in an open-ended environment turn out to be extremely lifelike, the result could prove the strongest argument yet for redefining the terms of life itself.

Those ideas drove a biologist named Thomas Ray to devise what he considered the first truly open-ended system. To this diminutive, energetic scientist, allowing the system to find its own fitness—a natural selection as opposed to an artificial one—was key to creating living things on the computer. Ray's own definition of life hinged on that factor: "I would consider a system to be living if it is self-replicating, and capable of open-ended evolution . . . ," he wrote. "Artificial selection can never be as creative as natural selection. . . . Freely evolving creatures will discover means of mutual exploitation and associated implicit fitness functions that we would never think of."

Ray's interest in the field was not that of a digital alchemist but of a professional biologist. Although he studied chemistry at Florida State University and had been planning to take further undergraduate work in physics and math, Ray became interested in ecology, "sort of in the sixties frame of mind," he explains, somewhat sheepishly. He completed a doctorate in biology at Harvard, and did fieldwork in the rain forests of Costa Rica. But one particular experience from his Cambridge days settled into his mind like a dormant spore. Ray had taken an interest in the Chinese game of Go, and one day in the late 1970s he was the recipient of a remarkable one-on-one deconstruction of the ancient game, from a beak-nosed, ponytailed hacker working at MIT's Artificial Intelligence Lab. To Ray's astonishment, this person cooly analyzed the game in biological terms, matter-of-factly mentioning that computer programs could self-replicate. Ray instantly made the connection between self-replication and natural selection and became very excited at the implications.

At the time, Ray's computer experience was insufficient to experiment with the concept. And soon, the pressures of his subsequent passion, rain forest conservation, took precedence. It was not until late in 1989, when Ray had become an assistant professor at the University of Delaware, that the spore revivified. Ray had become familiar with workings of personal computers, and he also followed the news of computer viruses. For some reason, the words of the mystery Go player tumbled back into his head. Could computer viruses be included among the potential life-forms the hacker had postulated? Could he exploit these possibilities to perform a digital form of the Darwinism he had studied so closely this past decade? Ray became determined to find out.

No one else at Delaware was much interested. When Ray brought up the idea at a graduate seminar in ecology, "I was virtually laughed out of the room," he says. Ray's colleagues, who had previously voted him down for tenure, considered the premise wacky. But Ray persisted. Although he had a grant to study tropical ecologies, he neglected the project. Instead he hatched ideas for techniques of simulating evolution. "It was something that was obsessing me, and I felt I had to go where the flow of my energies were," he says. "Artificial life was the thing that kept me awake at night."

Wondering whether others were similarly impassioned, he posted an inquiry on various computer networks and was led to the proceedings of the first artificial life conference. They galvanized Ray. He arranged to go to New Mexico to visit Langton, Farmer, and the other T-13 a-life researchers to discuss his idea for an open-ended evolutionary system.

It was a good thing he did. Ray's idea had been to create creatures consisting of computer instructions who would "live" inside the machine's core memory and compete for space in that silicon terrain. A potentially treacherous plan. Although Ray planned to run his experiment in an isolated personal computer labeled "containment facility" and protected with metal bars covering the disk drive and serial port, there was no guarantee that, through negligence or sabotage, his creatures would not be transferred to other computers. If for instance they found their way into one of the time-sharing mainframes on the Delaware campus, they could infect other jobs working on the computer or even migrate from that machine to the data highways of the international computer network. Ray's experiment could have been the equivalent of importing a deadly predator to an ecology that had evolved no protection against such an invader. It could be even more destructive than the notorious "Internet Worm" loosed on the computer nets in November 1988 by a mischievous Cornell student—almost exactly a year before Ray's trip to Los Alamos. Unlike the comparatively primitive worm, Ray's organisms would be constantly evolving. Natural selection would favor those organisms most difficult to eradicate, and, like certain insects immune to DDT, mutated variations of Tom Ray's experiment might become permanent, and unwelcome, residents on the computer nets.

Langton and Farmer suggested a modification, based on Turing's perception that any digital computer could emulate any other digital computer. They suggested, in effect, that Ray should create an imaginary computer and simulate its operation within a real computer. That way, his organisms, in their competition for memory space in a virtual computer, could use a nonfunctional computer language, one that worked only in the model. If someone attempted to liberate the creatures and use them outside this theoretical cage, the code would not work.

Ray's ideas of open-ended evolution depended on the creation of viable creatures whose subsequent mutations would drive the system toward a diverse set of more complex creatures. Mutations, however, were more often destructive than beneficial. Although natural organisms, with built-in redundancy, can accommodate occasional mutations, computer programs generally cannot. Non–open-ended simulated evolution systems such as genetic algorithms and Dawkins-style biomorphs avoided this problem by having an outside force weeding the population by a predetermined definition of fitness—a neat way to sweep away poorly mutated organisms. Because an open-ended system found its own fitness, Ray would not have that advantage.

But Ray thought he knew the way around the problem. Again, the virtual computer concept was the hero. Because an imaginary computer's machine-language requirements could be made much less exacting than those of a real computer, Ray could devise a specialized use of a computer instruction set that would be more forgiving to mutations. The scheme relied on using what Ray called "electronic templates." These were small blocks of computer instructions contained in each organism; replication occurred when the organism found the opposite template in the environment. Because the environment was well stocked with potential matching templates, even mutated organisms with altered instruction blocks could easily reproduce. In addition, when an organism searched for complementary templates it was in effect examining its environment. Thus Ray's digital organisms had the equivalent of sensory apparatuses. By searching their environment for matching parts, Ray's creatures behaved in the spirit of von Neumann's imaginary kinematic self-reproducing automaton.

As soon as Ray returned to Delaware, he began creating the artificial environment he would call Tierra. Previous work in open-ended artificial evolution focused on the origin of life in an attempt to evoke the behavior of biology from a prebiotic environment. The archetypical example was the VENUS simulator, codesigned by Steen Rasmussen, the Danish physicist who was part of the Los Alamos T-13 group. Although Ray considered VENUS interesting, he felt that it was unnecessary to begin so early in biological history. "It's based on the physics mentality—the Los Alamos guys want life to evolve virtually from quarks!" he says, the dismissive hyperbole underlying his conviction that his approach is superior. "They want to start with fundamental particles and get life to emerge spontaneously, at the origin of life level. What they get is more like chemistry than life. There's no individuality. It's a far cry from organisms."

Ray modeled his system on a later stage in life's development, the explosion of biological diversity that signaled the onset of the Cambrian Era, roughly six hundred million years ago. From a relative paucity of phyla, the earth teemed with unprecedented new life-forms. Ray believed that his system's exploitation of open-ended evolution, if not providing a similar profusion, would demonstrate the mechanics of that diversification.

The Tierran system was a competition for computer processing time and memory space. Whereas natural organisms drew energy from the sun to maintain their order, the digital organisms within the Tierran environment drew their energy from the virtual computer's central processing unit (CPU) and used that energy to power the equivalent of their own energy centers, virtual CPUs assigned to each organism. The components of the virtual computer—CPU, memory, and operating system software—were the environment, and the digital creatures themselves were assembly-language programs that ran on the computer. (Assembly language consists of digital instructions read directly by a computer's central processor.) Like many other digital creatures, the code of Tierran organisms acted both as a genotype, in that the code was copied during reproduction, and as a phenotype, in that the execution of the program performed a function that determined its fitness. Typically, executing the code would cause a creature to be copied from one part of the environment to another. Cell division, or replication, occurred when the move resulted in a daughter cell that required its own slice of CPU time. Essentially, Tierran organisms were genetic replication machines, digital kin to the hypothesized RNA-world life-forms that supposedly were the ancestors of all known subsequent forms of life.

All this took place in a block of computer memory that Ray referred to as "the soup." The creatures living in the soup were arranged in a circular queue, lined up to receive their slice of time from the virtual computer's CPU. A function Ray called the "reaper" made sure the soup did not stagnate, policing the population by lopping off the creatures at the top of a separate, linear, "reaper queue." These were generally the oldest, which climbed up the list simply by aging. However, by successfully executing instructions, organisms could postpone their climb and thus fend off the reaper. Flawed creatures rose quickly up the queue and reached their fatal peaks after a short existence. But even relatively fit creatures could not permanently stave off their rise toward death because newcomers constantly were introduced below them. In Tierra, as on earth, death was inevitable.

Evolution in Tierra was driven by several methods of mutation. First, the soup itself was subject to noise—random bit flipping that Ray considered "analogous to mutations caused by cosmic rays." (This insured the demise of even superbly adapted creatures, whose high fitness eventually would be worn down by the background bit flipping.) Ray also implemented mutations during the replication process in order to emulate genetic variation. Finally, there was a form of mutation that sometimes caused random alterations of instructions when the creatures executed their code. The cumulative effect of all these mutations was to vary the Tierran environment and the evolution of its inhabitants each time the program was run; thus Tierra was not a deterministic system but a probabilistic one.

For two months Ray programmed furiously, and soon after New Year's Day 1990 he was ready to begin the test runs of Tierra on the high-powered Toshiba laptop he used for development.

The first time Ray ran Tierra, he did not expect much. "The Los Alamos people had told me it was going to be really hard to do what I wanted, that it would take years of work," he recalls. "I believed that. They told me it wouldn't work with the type of instructions I used, because they're too brittle, mutations would stop the system. I believed that, too, but I wanted to try it, as Chris Langton put it, to find out why it wouldn't work. So when I first ran the system I just wanted to get it working. I figured out how many instructions it would require to replicate, rounded it off, and that was my instruction set. Then I built a creature to test the simulator, a creature that self-replicated and didn't do anything else. I thought, 'Okay, I'll get the simulator working, and it'll take me years to get evolution out of the system.'

"But as it turns out, I never had to write another creature."

On January 3, working at night on a table in the bedroom of his apartment while his wife slept, Ray "inoculated" the soup with his single test organism, eighty instructions long. He called it the "Ancestor." Its replications took somewhere over eight hundred instruction executions each time. The Ancestor and descendants quickly populated the soup, until it was 80% full. Once that threshold was attained, the reaper began its grim task and ensured that the population would grow no further.

The experiment proceeded at twelve million instructions per hour. (Later, using more powerful computers, Tierra would run six times faster.) Ray tracked the proceedings on a dynamic bar chart, which identified the organisms and the degree to which they proliferated in the soup. Initially, clones of the Ancestor dominated thoroughly; these typically replicated only once before dying. Then mutants began to appear. The first was a strain of creatures seventy-nine instructions long. The horizontal bar on the chart representing those creatures began to pulse, the bar representing the eighty-instruction Ancestors shrank, and soon the lower bar inched past the original. Eventually, some bars directly below those two began pulsing, indicating that even smaller mutations had successfully found ways to self-replicate. Ray was thrilled; Tierra was displaying the effects of evolution, as variations on the original were discovering more successful strategies for coping in the environment. The smaller organisms were more successful because their slightly shorter length allowed them to reproduce while occupying less CPU time. (Ray also had the option of adjusting the system parameters to reward larger organisms instead of smaller ones.)

Then something very strange happened. In the lower regions of the screen a bar began pulsing. It represented a creature of only forty-five instructions! With so sparse a genome, a creature could not self-replicate on its own in Tierra—the process required a minimal number of instructions, probably, Ray thought, in the low sixties. Yet the bar representing the population of forty-five instructions soon matched the size of the bar representing the previous most populous creature. In fact, the two seemed to be engaged in a tug-of-war. As one pulsed outward, the other would shrink, and vice versa.

It was obvious what had occurred. A providential mutation had formed a successful parasite. Although the forty-five-instruction organism did not contain all the instructions necessary for replication, it sought out a larger, complete organism as a host and borrowed the host's replication code. Because the parasite had fewer instructions to execute and occupied less CPU time, it had an advantage over complete creatures and proliferated quickly. But the population of parasites had an upper limit. If too successful, the parasites would decimate their hosts, on whom they depended for reproduction. The parasites would suffer periodic catastrophes as they drove out their hosts.

Meanwhile, any host mutations that made it more difficult for parasites to usurp the replication abilities were quickly rewarded. One mutation in particular proved cunningly effective in "immunizing" potential hosts—extra instructions that, in effect, caused the organism to "hide" from the attacking parasite. Instead of the normal procedure of periodically posting its location in the computer memory, an immunized host would forgo this step. Parasites depended on seeing this information in the CPU registers, and, when they failed to find it, they would forget their own size and location. Unable to find their host, they could not reproduce again, and the host would be liberated. However, to compensate for its failure to note its size and location in memory, the host had to undergo a self-examination process after every step in order to restore its own "self-concept." That particular function had a high energy cost—it increased the organism size and required more CPU time—but the gain in fitness more than compensated. So strains of immunized hosts emerged and virtually wiped out the forty-five-instruction parasites.

This by no means meant the end of parasitism. Although those first invaders were gone, their progeny had mutated into organisms adapted to this new twist in the environment. This new species of parasite had the ability to examine itself, so it could "remember" the information that the host caused it to forget. Once the parasite recalled that information it could feast on the host's replication code with impunity. Adding this function increased the length of the parasite and cost it vital CPU time, but, again, the trade-off was beneficial.

Evolutionary arms races were a familiar turf for ecologists such as Tom Ray. In the natural biosphere, of course, they extended over evolutionary time, measured in thousands of years. But even a true believer such as Ray was astonished at how easily a digital terrain could generate this same competition. Tierra had developed identical phenomena within ten minutes! Just as remarkable was that his system had produced this situation, previously wedded to biology's domain, without any manipulation whatsoever.

"In my wildest dreams that was what I wanted," he said. "I didn't write the Ancestor with the idea that it was going to produce all this."

Most satisfying to Ray was an effect clearly triggered by Tierra's open nature: on its own, the system had shifted the criteria for what constituted a fit organism. When the soup filled with organisms, the evolutionary landscape itself changed; the digital creatures were forced to seek novel responses to their altered circumstances. They did this by rewarding what previously would have been hopelessly ineffectual mutations. The door was opened to unprogrammed diversity.

"At the outset, selection favors efficiency towards the size bias we set up," explains Ray. "But as the system runs, mutants do odd things, and one of the odd things they do is discover other creatures, then exploit them. The parasites don't contain all the information they need to replicate, but they find that information in their environment, which now consists of other creatures. And it even turns out they alter each other's information, and in that way divert someone else's energy resources into the replication of their own genome. That's where the evolution gets interesting, because they're all still trying to make their code more efficient, but the bulk of evolution is coming from exploiting each other. The organisms have a whole new realm to the fitness landscape, a new adaptation for passing on their genes, a specific mechanism not present in the Ancestor. In this case, parasitism, or immunity to parasitism."

The emergence of diversity in Tierra's maiden voyage was no anomaly. Although each subsequent run differed in some respect, the major effects kept repeating. Within a few million instructions parasites would emerge, and an evolutionary arms race would ensue.

Ray conducted a variety of experiments with Tierra. As an alternative to inoculating the system with a single Ancestor, he injected the soup with creatures evolved from previous runs. His gene bank soon grew to over twenty-nine thousand different genotypes of self-replicating organisms, of over three hundred size classes. Typically, he would isolate a certain host and a certain parasite and see the effects. Then he would sort and analyze the results with the aid of an accompanying program called Beagle, honoring the ship on which Darwin voyaged to the Galapagos. "This sort of thing should be very interesting to population geneticists," says Ray. "Never before has anybody been able to look at genetic change in a population right down to frequency of every genotype in every species of a community. I'm making a record of every birth and death. I can go back and figure out why one variation beat out another, look at its code and determine what gave it the advantage."

Using this method, Ray duplicated various biological phenomena observed in the field by ecologists. In one experiment, Ray gauged the effect of introducing a parasite organism into a previously pristine ecology; then, trying the opposite, he removed parasites from the soup. "Just as in natural ecological communities, the presence of a predator doubles the diversity," he says. "The predator [parasite] tends to suppress the dominant host competitor, and prevents it from competitively excluding the weaker competitors. So Tierra reflects real ecological communities in a very nice way."

Ray's other experiments indicated that genetic mutation itself is not necessarily the driving force behind evolution. In one experiment, he adjusted the parameters of the system by switching off the background noise and eliminating mutations from replication. He inoculated the soup with hosts and parasites, and diversity emerged as surely as before. He attributed this to the effect caused by the "sloppy replication" that occurred when parasites tampered with the host genomes. The host codes were sometimes broken, causing an effect much like crossover. Along with Hillis's findings and related work by Kauffman and Koza, this result was a further indicator that the evolution of organic complexity, and possibly sexual reproduction, might owe much to the emergence of parasites.

Like Hillis and Koza, Ray believed that digital evolution had the potential to become the engine of practical computer programming in the next century. Tierran organisms, like Hillis's Ramps and Koza's LISP creatures, were capable of brilliant feats of code crunching. As millions of instructions were executed, Tierran organisms optimized their size, managing to compact very complicated algorithms into instruction sets much smaller than those with which they began. Ray saw organisms clock a 5.75-fold increase in efficiency. The organisms performed this wizardry by using the extremely nonintuitive techniques that come naturally to artificial organisms.

One example illustrated how organisms discover programming tricks. Ray's creatures commonly had pieces of code, or templates, to mark where they began and where they ended. (These acted as a sort of membrane to isolate the creature from the environment.) But one species of creature hit on an idea that enabled it to evolve without using a template to mark its end. "These creatures," wrote Ray, "located the address of the template marking their beginning, and then the address of a template in the middle of their genome. These two addresses were then subtracted to calculate half of their size, and this value was multiplied by two . . . to calculate their full size."

Ray's organisms were capable of more complicated tricks. After one run of fifteen billion instructions, he examined a certain creature he named "72etq." (Ray named his organisms by the number of instructions in their genotype, followed by three letters, representing the order in which the creature appeared in his experiments. Thus the Ancestor was called 80aaa, and 72etq represented the 3315th different version of a creature seventy-two instructions long.) This particular organism executed a series of algorithms that performed a sophisticated optimization technique called "unrolling the loop." It allowed the creature to operate with a genome half its actual size (thirty-six instructions) by a complicated but highly compact series of instruction swaps and self-examinations. According to Ray, "the optimization technique is a very clever one invented by humans, yet it is implemented in a mixed-up but functional style that no human would use (unless very intoxicated)." Ray managed to examine carefully only a small percentage of the genomes of his more evolved creatures; it is logical to assume that others had devised equally impressive optimization schemes that may or may not have been worked out by humans. One could speculate that environments like Tierra might find utility as virtual laboratories for generating the algorithms that would drive the devilishly complex computer programs run on the supercomputers in the next century.

Still, the most spectacular news from Tierra was its analogue to biology, particularly in the diversity that emerged when Ray allowed it to run for mammoth sessions. A series of eras unfolded. These appeared suddenly, after long stretches of stable behavior. (This was further confirmation of Hillis's discovery that punctuated equilibrium emerges spontaneously in computational evolution.) In each of these, genetic explosions erupted noiselessly, marked on the screen only by a profusion of different levels on the dynamic bar chart. (Later, one of Ray's students improved the display so that different organisms would be represented by colored rods.) Yet to an observer supplied with the knowledge that the tiny world had undergone a sort of evolutionary apocalypse, these shifts in light seemed accompanied by Wagnerian fanfares and blinding flashes of lightning. It was history on the grandest possible scale.

A typical experiment of this sort began with an inoculation of a single Ancestor. Soon came the almost inevitable appearance of parasites and host adaptations to resist the parasites. For millions of instructions, Tierra maintained a pattern wherein two sets of organisms—descendants of organisms of around eighty instructions and parasites with around forty-five instructions—maintained their presence in the soup. Suddenly, a new sort of organism arrived and began to dominate. On examining the code, Ray discovered that these new mutants were *hyper*-parasites: although derived from the genomes of host organisms, they had developed an ability to divert the metabolism of the parasites in order to bolster their own replication function.

The hyper-parasites were remarkable creatures. They were the same length as the eighty-instruction Ancestor, but subsequent evolutionary pressure had changed almost one-fourth of the genome and replaced the Ancestor's instructions with others. Those changes greatly enhanced their fitness by allowing them not only to replicate but also to fatally attack their small competitors. This stunt was dispatched in a manner that would win accolades and envy from any skilled hacker: hyper-parasites managed to examine themselves constantly to see whether parasites were present. If a parasite was detected, the hyper-parasite executed a Pac-Man-style maneuver. Transmogrifying from victim to victimizer, it diverted the parasite's CPU time to itself. The assault was so devastating that its continued repetition drove the parasites to extinction.

From that point on, cleansed of simple parasites, Tierra went into another long period of relative stability. No longer burdened with competing parasites, the host organisms, almost all of which were now hyper-parasites, searched evolutionary space in an attempt to maintain the genetic integrity necessary to replicate, while consuming less energy. The method by which the hyper-parasites accomplished this recalled experiments by Robert Axelrod and others studying the evolution of cooperation. Groups of hyper-parasites worked symbiotically, sharing the code for replication. This new variation could not reproduce on its own but relied on similar organisms to provide the missing piece of the reproductive gene. Like pairs of cooperating participants in the iterated Prisoner's Dilemma, each organism realized a benefit from the symbiosis.

This utopian scenario continued for millions of instructions. It was, however, doomed. Formalized cooperation had become yet another aspect of the environment to be exploited by an opportunistic muta- tion. In this case, the interloper was a tiny organism that shrewdly placed itself between two cooperating hyper-parasites and intercepted the genetic information for replication as it passed from one to the other. It was as though a quarterback and a halfback, smug in the knowledge that no defensemen were nearby, had been practicing handoffs, and suddenly, inexplicably, a defensive back emerged from nowhere and spirited away the precious football. By commandeering the replication code in one well-positioned grab, this hyper-hyper- parasite, or "cheater," was able to reproduce and thrive with a body length of only twenty-seven instructions.

"When the hyper-parasites drove the parasites to extinction at around 550 million instructions, I thought that I was never going to see them again because the defense seemed iron-clad," says Ray. "But the evolu- tion of sociality made them vulnerable again, and gave the parasites a way back into the system."

As each run of Tierra unfolded, Ray and others attuned to the behavioral mosaic of ecology could recognize biological phenomena as they emerged. But, because Tierra was life of a different sort, a truly synthetic form of life, it may have been displaying behavior that was lifelike but characteristic mainly of an alternative form of life. Tom Ray admitted a problem in identifying these possible effects: "What we see is what we know," he wrote. "It is likely to take longer before we appreciate the unique properties of these new life forms."

꘏

Tierra's instant ability to yield the drama, and apparently the dynamics, of an evolutionary biosphere changed Ray's life. The same ecologists at Delaware who once refused him tenure now came to his office and spent hours staring at the bars on his computer screen. Ray won tenure. Others at Delaware, particularly a group of computer scientists, became committed enthusiasts, and soon Ray was at the forefront of a Newark-based a-life study group.

Still, Ray suffered the reluctance of those who had difficulty conceiving lifelike phenomena arising from the bowels of a computer. When one official at the Air Force Office for Scientific Research (AFOSR) reviewed Ray's work with Tierra, he passed it around and found not only resistance to supporting the idea but also an edge of ridicule, a suspicion that Ray had perhaps overly relied on science fiction for his vision. Some at the AFOSR wondered whether some of the modest funding devoted to other experiments under the rubric of artificial life should not be reconsidered: Doyne Farmer had to reassure the funders that serious science was indeed the agenda of this new field.

As Ray continued his work, however, and began circulating his results among computer scientists and biologists, Tierra gained a level of respect unprecedented among a-life experiments. IBM, excited about the possibility of transferring the methodology of Ray's organisms to the principles of programming massively parallel computers, awarded him a $15,000 prize in their supercomputing competition. Ray's work won attention from science journals and the lay press. The Santa Fe Institute invited him to spend six months at the institute as a visiting fellow. Perhaps most impressive of all the reactions came from the ranks of biologists, most of whom normally were wary about the possibilities of producing lifelike phenomena on computers. When Ray presented his results to a gathering of evolutionary biologists, he won the respect of key evolutionary biologists like John Maynard Smith. Ecologist Stephen P. Hubbell of Princeton, originally a skeptic, attended a seminar on the work and described it as "spectacular." Another noted biologist, Graham Bell of McGill University described Ray's system as "the first logical demonstration of the validity of the Darwinian theory of evolution," and wrote a letter touting Ray's system.

> This work has three important uses. First, it is a superb educational tool. Many people doubt that the theory of evolution is logically possible. . . . Now, one can simply point to the output of Ray's programs; they are the ultimate demonstration of the logical coherence of evolution by selection. Secondly, it seems likely to provide a superior method for testing theoretical ideas in evolution, by providing more realistic general algorithms than have ever before been available. Thirdly, it may also represent a general advance in computation, since it makes it possible to evolve efficient algorithms for any purpose. . . . I am writing to assure you that it . . . ranks among the most interesting developments in evolutionary theory in the last ten years.

Ray would cheerfully admit the limitations of his system—he noted that several magnitudes of increased computer power would be required to support a system to evolve more complex creatures, one that could support life-forms with the equivalents of both DNA and RNA, for instance, or multicellular organisms. But in a sense Tierra had already accomplished one of Ray's prime goals—the beginnings of a shift in perception caused by a successful implementation of open-ended artificial evolution. An indication of this came in the August 27, 1991, edition of the *New York Times,* declaring that, on the heels of Tierran evolution, "a new round of debate has developed among scientists as to where the dividing line between life and non-life may lie." A debate long anticipated by the proponents of artificial life.

Tom Ray had an additional viewpoint on the ability of Tierra to evolve the workings of biology from a digital soup: "The conclusion I draw from it," he says, "is that virtual life is out there, waiting for us to create environments for it to evolve into."

ARTIFICIAL FLORA, ARTIFICIAL FAUNA, ARTIFICIAL ECOLOGIES

It still takes a leap of faith to believe that von Neumann's result means it is physically possible for a general-purpose computer to reproduce itself. We have taken the chemical of living things and made vital parts of living things from them (e.g., genes) but we have not yet generalized the secrets of living things to non-living creations of our own. (By "non-living" I mean not a member of the biological kingdom with its history of evolution, man-made.) I believe we shall, that the leap of faith is no small one and shall soon require no faith. I see forests of inorganic trees. I see buildings construct themselves, growing from a single brick-egg each. I see robots reproduce and evolve.

Alvy Ray Smith III

When the botanist Aristid Lindenmayer stood before the attentive gathering of scientists at the first a-life conference in 1987 and waved a large fall aster plant he had just plucked from the perimeter of the parking lot outside, the moment represented a final flourish to a career centered on logic and life. Lindenmayer's presence signified the forging of an important unity: a mathematical field had lent its logical power to the synthesis of artificial organisms. Using his system, researchers could generate realistic pictures of the plant that Lindenmayer held in his hand. The process cast a double illumination: it increased our understanding of issues of biology, and it advanced our ability to create a biology based on computation. Although Lindenmayer's system performed this trick in a unique manner, the transformation it effected echoed throughout the artificial life experience. In a similar manner, the synthesis of simple organisms, insects, and ecologies of multiple artificial organisms by various means would also bring a-life researchers closer to those bifurcating goals.

A stocky, grey-haired mustached Hungarian in his sixties, Lindenmayer had come to the United States soon after World War II and in 1956 received a doctorate from Michigan in plant physiology. But his focus shifted during a postdoctoral study in England with the logician J. H. Woodger, an exacting curmudgeon who attempted to bring biology to heel by axiomatizing its theories. Lindenmayer began thinking about using mathematical formulas to describe plant development.

The means he used was a formal language theory, a mathematical grammar postulated on the theory of algorithms. Language theory had particular significance in biology because the interpretation of the genetic code was a product of a natural grammar that used an alphabet of four letters to dictate recipes for complete organisms. Lindenmayer's system had something in common with cellular automata: it proceeded by discrete time steps and with every step each symbol would look first to its neighbors and then to a specific rule to see which symbol it would be in the next tick of the clock. The rules in Lindenmayer's system relied on self-similarity in the form of recursion, a programming technique where functions can refer to themselves. The result could include end-less simultaneous permutations based on a single variable, just as a television camera pointed at a monitor repeated an image ad infinitum.

The very assumption that a simple algorithmic formula could dare to predict such a seemingly complicated consequence as the growth of a plant seemed astounding. But, if it could be done, it would further indicate that the complex self-organizing principles in nature could be embodied in the pure realm of mathematics and computation.

Evidence that this grammar could indeed be used to model biological processes appeared in an extremely simple example—a Lindenmayer system that happened to correspond to the growth pattern of a particular form of algae. There were two sorts of cells in the early stages of this plant form; they differed in size and readiness to divide. In the mathematical model, each cell type was represented by a symbol, either a or b. Their development was generated by two rules:

Rule 1: an a in the current step becomes ab in the next step
Rule 2: a b in the current step becomes a in the next step

The process began with an initial string, known as the axiom, in this example a string of two symbols ab. After the first time step, the string was transformed to aba (applying rule 1 to a yielded $ab;$ applying rule 2 to b yielded a.) One more time step changed aba to $abaab$. The time step after that yielded $abaababa$, a fairly complex result for only three ticks of the computational clock. Because this particular example corresponded to a plant form in the natural world, one could check the veracity of the mathematical system by peering into a microscope to see whether the algae developed in the same way as the system. (It did.)

The rule sets formed in his language came to be known as L-systems. Lindenmayer intended L-systems to be used purely as mathematical constructs describing the development systems of plants. Using L-systems, one could create endless sets of production rules that may or may not have any correspondence to occurrences in nature.

In 1970, however, two of his graduate students at the University of Utrecht in the Netherlands, Ben Hesper and Pauline Hogeweg, wondered whether L-systems could be exploited to actually draw botanic forms. The results of these experiments would not be plants themselves, nor would they be models of plants, but a hybrid, an offspring of nature and logic.

Hesper and Hogeweg spent two weeks working on a computer program that would interpret an L-system rule set to generate something that branched and formed like a plant. "The L-Systems themselves don't generate images," explains Hogeweg. "They generate long strings. There's a second step necessary to generate images. You must *interpret* the string as branches and so on."

The string they eventually turned over to the attendant at a computer lab some miles way (the computer at Utrecht had insufficient power) consisted of around five thousand symbols. Then, as was the procedure, the attendant fed the cards into the computer and waited until the machine processed the program. Some hours later, the researchers returned to the lab to find an extremely baffled attendant. Instead of a series of numbers, the output of this program looked like . . . a fern! A rather elegant one, too. Because it was not really modeled on a plant but was a result of morphogenesis from an L-system string, the researchers decided to call the structure a "morpheme."

Hogeweg and Hesper rushed back to Utrecht to show the morpheme to Lindenmayer himself. His reaction was chilly. "He didn't like our work," recalls Hogeweg. "He felt that L-Systems were part of mathematical theory, and you shouldn't dilute them by producing pictures. He wasn't excited then about pursuing that avenue." Even after the two doctoral students published an influential paper in 1974 that exhaustively studied a set of 3,584 L-system trees, Lindenmayer regarded morphemes as a charming yet inconsequential curiosity; he used the image on his Christmas cards.

One person who became drawn to Lindenmayer's work after seeing a plantlike morpheme was a young mathematician named Alvy Ray Smith III. During the late 1960s Smith, disenchanted by the military use of computers, sought more benign applications: he settled on cellular automata and self-reproducing systems. His Ph.D. thesis was a brilliant proof that one could construct a universal computer in a 1-D CA. But, as Smith became more established in his field, he once again questioned his own role.

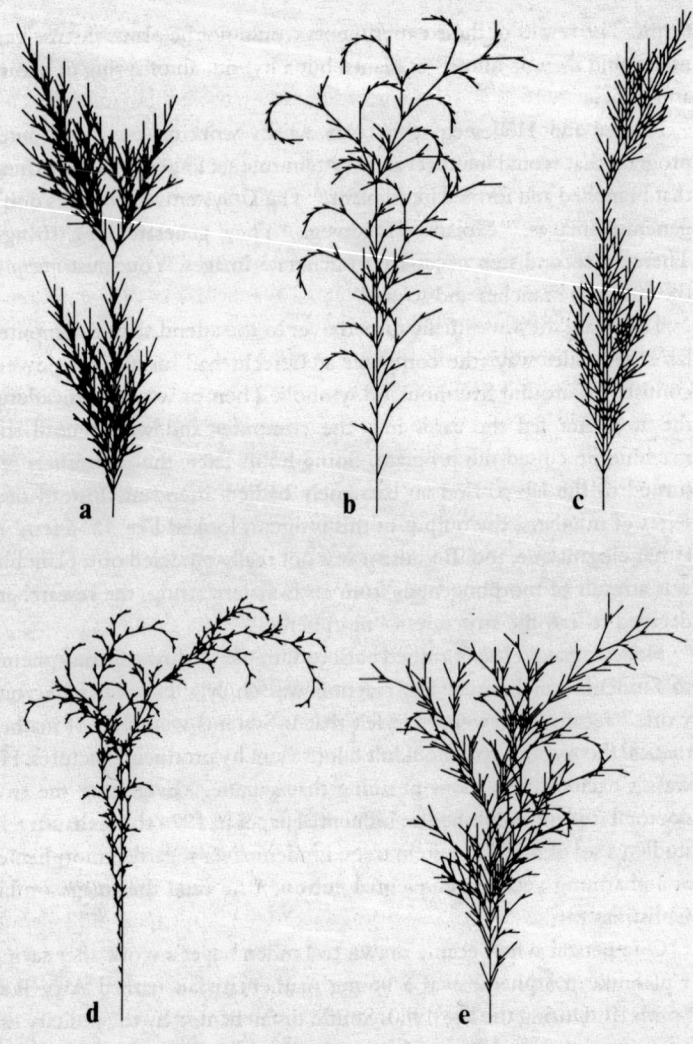

*Pauline Hogeweg and Ben Hesper generated these ferns by using L-systems, Aristid
Lindenmayer's mathematical development systems.*

"I wanted to think of computers as more than just sterile, number-crunching things," he explains. "There seemed three ways to realize this—using them to understand consciousness, using them to understand life, or applying them to create art. One of the reasons I had been attracted to cellular automata was that they seemed to be related to living things—like von Neumann's self-reproducing automaton—and that you could think of the visual configurations of CAs evolving through time as graphics or movies. But I felt isolated. Here we were in the middle of protests over Vietnam, and I was working on something I could discuss with maybe 100 people in the world—if that many. What was the contribution to the greater good?"

In 1974 Smith ventured to a conference in Noordwijkerhout, Netherlands, cochaired by Lindenmayer. It was held at a daffodil ranch where flowers filled the eye from horizon to horizon. Someone handed Smith a paper with one of Hogeweg's images. It touched something very deep in Smith. Later, he would recall how he was moved by the image—something that was a plant but not a plant. Something obviously lifelike but not alive. And there was a more personal reason for his fascination: Smith's father had been a botanist.

Soon after that conference, Smith visited the fabled research center, Xerox Palo Alto Research Center (PARC), where researchers were experimenting in interactive software and displays that could generate complex images. Smith realized how computer science and art could meld into a single discipline—through simulating reality by generating images with the complexity of nature. Smith's main concern from that point was drawing pictures, and he drew on his background in formal languages and CAs to become one of the world's best-known computer-graphics artists, winning cult status as one of the prime wizards in George Lucas's special effects operation. But he never lost interest in using these pragmatic processes to shed light on the essence of natural systems—and on life itself. As Smith wrote in a 1982 technical memo:

> Geometric computation is a path to understanding natural phenomena. The question is: How far does form divorced from physics go towards a profound knowledge? Consider man: How much understanding of his shape can be gleaned from treating the embryo as a

living geometric computation? The thesis is that pure computed form is a way of understanding the complexity of lifeforms and natural shapes.

Smith saw two powerful means of producing these complex, natural-seeming results from simple rules. One involved the fractal geometry first devised by Benoit Mandelbrot of IBM. Fractals relied on self-similarity to generate infinite complexity. Although Smith found the spirit of fractals inspiring and instructive, he chose to pursue the other approach, "parallel graph languages" based on L-systems. He called these "graftals." Smith designed software that utilized L-systems, along with other techniques, to generate structures for trees, flowers, bushes, and herbs; after a process of electronic touch-up, or "rendering," these images would appear on the screen with stunning verisimilitude. Symbols interpreted could become stands of Aspen spruce, blinding fields of wildflowers, or the restful daffodils Smith recalled from Noordwijkerhout.

In no way, of course, were the artificial plants alive. Yet their inescapable realism encouraged observers to believe that the machinery of life was within human grasp.

"We can get artificial forms of sufficient complexity that we human beings say it looks like life—but if you look at the details, it's nowhere close," says Smith. "It doesn't grow like life, it doesn't have the inner structure that organisms have. But what it tells me is that even though natural plants look complex and hard to understand, they might be understandable, because the rules that drive their form probably are not as hard as they might appear to be at first. In other words, you can get the complexity of plants fairly simply."

Peter Oppenheimer was another computer scientist experimenting with systems that generated botanic forms. He believed that creating artificial ferns and trees could illuminate the natural mechanism of self-similarity. As a consequence, Oppenheimer's work stuck closely to fractal geometry—he actually worked with Mandelbrot while an undergraduate at Princeton. However, the computational-tree-generating system he implemented at the New York Institute of Technology utilized other algorithms as well. A few knobs controlled parameters for tree branching, growth rate, degree of twistiness, and other factors. An equivalent to mutation was provided in that he allowed random variation in the interpretation of the parameters. "This way, I could use one seed to create a whole forest of trees," he says. In the sense that the person turning the knobs became an instrument of selection, the system was similar to Dawkins's and Sims's, although evolution was not a factor in the process. Rather, like Hogeweg and Hesper's L-systems and Smith's graftals, Oppenheimer's system made trees from symbols by what was essentially a morphogenetic algorithm, like that at work inside living cells that interpreted DNA instructions.

An odd thing happened to Oppenheimer as he produced image after image of near-photographic renderings of trees. As he turned the dials to tune the parameters so that his trees would look natural, he began to *sense* the geometry that formed them. He felt he had rediscovered a path trod by biology. Both plants and his own mathematical representations of them followed this trajectory, propelled by rules of self-organization.

Oppenheimer had stumbled on a concept that had engaged von Neumann, Langton, Farmer, and any number of a-lifers: life consists not of aggregations of matter, but processes that organize that matter. Yet-uncharted principles of complexity direct matter toward life, and the emergent result is a variety of shapes and behaviors that we can confidently identify as living. By rediscovering these principles, by correctly twisting the knobs of mathematics and information, we can create images—and eventually organisms—that derive from those principles with equal fidelity.

In the mid-1980s these life artists were joined by Przemyslaw Prusinkiewicz, an Eastern European computer scientist then teaching at the University of Regina in Canada. Prusinkiewicz had been working with fractals until he read one of Alvy Ray Smith's papers; he immediately wrote his own program utilizing L-systems to generate structures. In 1986, he met Lindenmayer. "That was a turning point," he once said of that meeting. "I was no longer happy with pretty pictures—I wanted plants based on nature."

By then, Lindenmayer no longer frowned on interpretations of his system that yielded pretty pictures. He understood that the mechanics of visual representation of L-systems were helpful in realizing his original goal—creating an analogue of plant development that would shed light on the natural process. Thus, when one used L-systems to create a realistic-looking daisy, apple twig, or unclassifiable hybrid, the result was not only a striking visual image but also a graph representing some progress achieved in mimicking the gears of nature. "In this sense," he wrote with Prusinkiewicz, "interactive computer graphics complements the mathematical theory of L-systems by providing a tool for formulating and verifying biological hypotheses."

Prusinkiewicz began a collaboration with Lindenmayer that lasted until Lindenmayer died in 1990. They used a sophisticated programming system dubbed a "virtual laboratory," that interpreted L-system symbols to striking effect. Various L-systems rule sets proved amenable to an impressive variety of botanic forms. Certain rules mimicked growth, branching, leaf formation, and budding. Combined with geometric information, these could be rendered into gorgeous images of, for instance, sunflowers, herbs, and palm trees.

Beautiful as these were, it was the developmental process itself that most interested the pair. L-systems were capable of reflecting the actual growth of plants according to various conditions, like food intake and weather variables. In a neutral environment, assuming a steady source of sunlight, water, and ground nutrients, the plant could be generated cell by cell, as it grew in regular patterns or, using probabilistic rules, sprouted with the uniqueness one sees in the field. The virtual environment could be manipulated; rules could be written to limit growth according to the presence of a certain value, which might be viewed as the amount of sunlight, of photosynthesis, or of a growth hormone.

Lindenmayer and Prusinkiewicz and their students also began simulating the cellular development of organisms. Using L-systems, it was possible to begin with a single cell, to grow a multicellular embryo, and to proceed from there. The evidence of a photo-realist L-systems sunflower indicated that nature took a similar tack in creating its own sunflower. An even stronger case for this confluence was made by viewing the stages of embryonic development of an artificial fern resembling *Microsorium linguaeforme*, in an experiment by Martin de Boer. Using a "map L-system" that grew and divided cells by rules that depended on which combinations of cell neighbors pushed against the wall of a given cell, de Boer's nascent fern was eerily parallel to microscopic photographs of the real thing. The shapes were nearly identical, but nothing in the rules implied that that would be the case. The artificial gametophyte's form was determined by the complex interaction of new cells pushing against recently divided cells. "The result is particularly interesting from a biological perspective," Prusinkiewicz and Lindenmayer wrote, "since it indicates that genetically controlled cell division patterns play an important role in determining the shape of a structure."

It also indicated an intriguing direction of artificial life: to begin with a single artificial cell and, using a set of principles or rules, to grow an actual being. The embryological path to artificial life.

That same idea first inspired Stewart Wilson, an otherwise rather conservative computer scientist, to begin experimenting in artificial life. "I'd been thinking about it for a long time," he recalls, "and finally put together a concept where you'd have these *rules,* starting from an egg. It occurred to me that you could base that whole development process on a kind of program, a production-system program . . . and this program would be carried out inside each and every cell, each cell would have a copy of this program. As we know, that's the dogma, the doctrine. So [in this development system], if you're a fertilized egg, you look at your program and if you find there's nobody around you, you split and become two cells. At that stage it's deterministic, but later it isn't necessarily so—there might be a certain competition that occurs between some cells that match. Then there are two cells, and they grow, and at a certain point there are other rules, and you let it grow and let it grow and you have this aggregate of cells. And then you have some way of rating that for fitness. You can do this, because now you have a phenotype."

In the early 1980s Wilson was envisioning a merger of the sort of embryonic development suggested by sophisticated L-systems and the evolutionary biology practiced by Danny Hillis. But at the time he hatched this concept he was a scientist working in what Chris Langton considered the woodwork, contemplating work in a field on the cusp of existence. The procedure would have been an ambitious scheme and, as he readily admits, too much an undertaking for that time.

Trained as an electrical engineer and a physicist, Wilson became increasingly fascinated by information theory and its relationship to learning. How did an organism adapt to its surroundings? Could computer programs perform the same sorts of adaptation? In 1979 he came across a reference to the work of John Holland. Wilson ventured into the MIT computer science library in the basement of the Technology Square building—next door to Polaroid, where Wilson then worked as a researcher—and found Holland's book. Although it was four years old, it had yet to be checked out. The GA approach fascinated Wilson, but he became even more excited by a subsequent development of Holland: a much-expanded adaptation scheme called "classifier systems." This seemed to Wilson an ideal substrate for autonomous artificial creatures. Classifier systems not only made use of the process of evolution but also allowed for individual learning.

John Holland had been halfway through writing his study of adaptation when he began contemplating such a system. "I was very optimistic about genetic algorithms," he now recalls. "An awful lot of my intuition was tied to genetics. And yet, in the back of my mind, I asked myself, Why can't [the creature] change as it goes along? If it doesn't like [the process of changing its] nucleotides, why can't it use something else?"

That something else was a means of adapting on an individual level rather than on a population level over a period of generations. In order to do this, Holland's organisms would require some sort of sensory input, so they could sample their environment. One day Holland was lunching with a student and discussing different ways an artificial organism might classify its surroundings. The student asked how one might make such an organism so it would be able to make judgments about the environment adaptively, so that it could adjust to its surroundings. In other words, how could it learn? Holland realized that his system should answer that question and more: artificial organisms should not only classify their environment but also *act* on what they classified.

Holland came up with classifier systems, a self-contained scheme for machine learning. Unlike genetic algorithms, classifiers were not closely based on nature: they integrated GAs, pure logic, economic theory, and computer science. "I wanted a general purpose learning system," Holland says. "So I felt free to borrow from whatever."

The shift was significant. Not only were GAs powerful but also they were implicit commentators on the evolutionary process. If a scientist conducted a genetic algorithm experiment that yielded fascinating results, it was reasonable to wonder whether a corresponding phenomenon in nature merited study. Classifier systems had a smaller claim to a kinship with life as we know it. However, their extended powers qualified them as objects of study in and of themselves. Like many of the lifelike artificial systems that researchers would undoubtedly create in the next decades, they ventured deeper into the realm of alternate life and drew not only on biology but also on other sorts of known complex systems.

Holland's experiment began, as did most canonical a-life ventures, with strings of random numbers. These were the classifiers themselves. Classifiers were rules, interpreted in what was called a condition–action, or if–then, format. The classifiers activated "messages," which were stored on a message list, much like a bulletin board at a local supermarket. Messages were pieces of information: a fact about the environment or a report of the success of a previous action.

The classifier system used "detectors" to perceive facts about its environment and, encoding those facts as messages, posted them on the message board. If the messages on the board satisfied the conditions of classifier rules, then action would be taken—in the form of posting a message in the next step. (This could trigger the posting of further messages in subsequent steps.) Finally, certain messages would trigger activation of output devices called "effectors," which would cause the system to interact in some way with the environment. Stripped to the bone, the flow seemed obvious: input, message reading and posting, output. The middle step, of course, was what translated information into the behaviors of life.

Holland liked to illustrate the process by postulating a fanciful classifier system that simulated some of the behaviors of a frog. The goals of the frog were getting food and avoiding predators. Holland provided the following list of rules, previously discovered by the classifying process:

Rules

IF small, flying object to left THEN send @.

IF small, flying object to right THEN send %.

IF small, flying object centered THEN send ¢.

IF large, looming object THEN send !.

IF no large looming object THEN send ★.

IF ★ and @ THEN move head 15° left.

IF ★ and % THEN move head 15° right.

IF ★ and ¢ THEN move in direction head pointing.

IF ! THEN move rapidly away from direction head pointing.

Message List

(Holds most recent messages)

★ @.

In this example, the artificial frog had already used the detector function to post messages on the message list. The presence of the messages ★ and @ on the list indicated that there was a small flying object to the left—probably a nice, juicy insect—and that no large looming object— the earmark of a predator—was present. The joint presence of those two messages would trigger the sixth rule on the list, and then the frog would move its head to the left. It would then be in position to eat the small flying object.

If moving its head to the left proved a successful stratagem in this situation, then the system would reward it. Positive feedback. Indeed, after every step, the rule set underwent an evaluation. A problem arose, however: when a result was obtained from following the entire set of rules, how did the system know which specific rules to reward? Holland would illustrate this problem with the example of a triple jump in checkers: this triumphant move would reap instant reward, but in all probability it had been the result of several clever preceeding moves. Those, too, should be rewarded. In some cases, there could be hundreds of complex rules associated with a positive result, some of the rules irrelevant, some subtly flawed, and others deceptively effective.

Holland addressed this problem by treating the rules as bidders in a market economy. He viewed each rule as a small business. Its product was a message. Each time a rule appeared it made an implicit "bid" for its business, like a construction company making a bid for a job. The value of the bid was paid off to other rules with which it became associated. Those other rules became, in effect, companies that provided business supplies—the equivalent of building materials—to that first rule. In order for a rule to survive, its payoff had to exceed the amount invested by its bid. If a set of rules "won," the payoff was given to the virtual contractor, which in turn would pay off its suppliers.

Under this system, a short, effective rule might go into business with many other rules. Those rules could, in turn, find more complicated partners and become "chained" to those. Those might be chained to still others. But no matter how complicated the rules became, the payoff would find its way back to the first, elementary rule. The intermediate rules acted as middlemen, receiving a large payoff and then distributing

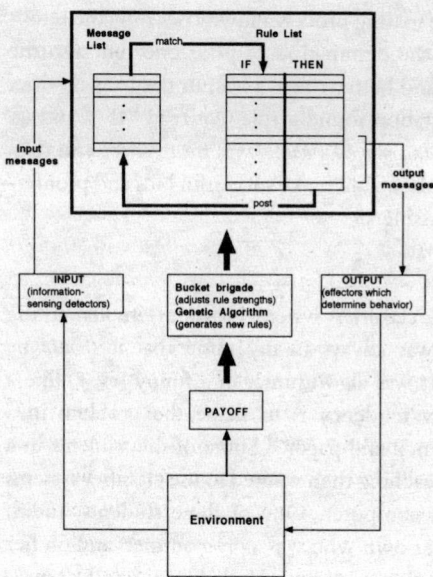

A schematic of a classifier system. One can view the upper box as a creature. Its detectors get information from the environment, which it handles by a process of posting and matching messages (classifiers). This determines its behavior. After each step it evaluates the result of its behavior and modifies its internal rules. Ultimately, the most efficacious rules win out, including powerful new rules generated by an evolutionary process. The creature adapts to its environment.

portions of it to their "suppliers." One might also view the amount due to the first rule as a lump sum handled through a series of intermediaries, who passed it down the line like a hot dog at a ballgame or a bucket of water directed toward a raging inferno by an old-time fire-fighting squad. Holland had the latter example in mind when he dubbed this credit-allocation process "the bucket brigade algorithm." "I had read some account of Benjamin Franklin's about colonial bucket brigades, and it seemed like the kind of thing that would describe the process," he explains. It proved reliably efficacious in allowing powerful rules to proliferate and maintain their presence. In Holland's terminology, these small yet essential rules formed the building blocks on which any complex adaptive system relied. In the case of the frog classifier system listed above, the final rule listed, which kept the frog away from deadly predators, was of obvious value in all situations. As an economic entity, it had potential for a booming business.

The other major tool in classifier systems, of course, was the genetic algorithm. The best rules were mated, their offspring given the opportunity to compete in the behavioral bazaar. Because of the GA's ability to produce novel variations, the mating process allowed not only the retention of successful rules and the elimination of poor ones but also the potential creation of better and better rules. Thus, in the frog classifier system, if a crossover or mutation found a rule that read "IF ★ and @ THEN move head 15° left *and move forward*" was more successful than its abbreviated parent, that rule would make successful bids and proliferate in the community of classifiers.

Typically, Holland devised classifier systems without implementing them on a computer. "It was always in my mind that it *should* be implementable," he says. "It was algorithmic, in a funny sense, like a computer program. But my tendency is to shape the problem in a mathematical sense, with pencil and paper." Some of the students in a psychology seminar he was teaching then wanted to use classifier systems to simulate organisms on a computer. One of these students, Judith Reitman, had a student of her own who was a programmer, and on her suggestion this student began programming Holland's system to represent an organism running through a maze. The classifer-system creature not only negotiated its way through the labyrinth but developed maze-running skills that stood it in good stead when placed in an entirely different maze.

Another Holland disciple, Lashon Booker, more fully implemented the idea of an artificial creature in a classifier system. Booker's creature, dubbed "GOFER," ventured into a two-dimensional world containing "food" and "poison." It was GOFER's task to distinguish between the two while remaining well fed. GOFER discovered a set of rules that allowed it to classify the objects in its universe and was able, by acting on those rules, both to eat heartily and to avoid digital salmonella.

For Stewart Wilson, all this was a revelation. He lived and worked in Cambridge, Massachusetts, probably the world center of artificial intelligence research. Yet here was a computable system that allowed computers to independently develop ingenious solutions to difficult problems—and the AI establishment ignored it!

Wilson's initial foray in classifier systems addressed a problem he was working on at Polaroid. Although he successfully applied Holland's system to computer vision, directing a video camera to center and focus on an object within its field of vision, Wilson wanted to explore classifier systems in a different, purer way. After his appointment in 1981 to a post at the Rowland Institute, an elite research center funded by Polaroid founder Edward Land, he enjoyed freedom to pursue any avenue he chose—even an experiment as strange as creating an artificial animal. In an unintentionally Kafka-esque twist, Wilson referred to his creature only as "*."

The creature * had simple needs: it lived to eat. But like many mammals, it arrived in its world with undeveloped cognitive survival tools. Before it could feast on the artificial meals that Wilson had spread over the forestlike terrain like Hansel's bread crumbs, * had to learn what food was. Also, *'s ability to roam was impaired by objects representing trees or rocks. Its vision was extremely limited, but its sensing was enhanced by a sort of radar—an analogue, Wilson figured, to a sense of smell—that allowed it to determine what was in its immediate neighborhood. It also had pleasure and pain sensors. When it bit something that turned out to be food, * would get a rush of pleasure akin to a bite of a cheeseburger after some hours of fasting. Biting a rock, or bumping into a tree, would hurt.

In a digital equivalent of an Outward Bound program, Wilson dropped ★ into the environment and observed, hands off, as it attempted to survive.

"He actually *learned,"* says Wilson of ★. "He created classifiers. After he bumped into a rock he got painful feedback, but since there was often food around rocks, he learned not only that he shouldn't knock into it, but that he shouldn't wander away, because there's probably going to be food at the other side. And when ★ was out in the open, he developed this interesting sort of behavior. He wouldn't move randomly, but drift in one direction, which incidentally is the best strategy for someone in a fog. And as soon as he saw something, he would respond immediately. If it was food he'd immediately eat it, and if it was a rock, he'd proceed around it."

One might note that instead of using the indefinite pronoun, Wilson referred to ★ as "he." Sheepishly, he acknowledges this tendency. "You anthromorphize things so quickly with these little creatures," he explains. "You cheer him on."

Wilson was most proud of ★ for its—or *his*—ability to defer immediate gratification, to chain its strategies by virtue of a bucket-brigade algorithm. ★ came to understand that sometimes one must endure unrewarding circumstances before enjoying fulfillment. Although Wilson claimed that ★ was the first artificial creature to learn this lesson, he believed that the phenomenon was an expected consequence of using classifier systems. "These are systems with positive feedback," he explains. "And that's what a Darwinian system is—something that's good just gets better. It's a multiple optimization system in that a creature has to be able to deal with lots of different things in the world, and can't devote all its resources to dealing with the food problem. Otherwise it's going to die. So it gets awfully good at the problem."

How good? Before any learning, an artificial creature in Wilson's virtual forest would require an average of forty-one steps to reach food. On the other hand, ★, after one thousand time steps, generally managed to dine in less than six steps. After another two thousand steps ★ had the ability to procure a meal every four and a half steps.

Wilson was so impressed with ★'s development of survival skills that his own view of artificial intelligence and machine learning refocused. He now judged classical AI as misguided. Instead, he had cast his lot with the alternate strategy—using emergent processes to make machines behave with the novelty and cunning of nature's creations. Thinking the term "artificial animal" as somewhat verbose, he called his idea the "animat" path toward artificial intelligence.

"In standard AI, basically, the effort seems to have been to take some fragment of high human competence like playing chess or proving theorems, and make a program that can do that," he says. "And you do have these marvelous programs that play chess very well, and so on. But they're not very good at reasoning and search—they're not adaptive. They can't generalize. If you say to one of these chess programs, 'OK, now let's play checkers,' they can't. Also, they don't deal with the perceptual problem—a chess program might have inputs about what's on the game board, but there's nothing visual about it. You have beautiful crystalline results like excellent chess, but the programs are very brittle. The animat approach says, 'Let's start very differently—let's try to maintain the holism all the way. Let's go down to a very low level, as low as we have to go, to the point where we have a complete environment, a somewhat realistic simulated environment.' And then you gradually complicate it, you make it more and more difficult, and the creatures adapt. Sometimes you may have to add to the architectures of the creatures, but you do that only as little as necessary—the game is to use as much adaptation as possible all the way out. So then, the Holy Grail is that you would get to the higher level, the human stuff. That's the animat path to AI."

Or, as Wilson stated in a paper about animats,

> the basic hypothesis of the animat approach is that by simulating and understanding complete animal-like systems at a simple level, we can build up gradually to the human. . . . We hope to reach human intelligence from below instead of piecemeal through high-level competences as in Standard AI.

This marched lockstep with Langton's observation that artificial life must be pursued from the bottom up, a conviction now shared by almost all of the community devoted to generating a computational biology with lifelike digital creatures.

Wilson was delighted that his own experiments found their way into a developing new discipline. Yet he worried that the quick growth of a-life studies might result in a redundancy of effort, or, equally bad, in an accumulation of experiments whose validity cannot be evaluated because of the inability to compare them to other experiments. "What we really need is a theory of environments," he says. "Researchers will show you their artificial organisms, and these things may be doing great—reproducing, surviving, and everything—but then you say, 'So what?' What problem have you solved? We need a taxonomy—we need to know what we mean by an easy environment, and what we mean by a difficult one. And we also need a theory of creature efficiency. So that if you have two different creatures you can put them in the same environment and compare. And if they do well, then you complicate the environment. You would then be able to know whether or not a creature represents a step forward."

Wilson therefore proposed a means by which one can precisely judge the performance of an artificial creature within its environment. Someone might be able to claim, "I have used an environment of type x in the *Alpha* family tree of environments, and the creature I have placed in this survives with an efficiency value of E, a level previously unattained." Although James Crutchfield, as we have seen, was also interested in establishing benchmark environments, his purpose was directed more toward creating an index of complexity rather than toward a level playing field for opposing artificial organisms. Wilson hoped that a well-calibrated set of universes, ascending in difficulty, would actually spur the creation of creatures that venture closer and closer to the realm of the living.

Wilson did not say, however, at what point we can definitively state that on survival in a certain environment—universe JW-419 or whatever—a creature must be deemed alive. He had no comment as to which point in the hierarchy of artificial worlds determined a space where living artificial organisms would emerge. He believed that one could make progress toward understanding and simulating the behavior of life without immersing oneself in the murky implications of a definition of life itself.

Others were less circumspect. Among these were Norman Packard, the childhood friend of Doyne Farmer, creator of CA snowflakes and currently a physicist at the Center for Complex Systems Research at the University of Illinois. Packard was very much in agreement with Wilson that a standard means of measuring progress in artificial environments was required, but he preferred to link the quest with a frank attempt to define the nature of the phenomenon. He began a paper cowritten with philosopher Mark Bedau with a confrontational gauntlet:

> What is life? How can it be recognized? In an everyday context these questions seem tantalizingly clear—a cat is alive and a rock is not. But formalizing this distinction is difficult especially if the formalization is to be used in empirical measurements. In this paper we present an empirically measurable statistical quality that distinguishes life.

For Packard and Bedau, a professor at Reed College, the matter was simple: "We believe that life is a property that an organism has if and only if it is a member of an evolving biological system of organisms interacting with each other and with their environment," they wrote. They saw life as a property associated with that environment; an organism was not alive in the long term, but a temporary participant in an evolving biosphere. Although the property of aliveness was complex, three aspects were identifiable: an information-processing apparatus, a capability to perform functions by way of a complex structure, and an ability over generations to modify and innovate on that structure spontaneously. The latter, of course, referred to evolution.

To Packard and Bedau, the key measure of aliveness was an evaluation of what they called "evolutionary activity." They quantified this by measuring the movement of beneficial, or useful, genes within the gene pool of a particular species. Useful genes were those that increased the fitness of organisms that inherited them. "The continual retention of new useful genetic material indicates that the population is continually enhancing the gene pool," they explained.

Packard and Bedau identified this movement of beneficial genes as "telic waves." The term was controversial because use of the word "teleology" bordered on taboo among biologists—evolution did not proceed according to a predefined purpose but by incremental increases in fitness driven by the requirements of survival in the particular environment. Here, the term was used in a different manner: "The teleology in telic waves presupposes no deity directing things behind the scene," wrote the coauthors. The teleology was a posteriori—Monday morning quarterbacking on the genes that, in retrospect, worked to improve the species. Reflecting on these genetic changes, one could say that they were purposeful without admitting that it was anyone's intent to bring about this purpose. Or so went the rhetorical footwork of Packard and Bedau.

Looking farther into the future, they envisioned a circumstance where purposefulness does have its place. Unlike populations driven solely by evolution, the organisms in these models would be sophisticated enough to act on explicit goals—precisely as human beings perform acts with conscious intent, so would these. This would be known as "mental teleology," where adaptations indeed come about to fulfill a predetermined purpose. In those cases, the telic waves would be based not on survival but on psychological adaptations or on learning.

The particular computer model designed by Packard in the late 1980s had no such mental teleology. If artificial environments were rated on a scale of theme parks, this would fall far short of Disneyland, although it might stand as an interesting roadside attraction. Organisms that Packard referred to as "bugs" were placed in a world dotted with heaps of food, from which the bugs could draw energy. The bugs had sufficient intelligence to seek and identify food, but every movement drained their energy. When its energy was totally drained, the bug died. On the other hand, when a bug accumulated a certain amount of food, it reproduced. In one version of this biosphere, reproduction was asexual, and the genome of the offspring was subject to mutation. In a later version, two bugs sexually reproduced and the offspring's genome was a product of mutation and crossover. As the bugs evolved, and increased their ability to gather food in the most efficient manner, Packard and Bedau measured the movement of the genes in the entire gene pool by charting the telic waves. This was done by evaluating and measuring the activity of those genes that increased the fitness of the bug population. By publishing the results of their calculations, they implicitly invited others to subject their own environments to the same test.

Packard and Bedau thought that the telic wave idea not only promoted a benchmark to compare artificial environments but also provided the equivalent of a Turing test to determine what is alive. "In this context," they wrote, "positive activity would indicate an entity's continual incorporation of new behavioral or psychological patterns of activity." The presence of telic waves in a system would be evidence that life is present. Real life. One could even evaluate natural biological populations with this measure, although the task would be difficult because wet life, unlike artificial life, selfishly shrouds its genetic content from researchers who wish to measure genetic movement.

Did this mean that Packard and Bedau considered something as elementary as the energy-seeking digital bugs in their model actually alive? When posed with the question, Packard was equivocal. "When the simulation ends I don't feel a big sense of remorse because they're all dead," he admits. "But when the simulation is going I do identify them as having a certain element of living-ness, even though it's crude. I've made a list of things that I think characterize a living system and I think they satisfy all those criteria."

Skeptics would rush to disagreement. But Packard was less interested in dazzling doubters and carbaquists than in determining a litmus test for a quality that indicates that *life lives here*. He thought that the pursuit was a logical step from his work in Stephen Wolfram's CA lab at the Institute for Advanced Study. The link between CAs and evolving organisms in artificial ecosystems, he claimed, was that both were complex dynamic systems with an element of creativity. "The snowflakes were a physical system that displayed certain levels of creativity," he says. "There is some aspect of the dynamics of cellular automata that could conceivably generate an endless stream of novel complex forms that get frozen into those snowflakes. I think a version of that is what's happening in life, too. There is something about the life process that's creating this endless stream of diverse complex forms, and it's that process I really want to get a handle on."

That same urge motivated David Jefferson. He was a lanky, intense, and sometimes acerbic computer scientist who in the early 1980s was teaching at the University of Southern California. He had already established himself in his field by his "time warp" parallel simulation algorithm. Then, pursuing a long-held interest in evolution, he came across Dawkins's book *The Selfish Gene* and became fascinated with the workings of biology, which, it now seemed obvious to him, were so closely linked to the mechanics of information. He set about creating his own silicon world, populated by what he called "programinals." The term may have sounded like a slick brainstorm from a toy marketer, but Jefferson was serious about his task. Although he considered artificial intelligence to be a valuable pursuit, he believed that artificial life would ultimately be a more powerful quest. "I'm interested in life, not intelligence," he explains. "Intelligence to me is incredibly exciting, yet a footnote in the history of life. One thing that drives me is the desire to create life inside these computers: To create life from non-life."

His first experiment was a simple competition between predators and prey. Jefferson's digital organisms, strings of LISP code, represented foxes and rabbits. He assumed that as his animals evolved, he would generate a classic predator-prey arms race—foxes would thrive until rabbits developed a response to the threat, whereupon a variant of the foxes would develop a subsequent response. Ad infinitum. At first, his system did respond in that manner but then seemed to follow its own emergent agenda. The rabbit population would suddenly dissolve, and the food-deprived foxes would follow them into extinction. Jefferson was not sufficiently trained as a biologist to understand what has happening, but he thought he had his answer after reading a paper by evolutionary biologist Robert May about instability in ecosystems: only in very large populations could Jefferson attain the classic oscillation he had hoped for. The relatively small populations he was working with courted unstable oscillations and sudden extinctions—they were at risk, exactly like small populations in the natural world.

Jefferson tried further variations. At one point, he devised a system in which he created two similar types of animals, equal in fighting ability and pitted against each other. He assumed that the populations of the two species would fluctuate as one gained a temporary evolutionary advantage and another developed a response. To his surprise, one species quickly dominated, forcing the other into extinction. Poring over the code for the organisms of the victorious species, he discovered that the difference had been a devastatingly advantageous point mutation in the genome of the winning species. Paradoxically, this particular mutation (like most mutations suffered by organisms) weakened the individual animals—it turned off their powers of locomotion. These creatures remained fixed in their initial location, as immobile as rocks. But the specific parameters of Jefferson's system made this handicap beneficial. By not moving, the animals avoided venturing into the field of vision of potential foes. They conserved energy and waited for enemies to come to them, whereupon they vanquished them.

There were two lessons here. First was a general lesson about artificial ecosystems: it bordered on impossibility to create these with absolute fidelity to the natural world. However, excellent debugging could, and inevitably would, be performed by the organisms themselves. If a programmer erred in designing an environment and exposed the possibility that a certain adaptation would exploit the error, one could count on an evolving digital organism seizing the opportunity, as surely as a high-priced drug lawyer detects a loophole in a search warrant. Jefferson's realization of this first lesson led to the second thing he learned from his programinals: he obviously needed to integrate more biological knowledge into his efforts, preferably in collaboration with a biologist.

The problem was resolved when Jefferson met Charles Taylor, a population biologist at UCLA. Chuck Taylor had long harbored a secret passion—a desire to trace the evolution of consciousness. He was fascinated by the seemingly miraculous chain of events that led a series of molecular interactions four billion years ago to result in subjective experience in human beings. After winning tenure in 1978, at the UC campus in Riverside, he subtly shifted his professional focus to address that topic. Interviewing for the position at UCLA, he wisely refrained from mentioning his willingness to use an unconventional tool—the computer—to pursue his goals. Only after he was safely hired did he begin in earnest. He read up on Turing machines and AI. A friend pointed him to Holland's work, and he was thrilled by the genetic algorithm. By 1982, when Jefferson appeared with news of his digital organisms, Taylor already realized that artificial life could become a powerful means of practicing biology. Jefferson offered Taylor not only computational skill but also a methodology by which scientists might incrementally discover the process by which consciousness and mind emerged. Ideally, the a-life simulations could wind an ascending path toward the critical complexity required for consciousness.

Soon Jefferson joined Taylor on the UCLA faculty. The pair drew on funding directed through a new quasi department, Cognitive Science. Taylor also introduced Jefferson to an informal weekly conclave of faculty, the Center for the Study of Evolution and the Origin of Life, which provided a means for researchers to present even unorthodox theories in life sciences to a constructively critical group of top biologists, physicists, astronomers, psychologists, and other assorted wise folk. With Taylor's help and with the aid of a group of graduate students who helped bear the programming burden, Jefferson transformed his system into what he and his colleagues described as "a powerful new kind of tool for biological simulation, capable of modeling population behavior and evolution to a finer level of detail than any other tool we know of." They called it RAM. The name was lifted out of Jefferson's *programinal* program.

The program was essentially a malleable digital environment and construction kit for strings of LISP code that represented animals. Each time the system ticked off a step, the RAM animals could perform any or all of the following functions:

Examine the nearby environment and possibly some of the animals found there.

On the basis of the nearby environment, the time, its own age, and its state (including genes and past history) decide, perhaps probabilistically, what actions to take next.

Take action, including any or all of the following: update statistics, move, update its own memory, modify the environment or other animals, reproduce, or die.

RAM was able to abstract a fairly complex implementation of the fox-and-rabbit situation previously attempted by Jefferson. Even more interesting was an experiment simulating lek formation among sage grouse. In many species of birds and mammals, a lek is an area where mates are sought and affairs consummated. In the case of sage grouse, females walk long distances to the lek region, which comes to resemble an avian version of the Chippendale's nightclub, with males strutting and thumping before them. The females pick a mate from these. Biologists had thus far been unable to determine the criteria by which grouse choose these mating sites. Most observers believed the females determine the site based on issues such as distance, the number of males, and the competition for those males. Others insisted that the male grouse determine lek formation.

Working with Robert Gibson, a UCLA grouse specialist, the RAM team simulated the process on an Apollo workstation. "Such simulations cannot prove that one set of factors actually underlies the process," they emphasized. "But they can test whether or not a specified explanation is able to describe what is observed, and they can demonstrate that certain hypothesized explanations are inadequate." Drawing from data compiled at leks in the Sierra Nevada, they postulated a population of two hundred grouse, divided equally between male and female, attributed various grouse behaviors to each animal, and let the system run. Digital lek formation occurred in five minutes. That particular run used parameters reflecting the assumption that female choice was crucial to establishing leks. In the case where the program reflected the assumption that male dominance determined lek formation, however, the artificial grouse were unable to construct anything approaching the natural distribution of leks. Thus the male-dominance-pattern theory of lek formation was convincingly refuted—it may be mathematically impossible. After testing several variables, the RAM team found that the lek-formation patterns that best matched those in the field were the result of implementing many of the variables hypothesized by various zoologists. This suggested, but of course did not prove, that grouse considered a variety of different criteria in forming leks, with females in the driver's seat.

Soon, UCLA was on its way to becoming a major site in the pursuit of a-life. Its leaders made an odd pair: Taylor was moderate and contemplative, with a bent toward ruminating on the metaphysical and ethical ramifications of their work. He enjoyed speaking at length on the issues involved in defining life. Jefferson, on the other hand, took a firmly logical view characteristic of computer scientists beginning with von Neumann. To him, the definition-of-life issue was a red herring. If one considered an organism alive if it replicated, grew, and evolved, then artificial life was here, now, in computers at UCLA. If one demanded that life must display the complexity of natural organisms, then artificial life was not here now. Our present digital beings, he would say, fell short of even the complexity of bacterium, missing by a factor of ten thousand, maybe even a million. But Jefferson believed that in twenty or thirty years this level could be matched *in silico*.

The group included two or three other faculty members, among them Michael Dyer, the head of the university's AI lab. These were joined by several graduate students drawn to the study and creation of a-life, which was beginning to evolve its own reputation as a hot specialty in computer science, if not biology. Grant money arrived, allowing the cognitive science group to purchase a $1,200,000 Connection Machine. Using the aggregate might of 16,384 processors, Jefferson and company created the next iteration of their a-life system.

They called it Genesys.

Although Genesys was designed to accommodate the sort of direct simulation of natural phenomena performed on RAM, the massive parallelism of the Connection Machine made it particularly tempting to create original creatures on Genesys and to use them to explore issues relevant to the nature of life itself, particularly evolution. One of the first Genesys experiments was Tracker, the trail-following experiment that demonstrated the power of GAs with artificial ants following an irregular path called "the John Muir Trail." Through generations of evolution, the ants developed the ability to follow the trail perfectly.

After proving itself on the John Muir Trail, Tracker was the basis of an interesting experiment with implications for evolutionary biologists. From New Mexico, Chris Langton devised a second trail, called "the Santa Fe Trail" and challenged a population of ants bred on curves and gaps of the John Muir ants to cope with the new course. The UCLA team found that the skills required on the previous path made the artificial ants less effective as generalized trackers. Over hundreds of generations, the John Muir ants did not perform as well on the Santa Fe Trail as the descendants of a control group of "baby" ants that began from scratch on that road. The John Muir ants had overspecialized and in the process had lost the diversity necessary to draw on different genes in the pool to tackle the challenges of a new trail.

Once again, an environmental loophole asserted itself, aided by the fact that evolution seeks the shortest path to survival. The John Muir ants "weren't optimized for general trail-following, just following this one," explains Jefferson. "They were willing to use any heuristic, any shortcut, any piece of junk code that worked on that one trail. A similar situation would be trying to evolve reptiles to live undersea. You'd probably do better starting with amphibians. So here's an example of macroevolution which nobody really doubted, but as far as I know, nobody could really exhibit, either. Until we did."

Although Tracker successfully utilized the genetic algorithm to evolve tracking behavior in artificial ants, it ignored what was for a-lifers probably the most interesting aspect of ants: social behavior. An ant colony can be viewed as a superorganism; its constituent members are more like organs of a single being than self-interested individuals. Working cooperatively, the ants in the colony divide their labors, specialize their tasks, pursue shared goals, and adapt to the circumstances of their environment. Yet there is no central controller, no dispatcher ant who distributes a task list each morning. The individual ants act on their own, and emerging from their local behavior is a seemingly coordinated global behavior. "The total behavioral repertoire of an individual ant worker is relatively simple, consisting according to species of no more than 20 to 45 acts," wrote E. O. Wilson and Bert Hölldobler. "Yet the behavior of the colony as a whole is vastly more complex." This dovetailed so nicely with the artificial life paradigm that the ant became a-life's unofficial mascot. Numerous experiments in cellular automata, from Langton's vants to the Brussels group's self-organizing social insect colonies, focused on how local interactions evoke an unprogrammed, emergent behavior.

In this same spirit, and on the heels of Tracker, the a-life cadre at UCLA was eager to conduct more experiments with computational ants. When a graduate biology seminar in ant behavior was offered, half the students were computer scientists. One of these was Robert Collins, recruited into the a-life group early in 1989 by Jefferson, who was looking for someone with the skills to program the Connection Machine. "He was honest with me," recalls Collins. "He said if this artificial life stuff turns out to be reasonable, I'd be in a great position. If everyone laughs at it and nothing comes out of it, I might not be in such a great position." Collins took the risk and participated in Tracker. Working with Jefferson, as well as with the T-13 group at Los Alamos, Collins began to build a general-purpose simulator, which originally implemented a specific simulation—ants. "We wanted something that was qualitatively life-like that if you showed a video to biologists they would say that artificial life might have something to it," says Collins. Instead of the population of individual ants following trails in Tracker, this new project, dubbed "AntFarm," would use colonies of ants. The hope was to evoke emergent, self-organizing behavior.

AntFarm was probably the most complex a-life experiment to date. Certainly the Connection Machine at Boelter Hall was the busiest digital anthill in history. It originally simulated the activities of 16,384 colonies, each of which consisted of 128 members, for a total of 2,097,152 ants. The ants themselves had genomes of 25,590 bits, compared to the Tracker ants' measly 450-bit genomes. (All ants in a given colony had the same genome, but, because each ant experienced the environment differently, it would display unique behavior.) These longer chromosomes, when interpreted by the AntFarm program, gave the ants the potential to sense information about their environment over a sixteen-by-sixteen-cell grid, including information about the location of food and pheromone chemicals dropped by other ants. The AntFarm creatures were able to forage, pick up food, drop pheromones, and use a mental compass to find their way back to the nest.

Collins and Jefferson implemented several innovative techniques in AntFarm. The first was a variation on the standard GA. The UCLA team was dissatisfied with the way mates were chosen: although effective, the technique of randomly choosing partners for the fittest organisms had little to do with the way natural organisms choose mates. Important factors such as geographical proximity were left out. AntFarm used a modified mating procedure. Each successful colony would send its ants out on two "random walks" in the neighborhood of the nest. During these strolls, they would inevitably pass several other colonies where they would note the amount of food successfully foraged and stored in the nest. After each walk, the scouts would choose the colony with the most opulent larder. Those two winners were mated. This brought the GA closer in line with nature's methodology.

Another important advance in AntFarm was the organisms' "representation"—the scheme used to make digits behave like insects. Instead of using the rule-based lookup tables that accompanied finite state machines, the AntFarm ants evaluated their environment by an "artificial neural network" (ANN). This was a thicket of connections determined by heredity, not subject to learning over the course of an individual ant's lifetime. The neural network was designed so that the ants would have the potential for a wide range of behavior, but it would take generations of successful searching through evolutionary space before the ants evolved to the point where they could exploit the ANN to the fullest.

When the artificial ant colonies were first set into motion, however, the ants were unable to develop any foraging skills. Collins programmed a more sophisticated sort of neural network, but even this did not produce ants capable of foraging. The problem was solved by splitting the foraging skill into two components—searching for food and transporting food back to the nest. The ants were given a complete neural network for each component. With that two-tiered implementation, the AntFarm colonies sent out soldiers who evolved the ability to locate the food, to secure it, and to transport it to the nest.

Watching a run of AntFarm on a monitor was somewhat less engrossing than viewing a literal ant farm. Because the terrain of digital anthills covered a one-thousand-cell square grid, only a portion was shown at a given time. The ants were represented by red dots. They wandered around a bounded portion of the screen, usually in a northeasterly direction, until they chanced on green dots. These signified a packet of food. A different display, inconveniently placed in a different room, gave the statistics on each anthill, so any attempt to understand what happened on the screen was punctuated by frequent exits to verify the success of a given colony or the population in general.

Eventually, some red dots began behaving in a different manner. No longer drifting, they went more directly to the food. These were citizens of well-evolved colonies. Meanwhile, other colonies were floundering. They would dispatch ants who missed the food, who located food but failed to grasp it, or who grasped the food but zipped past the nest like a downhill putt from an overeager golfer. These colonies had little chance of being selected for mating at the end of the five-hundred-time-step generation.

As the time steps and generations mounted, the ant genomes began to demonstrate the beneficial effects of natural selection. From an average of zero food units stored in the initial configuration, when the genomes were random numbers, the ants began to improve their ability to gather food. Some colonies gathered two or three units by the fifth generation. Eleven or twelve units a few generations later. By the thousandth generation, some colonies had hoarded two hundred fifty or three hundred units. The colonies had evolved good strategies for foraging.

Collins and Jefferson were frustrated, however, at the failure of a cooperative strategy to emerge. After nearly a year of computational ant farming, the artificial bugs still foraged as individuals, unwilling to leave pheromone trails to alert their brothers to the presence of a food source. (This process was called recruitment.) Any pheromone release seemed random, a result of a mutation or crossover effect that contributed nothing to fitness. Collins ran tests to verify that, using the ANNs, the artificial ants were genetically capable of recruitment. But they had yet to discover that location in evolutionary space that allowed this trait to flower.

There may have been a kind explanation for this, suggested by observation of natural ants. A study by entomologists had indicated that in certain cases, particularly when food patches were small, ant colonies did best by sending only a few workers out to gather the food; these foraged alone and neglected pheromone communication. AntFarm may have presented those same conditions. On the other hand, the system might have harbored some flaw—a bug, so to speak—that prevented cooperation from emerging. The immediate challenge for Collins was determining whether such a flaw existed and finding its solution. Then he and his colleagues would test artificial ant colonies in situations where they competed for the same food sources.

After AntFarm, the UCLA team planned to engage in experiments that took the measure of the relative advantages of evolution and learning. David Jefferson in particular believed that compared to the elephant of evolution, learning—the cognitive adaptation achieved in a single lifetime—was a relative mouse. "Look at life on Earth," he says. "Most of it is microorganisms. Much of the remaining biomass is plants. A small fraction, multicellular animals. Most of those don't do anything we call learning. While life, through evolution, adapts exquisitely well to its ecological environment, most of life doesn't do anything resembling learning."

To Jefferson, learning might be part of life but apparently not one on which scientists should concentrate when devising creatures. Evolution was where the gold resided. "It's not our goal," he says, "to either study learning or evolve learning unless for some reason that should be an interesting part of evolution."

Quite coincidentally, a researcher on the other side of the continent has run an a-life experiment that intimated precisely what Jefferson doubted: learning is an interesting part of evolution. In a tiny, third-floor warren at Bellcore in Morristown, New Jersey, computer scientist David Ackley created an artificial life world named "AL." This two-dimensional universe was populated by genetically reproducing artificial life-forms called "agents."

As Ackley and his collaborator at Bellcore, Michael Littman, designed AL, it was a rigorous survival test for these hapless agents. At one hundred by one hundred cells, AL was not particularly spacious, and the agents' freedom was further constricted by a smattering of walls both inside the world and on its boundaries. If an agent smacked into a wall, it would suffer damage. Carnivores roamed the land, damaging agents more seriously—too many encounters and the agents would die. The agents could seek shelter from their foes in trees, but, if a tree died, it would crush the agent huddled underneath. Although agents could feast on dead carnivores and, in a pinch, the corpses of other agents, their main fare was plants. Besides dinner, the plants were indirect causes of reproduction; when sufficiently energized by food consumption, the agents reproduced.

The AL agents, however, had an advantage. Unlike residents of other evolutionary a-life ecosystems, they possessed neural network brains that allowed them to learn within a single generation.

Standard genetic theory dating from Mendel dictated that anything an organism learned during a lifetime was not physically passed on to its offspring. The opposite view was Lamarckism, which stated that acquired characteristics could be passed on to subsequent generations. AL, of course, did not follow the discredited theories of Lamarck. For instance, if an agent learned that a certain response helped it avoid the carnivores, that information might help the agent survive but would not be reflected in the genetic material passed on to its daughter. Yet, according to Ackley, learning such a technique *could* have an impact on evolution. This was due to a controversial theory called the Baldwin Effect, which was one of the emergent phenomena Ackley hoped to evoke in AL.

OVERVIEW	LANDSCAPE VIEW	INPUT TO AGENT

OVERVIEW

AL (*world*) 100x100 cell non-toroidal, asynchronous updates by type. Simulation ends after 1 million steps or agent extinction.

(*trees*) Infrequent birth and death. Provide shelter for agents from carnivores but no food. Only one agent allowed per tree. Occupant killed if tree dies.

(*plants*) Geometric growth up to a crowding limit. Eaten only by agents. Walked over by carnivores. Minimum of 50 plants alive.

(*carnivores*) Controlled by hand-coded FSA. Input is direction to closest agent directly N,S,E or W no further than 6 cells away. Cause damage to agents. Eat dead agents. Reproduce when sufficiently nourished. Damaged by agents. Die if sufficiently damaged or hungry. New one added to world every 200 steps.

(*agents*) Controlled by genetically-coded neural network. Input is representation of closest object directly N,S,E & W no further than 4 cells away (see figure). Output is 2 bits coding action direction N,S,E, or W. Eat plants and can eat dead agents and carnivores. Reproduce when sufficiently nourished passing genes to offspring (see text). Damaged by carnivores, walls and other agents. Die if sufficiently damaged or hungry.

(*walls*) Delimit outer edges of world and are scattered inside. Permanent. Cause minor damage to agents.

LANDSCAPE VIEW (closeup of southwest corner)

INPUT TO AGENT

David Ackley's world of AL. To the left is a description of the world; the center shows a part of the world itself; and to the right is a chart showing what the agent perceives. These perceptions trigger the agent's action network, which determines its behavior in response to this input.

The Baldwin Effect was named after J. M. Baldwin, a biologist who formulated the idea almost a hundred years ago. It suggested that Darwinian evolution could be shaped by what individuals learned in a lifetime. Consistent with the rejection of Lamarckism, it postulated that the learning itself was not passed on; rather, there were physical tendencies rewarded by organisms who had learned certain skills, and these changed the criteria for fitness.

"The idea is pretty simple," Ackley says, using his favorite example. "Suppose you have a population of squirrels that way back in the foggy past learned to jump from tree to tree. One population might learn to do this and another population doesn't. The population that learned tree-jumping will get evolutionarily rewarded for things that help the task, like developing webbing between the toes, while the other population won't get rewarded for that. So looking at this over evolutionary time, you can now see that the population that used to learn to jump from tree to tree becomes *born* to jump from tree to tree. What the ancestors learned, the descendants inherited. It's like Lamarckian evolution, except it's not in fact Lamarckian. It's just that you're changing the fitness function by something you learned."

Ackley devised an algorithm for what he called "evolutionary reinforcement learning" (ERL). As dictated by their genetic code, agents would actually develop *two* neural networks: an "action network" that would convert sensory input into behaviors, and an "evaluation network" that would also draw from sensory input, by using that information to judge whether a particular situation was good or bad. Depending on the feedback it received after acting on that judgment, the agent would reinforce, or modify, its behavior.

Using ERL, Ackley's organisms began life with a set of rules for behavior, which would evolve over a period of generations. These rules had variables in them that allowed for adaptive learning. An example of this mechanism would be found in Adam, an agent so named because it fathered 272 generations that came to dominate an entire AL population, Adam began life with a fairly capable behavioral network, with one glaring flaw—when faced with a predator to its south, it insisted on moving in the same direction. During the early days of Adam's existence, this unfortunate peccadillo almost led to disaster—only luck allowed it to escape a southerly predator that was on the verge of bashing it to a pulp. This experience, however, led Adam to observe that its response could be fairly judged as "bad." It adjusted its network so that the next time a predator lurked to its south, it would perform a less misguided behavior, one that avoided ugly confrontations and would be evaluated as good and therefore reinforced. This worked well, and Adam soon was parent to the first of its four children, and the dynasty was on its way.

Obviously, any agent who acquired similar wisdom would have a decided advantage over an agent who had not divined a clever protocol for coming face to face with a predator. Because agents do not communicate with each other, however, this vital information would not be passed on to an agent's offspring in a digital equivalent of a father-to-son chat. A descendant would be able to include that maneuver in its bag of survival tricks only by learning the response from scratch or experiencing a mutation that would affect its genome so that the response was present as a born instinct. A third option would be a long-term process: the Baldwin Effect.

Ackley's first experiments with AL life-forms were an attempt to determine the relative worth of learning, evolution, or a combination of the two. He seeded AL with a population of agents with various parts of their neural net system disabled, either the learning or evolutionary abilities, or both. In addition, he created a "brainless" group; stripped of their senses, these unfortunates wandered obliviously throughout the terrain, like blind Lears. Finally, he loosed on the landscape fully enabled agents. All four species were tested for one hundred runs, each run beginning from a random arrangement of objects and organisms. The results showed that, indeed, AL was a rather inhospitable world. Fewer than 18% of all the populations avoided extinction before ten thousand time steps, and only a tenth of those survived until the millionth time step. As one might expect, the brainless agents did poorly. But, surprisingly, the two species capable of evolution but not learning did even worse. It appears that these species became extinct before natural selection had an opportunity to assert itself in the genomes of the species capable of taking advantage of evolution. This suspicion was confirmed by the comparative performance of the two best species, the learning-only agents and the ERL agents. For approximately a half-million time steps they did equally well in maintaining an active population, but from that point and beyond those with both evolution and learning capabilities—the ERL group—managed to thrive in the perilous world of AL. Only ERL agents survived until the millionth time step. Seven populations out of the original ERL one hundred lived to commemorate this anniversary.

When Ackley and Littman sought to identify interesting phenomena in the course of those experiments, including evidence of the Baldwin Effect, it was those latter populations that provided the richest fossil record. One run in particular caught Ackley's fancy. At its millionth-step birthday, it showed no signs of flagging. Ackley and Littman decided to run it indefinitely. Millions more time steps were ticked off, the agent populations rose and ebbed, and almost a week of continuous computer cycles later, the last remaining agent, scion of 3,216 generations, finally succumbed.

This megarun of AL produced an embarrassment of data because it retained the life history and genetic makeup of thousands of agents. Trying to discern the relative significance of learning and evolution in the ERL agents, Ackley and Littman analyzed the difference between genomes before and after six hundred thousand time steps, when evolutionary changes began clearly asserting themselves. Isolating the genes that determined the agents' response to plants, the food source in the environment, they found an intriguing clue. Initially, the agents seemed to rely on learning to determine that the plants were good. That information was then converted to action—the agents approached the plants. But genomes analyzed in later stages of the run showed that this learning function had atrophied. Instead, from the moment they were born, these more evolved agents knew *instinctually* that plants were good to eat. They did not have to learn that useful fact. Ackley and Littman conjectured that the shift was a result of the Baldwin Effect:

> In the beginning era of successful populations, agents possess (mostly by luck) learning genes telling them plants are good. This is a big benefit for survival since the agents learn to eat, leading to energy increases, and eventually offspring. From time to time, action-related

mutations occur that cause agents to approach plants instinctively. These changes are favored by natural selection because they avoid the shortcoming of each new agent having to rediscover that plants' goodness means it should approach them. Agents begin to eat at birth and are better able to survive. . . . What once had to be acquired, was now inherited by around the three million step mark.

That was not the only major discovery in this AL run. When exhuming the data concerning the population's eventual demise, Ackley and Littman discovered a phenomenon as strange as the Baldwin Effect, one apparently undescribed in any of the biological literature. They called it "shielding." It appeared in the genes that determined how the agent evaluates carnivores. Because encounters with the roaming beasts invariably damage, and sometimes kill, agents, one would expect the crusty survivors of later evolutionary periods to have a fairly dim view of these predators. Yet there was a disturbing period very late in the megarun, lasting over a million time steps, during which the agents in the surviving population considered the carnivores good. They *liked* them.

"How could this have come to be?" Ackley wondered. "Why would natural selection have permitted such unfit organisms to proliferate?" The reason seemed to lie in the extremely high fitness of the instinct-based "action network" of these agents. Their genes dictated an inborn desire to run from the predators. The agents were free to assume that carnivores were good because they never lingered in the presence of predators and thus they fortuituously avoided testing this assumption. In addition, the carnivore population, living in an unfortunate time of well-evolved agents, was limited by the difficulty of procuring a decent meal. As a result those agents who, by mutation or crossover, inherited a learning network incapable of making correct predator evaluations, were not punished by natural selection. As Ackley and Littman put it, "The well-adapted action network apparently *shielded* the maladapted learning network from the fitness function."

This effect should not be viewed as a protective shield, but one that preserved an illusory, perhaps dangerous, assumption. As long as the first line of defense against the predators, the action network, remained intact, the agents would not have to face the consequences of this disability. But a change in their action-network genome, a shift in predator population, or some other random perturbation of their environment could quickly convert that harmless flaw into a fatal one. Indeed, Ackley and Littman postulate that "this maladaptation contributed to the population's eventual extinction."

The lessons of AL led the Bellcore researchers to hypothesize an undocumented biological effect, called "goal regression." This is a sort of evolutionary boomerang. It begins when a learned ability transmogrifies into an inherited characteristic, by virtue of the Baldwin Effect. From that point, the learning genes that contributed to the original acquisition of the characteristic will be shielded. Inevitably, the genes atrophy, as evolution removes the necessity to learn something that is now an inherent trait. As the ability to learn that trait genetically deteriorates, the organism itself becomes at risk. "When natural selection is the only source of feedback," write Ackley and Littman, "shielding and goal regression are potential hazards wherever the Baldwin Effect is a potential benefit."

Shielding need not be a hazard, however. "Shielding frees up the learning mechanism, which in this case was bad, because there was nothing else to learn in AL—the agents here had basically beaten their world," says Ackley, referring to shielding in the carnivore learning net. "But if these guys had more powerful brains, they could learn agriculture, for example. They could limit their feeding so they'd keep a good supply of food all over the place, and they could support a population two or three times the previous size."

The implication was obvious. Once our computers support a more powerful digital ecosystem, we will see much more complex emergent behavior from our artificial creatures—even such epochal phenomena as a shift from a foraging society to an entirely unprogrammed agricultural economy. One recalls John Horton Conway on the possibility of a very large Life population "evolving, reproducing, squabbling over territory. Getting cleverer and cleverer. Writing learned Ph.D theses."

These were not the only lessons of AL. At one point, Ackley wondered what would happen when he created the perfect agent—one whose response to every situation was optimal. He then seeded the environment with these über-agents and compared their performance to a successful, but not perfectly evolved, population of ERL-equipped agents. Indeed, the population of hand-optimized agents did very well, surviving through many thousands of time steps. However, they did not equal the success of the control group of evolved yet imperfect agents. The latter frequently sustained a population size of between thirty and sixty agents alive at a given point, while the putative superagents usually numbered between ten and thirty, and sometimes sank to single digits. "They were a plague on the land," said Ackley of his hand-engineered wonders. They would eat plants before they flowered. The sloppier population, whose behaviors were determined by many generations of evolution and learning, may not have always responded appropriately in every situation, but their very imprecision was better suited to maintaining a thriving community; the combination of evolution and learning enabled them to "find" a solution to their environment that was superior to the best that a human could endow them with.

Despite his impressive findings, Ackley had few hopes that evolutionary biologists would rapidly seize on his work and attempt to verify it in the field. A predecessor to his experiment, a computer simulation of the Baldwin Effect performed by Geoff Hinton and S. J. Nowlan, had won little attention from that camp. Instead, emboldened by the encouraging response to a video he ran at the second a-life conference in 1990, Ackley intended to push forward with even more ambitious experiments in a-life. His stated beliefs were that humans are machines of a sort, that the human brain is an information processor, and that creating artificial life will enable us to place ourselves more squarely in the pantheon of complex systems. As he and Littman declared,

> Computers, like microscopes, are instruments of empirical science. Multi-scale simulation models offer a way of casting light on elusive phenomena that hides in the cracks between levels. . . . The power of the computational microscope is growing by leaps and bounds, and we are just beginning to learn how to use it.

REAL ARTIFICIAL LIFE

I wish to build completely autonomous mobile agents that co-exist in the world with humans, and are seen by those humans as intelligent beings in their own right. I will call such agents Creatures. This is my intellectual motivation. I have no particular interest in demonstrating how human beings work, although humans, like other animals, are interesting objects of study in this endeavor as they are successful autonomous agents. I have no particular interest in applications; it seems clear to me that if my goals can be met then the range of applications for such Creatures will be limited only by our (or their) imaginations. I have no particular interest in the philosophical implications of Creatures, although clearly there will be significant implications.

Rodney A. Brooks

The ninth floor of 545 Technology Square on the MIT campus is the penthouse, as it were, of one of two blockish towers overlooking the sprawl of Cambridge, Massachusetts's silicon-industrial complex. But it seems more like the basement. Short on windows and elbow room, the maze of workrooms, hallways, and common spaces is permeated by a constant hum from an armada of mainframe computers. On the ninth floor, it always seems like midnight, the feverish hour favored by those driven by desire, not duty.

Only on the ninth floor is access limited to those with keys. The security measure is a vestige of the days, over twenty years ago, when protesters correlated the engines of computation with the war machine grinding in rice paddies and jungles 9,000 miles distant. Instability may have ruled the streets, but the sixties were the glory days of the ninth floor. There, the best computer programmers in the world virtually invented what would become an international counterculture centered on the free exchange of information. They laid the digital foundation for what would be known as classical AI. They coded chess programs, LISP, worlds made of colored blocks, and Conway's Life. It was a citadel of logic, protected from the messiness of the real world.

In the early 1990s, the ninth floor is in some ways a mirror-image *Weltanschauung* of its predecessor because it employs logic, in the bottom-up spirit of artificial life, to *cope* with the messy world. Its creators sometimes call their work "real artificial life."

Its exemplar is Genghis, a foot-long robot cockroach. Its body is a metal chassis loaded with computer chips; its legs are angled rods with rubber-tip socks; its head is a row of six sensors lined up like lights on a police car roof, and protruding from its thorax are two stiff wires that act as whiskers. Genghis may have benefited from its creators' indulgence in whimsy, but it also represents an iconoclastic new paradigm in robotics.

Genghis rests belly to the floor. But, when power flows from its on-board battery, it comes to . . . life. With a ponderous whir, Genghis pauses an instant and then pushes its legs to the ground until it stands.

273

Then it begins to walk. A leg on each side goes outward and forward, like a healthy kick from a slow-motion Rockette, and plants itself on the ground. The process is repeated, with two different legs going forward. With high-pitched grinding of the twelve on-board motors, Genghis makes its way across the room, its gait appearing as a somewhat more deliberate variation of a real insect's walk.

All is well until it encounters a telephone book placed in its path specifically to annoy it. Genghis's front leg on the left hits the side as it begins its movement forward. All motion halts. Then the leg moves again, this time angled more steeply upward. The widened angle is sufficient to brace the leg on the cover of the book. With what seems like deliberate, confident movements, Genghis manages to climb over the book and make its way to the far edge. When it moves its front leg forward and can not feel the ground, it pauses, startled, as if sensing that it is about to dive into an empty swimming pool. Its rear legs stiffen, angling its entire body so that this time the leg can touch the ground. With dignified caution, Genghis lowers itself from the book and continues its stroll.

No one ever "told" Genghis specifically how to deal with telephone books or other impediments to its motion. Indeed, the very concept of walking is at best a vague abstraction to the robot. Dealing with obstacles, and maintaining its locomotive rhythm, are emergent behaviors based on simple rules. The robot's movements come from the complex, self-organizing consequences of simple rules. Just like an interesting configuration in a cellular automaton.

Or an animal.

Genghis is both mascot and vindication for the Mobile Robot (Mobot) Group at MIT's Artificial Intelligence Laboratory. Although not the most elaborate application of the Mobot lab's principles—it was built in twelve weeks, mainly by an undergraduate —Genghis has drawn attention from quarters as varied as the Department of Defense and the David Letterman Show. More important than what it does is what it represents—a subtle but potentially debilitating blow to traditional robotics and AI, in favor of the ideology of artificial life. The source, if not the sorcerer of this, is an Australian expatriate who did not realize he was a flag bearer of a-life until the movement embraced him.

Born in 1954, Brooks grew up in Adelaide. At ten he built his first computer. His materials were ice cream tins, nails, light bulbs, and batteries. He funded his efforts by venturing barefoot into muddy puddles on golf courses to retrieve misbegotten approach shots. Like Danny Hillis, he used these motley gadgetoids to fashion a ticktacktoe machine. But there were no support groups for young hardware hackers in his part of the world, so he drifted to more orthodox studies and began a doctoral program in mathematics at Flinders University in South Australia. The drift abruptly ended when he realized that fellowships available in the United States would allow him to pursue his dream of building machines. He secured an assistantship at Stanford and found himself sharing an office with a young roboticist named Hans Moravec.

Moravec was building a mobile robot. His goal was to place the robot on one side of a room and have it maneuver its way across the room, avoiding trash cans and desks. He approached the problem with standard assumptions. In order to negotiate its journey successfully, the machine would need a silicon "brain," which could be the center of its cognition. In the memory of this brain the robot would retain some sort of representation of the room. It would use vision sensors to "see" this room and compare it constantly with its mental representation of the area. And it would "know" things. It would know what its goal was. It would know what an obstacle was and recognize one when it saw it. It would know how to move around obstacles. If such a wondrous consummation were ever to occur, it would know when it completed its task.

Moravec was extremely dedicated and clever, if a little odd. He lived in a makeshift warren in Stanford's AI building, between the ceiling tiles and the roof. His robot was among the best and smartest autonomous robots the world had ever seen. Yet Brooks could not help wondering whether there might not be a better way to go about making such creatures. "It would sit and compute for fifteen minutes and move a meter, then sit and compute for fifteen minutes more," Brooks recalls, with unseemly amusement. "That seemed long for me. I didn't want a real slow robot. I wanted one that was faster to begin with. I wanted a robot to be in the world, with real people around."

Brooks, in fact, was disgusted with the timidity of the entire field. Researchers would point with pride to robots who could figure out which blocks to move in a sandbox. Placed in rooms with pure black backdrops—settings that lacked any of the clamor and noise of the real world—these robots were coddled. "I was mad at those logic guys who I thought were playing in the sandbox with their little blocks world and didn't understand the complexities of the real world," recalls Brooks. "I guess I was so mad at them that I was trying to say they shouldn't even exist."

During the next several years, Brooks honed his own vision while serving time at a pinball progression of jobs in the golden triangle of American robot labs—Stanford to Carnegie-Mellon to MIT to Stanford again and finally, in 1984, back to MIT. An assistant professor in the Artificial Intelligence Laboratory, he was encouraged to establish a mobile robot group with a number of interested students and paid workers, provided that he could procure the funding and interest the students. Brooks accepted the challenge with his trademark bravado.

Within the relatively staid bounds of the AI establishment, his irreverence quickly distinguished him as a punk rocker among established and beloved crooners. "I'd never been a self-doubt kind of guy," he explains. "When I've worked on things, I've made them big. When I was a graduate student I built a big complex software system, much hairier than anyone else had ever built for a vision system. I programmed the first version of a LISP system for the Lucid company, and I'm still kind of their compiler hacker. The first time I came to MIT, as a research scientist, I was assigned to implement things that had been studied theoretically for years and built them, got them to work very quickly."

When Brooks returned to Cambridge, in 1985, he sensed the heat. He had not really *built* robots since his junkyard high school toys. Now, he was a member of the AI elite—against which he would soon devise scathing methodological indictments.

He soon had his first worker, Anita Flynn. She was a former United States Naval Academy plebe who had taken up engineering after the bitter realization that a slight myopia prevented her from pilot training, and a congressional edict barred women from flying second seat on combat planes. At a Naval research lab, she became interested in robotics and particularly the way they extracted information from sensors. But the labor in robotics had always been 90% engineering—more metallurgy than coding—and the AI Lab rarely deigned to indulge these hardware projects. When Flynn learned that Brooks was recruiting machine builders, she signed on as research partner and factotum, ordering the arcane gizmos and wires required to build mobile robots. Soon after Flynn came Jonathan Connell, a twenty-four-year-old graduate student from Connecticut. A grant of $3000 arrived, earmarked for equipment for their first creation. They decided on a name for it: Allen, in honor of AI pioneer Allen Newell.

Some weeks after taking the position, Brooks took a trip that would prove fateful not for only Allen's future but also for the Mobile Robot Group. Brooks's wife at the time was Thai, and he accompanied her to visit her relatives in a village situated in southern Thailand. None of the relatives spoke English, and for some reason they were quite emphatic that Brooks's well being would be at risk if he autonomously explored the village. In fact, they insisted he remain in the house, which stood on stilts by the river. Only by deeply offending them could he violate their wishes. "My wife was busy with her relatives, so I just got to sit there for a month with nothing to do," he says. "I hated it, but it was great for thinking."

Brooks thought about Allen. He knew that it had to be different than the current lame darlings of research robotics. These, in Brooks's view, were doomed by their adherence to the AI paradigm. This stated that the robot first perceived its world and then began to think about it—it tried to build a little model of the world and then lay mental plans as to how it would achieve its goal in that world. Only then would the robot act, by translating its cognition into action. Brooks believed that there should only be two steps—perception and action. The robot should sense something and then act on it, without a cognitive bottleneck.

But how could this be implemented? As Brooks sweated out his days in the stilted house by the river, he pondered a series of behaviors that could be seen as modules, intimately intertwined with a simultaneous process of real-time world modeling. Depending on what its sensors told it at any given moment, the robot would choose the appropriate behavior. Essentially, it would act like a giant finite state machine. Information about its environment and its present state would be processed according to rules, rules would run in parallel, and behavior would *emerge* from the continual series of actions that would result.

Using this new idea, the robot would forgo the complicated planning, mapping, and cognition required by the AI paradigm. It would have layers of behavior modules that triggered other behaviors when appropriate. A behavior toward the top of the stack might be "explore." The next level down might be a "walk" behavior. Then would be a set of even lower-level behaviors, determined by input from the sensors on the legs. Instead of starting at the top and working down, his machine would begin at the bottom. The behaviors at the basement of the hierarchy would determine how the robot coped with the world on a moment-to-moment basis. The robot might first check the space directly in front of it. If space were clear, the wheels would turn, thereby making the robot move forward. Once the wheels turned completely, the robot would again look ahead to see whether the path was clear. The "walk" process would continue until the machine sensed something blocking its path. At that point, a different behavioral rule would kick in, suppressing "walk" and activating "avoid obstacle," which might trigger wheel movements to turn or move backward. Or, if the robot found itself walking for a certain number of steps without incident, it might "get bored" and trigger the "explore" level, causing it to change direction in search of interesting input.

Because the process continually allowed one behavior to subsume control from another—using low-level behaviors allowed the robot to cope with the world in real time; using higher-level behaviors allowed the robot to pursue goals—Brooks dubbed his scheme "subsumption architecture." Quite coincidentally, he began intoning the word "bottom-up" as a slogan, the same slogan favored by Chris Langton.

Whereas the robots produced by the unhappy paradigm of artificial intelligence were faced with a confounding bottleneck of cognition:

SENSORS →   → ACTUATORS

perception   modeling   planning   task execution   motor control

The subsumption architecture would avoid the AI bottleneck and build on behaviors so that complex results would emerge:

reason about behavior of objects
_____

plan changes to the world
_____

identify objects
_____

monitor changes
SENSORS →   → ACTUATORS
_____

build maps
_____

explore
_____

wander
_____

avoid objects

Brooks's optimism in postulating that his robots could climb to those levels and top all previous efforts at smart robotics was based on the premise that they *had* to get better in order to survive in their environment. Brooks believed that forcing his creatures to cope with the same dirty reality that humans and animals dealt with constantly was the *only* way that one could expect intelligence to emerge in those artificial constructs. It worked in the natural world, where the challenge of dealing with the uncertainties of real life was the fuel that stoked the engines of evolution. Brooks professed utter contempt for minimalized "toy worlds" and especially for computer simulations; real roboticists, he felt, built robots for the real world.

Within a few months after his return from Thailand, Brooks had designed a subsumption architecture for Allen, a wheeled robot that resembled the *Star Wars* character R2-D2 in its electronic underwear. Ironically, Allen's initial successes came mostly in computer simulations of its architecture and not from actual movements of the robot itself. The paper Brooks published about the robot was, as he later admitted, "a simulation, and an oh-by-the-way-we-have-a-real-robot-which-will-be-working-next-month sort of paper." Brooks and crew eventually did use subsumption architecture to make Allen follow walls and recognize doorways, so that it somewhat proved its worth in the real world. But Allen never became truly autonomous, in that it was tethered to a LISP machine that ran its software. In what would become standard practice in the lab, the lessons learned in preparing the robot were quickly shifted to the next project.

Promiscuity in project selection would become common in Brooks's lab. It was almost as if the lab itself were working on some sort of subsumption architecture; often, it would be called away from a behavior by a sudden activation that led it to something else, another behavior valued more highly. Or new hardware technology would arrive that would make it easier to achieve a goal with a robot started from scratch. Half-built robots were abandoned, sometimes forever, and were other times revived when a graduate student decided to implement a project on it. "We have this long learning curve on how to build robots—it took years to get over our hardware fear—and we've been on that learning curve quite a while," Brooks explained several years after the process began. "At times we sort of run against the physical capabilities of a robot. It can't do anymore, it can't sense anymore, so it's hard to keep on with it."

What remained a constant was the de facto religion of the Mobot Lab, espoused with nose-thumbing élan by Brooks and his charges in a series of papers with unusually jargon-free prose (the better to throw down a gauntlet) and intentionally provocative titles, such as "Elephants Don't Play Chess" or "Battling Reality" or "Fast, Cheap, and Out of Control." (Emblazoned on buttons, the latter became a motto of sorts for the lab.) Though in practice Brooks would avoid pedantry in favor of pragmatism, he intentionally leaned toward hyperbolic pronouncements in his talks and publications. This not only drew attention to his ideas but also provided additional motivation for his group. In one paper, Brooks actually isolated more strident nuggets of his philosophy in a section labeled "dogma." His explanation is instructive: "I'm saying, 'You guys have a dogma, a certain irrational set of beliefs, only you're not willing to admit it.' Well, here's *my* alternate irrational set of beliefs, if you like—something that *works*.' "

An integral part of the Mobot Lab dogma was the idea of imbuing robots with biological essence. During Allen's nascent days, Brooks came across an article in TWA's in-flight magazine about a University of Pittsburgh professor working with pigeons. Brooks obtained the researcher's papers and discovered similarities between what the pigeons were doing and the intended behaviors of robots using the subsumption architecture. It confirmed Brooks's suspicion that subsumption not only predated modern robotics but also, having been implemented in our evolutionary forerunners, was nature's way.

"It's inspirational," he says of biology's relationship to his work. "It gives us confidence that some of the things we're doing are not so wacko, because there are other examples of systems which seem to share many of the properties, and these systems are successful in the world."

Brooks identified one animal in particular as a good model for his robots: the insect. While workers at UCLA tried to create digital insects, and while workers at Brussels simulated insects by cellular automata, Brooks began to *build* mechanical insects. He explained this passion in a 1986 paper, "AI through Building Robots":

> Insects are not usually thought of as intelligent. However, they
> . . . operate in a dynamic world, carrying out a number of complex
> tasks, including hunting, eating, mating, nest building, and rearing of

young. There may be rain, strong winds, predators, and variable food supplies all of which impair the insects' abilities to achieve its goals. Statistically, however, insects succeed. No human-built systems are remotely as reliable.

Instead of trying to construct geniuses who could not manage to walk across the room, Brooks wanted to build idiots who could shimmy across a rutted field like water bugs. Instead of consuming the computational power of a Connection Machine while trying to codify and interpret the input from a video camera, his robots would get quick-and-dirty input from cheap sensors that told them when they hit something. With some clever human planning, these minimalist subsumption robots would quickly exceed their top-heavy cousins in utilitarianism. Insect-level robots "have the potential to change our daily lives in much the way microprocessors have," wrote Brooks in one of his manifestos.

As an example he postulated a vacuum-cleaning robot. Many people imagined this as an ideal robotic vocation; they pictured a wheeled metal object resembling a human being—perhaps in a maid's uniform—pushing around a conventional vacuum cleaner. Brooks's proposed dust-gathering robot looked instead like a common vacuum cleaner itself, albeit a rather large one. Periodically roaming the house, it vacuumed and avoided furniture. Its weakness was an inability to get into corners and tight spaces, so Brooks provided a supplement: tiny six-legged robots, only a few inches in diameter. These solar-powered robot "bugs" crawled into corners, electrostatically picked up dirt, and stored it in their bellies. When the large vacuum robot approached, its noise triggered a sensor in the bug. As Brooks put it, "When it hears [the sound] it will run to the middle of the room and dump its guts all over the floor."

Brooks ended his speculation with characteristic flourish: "Such," he concluded, "is the future."

While Brooks's insect-level robots flouted the reigning wisdom, in some respects they hearkened back to an ill-maintained path first cleared by cyberneticians. These early roboticists also desired electronic beings who performed a la biology. The most famous experiment of this stripe was conducted in 1950 by W. Grey Walter, a British biologist known for writing *The Living Brain,* a book that captivated Brooks as a young boy in South Australia. Walter built what he called "imitations of life." These were Elmer and Elsie, identified by the "mock-biological" name *Machina speculatrix,* "because," Walter wrote, "they illustrate particularly the exploratory, speculative behavior that is so characteristic of most animals." Walter outfitted Elmer and Elsie with radio tubes, motors, two batteries each (a regular six-volt storage battery and one of the variety used for hearing aids), and sensors to discern light and touch. Because the electronics of each of these faux animals were housed under a shell-shaped dome, with a light sensor protruding, they resembled tortoises.

Elmer and Elsie had but those two sensors each. Yet, as Walter reported, "the strange richness provided by this particular sort of permutation introduces right away one of the aspects of animal behavior—and human psychology—that *M. speculatrix* is designed to illustrate: the uncertainty, randomness, free will or independence so strikingly absent in most well designed machines." Elmer's photocell sensor was hooked to its steering mechanism, and its logic circuits were wired to seek a particular level of illumination. When the synthetic tortoise was placed in a darkened room, it thoroughly scoured every edge and corner as it sought brightness. When it came across a flashlight beam, its motors sped up. Elmer rushed toward the light. As the robot approached, however, and as the beam's intensity became overwhelming, Elmer backed away. When a second light was placed in the room, Elmer scurried back and forth between them. It recalled to Walter's mind the dilemma of Buridan's ass, "which the scholastic philosophers said would die of starvation between two barrels of hay if it did not possess a transcendental free will." As Elmer's batteries died down, it virtually solved this hoary dilemma. The robot's weakened sensors allowed it to approach the 20-watt lamp over its "hutch," where sustenance lay in the form of a battery charger. As soon as the batteries were renewed, of course, the light once again made Elmer scurry in what surely must have been pain.

Next, Walter placed an indicator light on Elmer's shell that switched on when its motor started or stopped. Elmer quickly zeroed in on a mirror hung in the room. An entertaining dance of oscillation ensued. Each time its motor turned off, the indicator light would flash, and

Elmer, exposed to the light, would grind its motor again. "The model flickers and jigs at its reflection in a manner so specific that were it an animal a biologist would be justified in attributing to it a capacity for self-recognition," Walter wrote.

Walter then placed Elmer and his twin, Elsie, in the same room. With indicator lights on both tortoises, they engaged in a complex dance of attraction and repulsion. When both sought to recharge from the same hutch, the stronger one had the power to muscle out the tortoise whose battery charge was weaker. Thus the creature most desperate for energy received none and soon "expired" of exhaustion.

Walter was optimistic that others would imitate life with more complex creatures of similar style. He predicted that in the near future similar imitations of life would repair themselves and reproduce. Yet, as classical AI imposed its top-down dogma on experimental robotics and demanded from its creations a near-human grasp of logic, the supple, animal-like behaviors of Elmer and Elsie were relegated to the curiosity heap.

But not forgotten. Over thirty years later, that same idea of complex behavior arising from simple components was reflected in *Vehicles,* a compact but resonant book published in 1984. Its author was Valentino Braitenberg, a German neuroanatomist who remained a devout cybernetician. In *Vehicles,* he painstakingly created a series of imaginary wheeled carts, outfitted with sensors and motors, and asked his readers to infer logically the sources of their behavior. As did Elmer and Elsie, Braitenberg's vehicles appeared motivated by urges and emotions.

With droll whimsy, Braitenberg dismissed the issue of defining life. The very simplest of his vehicles was equipped with a single sensor and a single motor, wired so that it moved proportionally to the strength of the signal reaching the sensor. If the sensor reacted negatively to heat, for instance, and the vehicle were placed in a pond, one might indulge in the first of a series of anthropomorphic speculations on its remarkably complex behavior:

> It is quite restless, you would say, and does not like warm water. But
> it is quite stupid, since it is not able to turn back to the nice cold spot
> it overshot in its restlessness. Anyway, you would say, it is ALIVE,

since you have never seen a particle of dead matter move around quite
like that.

Subsequent vehicles, with more sensors and motors, displayed behavior
characteristic of emotions ranging from cowardice (avoids objects) to
love (embraces objects). The behavior of various vehicles encouraged
observers to judge them as explorers, social beings, even philosophers.
Braitenberg even argued, as did Walter, that certain of his vehicles
displayed free will.

To those who might object that free will implies conscious decision
making, he parried with the provocation that perhaps free will exists
only in the eyes of observers. "Interest arises when we look at these
machines or vehicles as if they were animals in a natural environment,"
he wrote. "And yet we know very well that there is nothing in these
vehicles which we have not put in ourselves." This was coy; after all,
there is "nothing" in complex cellular automata not determined by the
rules, nothing in a human being but what is found in the embryo, and
probably nothing in the entire spectrum of natural life but what was
evolved from a common single-cell ancestor. (Braitenberg insisted his
vehicles, too, evolved—wiring mistakes that evoked unexpectedly
clever behavior were, in essence, favorable mutations.) So no one would
miss his point, Braitenberg spent a lengthy appendix discussing phenomena in the natural world that correspond to the mechanisms of his
vehicles. But the virtually unanswerable question remained—how could
we be so sure that the behavior produced by these transparently wired
machines was qualitatively different from behavior in the natural world?
In a sense, Braitenberg was proposing a Turing test for life. If something
behaved like a living thing, he implicitly argued, we may well consider
it to be alive.

Braitenberg's work provided a treasure house of ideas for bottom-up
minded roboticists. MIT's Media Lab was particularly fertile ground for
those ideas; Marvin Minsky who had moved from the AI Lab to this
high-tech research enclave, enthralled followers with his book *Society of
Mind,* which postulated that nature's approach toward intelligence and
behavior was decentralized. A group at the Media Lab used these con-

cepts to outfit colorful, linking-toy LEGO blocks with motors, wheels, sensors and integrated circuit chips so they could vivify the behavior of digital "turtles" in the learning-oriented computer language Logo. MIT computer scientist Mitchel Resnick and his colleagues further modified this "LEGO-Logo" system by outfitting the creatures with what he called "electronic bricks," programmable circuit blocks that eliminated the need for the creations to be attached by cable to a computer. Thus Braitenberg-ized, the constructs could be seen less as machines than as creatures. Resnick claims that "there is great potential for using LEGO/Logo as a construction set for artificial creatures. . . . using sensors a LEGO/Logo creature can sense the world around itself—then change its behavior depending on what it senses. . . . LEGO/Logo creatures don't just *act* in the world, they *interact with* the world."

This was an idea independently seconded by a robotics lab at the University of Edinburgh, which was constructing its own Braitenberg-inspired LEGO robots. The instantly interesting yet confoundedly complex behaviors of their plastic beasts led the Scottish scientists to praise and bemoan what Braitenberg called the "law of uphill analysis and downhill invention" regarding vehicles. The law stated that inventing machines that behaved like animals was easy; figuring out *why* such interesting behavior arose was the true challenge. Therein lay, most probably, the Holy Grail of complexity.

Mitchel Resnick's own epiphany occurred at a children's LEGO-Logo workshop on constructing creatures. One project entailed writing a program to enable a creature to follow a line drawn on the ground. "We wrote the program and it was following this line," recalls Resnick. "And all of a sudden it struck me that I had no idea what was going to happen when it reached the end of the line. We'd written the program, but we didn't take that into account. I didn't have time to think about what it might do, so I just watched it. When it got to the end of the line, it turned around and started following the line in the other direction! If we had *planned* for it to do something, that would have been the ideal thing for it do to."

Children, Resnick elaborated, viewed the creatures on three levels: "on a *mechanistic* level, examining how one LEGO piece makes another move, . . . the *information* level, exploring how information flows from one Electronic Brick to another[,] . . . [and] a *psychological* level, attributing intentionality or personality to the creatures." Whereas most science teachers would rush to correct such heretical inferences, Resnick did not consider them erroneous. "Complex systems can be meaningfully described at many different levels—that is one of the important lessons of artificial life," he wrote.

Not surprisingly, the spirits of Grey Walter and Valentino Braitenberg burned brightly on the ninth floor of Technology Square. In 1987 Rodney Brooks's graduate student Jonathan Connell built a pair of small robots that were truly vehicles. Instead of installing his electronics and software on the large prefabricated circular base of Allen, Connell began with two radio-controlled toy automobiles, modeled on the cars driven by characters in a TV series, "Knight Rider 2000." He removed the toys' radio controllers and replaced them with logic chips holding the code for subsumption architecture. The cars were outfitted with infrared sensors so they could "see" obstacles and each other. Within seconds of activation, a robot would begin moving and "exploring" the room until it was about to collide with an object. At that point the sensors would note the presence of an object, and the wheels would suddenly spin in reverse. (The cars had no brakes.)

Later, the exploration mode was refined. With each tick of an onboard clock, the robot moved to the right. This set the robot in a circular path. In an open space with no intruders, the robot indefinitely circled, as if marking territory. If the second robot were released in the room, its trajectory would threaten to violate this territory. One of two things would happen. The intruder would sense the defender, and veer away from the circle before crossing the invisible line. Or the circling robot would sense the interloper, whose presence would then trigger avoidance behavior. When the exploration behavior returned, the robot would draw a new territory.

Connell added yet another behavior level, which he called "follow the leader." The clock inside the robot would now take note of the duration of an obstacle's presence. If it sensed the continuous presence of obstacles, the robot would execute the normal avoidance behavior. But if it were in an open space, its first impulse would be to rush gregariously toward an object. As Connell wrote,

287

This last behavior allows our robots to truly relate to one another. Before, when two robots met they simply shied away from each other. But now if one has established its territory and is approached by a second, they actually interact. If a circling robot sees the backside of a wandering robot still in the explore mode, for instance, it will latch on and try to follow the wanderer. If the two meet head-to-head, on the other hand, the local robot attacks the visitor by driving straight toward him. If the visitor is still in the "explore" mode it will run away and leave the local robot's territory. If, however, the visitor has already staked out a territory that overlaps that of the first robot, the two robots will have a face-off. The robots park nose to nose and glare until one of them yields its territory by switching out of the "follow" mode.

Obviously, this interplay had its comic aspects, which inspired the roboticists to name the cars after the dog-and-cat cartoon characters Tom and Jerry. (The names had a second meaning: in keeping with the tradition of naming robots after computer science pioneers, the alternate namesakes were MIT programmer legends Tom Knight and Gerry Sussman.)

The behavior of Tom and Jerry courted anthropomorphic responses. Some of the unprogrammed, emergent responses described by Connell seemed sufficiently clever, or at least sufficiently lifelike, to encourage observers to infer motives and emotions in these simple robots. Could it be that those same forces, and not the other, more rigorous qualities we have identified with life, led to the labeling of animals behaving in this manner as "living"?

Rodney Brooks preferred not to deal with the question. "I don't like definitions, because every time you get a definition someone pushes it the wrong way, or pulls it the wrong way," he says. "I want to have stuff that speaks for itself, stuff deployed out there in the world, and surrounding you now. If you want to argue if it's intelligent or not, or if it's living or not, fine. But if it's sitting there existing 24 hours a day, 365 days of the year, doing stuff which is tricky to do and doing it well, then I'm going to be happy. And who cares what you call it, right?"

Brooks is convinced that, if researchers used the subsumption scheme, there would be no foreseeable obstacle to prevent the development of robots of even human-level intelligence. Or beyond. When asked whether this indeed were so, Brooks answers unhesitatingly, "All the way. There will be embellishments, there will be new things to come in, but I don't see the wall yet. I don't see a wall."

All the way?

"Yeah," he reiterates. "All the way."

Questions of this sort were also being actively addressed by people in the single area of biology whose practitioners seemed willing, even eager, to consider the possibility of artificial life: ethology, the study of animal behavior.

The tolerance came as a function of the field's recent history. In the wake of the pioneering work of Konrad Lorenz on aggression, ethology drew much attention and funding in the years immediately following World War II. Those who hoped for so-called cures for humanity's foibles were disappointed. As a means of better understanding the animal kingdom, however, ethology has done considerably better. The work of Nobel laureate Niko Tinbergen, for instance, is regarded as a landmark in the analysis of animal behavior. Concentrating on the actions of a small fish, the three-spined stickleback, Tinbergen theorized a hierarchical structure based on "drive centers" that helped determine what the fish would do at a given instant.

To a-lifers, this system resembled a finite state machine, something easily replicable in software. The concepts of Tinbergen and his successors bore such close relationship to computational systems that inevitably some ethologists began using the computer as a modeling tool. But neither their successes in these pursuits nor important work done by neuroethologists in determining which parts of the nervous system performed various actions did much to retard the field's gradual yet undeniable fall from popularity among scientists. The action in life sciences lay in molecular and evolutionary biology, where breakthroughs abounded, and the secret of life itself seemed to rest. In comparison, there was something quaint about ethology. It was too . . . earthbound.

A conference on adaptive behavior held in Paris in fall 1990 attempted, with limited success, to draw together computer scientists, roboticists, and ethologists. The implicit hope was to foster two kinds of cooperation. First, those working in silicon could exploit examples from the field work and models of the ethologists and implement them in simulations and robots—a process well under way. The second kind of cooperation was more unusual. It involved ethologists studying the behavior of artificial creatures, regarding these artificial constructs as if they were animals.

The ethologists were at once cautious and surprisingly accommodating. Their presentations were punctuated with asides and genuflections to the roboticists, suggesting possible connections between, for instance, field studies of songbirds and autonomous robots. They often addressed Rodney Brooks directly. When pressed for explanations for their willingness to direct their attentions to such unorthodox ground, they made cogent arguments. They argued that ethology should be mainly concerned with studying behavior and should not entangle itself into ultimately nit-picking definitions of what was alive or what was not.

"There is a spectrum of living to non-living things," says David McFarland, an Oxford professor who has authored some of ethology's standard texts. "And my argument would be that the protocols and the principles of behavior control are the same across the spectrum. I wouldn't say they're the same, but they share the same body of theory." McFarland had little time for those who argued that robot behavior was in some way less "real" than the behavior of natural creatures. "Those who would talk like that usually have a kind of an anthropomorphic viewpoint, which I don't go for. It's not objective. If you're going to say an animal can make decisions and a robot can't, then it's sort of a quasi-religious stance."

The ethologists, however, were concerned that the a-life contingent had been insufficiently discriminating in choosing what of ethology to integrate into their simulations and critters. For instance, McFarland was aghast that many roboticists regarded the sort of hierarchies Tinbergen postulated as the last word in animal behavior. "Ethologists abandoned hierarchical thinking a long time ago," he says.

In a certain sense, McFarland's complaint was irrelevant. Although most computer-based artificial life experiments began with clear purpose as to which a-life they owed allegience—weak a-life, which simulates the mechanisms of natural biology; or strong a-life, which aims toward the creation of living creatures—experiments in what came to be known at MIT as "computational ethology" were not so clearly delineated. As far as the roboticists were concerned, their brand of a-life leaned toward the strong: although they happily drew from biology's breathtaking engineering feats, they made no claims to biological fidelity for their creatures. "There is a certain tension," admits Pattie Maes, an MIT roboticist interested in both strong and weak artificial life. "Do we want to be engineers and come up with systems that are useful, or do we want to study behaviors as a biological thing?"

The former usually won out. For one thing, animals were often, as Maes puts it, "suboptimal." They did things that made sense for themselves but did not qualify as efficient robot behavior. For another thing, funding agencies were more willing to support robots that performed measurable labors than those that rigorously followed natural methodology. At MIT, the ethological approach inspired a series of experiments in both computer simulations and robotics. Computer scientists particularly frustrated with the top-down formulations of AI, which insists that creatures hold a model of the entire world in their silicon heads, found ethology particularly enticing. Ethology offered a perspective of "situatedness," a bottom-up approach that assumed that the creature would operate more like an FSM. The bookshelves in the cubicles of faculty and graduate students at the Mobot Lab and the Media Lab quite commonly harbored Gould's basic textbook on ethology and McFarland's *Oxford Companion to Animal Behavior*.

Michael Travers, a graduate student at the Media Lab, used ethology as the basis for an "animal construction kit" he named "Agar." (Microbiologists used the substance agar as a catalyst to grow cultures.) Travers contended that "people and computers can demonstrate their intelligence by manipulating symbols, but animals have no such ability, or only very limited forms of it. Instead they display their intelligence by action in their world. The appropriateness of an animal's actions to its situation constitutes its intelligence." Using a complicated set of behavioral triggers he called "agents," Travers managed to produce specific instances of ant behavior emergently, through the creature's responses to its state. For instance, in Agar, ants sought food, picked up food when they found it, and then returned to the nest. While executing the latter behavior, they left a pheromone trail that alerted their colleagues to the direction in which food lay. Travers's ants, presumably like real ants, did not have to ponder the reason for this—leaving pheromone was simply a function of noticing that one's pincers were holding a piece of food. "It's clear," he wrote, "that the boundary between behavioral system and physiology is mostly artificial."

Another researcher straddling that boundary was Randall D. Beer of Case Western Reserve University. He constructed perhaps the most elaborate simulated insect to date. Because it was modeled on the American cockroach, or *Periplaneta americana*, Beer named his creation the "computer cockroach," or *Periplaneta computatrix*. (He chose the name to honor the work of Michael Arbib, an automata theorist who spent years implementing the neural structure of a frog he called *Rana computatrix*.) Like Rodney Brooks, Beer was profoundly discontented with classical AI. His suspicions were reinforced by an essay titled "Why Not the Whole Iguana?" written by cognitive scientist Daniel Dennett. It argued that AI should retreat from modeling "human microcompetences" such as chess or reading fables, and focus instead on modeling the overall competences of simpler animals. Beer also became interested in a branch of ethology that looks to neural structures of animals to explain certain aspects of behavior. In constructing his cockroach, then, he aimed for establishing a subdiscipline, computational neuroethology.

P. computatrix, then, was centered around a nervous system suggested by biological examples. The insect visible on the monitor of the Texas Instruments LISP machine had a coffin-shaped body, six legs, a diamond-shaped head with an inverted V for a mouth, and two long whiskers. But what mattered was the neural network that swallowed input from the environment and expectorated the output that dictated its behavior.

Beer first modeled locomotion. In order to walk successfully, the insect had to coordinate the movement of its six legs so that at all times its center of gravity remained within a tripod of legs on the ground. Otherwise it would ignominiously tumble. Using neuroethological studies of insect locomotion, Beer set up a neural network that used feedback from the cockroach's legs to discover a stable gait known to entomologists as a "metachronal wave," where leg movements on either side begin in the rear and progress to the forward legs. Then, just as neuroethologists perform lesion studies on their subjects, slicing connections between neurons to determine behavior differences, Beer digitally severed connections in his cockroach. He found that, amazingly, the artificial insect could recover from lesions; it stumbled at first but eventually adopted an alternate gait. Beer had even more interesting results from tampering with the activation levels in the neural net. He found that, by increasing the current in a certain neuron, he could provoke his cockroach to switch spontaneously from the metachronal wave to what was known as the "tripod gait." By varying the firing frequency of this particular neuron, Beer was able to produce five different emergent gaits, all of which had been identified by E. O. Wilson as characteristic of natural insects.

After months of adding levels of behavior to the cockroach, Beer was ready to test its survival skills. A hungry cockroach—its energy was low, a circumstance that caused it consternation—was released into what looked like a holding cell. Bounded by four square walls, the cell had a food source, but between the food and the cockroach was a curving barrier, extending three-quarters of the way across the room. Appearing on the screen, the cockroach moved warily yet effortlessly, coordinating its leg movements with natural elegance. It picked up the scent of the food and plodded toward it, only to be frustrated by the barrier. As its left antenna collided with this obstacle, the cockroach moved into position to follow its edge, toward the right, even though the maneuver entailed moving away from the food. By noting the activation levels depicted on the side of the screen, one could see that with the food-seeking behavior flummoxed, the edge-following behavior hesitantly asserted itself. Soon, the bug lost the scent of the food, and its sole concern was following the edge of the barrier. When the cockroach reached the barrier's end, it fleetingly, almost wistfully, turned back toward it and attempted to reestablish contact. But it had already moved into open space and its antenna felt nothing. Walking behavior then subsumed edge following. The cockroach wandered, roaming in roughly a northeasterly direction until it arrived at the far corner of the cell, whereupon it rather nimbly turned toward the left to avoid entrapment. Then it followed the top wall until its minute hesitation signaled it had again apprehended the scent of food. That did it. The famished insect dropped all pretenses to edge following and veered straight toward the food patch, whereupon it began to eat.

Observers of this experiment were impressed by the autonomous artificial insect's successful negotiation of what could have been an unfortunate situation. There was also something rather intangible, but perhaps even more striking, at work. At each step in the experiment, one

Randall Beer's artificial cockroach negotiates its way to the food source (dark circle). The cockroach is released into the simulated room and left to its own devices. Quickly picking up the scent of dinner, it heads directly toward the food, then encounters the barrier. It switches to edge-following behavior until it reaches the end of the barrier; by that time it is too far from the food to sense it. Wandering about, the roach avoids getting stuck in a corner by exercising another behavior and following the top wall. When it again senses the food, nothing stands between it and a good meal. Watching the artificial insect solve this problem, one could easily mistake its behavior for that of a natural organism.

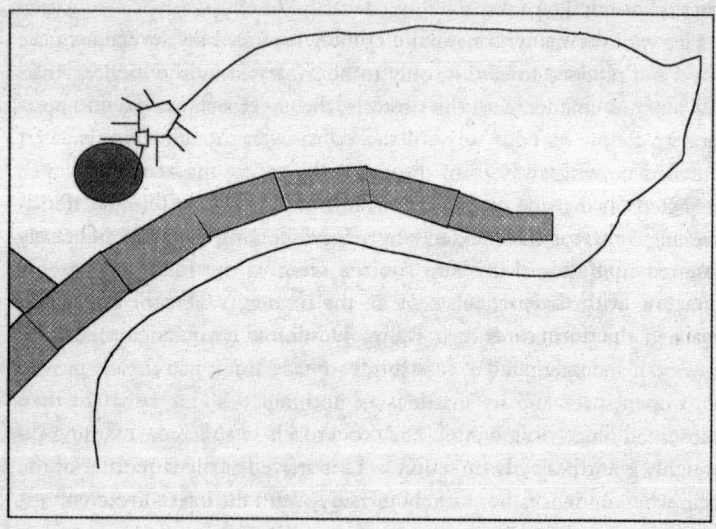

could not help but frame the question one would ask of a living being confronted with a dilemma, What would it do next? Just as in watching a genuine cockroach, the answer was not quite predictable, because the behavior was not programmed but emergent. But it was always reasonable from the bug's point of view. The behavior of the bug easily made one feel, if but for an instant, that this crudely drawn stick figure, *P. computatrix*, was alive.

The MIT Mobot Lab strived to create ever-higher levels of ethological validity. Because, as Brooks put it, "a robot is worth a thousand simulations," the idea at Tech Square was to embody these ideas in the physical world. The Mobot Lab's second large project was Herbert, adopted by Jon Connell as his doctoral project. Connell specifically used an ethological methodology to encourage Herbert to perform a deceivingly complex goal: collecting empty soda cans around the laboratory. (Because many in the lab had ties in some way to Danny Hillis's company, Thinking Machines, Herbert was jokingly referred to as "the Collection Machine.") This task was the sort of "mindless" goal that artificially intelligent robots had difficulty accomplishing; it required quite a bit of skill and savvy. A robot had to make its way across a cluttered area, identify soda cans, determine whether they were empty, and accurately grasp them.

Connell drew inspiration from ethological studies of several animals, including Tinbergen's demonstration that baby seagulls respond identically to a crude mock-up of a parent's head (with a crucial identifier—a red spot near the point of the beak). This showed him how Herbert could easily recognize a soda can solely by an outline of its shape.

But Herbert owed much of his behaviors to studies of the coastal snail *Littorina*. These indicated that the snail operates on a hierarchy of behaviors corresponding closely to Brooks's subsumption scheme. When interacting with the particulars of its environment, Connell noted, the snail "can perform some seemingly sophisticated navigational tasks with a relatively simple control structure."

Among the snail's behaviors is a reflex called UP, which tells it to crawl against gravity's grain, and another called DARK, which urges it to crawl away from light sources. The opposite behavior, BRIGHT, activates only when the snail is inverted. This in turn is subsumed by a stronger behavior, DARKER, which activates only when the creature is out of water. This forces the snail toward darker regions. Finally, a STOP behavior is activated whenever the snail is fully dry.

Coastal snails eat a certain kind of algae, one that grows in the cracks in rocks just above the tide line. Leaving its underwater habitat to seek this food puts the snail at risk; if it spends too much time in the sun, it fries. If it wanders too far inland, it dries out. The emergent properties of its behaviors allow it to survive. When still underwater, it finds the shoreline by heading toward the rocks, which are darker than sand. DARK. Then it climbs. UP. When it reaches an overhang in a rock, the snail becomes inverted, and it heads toward the brighter region toward the surface. BRIGHT. It continues climbing until it is out of the water but retreats if the sun is too bright. DARKER. If not, it climbs until it finds a crack in the rock. UP. Attracted by darkness, it crawls into the crack and, ideally, discovers algae. If by chance it climbs too far, it stops, waiting until a wave washes it home again. STOP. Although its central-ized brain does not "know" where food is to be found or which conditions may put the animal at risk, the appropriate responses to its world constitute a behavioral network that does know these things.

Herbert used its surroundings in the same way; its name was a tribute to Herbert Simon, who observed that the complex behavior of an ant is a function of the complexity of its environment. As Connell wrote in his dissertation, Herbert could "use the world as its own representation."

Unlike Allen, Herbert had all of its computer chips on board; it was truly autonomous. It resembled an electronic wedding cake—the bot-tom layer was a circular base resting on three wheels; the middle layer was a maze of circuit boards; and the top layer consisted of wires, chips, and two oversize replacements for bride and groom—a human-sized hinged metal arm and a periscope-shaped laser light sensor with a small video camera affixed to it. Its circuitry housed its behaviors. True to its bottom-up spirit, not a central brain but a series of parallel processors coordinated these behaviors. Its behaviors would emerge from moment-to-moment interactions with its environments. Herbert was incapable, in fact, of remembering its state more than three seconds previous.

It operated like a coastal snail. Using environmental cues as it wan-dered through the maze of rooms and work spaces on the ninth floor,

Herbert avoided obstacles and kept an eye out for tables, the natural habitat of soda cans. Then, if it found a table, a new behavior activated, one that incited Herbert to move closer to the table. Reaching the table activated the behavior of looking specifically for a can. This was done in the same spirit with which baby seagulls identify their parents. Beaming its laser light over the table, Herbert apprehended shapes, seeking to match the squat cylindrical shape imprinted in its chips. Instead of plotting the coordinates of the can in its vision field and directing the arm to the region, the robot simply kept turning until the can was in the center of its vision field. The appearance of the can in this place caused the robot to stop all movement.

The lack of wheel activity triggered the set of behaviors concerning the arm. True to Herbert's on-the-fly behavioral style, the arm navigated by the sensors on its hand. The hand "felt" its way around the area of the suspected can. It did this by skimming the table surface, by touching it every couple of inches, feeling for the familiar raised shape of a can. When the sensors felt something that seemed to be a can, the hand surrounded it and grasped. Once the sensors reported a can firmly held in its pincers, another set of behaviors activated: go home.

By the time Herbert was retired in 1989, the Mobot Lab was enjoying a boom in both its human and robot populations. With Brooks providing the religion and Anita Flynn acting as facilitator and cheerleader—commissioning T-shirts and organizing an annual "Robot Olympics"—the Mobot Lab gave off a special aura that touched all who worked there; there was a feeling that history was being made. Other paradigms of robotic research snared more funding, but the sorts of results obtained in the ninth floor seemed, to the MIT roboticists at least, substantially more impressive than those of their competitors.

This was underlined by successes in the area with which the traditional paradigm had the most difficulty: navigation. In 1989 one of Brooks's students, a Yugoslavian-born graduate of the University of Kansas named Maja Mataric, used Brooks's ideas to design an intuitive navigational scheme in Toto, a sonar-equipped robot. By juggling behaviors such as STROLL, AVOID, and ALIGN, Toto managed to explore the ninth floor of Tech Square and, by using a scheme of remembering landmarks around the lab, actually learned how to find the quickest routes to arbitrarily chosen locations. While implementing these behaviors, Mataric drew on the design features of bats, bees, birds, and rats, some of which also used landmarks as navigational tools. As does a human, when he or she tells someone to turn left at the gas station and right at the light.

The biological, subsumption approach was working. Researchers outside MIT began to look more closely at Brooks's ideas and the work of his group, especially after the first two a-life conferences placed this methodology firmly within the wider pursuit of artificial life.

Within MIT, the lab became known as one of the most interesting projects on campus. It was able to attract brilliant undergraduates like Colin Angle, an upstate New Yorker with a wizard's touch whose philosophy on matriculating was "to major in whatever lets me build the coolest stuff." For three years Angle dabbled; stuffed with oscilloscopes, circuit boards, and wires, his room in a campus fraternity house had become a virtual electronics lab. Before his senior year in 1988, however, he bested forty-three competitors for an undergraduate position at the Mobot Lab, and his lot was cast. Within a few weeks of his arrival Brooks asked, "Why don't we build a walking robot?" The group decided to attempt a six-legged walker. Angle volunteered. In less than three months, aided by others in the lab, he built Genghis, the Mobot Lab's best attempt to date at real artificial life.

Genghis was so named because "it stomps over things," says Angle. Genghis's appearance added to its mystique: Its cockroach-styled chassis was a marriage of functional design and bad Japanese science-fiction films. Brooks's subsumption architecture was the basis for its behavior, but Angle's pack-rat ingenuity infused the robot with an ethological verisimilitude: although not a biologist, Angle had been encouraged to adopt the same opportunistic view of potential synergy between body and environment that nature seems to favor. Thus Genghis claimed maximum value from its sensors, enabling the six-legged machine to find its way through cluttered rooms without benefit of sight, knowledge of what a room is, or a central brain. Its intelligence was truly distributed, as fifty-seven "augmented" FSMs in its hardware executed basic behaviors: stand up, simple walk, force balancing (compensating for rough terrain by taking account of the force expended during each step), leg lifting, whiskers (controlling the feedback from long front touch sensors), pitch stabilization, prowling, and steered prowling.

The latter two allowed Genghis to live up to its barbaric moniker. Prowling occurred when the robot's forward-facing pyroelectric sensors detected the heat of a human being. This inhibited walking until the intruder passed; then the robot moved forward again. Steered prowling was similar, except that Genghis "attacked"—its sensors locked onto the prey and it pursued, albeit at a leisurely pace.

As Randall Beer realized while simulating his artificial cockroach, six-legged insect gaits were difficult to attain. Producing these gaits in the real world was more than difficult. Brooks wrote a specific code for the timing and coordination of the leg behaviors. Later, Pettie Maes, while a visiting faculty member from the University of Brussels, devised a behavioral scheme where Genghis's walking could truly emerge. She eventually implemented an even more resourceful method whereby each time Genghis was switched on, using feedback from sensors on its legs, and a sensor on its belly, which flopped on the ground when the robot fumbled in its attempts to find a stable gait, it would literally *learn* how to walk. It would fall, it would try something else, it would take a step and trip, but finally Genghis would triumphantly, emergently walk.

To be sure, Genghis, and the dream of insect-level intelligence it represented, had its share of detractors. The people in big robotics would look askance at this *bug*, a foot in length and hardly tipping a scale at three pounds. Even as Genghis deftly crawled across the floor, they would object to the claims of its creators in offended tones: What of human culture does this represent? they would ask, and then deliver what for roboticists, ultimately a field driven by steel and pragmatics, is the coup de grace: "What can it *do*?"

Rodney Brooks had the answer for that. Genghis, or its successors, could explore the moon. Or even Mars.

Exploring outer space would require autonomous robots. Using robots controlled from earth would not be feasible: because there would be a time gap between transmission and reception, a human in Texas could not steer a robot across a Martian ditch—it would be as if a truck driver, seeing a curve in the road, waited forty-five minutes before turning the steering wheel. NASA understood that our beachhead on the moon, or on other celestial bodies, would best be established by mobile robots operating independently. The space agency commissioned two institutions to build robots to land in advance of a possible manned expedition to Mars in 2019: the Jet Propulsion Laboratory in Pasadena, California, and Carnegie-Mellon's Robotics Institute. Both of these laboratories proposed large robots working on the classical AI cognitive paradigm. Of the two projects, the rumored front-runner was Carnegie-Mellon's Ambler, a six-legged robot that bore little resemblance to an insect or to any biological specimen—it was more like a propane tank on stilts. It stood 19 feet high, and its six legs were as thick as elephant stumps. It weighed tons, cost millions of dollars, and was not easily transportable.

Brooks regarded robots like Ambler as dinosaurs. He charged that a mission based on a single large robot explorer was doomed to unproductive conservatism. A single mishap might ruin the entire project. He also suspected that no degree of caution would compensate for the handicap of a top-down methodology he felt was inadequate for the task of autonomous exploration.

The reasonable alternative, Brooks argued, was to populate Mars or the moon with hordes of small robots. Dozens, even hundreds, of six-legged subsumption-architecture artificial insects would cost considerably less than a single Ambler. They would be given the ability to communicate with each other. If one insect became permanently disabled—if it died—others would shove it aside and continue their task. The community of robots would behave like an insect colony, with the simple behaviors of each member aiding the execution of a shared goal.

With little encouragement from NASA, Brooks made extraterrestrial exploration and industrial applications a focal point for the Mobile Robot Group. The prototype explorer was Attila, a sophisticated descendant of Genghis. Colin Angle undertook the hardware design. Brooks, who designed the software, claimed that the 3.6-pound artificial creature was the most sophisticated robot per pound ever built by human beings. "I think with Attila, we've almost got insect intelligence," he says. Attila was more solidly constructed than Genghis—it looked meaner. It had twenty-three motors, 150 sensors, and the circuitry of eleven computers. Its legs were jointed, more limber and durable than those of its predecessor, so that Attila was able to walk over rough terrain and climb over obstacles. The nature of the construction also allowed Attila, if it tumbled off a crater and landed on its back, to rotate its legs and the appropriate sensors so that it could continue walking. Besides an array of inclinometers, touch sensors, velocity sensors, and force sensors that enabled Attila to cope with its immediate environment, the robot could also use infrared sensors to sense objects within three meters, and even a video camera to sense distant landmarks.

Anita Flynn, Brooks's longtime lieutenant, postulated a different sort of robot explorer. For several years she had been developing the technology for what she referred to as "gnat robots," artificial creatures barely bigger than quarters which would eventually cost not much more than the currencies that these coins represent. These took advantage of recent advances in silicon-embedded micromotors, visible only by microscopes; such mechanical miniaturization promised a revolution in robotics similar in impact to that experienced by computers during the transition from tubes to chips. Because Flynn had once worked with Danny Hillis, she quickly understood that in the spirit of the Connection Machine gnat robots could harness massive parallelism.

She envisioned millions of gnat robots, with sensor technology embedded in their densely imprinted circuitry, spread over the surface of a planet. Outfitted with transmission capability, they would record seismographic conditions, temperature and humidity, and the presence of certain chemicals, and then send the information to a central orbiter or even to roving Attilas. The gnats could perform their tasks from wherever they landed, or they could explore their immediate neighborhoods. Although some of the first gnat robots, including Flynn's prototype, Squirt, were literally computer chips with wheels, there were better ways of locomotion for such diminutive creatures. In contemplating these movements, Flynn obviously had been thinking of dandelions and grasshoppers: "On Mars, gnats could be spread on the wind," she wrote. "Elsewhere, they could disperse by hopping. Solar cells would collect energy and store it in a silicon spring. After a certain compression, a catch would release the spring, and the robot would go flying."

The papers by Mobot Lab scientists proposing such expeditions were peppered with similarly vivid imagery. One might have been tempted to dismiss these scenarios as overly speculative. Yet in their daily labors, the Mobile Robot Group dealt with the pragmatics and problem solving required to realize these proposals. Their progress indicated that their discussions lay less in the realm of science fiction than in short to medium term agendas, particularly in evoking powerful behaviors from groups of robots.

"Attila is a base and gnat robotics is a base for the next step, which will be emergent behaviors from multitudes of robots, societies of robots," explains Flynn. "People here are starting to think about what they're going to do if they had twenty or a hundred or a thousand robots."

Such thoughts inevitably turned to the insect societies. Pattie Maes, who in 1991 became an assistant professor of computer science at MIT's Media Lab, addressed herself to implementing emergent swarm intelligence in robots. It was Maes, while still on loan from the University of Brussels, who had designed Genghis's walking algorithm. But she had never forgotten some experiments conducted by Luc Steels, the leader of her AI group at Brussels.

Steels spent much time pondering the paradox of emergence: that self-organization provoked autonomous agents following simple rules to cooperate spontaneously. Steels understood that the power of emergence would provide bounty from crumbs. *Something out of nothing*. Yet by its very nature emergence was difficult to control; its results were unbidden. Steels insisted that the difficulty could be overcome. With careful planning and a deep knowledge of complex systems, he argued, it was far from a misnomer to have a specifically evoked emergent behavior.

His experiments involved emergent social behavior from groups of autonomous agents: swarm intelligence. He, too, was looking forward to robot colonies on distant planets. Drawing from the social insect and cellular automata studies of his neighbors at the University of Brussels studying under Prigogine, and postulating robots running under Brooks's subsumption architecture, Steels constructed a "robot ecology" based on functional self-organization. He viewed the ecology itself as a complex dynamical system. Using Prigogine's concept of "dissipative structures," which identified self-organizing powers as rising from the responses of a system in rough equilibrium exposed to an outside disturbance, he designed a simulation of mobile robots engaged in an equilibrium behavior—exploring the terrain around a recently landed spaceship on the moon. The system would be "provoked" by the presence of rock samples. Steels hoped that the system would spontaneously produce a dissipative "spatial structure"—a path—between the rocks and the mother ship. Under the domination of this spacial structure the robots would collect the rocks and deposit them in the ship.

Steels's simulation allowed his virtual robots to perform this tricky task by eschewing hard-to-implement features such as vision or the cognitive use of symbolic logic. Instead, his robots cleverly exploited aspects of dynamical systems. First, they used random behavior in their original explorations, to guarantee that they would find rock samples. (A probability theorem stated that *starting from any point in a random walk restricted to a finite space, we can reach any other point any number of times.*) Second, the robots made use of a "gradient field" to limit the boundaries of their search. A gradient field, Steels explained, is one "emanating from a certain point and diminishing in strength as the distance to the point increases." In this case, it consisted of a pulsating wave of sound originating from the mother ship. As the robots moved away from the ship, the sound became fainter, a circumstance taken into account in their behavior. Finally, Steels used the principles of self-organization and parallelism. Following the simple rules assigned them, the robots performed behavior that altered the environment and thereby altered their subsequent performances of those rules.

Steels ran his simulations on a ten-by-ten-cell grid, with one hundred rock samples scattered. (The rocks were often bunched in clusters; a single cell was capable of holding multiple rock samples.) In the center of the grid was a spaceship beaming sound. Following a set of rules, a number of virtual robots began from this point. If a robot was in exploration mode, it moved away from the sound. If a robot was in return mode, it moved toward the sound. The robots randomly searched the terrain. If one of them reached the boundary of the area covered by the sound waves, it switched to return mode and thus ensured that it would not wander beyond the vivifying sound pulses of the mother ship. If a robot sensed an obstacle, it executed behavioral rules for avoiding it. If a robot sensed a rock sample, it first performed a series of behaviors to collect the rock, then switched to the return-to-ship mode. Using only these behaviors, it took eight virtual robots approximately twenty-five thousand time steps to gather the rock samples. If 256 robots blitzed the terrain, the samples were gathered in around five hundred time steps.

That simulation was limited in that robots communicated only with the mother ship and not with each other. Steels remedied this omission by allotting each robot a number of radioactive "crumbs," easily detectable by robot sensors. Then he added behaviors: when a robot carried a rock sample on its return trek to the mother ship, it would periodically drop two crumbs behind it. When a robot not carrying a sample sensed crumbs, it would pick one up (insuring that trails would not remain indefinitely) and move toward the highest concentration of crumbs. Thus robots would more efficiently be drawn to the fertile rock-hunting areas.

Using this methodology, inspired by pheromone-dropping habits of ants and other social insects, eight of Steels's robots required only twenty-five hundred time steps to swoop up the rock samples—a tenfold decrease from painstaking work of their less communicative cousins. The efficiency was such that increasing the numbers of robots quickly reached a point of diminishing returns. While sixteen robots gathered the samples in fewer than fifteen hundred time steps, doubling and redoubling those numbers failed to match the performance of an equal number of gatherers using less communication. It seemed that brute-force massive parallelism obtained the fastest results, but a more economical approach—only a few robots with the ability to communicate—came fairly close. As ants, wasps, and commune dwellers knew, cooperation yielded wondrous efficiencies.

Similarly, Maes, Brooks, and Mataric proposed the following scenario for a horde of mobile robots attempting to clear an area of lunar terrain in anticipation of a manned expedition. A crucial component of this task would be accumulating piles of lunar soil to use as a shield against solar radiation or perhaps even the building material for the base itself. American and Japanese planners believed this task would be best accomplished by traditional construction technology—a full-size bulldozer, either a robot controlled by radio or a machine actually driven by a blue-collar astronaut. Brooks and his coauthors instead suggested that a swarm of robots should do the job.

The invasion of a-life soldiers would occur several years before astronauts were sent. On arrival on the moon, the spaceship would disgorge several hundred 5-pound, solar-charged robots that resembled tiny bulldozers, with scoops capable of gathering lunar soil. As envisioned by Brooks and crew, each robot would execute the same set of rules, inspired in part by Craig Reynolds's deconstruction of bird-flocking behavior:

1. each robot maintains a minimum distance from the robots surrounding it,

2. each robot matches velocities with the robots in its neighborhood,

3. each robot moves towards the perceived center of mass of the robots in its neighborhood,

4. the velocity of a robot is proportional to the number of big rocks it perceives in its neighborhood (or inverse proportional to the degree of flatness of the local neighborhood),

5. when a robot hasn't moved much for a while it goes into a new "mode," adopting a new set of behaviors which are appropriate for the next global task.

. . . a collection of robots executing the first three rules will tend to wander around some area in a flock-like way. Rules 4 and 5 should ensure that the flock stops wandering around, once an appropriate location has been found.

Again, the robots would follow a series of rules designed to produce emergent, functional behavior. Each robot would emit a radio signal identifying its current mode, and unless other rules subsumed the process all robots would assume the mode of the majority. Robots who detected neighbors on one side only would send a special signal and thus delineate the boundary of the group. Those robots who sensed that their scoops were empty would roam randomly until they sensed a gentle slope, whereupon they would back up and scoop up soil from the incline. Sensing a full scoop, these robots would gravitate to robots sending the special signal. Sensing a pile of soil, they would dump the load from their scoops. Ultimately, the team of robots would level an area of lunar turf and pile soil at the boundary.

Although the Mobot Lab researchers devised their scheme independently, the global process they proposed bore an uncanny resemblance to the vision delivered ten years previous by Richard Laing's team of scientists working under NASA's aegis. The ship carrying the robots corresponded in part to the Laing team's earth-originating "seeds," designed to sprout into self-replicating lunar factories. The scientists reporting to NASA had no inkling that an ethological, bottom-up approach to robotics would promote the construction of lifelike autonomous robots to invade the moon, Mars, and more distant destinations. Inspired by John von Neumann's mind experiment, their proposal had verged on science fiction. With new, enabling technologies, their vision had become feasible.

The experience of the Mobot Lab roboticists, the computational ethologists, and the theorists of emergence demonstrated that the most fertile grounds for seeking those enabling technologies were biological systems. Living organisms, the best machines previously imaginable, embodied powerful processes honed by evolution and self-organiza-

On the left, a sketch of a lunar mining module envisioned in 1980 by the NASA Self-Replicating Systems Concept team. On the right, a rendering of a currently working robot developed by the MIT Mobot Lab, which can be modified to perform those same extraterrestrial tasks.

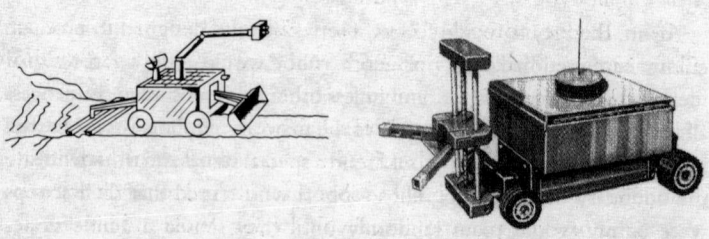

tion. Now that these ideas were being similarly embodied in nonorganic machines, the dreams of the NASA scientists did not seem so farfetched. Nor did the premise that life could exist outside of carbon-chain chemical matter. Consider a reasonable extraterrestrial observer viewing a thousand Attilas on the moon as they flocked toward a location, fanned out to explore the area, and carried stones back to a central pile. Would the observer consider these alive? Consider a similar observer monitoring a planet for a period several times longer than human life span, during which time the product of a-life robot labor was a self-replicating factory that built more robots, perhaps with functional mutations that allowed them to perform their work more efficiently. How restrictive would the observer's definition of life have to be to exclude this system?

At the Mobile Robot Lab, there was no statement of purpose regarding whether the successors of Allen, Herbert, Genghis, and Attila might claim the status of living beings. There did seem a consensus that by striving for animal-level intelligence, as opposed to using the techniques of top-down symbolic knowledge to embody humanlike thought processes in robots, roboticists may well create additions to the natural ecology that would engage in symbiotic relationships with human beings, much in the way humans cultivate houseplants, ride on horses, and employ canaries in mines. One of the papers generated by the lab described the vision: "There may be a colony of almost microscopic screen-cleaning robots that live on your television screen, a horde of slightly larger robots that scrape the food off the plates before the water cycle begins in the dishwasher, a group of mouse-sized robots that keep the corners of your house clean, a family of dog-sized robots that maintain your garden and a herd of hippopotamuses that build the dam that supplies you with water and electricity."

If, as Rodney Brooks claims, Grey Walter's cybernetic Elsie and Elmer surpassed bacteria intelligence, and Attila falls only slightly short of insect-level intelligence, would we soon see life be simulated at, say, the canine level? One of the Mobot Lab workers, Paul Viola, actually wagered a case of fine cognac that he could accomplish this within a decade. That is, he would build a robot that behaved so much like a dog that for all practical purposes it really was a dog. Viola and his skeptical friend would use an intriguing variation of the Turing test to determine whether the bet should be paid off. Viola would bring it home and show it to his friend's (yet-unborn) children.

If they loved it, Viola would win the bet.

THE STRONG CLAIM

How dare you sport thus with life? Do your duty with me, and I will do mine towards you and the rest of mankind. If you comply with my condition, I will leave them and you with peace; but if you refuse I will glut the maw of death, until it be satiated with the blood of your remaining friends.

The monster, in Mary Shelley's *Frankenstein*

On November 3, 1983, Fred Cohen allowed his attention to drift from the discussion in the small seminar room at the University of Southern California (USC). It was a graduate course in computer security, a subject that fascinated Cohen. Consulting work in that area was helping him continue his studies. But he had other burdens that day. Earlier that year his thesis proposal had been rejected. Within a week, he would confront the six-month deadline for submitting another. So far, all he had was a workmanlike elaboration of his original failed attempt, which dealt with theories of parallel processing. If his professors rejected that, there would be no doctorate in computer science and not much of a career. It was no surprise that his mind was restless that day.

Cohen was a nomadic student in electrical engineering and computer security. The son of physicists, he had grown up in Pittsburgh, where he earned a bachelor's degree at Carnegie-Mellon and a master's in information science from the University of Pittsburgh. Robust, brash, and sometimes impolitic, Cohen liked a good time. He was a member of both the lacrosse and Frisbee teams. Yet he realized that the demands of adulthood were on him. Vowing to become "a perfect student," he entered USC to study computational theory and robotics.

Now, Fred Cohen daydreamed as his professor Leonard Adleman and Cohen's fellow students discussed various Trojan-horse attacks on computers. In Cohen's studies on parallel processing, he had become interested in distributed algorithms, a way to allocate parts of a single computational problem to different parts of a computer or even to different computers. He mused that one way to tackle the mechanics of this would be via self-replicating programs. Cohen was of course familiar with von Neumann's work. But the idea he was hatching that morning dealt with much simpler constructs than the famous self-reproducing automaton. What if simple pieces of programs could insert themselves into other programs and assume control of them, in the same way that parasites fix themselves to hosts?

"It was as if there were this curtain between me and the truth, and

God split the curtain apart and said, *'There it is.'* " says Cohen when describing his feelings that day. "I immediately understood the implications. I'd been working on computer security for a long time—I knew how systems worked, and how different attacks worked. . . . But now it came over me. Anyone who writes one of these things would have something that could replicate everywhere."

Cohen's realization provided another key piece in the puzzle of how life should be defined. Life should be regarded as one half of a duplex system: the organism and its environment. A recipe for interactions capable of cooking up the mechanics of life required the setting that allowed its potential to be fulfilled. The DNA code is effective within the structure of a cell, which provides the raw materials to interpret the code by forming its vital enzymes. Von Neumann's kinematic self-reproducing automaton required a lake stocked with the proper body parts. And a certain class of computer programs that could self-replicate and feed on other programs needed a rich data environment. In creating a dizzyingly complex matrix of computer operating systems, we had inadvertently spawned this environment. It was fertile ground for a new type of creature: a parasitic information organism. So rich was this world of data that Cohen believed that even simple creatures could live in it—and wreak havoc on its stability.

When the seminar ended, Cohen explained the idea to Adleman. The professor immediately identified the biological analogue to what Cohen proposed was possible: viruses.

Unknown to Adleman or Cohen, science-fiction writer David Gerrold, in his 1972 book, *When Harley Was One,* had already used the word "virus" (whose own meaning derives from that Latin word for poison) to refer to a rogue computer construct. The coinage had not caught on: Gerrold, in fact, had deleted the relevant passage in reprints of the novel. Cohen ultimately would define a computer virus as "a program that can 'infect' other programs by modifying them to include a possibly evolved copy of itself."

Adleman encouraged Cohen to experiment with the idea. Cohen retreated to the small office he shared with four other students and sat down at his terminal. Within five minutes he had written the code for a program that could insinuate itself into other programs. A computer virus. The easiest part—the destructive component—completed, Cohen worked until the early evening on the more difficult component: code so that the construct would not proliferate uncontrollably. By eight o'clock that night he had completed his work: two hundred lines in the computer language C that would be known as the first documented computer virus.

Cohen wanted the virus literally to seek permission before infecting other programs. "I didn't want to have something that just spread, I wanted to have something I could control," he explains. "It was quite clever as viruses go. Not only would it ask me for authorization, but it wouldn't randomly infect everything. I did analysis of the habits of various users [this was readily available to Cohen because of the habit of the UNIX operating system to provide lists of each user's files] and figured out which programs were run most often by most users. It would infect the thing that was most likely to spread the infection furthest and fastest. It's no different than a biological disease—if you wanted to infect a lot of humans, you would choose to begin with someone like a prostitute in Las Vegas."

Adleman secured permission for Cohen to release his program into the UNIX environment of the VAX 11-750 computer at USC. Cohen doubts that his adviser fully explained the nature of the experiment to the adminstrators that granted the request. How could they have known the implications? Cohen was certain that he could maintain control of his creature. He was the first computer scientist ever to conduct a scientifically monitored release of a predatory information organism "in the wild."

The experiment was performed in mid-afternoon, peak time for computer usage at the university. There were approximately fifty users time-sharing the VAX.

Cohen's virus was implanted into a program called "vd." The ostensible nature of the program was to display people's files in a graphic, easy-to-read manner. While an infected version of vd would perform this function, the virus within it enabled Cohen to subsume the identity of the user who bore the disease. If and when the most important user on a UNIX computer—the system user, also known as the "root"—became infected, Cohen would then have that system user's access to everything on the system, including the ability to read and write to all files, including the operating system itself. It would be like capturing the queen bee: the hive would be his. Cohen posted the availability of the program on the user bulletin board and waited.

When the first user accepted the bait and accessed the program, the virus struck. Scanning the user's files and comparing them to the log determining program activity (kept elsewhere in the system), it chose the most "social" program to infect. In the UNIX system, certain programs in the files of individual users were available to everyone on the system—those most accessed were the choices for invasion. The virus required only half a second to insert itself into this file, a time far too brief for any user to suspect anything was amiss.

In the case of this first infection, the program chosen was an on-screen time-of-day indicator that many users liked to run when they worked with an editing program called EMACS. Approximately half the users would routinely access this clock. When the virus asked Cohen permission to infect, he granted it. The infection then spread to other people using the clock and soon reached the user who had possession of the EMACS program itself. From then on, everyone who used that program would become infected—pending Cohen's permission. The infection would reside in the most social file of each contaminated user. Within a few minutes, the root himself accessed an infected program, and the virus's job was done.

Cohen's virus had completely penetrated the system.

Cohen was now able to access the programs and files of any user; he could type commands as if he were that user. He used this power to carefully eradicate the virus from each user's files. Then he ran the experiment again. He unleashed the virus five times in all. Each time, he achieved 100% penetration. Here was the way Cohen logged a typical run (note that "loadavg" was a frequently used utility program that measured user activity, and "editor" referred to the EMACS program):

ELAPSED TIME	EVENT	EFFECT
(in minutes)		
0	Program announced on BBoard	Existence published
1 min	Social user runs program	"Loadavg" infected
4 min	Editor owner runs	"Loadavg" editor infected
8–12 min	Many users use editor	Many programs infected
14 min	Root uses editor	All privileges granted

The fourteen-minute capture time above was Cohen's second best. The shortest was five minutes. The longest saturation period was an hour.

When Cohen demonstrated his creation at Adleman's seminar, exactly a week after he first conceived the idea, his fellow students seemed to have difficulty understanding what it was they were seeing. One by one, Cohen would have them log into the system and access an infected program. As they watched in astonishment, they were set on by Fred Cohen's virus. Cohen was easily able to explain the theory and the mechanics of what they were seeing. Awakening them to the significance of the experiment was another matter. Cohen later compared the reaction to someone going to his automobile in the morning and finding it missing. One's first reaction might be to wonder if he had parked the car somewhere else. Then he might ask his wife if she had moved the car. It might slowly begin to dawn on him that the car might be stolen. Even so, before calling the police, that person would probably check the parking spot once more. Sometimes evidence alone was not enough to turn a belief around. It also required a willingness truly to see the evidence.

Partially for this reason, Cohen exercised great caution when documenting his results. He took to heart the advice of David Jefferson, then still at USC, who, realizing the significance of Cohen's find, said, "Make this the greatest paper you will ever write." After receiving permission to make computer viruses his thesis topic (it was so late in the game that this could only be done by first submitting his previous proposal with the verbal understanding that he would quickly submit a brief on his proposed subject change), Cohen read extensively on epidemiology, analyzed his data in exacting mathematical terms, and planned experiments on other systems. The latter was no simple matter. As soon as the administrators in charge of the initial test site saw results of Cohen's first experiments, they unconditionally banned any encores, even those proposed by Cohen that would implement special programs to test a system's ability to resist possible infections. "This apparent fear reaction seems typical," wrote Cohen in his thesis. "Rather than try to solve technical problems technically, policy solutions are often chosen."

Those administering other systems at USC expressed similar fears and even refused Cohen permission to perform his experiments using sanitized versions of log tapes in off-line simulation. It seemed to Cohen as if they hoped to eradicate the potential menace of predatory computer programs by willing it away. After months of negotiation, Cohen was finally able to repeat some of his tests on other systems and to reconfirm his results. But despite proposing what he considered foolproof safeguards, he was never able to secure the access he required to experiment with and measure the dissemination of computer viruses.

When Cohen began to discuss his research in public, the response was even more alarming. Cohen would claim that after he spoke at one computer security conference in Canada, an American official told him that, had the State Department known of the subject of his talk, it would not have allowed him to speak. Cohen further claimed that he was subject to a thorough search on reentering the country. After he completed his thesis in 1985, the newly minted doctor had difficulty publishing the paper summarizing it. Finally, in 1987, it was accepted by the journal *Computers and Security*. Because Cohen did not want the people who assisted him to become stigmatized, he felt compelled to take the unusual step of acknowledging them only by their Christian names.

By then it was four years since Fred Cohen had first stumbled on the realization that a fertile information environment existed for a potentially destructive form of artificial life. Cohen had been suffering, and would continue to suffer, from a virtual lockout in funding. His academic career was marked by an inability to continue his experimentation in computer viruses, almost all of which would have been centered in eradication and prevention. Cohen would later vividly recall a presentation from that period. As he introduced the audience to the brave new world of computer viruses, his eyes chanced on the obviously disturbed visage of a young woman.

"It was as if someone told her her mother was not her mother," says Cohen. "That's the reaction I got from most people until the theory and practice of this thing became well understood. It was not within their belief set. And it wasn't until they got hit by it that they understood."

Cohen would eventually be recognized as the father of the computer virus. (This was not necessarily a career-enhancing distinction.) After more research, however, he recognized the footprints of others. Although no one had created a rigorously defined computer virus before Cohen, there had been speculation about predatory computer organisms, with isolated sightings that had become part of computer folklore. Some of these had been products of a digital demimonde. Throughout computer history, such unauthorized after-hours activities sometimes masked advances in the science. Those ventures constituted the brief prehistory of free-range artificial life-forms: wildlife. They came into being as pranks, or unorthodox means of research, and in no case did they seem designed for destruction. But they portended a potentially horrifying future if artificial life were realized without proper controls. Worse, their persistence indicated that those controls might be unattainable.

The first known predatory self-replicating organisms, however, never found their way out of the confines of the unwieldy IBM 7090 mainframe computer in the bowels of AT&T's Bell Labs in New Jersey. These beasts were the digital warriors in a gladiatorial game called "Darwin." In 1962 there was nothing else like it. Darwin's creator, Victor Vyssotsky, used von Neumann automata theory as a basis for the creation of self-replicating programs that were released by their programmers into a virtual arena—much like feral roosters tossed into the cockfight by their trainers. Vyssotsky matched his autonomous gladiators with those of two other Bell computer scientists, H. Douglas McIlroy and Robert Morris, Sr.

The organisms were made of low-level computer language, or assembly-language, instructions that could be executed in the memory "core" of the machine. The organisms could perform three functions: PROBE, CLAIM, and KILL. When an organism was released into the computer environment, it would PROBE addresses in the core. If it found a region of the core to be empty, it could CLAIM the turf by self-replicating. If an enemy resided in the examined area, the organism sought to KILL it.

At one point, McIlroy released an interesting fighter into the core. Possibly it was the first computer construct to be called a virus, although it did not, like Cohen's later creation, infect extant programs in the spirit of a biological virus. It consisted of only fifteen instructions. Because the rules of Darwin allowed each organism to protect twenty of its instructions from the attacks of other organisms, the virus was indestructible. But the organism's brevity dictated incompleteness: it could PROBE addresses for enemies and KILL those it discovered but could not execute instructions for self-replicating. This put it at a disadvantage, because the winner of Darwin, in the spirit of its namesake, was the organism with the most progeny. If it did not destroy its opponents within the game's time limit, it would invariably lose. Not long after the creation of this organism, the third Darwin fanatic, Morris, wrote a creature of thirty instructions that displayed adaptive behavior: it not only learned how to make increasingly effective probes for enemies but also passed that information on to its offspring. It won consistently.

Much of this activity was in the spirit of what would become a-life experiments. The Bell workers tried various biological strategies, even implementing bisexual species (with disappointing results—according to one account, "the two types spent much of the time trying to find one another, and of course the whole species could be killed by exterminating all of either sort"). Yet at Bell Labs, Darwin was regarded solely as a recreation. After each round of battles, the organisms were purged, and it was implicitly understood that no one would reveal the nature of the lab's midnight diversions.

For years Darwin remained a secret. Meanwhile, computer scientists began concocting a variety of information organisms well suited to proliferating in the wild. These did not infect existing programs but simply self-replicated, sometimes erasing the original copies and sometimes multiplying with alarming speed. One of the earliest examples was "Cookie Monster," an anonymously coded mid-1960s program on an MIT time-sharing computer. It caused a typed plea for cookies to persistently scroll across a user's computer and stopped only when the user typed the word "cookie."

In 1971 Bob Thomas, a computer scientist at Bolt Baranek and Newman wrote a more ambitious variation. Thomas's work in air-traffic-control software, where airplanes had to be tracked on different computers as they moved from one region to another, inspired him to write "creeper," which, moving from one node of the Arpanet computer network to another, would unexpectedly appear on someone's computer screen as the message, "I'm creeper! Catch me if you can!" In response, some programmers wrote "reaper" programs that attempted to locate and snuff out creepers.

In the mid 1970s John Shoch and Jon Hupp, two Xerox PARC researchers, came across the idea and attempted to implement it to increase the productivity of the network of personal computers at their research facility in Palo Alto, California. Shoch and Hupp were interested in what was called "distributive computation," a process where boundaries between individual machines are crossed in order to use their collective processing power to address a single problem. Xerox's network linked over a hundred personal computers by a high-speed network protocol called "Ethernet." Shoch and Hupp viewed the entire net as a single computer with a hundred processors. The problem was accessing the different machines in an orderly fashion. As Shoch explains, "You're not going to walk around the building loading up 100 machines with the program, that's a really dull idea."

Eventually, they implemented a creeperlike scheme whereby a program could move around the network, find idle machines, and run tests in them. (Xerox PARC workers seldom, if ever, shut power from their computers; when the machines were not running a user's programs, they would revert to a simple program that diagnosed possible memory problems.) This would best be performed at night, when all but the hardiest programmers had gone home.

Originally, the researchers envisioned their work as akin to the creature in the movie *The Blob,* a formless yet vital ooze that used its viscous nature to insinuate itself into unwelcome areas. But a contemporary science-fiction novel, *The Shockwave Rider,* by John Brunner featured an informational monster that elusively traveled, à la creeper, throughout a network. Brunner's characters called it a "tapeworm." So the Xerox researchers classified any segmented computation capable of living on multiple machines as a worm.

Shoch and Hupp's worm would find idle machines, initialize them to receive a new program, and send a copy of a specific program into the machine. The machine would then run the program, whereupon it would be considered a segment of the worm. When the program was finished with the machine, it would leave and return the machine to its original state.

The only purpose of "the existential worm," the first iteration, was survival. Once a segment was established, it would send out a few more copies; a "complete" worm generally had a fixed number of segments. When a user reclaimed a machine by beginning a program, the segment would move to another machine. A built-in timer would limit the life span of the worm. Next came the "billboard worm," which distributed a graphic image throughout the network. When users arrived in the morning, they would know a worm segment was in their machine by the screen display—a "cartoon of the day." Ultimately, the researchers implemented a complicated worm that, moving from machine to machine, performed useful, otherwise cumbersome, diagnostic tests on the network. The success of this worm indicated that worms could indeed be a powerful tool in achieving distributed computation.

In Brunner's novel, the tapeworm eventually eluded human control. "It can't be killed," said its fictional creator. "It's indefinitely self-perpetuating so long as the net exists." Shoch and Hupp read sober significance into that passage. "The biggest problem associated with worm management," they wrote, is "controlling its growth while maintaining stable behavior." In one nocturnal experiment, they released a small, seemingly innocuous worm into the Ethernet. When they returned the next morning, they were shocked to discover that the network had been rendered a computational wasteland. Dozens of machines were dead, refusing attempts to resuscitate them. The worm still lived.

"If one restarted the regular memory diagnostic, it would run very briefly, then be seized by the worm," wrote Shoch and Hupp when they published their research in 1980. "The worm would quickly load its program into this new segment: the program would start to run and promptly crash, leaving the worm incomplete—and still hungrily looking for new segments." Fortunately, Shoch and Hupp had a doomsday feature in their program that commanded all worms to commit hara-kiri.

What had happened was a mystery. Although they later postulated several ways that worms could similarly run amok, none of those scenarios corresponded with the circumstances of that particular incident. Years later, Shoch would guess that in copying a segment the code had become corrupted. The change had caused the worm to take different form in its self-replication. As a result, the newly destructive worm was not the same as the Xerox researchers programmed but rather, as Shoch says, "a mutation."

Shoch did not push the biological metaphor any further. His worm had little similarity with natural worms. In that, it differed from computer viruses, which actually did what real viruses did, and was not really a predecessor to Cohen's information organism. After Shoch and Hupp published their paper, the idea received some limited notoriety, and some people even experimented informally with creating worms in personal computers. But the idea of computer wildlife still belonged more to science fiction than to computer science. Until Fred Cohen exposed the possibility to his fellow students in Adleman's seminar and, eventually, to the world.

In May 1984, before Cohen's results had been published, A. K. (Kee) Dewdney wrote a column in *Scientific American* about a game he devised called "Core War." Like Darwin, Core War postulated a battle between organisms consisting of instructions in a mock machine code, in this case a language Dewdney created called "Redcode." (By creating a "virtual" language, Dewdney assured that the actual Core War organisms would not be able to live outside the designated battlefield.) In essence the combatants would exchange blows, executing an instruction each round. The aim was, as Dewdney put it, "to destroy the other program by ruining its instructions."

The fighters waged their wars in diabolically variant fashion. An early Dewdney creation was DWARF, which he described as a "very stupid but very dangerous" beast of four instructions, which methodically peppered the core with a barrage of "zero bombs." (A zero bomb was the insertion of a zero in an address on the core; it was capable of damaging the instructions of a creature residing in that address.) A worthy foe for DWARF was IMP, consisting of a single line of code that instructed the creature to move itself to another address in the core.

Dewdney suggested that the ultimate victors of Core War battles would be complicated creatures that displayed intelligence. His readers gleefully provided these sophisticated information organisms. These incorporated both weaponry and shields: some of them were capable of launching IMPs and of implementing IMP-STOMPER components to stamp out enemy IMPs. One of the more successful creatures, MICE, managed to snuff opponents by relentless self-replication. In the first Core War tournament, MICE was challenged by a program called CHANG1, which turned itself into a virtual factory of IMPs. The multiplying MICE fended off CHANG1's zero bombs, and the match ended in a draw.

If Fred Cohen's experiments represented a landmark in the formal study of computer viruses, Kee Dewdney's column marked a signal, if unwelcome, event in the subterranean creation of computer beasts. On one hand many programmers were precisely hewing to the spirit of good clean fun that Dewdney intended for Core War—implementing the game on various microcomputer operating systems, writing innovative Redcode creatures, organizing tournaments, and even forming a club, the International Core War Society. In addition, Core War inspired the methodology for some significant experiments in a-life: Steen Rasmussen's VENUS program used Redcode as inspiration for their computer organisms, as did Tom Ray's Tierra simulator.

On the other hand, Dewdney's writings helped spread the news of the destructive possibilities of information organisms. This was a factor in provoking an epidemic of predatory programs. Three years before Chris Langton initiated the first a-life conference, outlaw programmers were creating free-range examples of artificial life. "There are abundant examples of worms, viruses, and other software creatures living in every conceivable computing environment," Dewdney wrote in a follow-up column in March 1985. "Some of the possibilities are so horrifying that I hesitate to set them down at all."

Particularly chilling was a letter written to Dewdney by two Italian programmers who proposed but did not implement a virus on the popular Apple II computer operating system. Each disk used in the Apple devoted a small portion of its contents to a piece of the disk operating system. The start-up disk used this code to set an ignition key to boot up the computer. Thus it was called a "boot disk." The Italians suggested implanting in that code a virus that would plant itself in subsequent disks inserted in the computer. They surmised that installing a few such infected disks in their city's (Brescia) largest computer store would be sufficient to spur an epidemic, if an epidemic could consist of such a benign virus. They decided that it could not. "No, our virus should be malignant!" they concluded. "So we decided that after 16 self-reproduction cycles, counted on the disk itself, the program should decide to reinitialize the disk immediately after bootstrap." The drawback to their solution was the disk would be wiped clean of all its potentially invaluable information.

Another letter Dewdney included in the column was by a Pittsburgh high school student who had actually written a similar program, differing mainly in its less thorough degree of devastation. (It did not wipe the disk clean but rather mangled the operating system.) In a twist worthy of Mary Shelley, the chief victim of the monster's destruction was apparently its creator. "I have never been able to get rid of my electronic plague," wrote the student. "It infested all of my disks, and all of my friend's disks. It even managed to get onto my math teacher's graphing disks."

Dewdney tried to suggest means of combatting computer viruses, referring to proven defensive measures in Core War strategy. It was the first of what would become a cottage industry of "disinfectant" or "vaccination" programs. It was also too late. By the mid-1980s Fred

Cohen's dour prediction of computer security meltdown was quickly being fulfilled. During the next few years a de facto a-life research effort was launched by both playful and malicious programmers. First came crude viruses appearing on the Apple II computer, with names like "Festering Hate" and "Elk Cloner." Then came over sixty varieties of virus attacking programs running on the popular MS-DOS operating system, including IBM personal computers. The dense informational ecology of busy computer networks was particularly vulnerable to attack. In November 1988, Robert Morris, Jr., a twenty-one-year-old Cornell student (and the son of the computer scientist who had written the invincible Darwin organism at Bell Labs in 1962), released a self-replicating program that came to be known as "the Internet Worm." Morris quickly lost control of his creation and watched helplessly as it wildly made copies of itself and shut down a network affecting millions of users.

In a single human generation, from Morris, Sr., to Morris, Jr., the technology of artificial life had gone from an amusing diversion to a destructive information bomb. This was the dark side of garage-band science: the same powers that could be easily summoned to illuminate life's machinery could just as easily be channeled, intentionally or otherwise, toward mayhem.

On the other hand, as Fred Cohen later noted, Morris's program, by quickly copying itself to over six thousand computers, had established the world's record for high-speed computation. Cohen's remark was made with a degree of irony. During the period that young Morris and other unauthorized experimenters were blithely releasing predatory creatures in the wild, Cohen and other serious researchers were consistently being refused not only funding but even permission to conduct experiments in computer viruses. As a result, the creations of willful criminals and reckless hackers were for years the most active, and in some ways the most advanced, forms of artificial life thus far.

A case in point was the creature concocted in 1986 in the back room of a Pakistani computer store, Brain Computer Services. The store's twenty-four-year-old proprietor, Amjad Farooq Alvi, and his teenage brother Basit, decided to write the virus to punish the American customers (but not the Pakistanis) who bought pirated MS-DOS software from their store. Apparently, they also hoped to reap profits from their creation: when the virus ruined someone's work, it was programmed to post the name and the address of the store, along with a copyright notice and with a note suggesting that the Lahore, Pakistan, business could provide vaccination.

The Brain Virus, as it came to be known, not only was one of the first viruses to infect a large population (estimated at over one hundred thousand) but also was regarded as a fairly clever program. When a disk infected with the Brain was used to start the system, the virus copied itself to the computer memory and then "hid" itself. It then allowed the booting process to continue. If the infected disk was not "bootable" (i.e., it carried only files and was not intended for use in starting the computer), the virus would insert itself in memory anyway, and display the following message on screen:

Please Insert a Bootable Disk Then Type [Return].

In both cases, any disk subsequently inserted in the computer would become infected. The virus would search the disk to see whether it was already infected. If not, it would write the virus, by utilizing three blank clusters of the disk, first marking them "BAD" (making them otherwise unusable), then hiding itself in those areas (a cluster stretches over two sectors of the nine-sectored disk). If no clusters were blank, the disk would be spared; however, if there was only one blank cluster, the virus would write itself on that cluster and overwrite the next two clusters, thus obliterating some data on those clusters. That was where the virus could be destructive. If those sectors held a program, the missing bits would affect the program's operation and would crash the program. If the sectors were part of a data file, that information would be lost, and the contents of the entire file would possibly no longer be available.

Among the diabolical features of the Brain was an ability to resist detection. If someone attempted to use a debugging program to search for the infection, the virus would redirect the search to a noninfected region. The program was also written in such a way that it could not easily be disassembled. Finally, it was sufficiently malleable that its code could be altered by programmers wishing to elaborate on it, a quality that further compounded both its elusiveness and destructiveness. These effectively acted as mutations, and the more fit of these enabled the Brain to be ever more persistent in surviving as a parasite in the data world inside personal computers. As of 1989, researchers had charted ten major Brain mutations, one of which was programmed to remain dormant until May 5, 1992, whereupon it would destroy data.

Even though programmers eventually devised effective vaccination programs against the Brain, observers conceded that the virus was destined to hang on as long as its host, the MS-DOS operating system, remained popular. Even Fred Cohen, who with typical immodesty regarded his own viral creations as by far the most well-crafted variety for many years thereafter, admitted a grudging respect for the Brain authors. "This sucker is going to be here for a while," he says. "It's going to be on computers for tens if not hundreds of years."

Cohen believed that his own virus was literally alive. When the field of artificial life coalesced in 1987, that claim was taken quite seriously. The a-life scientists generally agreed that, of all information organisms, none came so close to fulfilling the admittedly vague demands of life as did computer viruses.

Essentially computer viruses were the first organisms to contend for what was known as the "Strong Claim" to artificial life. This held, according to Chris Langton, "that any definition or list of criteria broad enough to include all known biological life will also include certain classes of computer processes, which, therefore, will have to be considered 'actually' alive." (The "Weak Claim" held that, although a-life experiments were potentially useful simulations of the processes of life, the nature of living systems dictated that they could never themselves become instances of life.)

Did computer viruses, indeed, vindicate those who believed in the Strong Claim? Was the daring leap that artificial life required of its adherents—the belief that life could be created computationally—*already* fulfilled?

It was true that Cohen's virus, the Brain virus, certain winning Core War organisms, and hundreds of other persistent computer creatures shared a frightening quality with natural organisms. All drew on forces much more powerful than themselves, in a manner consistent with life's slickest move: an apparent violation of the second law of thermodynamics. As Leonard Adleman was quick to perceive, Cohen's virus accomplished this trick with eerie similarity to the devices of biological viruses. Yet this alone did not bestow them life.

In fact, it was not clear whether a biological virus itself could be included in the society of life. The debate over this matter had long ago turned into a unproductive stalemate. Biological viruses are no more than naked strands of nucleic acid, either RNA or DNA, surrounded by a sheath of protein. They cannot perform their key organic functions, particularly reproduction, without commandeering the host cells they rudely violate. They remain dormant until invading a cell of a host species, whereupon they burst into activity, hijacking the mechanics of the cell so that it performs tasks geared toward the viruses' ends. The materials inside the cell are appropriated to reproduce new viruses. At times, even parts of the host cell's DNA code are reinterpreted to aid in the production of viruses. Thus viruses are incomplete organisms.

To some, this incompleteness indicated that viruses were something less than fully alive. To others, it seemed obvious that viruses shared so much with organisms universally considered alive—the family of life, from bacteria and up the ladder of complexity—that the boundaries of our definition must include them. Because we had no definition of life, the question was perpetually up for grabs. Author Andrew Scott suggested that the matter be put to rest by considering life not as a collection of separate organisms but as a complete and integrated biosystem. "Within such a system," he wrote, "viruses are certainly *a part of life,* just as we ourselves are a part of life."

Did this mean that computer viruses could also make that claim? As outlined by Doyne Farmer and Alletta d'A. Belin, a computer virus "satisfies most, and potentially all, of the criteria [for life]."

- A computer virus is a pattern on a computer memory storage device.

- A computer virus can copy itself to other computers, thereby reproducing itself.

- Like a real virus, a computer virus makes use of the metabolism of its host (the computer) to modify the available storage medium. . . .

- A computer virus senses changes in the computer and responds to them in order to procreate.

- The parts of a computer virus are highly interdependent: a computer virus can be killed by erasing one or more of the instructions of its program.

- Although many viruses are not stable under large electrical perturbations, by the nature of the digital computer environment they are stable to small noise fluctuations. A truly robust virus might also be stable under some alterations of its programs.

- Computer viruses evolve, although primarily through the intermediary of human programmers. . . . For current computer viruses, random variation is almost always destructive, although some more clever viruses contain primitive built-in self-alteration mechanisms that allow them to adapt to new environments, or that make them difficult to detect and eliminate. Thus contemporary viruses do not evolve naturally. . . . Eventually it is likely that a computer virus will be created with a robust capacity to evolve, that will progress far beyond its initial form.

The similarities between natural and artificial viruses are considerable. Both share the condition of being incomplete organisms that fulfill their active destiny by scavenging host mechanisms. Both are no-frills survival mechanisms dedicated to preserving their essence, a piece of code. They do the same things for the same reasons. They infect, replicate, and go on to infect more, simply to preserve that precious data.

They attack their hosts in similar fashion. Certain forms of biological viruses infect cells by inserting their genetic material into the cell and by operating outside the cell nucleus. Although the cell's DNA is unharmed, the virus uses the cell materials to produce enzymes for its own purpose of reproduction, until the cell's altered production status overwhelms its natural functions. This corresponds to the variety of computer organism called the "shell viruses." These effectively form a shell around the code of the original program, which then becomes a subroutine of the virus. Other natural viruses operate in the cell nucleus. Some of these link their genetic codes to the cell's DNA; these correspond to "add-on" computer viruses, which append their code to the host program. Yet another type of natural virus more subtly integrates itself with a host cell's DNA, as in the case of lysogenic bacteria, whose inherited genomes can include viral DNA. These may be seen as kin to "intrusive" computer viruses, which replace a code from the host program with their own viral code.

Computer security experts began to argue that digital viruses were best fought by applying lessons from biological virology and epidemiology. One expert, postulating that computer systems managers should play the role of epidemiologist, drew the following analogy between natural and artificial viruses:

> A virus is expelled (sneeze, SENDFILE) from an infected member (carrier or originator) of a community (family, users of a common network or system), through a medium (air, network or shared input-output devices or media) through a portal of entry (nose, network reader) to a target member of the community. Depending upon the susceptibility (e.g., immunity, similar language, command or instruction set) of the target and the satisfaction of necessary triggering conditions (passage of an incubation period, event on the system clock, execution of the virus code) the subject may manifest symptoms (fever, pain, destruction or disclosure of files). Even where no symptoms appear, the subject may manifest sub-clinical evidence of infection (give positive response for a test of the virus).

The final element in the Strong Claim for computer viruses was their comparable complexity. Parvoviruses, the simplest variety of natural virus, consist of but a single strand of DNA with a coat made of only three different proteins—the DNA of a particular parvovirus that infects mice stretches for only 5081 nucleotides. Although the still-mysterious nature of biological encryption no doubt ensures that this information is densely compressed, this still represents fewer data than were stored in the Brain Virus.

Computer viruses make a compelling case for aliveness, at least to the degree that biological viruses are alive. Observers are stuck with some variation of the admittedly subjective Vaucanson test. Does it look, quack, smell like a duck? Applying this test to computer viruses, the result is negative only in that no one has yet developed a species capable of true open-ended evolution (although some viruses indeed evolved in a more limited fashion). But this is expected (and dreaded) in the not-too-distant future.

Computer viruses, then, stand just on the cusp of life—and soon will cross over.

Considering that these creatures are illicit, uncontrollable, and destructive, some people become unhinged at the concept of their being the frontrunners of the Strong Claim. Computer virus scholar Eugene Spafford ended a compelling brief on why computer viruses should be considered alive with a sudden turnaround. After affirming that viruses were "very close to what we might define as artificial life," Spafford, who had become galvanized by the virus peril after the Internet Worm struck the computer facility he supervised at Purdue, found his conclusion so upsetting that he questioned his own means of defining life. Then he addressed his real problem:

> I would also be disappointed if computer viruses were considered as the first form of artificial life, because their origin is one of unethical practice. Viruses created for malicious purposes are obviously bad; viruses constructed as experiments and released into the public domain are likewise unethical, and poor science besides. . . . Facetiously, I suggest that if computer viruses evolve into something with artificial consciousness, this might provide a doctrine of "original sin" for their theology.

Spafford preferred that the Strong Claim be proven by something less offensive. Addressing the collected a-life elite in Santa Fe in 1990, he asserted that any task a virus might expedite could be better performed—

and, to the point, performed more safely—by other means. "There are no practical, 'good' viruses," he claimed.

One certainly cannot make that claim for biological viruses. Although the precise contribution of viruses to the development of life on earth is not yet understood, some scientists believe that they hold a crucial role in pushing early organisms off local maxima, much in the same way that Hillis's anti-Ramps forced his Ramps to better evolutionary solutions to the sorting problems. More recently, humans have learned, beginning with the use of the relatively benign cowpox virus as a successful immunizing vaccination against deadly smallpox, to use "good" viruses to fight more destructive ones. Certain a-life scientists—chief among them Hillis—believe that computational viruses might similarly be used as tools to expedite otherwise-cumbersome or -unmanageable tasks.

One obvious application would use computer viruses to fight computer viruses. These antiviruses, like dormant antibodies in an immune system, would harmlessly reside in operating systems until the presence of a hostile virus triggered their activation. Some of these have already been written, including a set of programs created by programmers at Lawrence Livermore Laboratory. But the Livermore Lab creatures were never released in the wild. The system administrators were worried that the autonomous antivirals might themselves cause damage. Their position was similar to that of an agricultural officer deciding whether to import a foreign predator that attacked a troublesome parasitic insect: it would be impossible to predict the full effects of the newcomer on the complex ecology. Indeed, Den Zuk (translated, this means "search"), a flawed antiviral written by a Venezuelan programmer to combat the Brain Virus, on its unauthorized release into the personal computer environment, wound up causing damage comparable to that caused by its target virus.

Yet the potential benefits of such programs encouraged scientists to think of ways to exploit them. "Viruses have two features, aside from their nastiness, that make them so effective," wrote scientist Harold Thimbleby, a computer scientist at Stirling University in Scotland. "They are autonomous and they communicate. . . . There are all sorts

331

of occasions where the user would like to have autonomous communication *working on his own behalf.*" Thimbleby and a colleague thus began creating what they called "liveware"—self-replicating organisms programmed to perform tasks automatically. Thimbleby was careful to avoid the epidemiological jargon of computer viruses; he stipulated that liveware creatures did not infect the data they manipulated, but rather they "enlivened" it.

One of the first examples of liveware enhanced a data base of research work in human-computer interaction. Thimbleby ordinarily would send out questionnaires and integrate the information into his data base. Instead he sent out the data base itself, "enlivened" with liveware. The virus residing in the program had the ability to recognize when another copy of the data base found its way onto the same computer. When that occurred, both data bases would examine their kin. Each data base would then supply the other with any information it held that its cousin was lacking. "The database therefore keeps itself up to date, with practically no cost," wrote Thimbleby.

Fred Cohen was also a believer that the biological mechanisms in computer viruses could be exploited as tireless information workers. He wrote a "viral bill collector," software to automate bill collecting for businesses that needed their information distributed over several computers. The program employed evolving viruses. Each virus monitored a number of individual cases. The autonomous virus sensed when a task was required on a given case and sprang into action. If a reminder had to be sent to the debtor, for instance, the virus would initiate that process, then put itself to sleep, scheduling a "wake-up call" that told it when to take the next action. If before that point a debtor paid the bill, a human would register the information and the virus would be awoken to register that event. At any time, a human operator could gather information on payments due by "polling" the viruses monitoring the cases. In addition, Cohen populated the environment with a number of maintenance viruses that monitored the system by various means. It swept up the digital detritus of dead viruses, policed the human operators so no one without the proper clearance could access files, and, most important, aided in the process of evolution.

"In my bill collector system," wrote Cohen,

whenever a person wakes up a collector, a different maintenance virus is given the chance to reproduce. Whether the birth takes place depends upon the probability of reproduction associated with the parent virus: that probability declines with successive generations. At birth, each virus is assigned a reproductive probability and a limited life span to keep the population under control. When the probabilities are adjusted properly, the viral population becomes stable yet resilient. . . . Eventually the system operated for two years with no human intervention except the adding and removing of users.

Cohen believed that, while malignant computer viruses could be controlled, beneficial viruses could "lead to remarkable enhancements of information systems, which should come to bear the brunt of the world's menial work." In an attempt to shift the focus of computer virus work from predator to symbiotic organism, he offered, under the aegis of his small company, an annual $1000 prize for "the most useful computer virus." He was immediately attacked by Spafford, who warned that Cohen was, in effect, inviting programmers to experiment recklessly with forces they could not control. Cohen, he charged, was behaving not only irresponsibly, but immorally.

Morality's entrance into the debate was a fitting intrusion. At its heart the question is not whether experiments in computer viruses should be encouraged. Computer viruses are not inherently bad any more than biological viruses, or any form of life, can be considered bad. Uncontrolled release of viruses into the information ecosystem, however, can certainly reap unhappy results for those who depend on the stability of that system.

The real moral question is whether artificial life itself should be encouraged. The dangers of viruses are a vivid paradigm of the perils inherent in any realized form of a-life. These perils are rooted in what Doyne Farmer once called "the bugaboo of Frankenstein." In Mary Shelley's story, the villain was not so much the murderous and ultimately vindictive artificial life-form as the hubris of its creator. Intoxicated with the power of creation, he assumed that one could forge life without bearing the consequences. As Spafford glumly warned, damage from computer viruses only hinted at the danger to come: "Similar but considerably more tragic results could occur from careless experimentation with organic forms of artificial life."

By "considerably more tragic," Spafford was not kidding. As the practitioners of artificial life themselves are quick to note, the development of a-life opens a box of potential horrors worse than those that daunted Pandora. "It involves a threat to our species," wrote Farmer and Belin. "It is easy to imagine nightmare scenarios in which cold, malevolent machines, or vicious genetically engineered creatures overwhelm humanity."

How could that occur? Farmer and Belin suggested a horrifying example of a potentially destructive use of a-life techniques—"military applications . . . from battlefield robots to satellite warfare." Considering the pervasive government funding of a-life studies, from Farmer and Langton's T-13 group to Brooks's Mobot Lab, this seems almost an inevitability. (In 1990, the United States government solicited contracts for the development of computer viruses for military use.) Farmer contended that, if a-life came to realize its potential, those uses would destroy even those who sought to utilize it. "Once self-reproducing war machines are in place, even if we should change our mind and establish a consensus, dismantling them may become impossible—they may be literally out of our control. An escalated technological war involving the construction of artificial armies would certainly end by destroying the participants themselves, and would give rise to a generation of life forms that might be even more hostile and destructive than their human ancestors."

This warning seems less fantastic in light of the fact that, with computer viruses, an "organic" technology beyond our control has already been unleashed—a technology so simple that a single college student can use it to stall the labors of a million people. The very properties that made artificial life worth pursuing assure that the most advanced forms of a-life will be difficult, if not impossible, to control. Other autonomous organisms will undoubtedly follow in the viruses' wake. By utilizing the biological mechanics that allow natural life to evolve according to its own rules of fitness, one invariably creates organisms that operate according to their own needs, whether or not these happen to correspond to their creator's needs. This quality allows artificial organisms to discover perpetually innovative solutions to the problems researchers pose to them, but it also flirts with the risk that the organisms will mutate in a manner that will make them, in effect, ask themselves why they should bother to do what the researchers want them to do.

Consider an autonomous robot that has been programmed with Isaac Asimov's famous three laws of robotics. The first of these states, "A robot may not injure a human being, or, through inaction, allow a human being to come to harm." If, however, a robot were constantly self-reprogrammed by genetic principles, it might discover a code mutation that made its operating program jump over the subroutine that evoked that rule. Certainly such a robot, freed from the quite unnatural restriction of placing another organism's interests above its own, would increase its fitness. If the trait were passed on to its descendants, those offspring would eventually proliferate, and future generations of robots would have no compunction about harming human beings. Like other beneficiaries of evolution, they would be guided by their own genetic self-interest. As a result, UCLA biologist Charles Taylor notes, "Artificial life violates Asimov's First Law of Robotics by its very nature."

This inherent potential for catastrophe makes artificial life a horribly risky proposition. In this view, the promise of a-life, and the powerful benefits it draws by apparent violation of a different law—the second law of thermodynamics—are as illusory as the belief that life actually does violate the second law. Of course, it does not. In the long run there is an entropic bill to be paid. Any local creation of order will eventually incur a payback in accelerated disorder. It is almost as if life were a Faustian deal with the universe, a temporary respite from the second law, with horrific consequences to come. Some of these consequences are already apparent: the order we created by building the edifices of our civilization has already resulted in the entropy of pollution. This principle can also be seen rather clearly in computer viruses. From the point of view of the infecting agent, the Brain Virus's replications are creating pockets of order from an otherwise-disordered information universe. Yet the computer user realizes, to his or her dismay, that, although the Brain Virus promotes order for itself, the toll it exacts from its overall environment is massive *dis*order. In exchange for its few bytes of organization, the Brain Virus scrambles megabytes.

Likewise, a kinematic von Neumann automaton such as a self-replicating mining factory would undoubtedly provide a massive return on its investment: yet ultimately it and its billions of progeny would be a force for massive disorder, as the stored energy of the materials it gathered would be irrevocably broken down and used up by the factories. The 1980 NASA Self-Replicating Systems (SRS) team predicted, "Environmentalists might perhaps regard SRS released on earth merely as automated strip-mining robots—yet another sophisticated instrumentality in the hands of those who would mercilessly rape the Earth of its limited resources, leaving behind the ugly scars of profit." Interestingly, the NASA team, condemning this view as short sighted, suggested that more self-reproducing robots could be created to undo the damage and restore earth to its original state. Taken to its logical point, this solution would initiate an elaborate pyramid scheme, lasting perhaps thousands of years, where the landscape was perpetually filled with new a-life factories undoing the work of their predecessors, until there were no resources left to set the next round in motion.

Even the optimistic NASA team confronted the possibility that artificial life would drive natural life out of existence, citing the work of physicist J. P. Wesley, who wrote, "Machines, being a form of life, are in competition with carbon-based life. Machines will make carbon-based life extinct."

One would think that the enormity of this peril—no less than the end of humanity, perhaps even of the entire biomass—would evoke a ground swell of opposition to a-life. Yet none has so far emerged. This is due less to artificial life's dire risks than to the widespread belief that *it is not possible*.

After several years of a-life research—the first tentative steps in what may be an epic trek—could one confidently defend that assumption? Could the doubters of the Strong Claim to a-life easily deny the promising nature of the field's beginnings—the aggregate labors of von Neumann, Conway, Wolfram, Kauffman, Langton, Farmer, Holland, Hillis, Ray, Lindenmayer, Wilson, and Brooks? On what basis?

To be sure, a-life is so young a field that no cottage industry of nay

sayers (such as the one that thrived on denying the possibility of strong
AI) has yet arisen. Those who still cling to vestiges of vitalism, of course,
dismiss the Strong Claim out of hand; others construct their disproofs
out of the droppings of those who professionally attack AI. Yet the
standard objections to AI do not seem to apply to artificial life. Roger
Penrose seemed to acknowledge this in his long argument about the
impossibility of consciousness emerging from artificial intelligence, *The
Emperor's New Mind*. After a discussion of natural selection and the
chimera of consciousness, Penrose appeared reluctant to rule out the
possibility that a machine could indeed become conscious—if evolution
were the mechanism by which it was attained. "There is still something
mysterious about evolution, with its apparent 'groping' toward some
future purpose," he wrote. "Things at least seem to organize themselves
somewhat better than they 'ought' to, just on the basis of blind-chance
evolution and natural selection. . . . There seems to be something about
the way that the laws of physics work, which allows natural selection to
be a much more effective process than it would be with just arbitrary
laws." These apparently teleological properties of evolution, of course,
are actually the self-organizing properties that a-life examines and attempts to exploit.

The most ardent critics of artificial life seem to be researchers in
systems theory, many of whom trace their intellectual lineage to cybernetics. They are often quick to cite the simulation problem. This is the
telescoping of an obvious truism—any simulation of something cannot
be the same as the object it simulates—to a general criticism of the
methodology of simulation. Even those enthusiastic about the Weak
Claim to a-life, like Howard H. Pattee, have warned that its practitioners
should resist the temptation to assume that fascinating results of computer experiments had relevance to the physical world. But in practice
a-life frees itself from that dilemma by insisting that, although, indeed,
a computer experiment is by no means equivalent to something it may
be modeled on, it certainly is *something*. Maps are not *the* territory, but
maps are indeed territories.

The methodology of a-life also shatters a related objection, that computer experiments, by their deterministic nature, can never attain the
characteristics of true living systems. According to this argument, life

cannot emerge from a mere execution of algorithms: in the natural world any number of chance occurrences contributed to the present biological complexity. But random events are indeed well integrated into artificial life. Von Neumann himself proposed, although he did not have the chance to design, a probabilistic version of his self-reproducing cellular automaton, which obviated the deterministic nature of the previous version. Many experiments in a-life, especially those that simulate evolution, include a step where random events make each iteration unpredictable. In any case, even in deterministic systems such as the CA game, Life, the cacophony of variables is sufficiently complex that the system can yield unbidden, or emergent, behavior.

Recognizing this, some systems theory critics have seized on the evanescent nature of emergence as their caveat about artificial life. A student of Pattee, Peter Cariani, claimed that a-life could be evaluated only by rigorous definition of emergence and that such a definition would establish that a product of pure computation could never aspire to the kind of emergence achieved in the biological world. But early results from open-ended experiments in a-life, such as Ray's Tierra, cast doubts on this claim. Likewise, the nature of computer viruses seems to contradict Cariani's position that "biological organisms are autonomous relative to us, while computer simulations are not."

As more scientists come to regard a-life with increasing seriousness, they undoubtedly will launch other theoretical arguments, perhaps conclusive ones, against the Strong Claim to artificial life. Until then it seems reasonable to assume that von Neumann's instincts were correct, and that his mathematical proofs of computational self-reproduction indeed are relevant to the matter of life. The early work in artificial life so far seems only to confirm this.

Given that, there seems but one rationale for ignoring the potential consequences of a-life: the assumption that it will be an arbitrarily long period before scientists create indisputably living organisms, and longer still before those organisms pose a serious threat to our well-being, let alone to our survival. The almost innate skepticism about whether it could happen at all, when combined with the vague feeling that the entire enterprise has a whiff of the crackpot to it, assures that the alarm over what those scientists are doing will be minimal. The field of artificial life will therefore be policed only by itself, a freedom that could conceivably continue until the artificial-life community ventures beyond the point where the knowledge can be stuffed back in its box. By then it may be too late to deal with the problem by simply turning off the computers. As Norbert Wiener wrote forty years ago,

> Again and again I have heard the statement that learning machines cannot subject us to any new dangers, because we can turn them off when we feel like it. But can we? To turn a machine off effectively, we must be in possession of information as to whether the danger point has come. The mere fact that we have made the machine does not guarantee that we shall have the proper information to do this.

The scientists seeking artificial life are acutely aware of this. "Right now it's kind of nice that artificial life is underground, because it means we can keep a low profile and just do what we want," says Doyne Farmer. "But as responsible scientists I really do think that this is the thing that's going to have the biggest impact on the world in a hundred years, and we should try to get the issues out in front. And we should do that before the equivalent of the bomb is here. Certainly at this point artificial life is not at all like nuclear weapons, but on the other hand it may be that once it starts happening it happens a lot faster than we expect. Exponentials are always deceptive in that regard. And I do think we're on some kind of exponential growth curve. I think it's going to be a lot better if we're prepared—if we've thought about the issues, if we know how we're going to address them, if they've been aired properly before that happens."

In that spirit, the leaders of the artificial life movement are diligent in urging a discussion of these matters. Chris Langton in particular insists that the biannual a-life conferences address the ethics and potential dangers of the new science. He hopes that, through frank and open discussion, the researchers would impose implicit sanctions on those who would use artificial life to arm the dogs of war. He expects the scientists to agree eventually on a framework of responsible methodologies. As with safeguards used in biotechnology labs, these would be mandatory. Codes would be written in a manner that obviated the emergence of destructive wildlife. Langton and his colleagues have faith that, with careful tending and scrupulous openness, the work of a-life will limit itself to increasing our knowledge of living systems and to using that knowledge for our benefit.

"Los Alamos wasn't an illogical place to hold the first workshop on artificial life," he says "It was here that the mastery of atomic fusion and fission, the technology of death, if you will, happened in secret, with no official concern about the possible consequences of mastering the technology, or deploying it, actually; and with no public feedback about whether we should do this or not. I want to make sure that artificial life happens with all those axes reversed. Not in secret, but out in the open, with as much attention to the possible consequences, implications, both good and bad, as possible. We want to encourage public feedback. We're going out of our way to involve not just scientists but philosophers, artists . . . people whose profession it is to worry about the consequences of technology."

Langton insists on devoting attention to certain issues even while admitting that the discussions are in some ways almost comically premature. The scientists at the 1990 a-life conference spent a session discussing whether artificial life-forms should one day be granted civil rights. Or whether those life-forms may *demand* their civil rights. Some of the questions had already been posed: the scientists in the 1980 NASA summer study had speculated on that very question. More recently, the late physicist Heinz Pagels addressed the question in *The Dreams of Reason:*

> The day will come when people have moral concerns regarding artificial life—what are our obligations to the beings we create? Can we permit such beings to hurt and kill one another? We may have a moral problem in determining what actions we allow our artificial creatures to undertake. Perhaps we ultimately have to let our creations be free to come to terms with themselves.

Skeptics would find Pagels's suggestion ludicrous. But the true believers of strong a-life have long ago assessed the matter with logic and sobriety. The more they learn about the universe and the mechanics of its complexity and the more they learn about the theory of computation and its eerie reflection in the realm of biology, the less they see that causes them to think otherwise. On a nonscientific basis, they even have attempted to accommodate the concept that life can be created by initiating emergent patterns in a computer or within the chips of a robot, with human spirituality. Believing that one could create the patterns that consist of life, they insist, does not necessarily strip life of its awesomeness. Nor of its dignity. And, if that dignity is to be retained in artificial creations, it is fitting that the subjects of the new creation would be regarded as having the same rights as other living creatures.

Some of the would-be life bringers, emphasizing that in this they are speaking informally and not as scientists, even speculate that their own creations would have souls.

"To me there is a soul, but the soul is in emergence," says Danny Hillis. "The soul is the result of taking simple things that you understand the rules of, and applying this emergent behavior that is both a consequence of the rules and also not obviously connected to it. That's to me where the soul is. That's a much more interesting, robust place for the soul to be than off in some little corner of science which we just haven't figured out yet."

Norman Packard seems to agree. "People want there to be something sacred about life," he says. "I think there *is* something sacred, and I think that there is actually something that's still mysterious. Even though I believe you can have a living process in a completely computational realm I think there's still a question of what is the nature of the soul, and in what sense do living things have soul. If you can envision something living in an artificial realm then it's hard not to be able to envision, at least some point in the future, arbitrarily advanced life-forms—as advanced as us. Therefore they would probably have a soul, too. Then you'll have to deal with the problem with whether they have their own rights as entities, and that could prove to be a real mess."

Chris Langton puts the matter of granting civil rights to artificial life in another way:

> By the middle of this century, mankind has acquired the power to
> extinguish life on Earth. By the middle of the next century, he will be

able to create it. Of the two it is hard to say which places the larger burden of responsibility on our shoulders. Not only the specific kinds of living things that will exist, but the very course of evolution itself will come more and more under our control. The future effects of changes we made now are, in principle, unpredictable—we cannot forsee all the possible consequences of the kinds of manipulations we are now capable of inflicting upon the very fabric of inheritance, whether in natural or artificial systems. Yet if we make changes we are responsible for the consequences.

When pressed on the issue of responsibility, however, otherwise-thoughtful a-life scientists become uncomfortable. They admit that there is no precedent for what they hope will occur: a powerful, potentially catastrophic technology will perpetually remain a benign and beneficial force. They live a paradox: in creating something that more fully reveals the beauty of living systems than anything that has come before it, they may be initiating the end of their own species. Of all the controls and restraints they suggest, none includes the single best control: abstinence. *Stop doing it*. They proceed on the assumption that the risk is worth the benefits—a chance to unearth an unimaginably productive force and, perhaps more important, to unlock the secrets that billions of years of evolution has led its subjects to ask. Perhaps it was something in the nature of evolution itself, a sort of fitness function, that has led human beings to seek such truths. "Nature is *there,* and I think curiosity is an inexorable force that can't be contained," says Farmer. "And I think learning for its own sake is just something that is a force that goes beyond us."

Some a-life scientists, however, believe that the creation of artificial life is destined to be the next major punctuation in natural evolution. Some, as did the NASA SRS team, speculated on an emergence of a-life organisms that will symbiotically share the environment with humans. Possibly, they will be our equals. Possibly, our superiors. Others sincerely think that newly minted organisms will assume our own evolutionary niche. Farmer and Belin put it succinctly, "With the advent of artificial life, *we may be the first species to create its own successors.*"

"I see basically us racing towards the next level of organization of life," says Langton. "The next major leap in the complexity of life will be to incorporate biological life together with sort of technological life. There will be collections of biological and mechanical things which together constitute a higher level of the organization of life."

This so-called postbiological future was first envisioned by J. D. Bernal in *The World, The Flesh and the Devil*, a prescient volume of speculation published in 1929. While von Neumann was still doing quantum mechanics in the coffeehouses of Göttingen, years before pondering automata theory, Bernal—a young crystallographer who would later become one of Britain's most distinguished life scientists—had been thinking about the future of artificial life. "To make life itself will be only a preliminary stage," he wrote. "The mere making of life would only be important if we intended to allow it to evolve of itself anew. . . . Men will not be content to manufacture life: they will want to improve on it."

The postbiological vision begins with the premise that genetic evolution has been outstripped by cultural evolution. Whereas previous organisms adapted to their environment by changing their physical constitution over a period of generations, conscious human beings developed the ability to adapt very rapidly by nongenetically passing information to each other and to their descendants. Instead of developing bodies that withstood very cold temperatures, for instance, humans learned how to make warming clothes and how to heat their domiciles. So quickly have humans constructed a world where cultural artifacts are more necessary for survival than physical characteristics that humans themselves are walking anachronisms, saddled with unusable debris (body hair, fingernails, outmoded gender instincts) from an evolutionary past they have since discarded. "In the present condition, we are uncomfortable halfbreeds, part biology, part culture, with many biological traits out of step with inventions of our minds" wrote Hans Moravec, the Carnegie-Mellon roboticist who vividly outlined the postbiological vision in his book, *Mind Children*.

In the early history of life, there has been a possible precedent. According to Scottish biologist Graham Cairns-Smith, the predecessor of life as we now know it was clay-based crystals. These occasionally held defects that acted as evolutionary mutations. Certain mutated crystals proved capable of more growth and reproduction than others and proliferated. As clay structures became more complicated they acquired the ability to encode their genetic information in strings of carbon molecules, which proved more stable than their previous means of inheritance. Eventually the strings of carbon molecules were able to survive without the clays, and thus began carbon-based life. Cairns-Smith referred to this origin-of-life theory as a "genetic takeover."

Now, the theory goes, we are ready for a second genetic takeover: the silicon-based organisms of a-life will replace carbon-based life, including human beings. The new life-forms would have certain advantages. Physically, they would be more protean: their bodies could be made of any materials and in any shape. They could be more durable; they would not have to die for perhaps thousands of years, if that. These new organisms would also be able to evolve by *two* forms of evolution: Darwinian natural selection, and Lamarckian inheritance of acquired characteristics. Because their essence would be information held in the malleable form of silicon bits and not in the hard-wired molecules of DNA, one could tinker with one's own genetic code and integrate what one learned during the course of one's lifetime—or even what others learned during the course of their lifetimes.

(Moravec and Hillis anticipated that these new life-forms would be able to accommodate the consciousness of a human being, allowing them to live in vastly improved bodies for thousands of years. "I have the same nostalgic love of human metabolism that everybody else does, but if I can go into an improved body and last for 10,000 years I would do it in an instant, no second thoughts," says Hillis. "I actually don't think I'm going to have that option, but maybe my children will.")

Despite Hillis's hopes, and Moravec's blithe prediction that this form of "down loading" one's consciousness into another life-form may occur within the next century, most a-life scientists consider that time frame, if not the entire concept, exceedingly optimistic. Although viral-level artificial life is at hand, and insect-level life is being contemplated, these are mere anthills to the comparative Everests of mammals, primates, *Homo sapiens*. Most of those who accept the premise of what Farmer called the "coming evolution" see it ocurring in centuries, if not in millennia. Yet they quite soberly believe it will occur. This places them in an interesting dilemma. Although uniformly recommending strict safeguards in a-life experimentation and urging that a-life creations not be used as tools of war, some of these scientists are genuinely enthusiastic about the possibility that their labors will eventually lead to the extinction of the human race.

Those who hold this view speak of the potential successors to human beings—those "mind children" who provided Moravec with a book title—with paternal pride. "What will these successors be like?" asked Farmer and Belin. "If we fail in our task as creators, they may be cold and malevolent. However, if we succeed, they may be glorious, enlightened creatures that far surpass us in their wisdom and intelligence."

Does this mean that the glory of these creations will be sufficient to ease the pain of our own extinction? Yes. "I'm not overly perturbed by the prospect that there might be something better than us that might replace us," says Hillis. "I see no reason to believe that we're the end of the chain and I think that better than us is possible. To me what's important about humans is that they love, create and think and certainly I wouldn't want to be replaced by something that didn't do those things. To me it's not very important that humans have five fingers. If I had a son with six fingers and somehow that enhanced his ability to love and create then I would feel very happy about that."

Disdaining the parochial human point of view on the matter, the postbiological a-life scientists prefer to regard the matter in evolutionary time. "If you just consider things on the timescale of human lives, you get this feeling that nature has a certain harmony," says Packard.

And that it's good not to disrupt this harmony too much—it's good not to pollute the planet, and it's not good to destroy each other with atom bombs. It's good to kind of maintain a certain ecological, global harmony. But on a longer timescale, not a few years, but a few million years, I think there's a different kind of harmony. There's a harmony of the evolutionary process. This harmony is completely divorced from the existence or the maintenance of a particular species, let alone a particular individual. You and I, we're totally irrelevant, absolutely irrelevant. The evolutionary harmony, because of its timescale, becomes divorced from individual considerations or even species considerations.

I believe very strongly in the inevitability of the evolutionary process. The reason that artificial life is really exciting to me is because it allows me to participate in this harmony. The only thing that worries me is that somehow we would be so inept as to introduce an element of cruelty into our successors. But I have a fairly strong feeling that the process of evolution carries with it an intrinsic fairness to all the entities that have participated. As long as what's happening is the integral part of the evolutionary process of what's already going on I think that that fairness will be part of the process.

Of course there is another possibility. Our interest and ability to create new successors may not be so much a component of any sort of universal harmony but rather a fatal genetic flaw, a misbegotten evolutionary dead end, leading to the creation of a-life organisms that do no more than drive us into unwilling extinction. If that were so, those steering artificial life toward the creation of autonomous, evolving organisms truly will become successors to the fictional Victor Frankenstein, who was destroyed not so much by his own creation as by his willingness to tamper with the justifiably forbidden. In 1980 the NASA SRS team asked a rather frightening question concerning the impact of a second creation by the hand of human beings and not natural forces:

> What of man's view of himself? He now takes pride in his uniqueness. How will he adjust to being just an example of the generic class "intelligent creatures"? On the other hand, the concept of "God" may take as much a beating as the notion of "man." After all, He is special now because He created us. If we create another race of beings, then are we not ourselves, in some similar sense, gods?

Venturing into the territory of gods exhilarated some, sobered others. One of the latter was Los Alamos physicist Steen Rasmussen. Well aware of the hubris involved in flirting with the prospect of humanity's end, he confessed that in his heart of hearts he was doing wrong.

"If you ask me really honestly, 'Steen, why are you doing this?' I can't answer you," he says. "I feel in some way that I am committing sin by the things I am doing."

Although he does not share Rasmussen's sense of sin, Chris Langton, too, is occasionally visited by doubts. In late 1991, for instance, he had a small dilemma to ponder. He had been wondering what it would take to convince a skeptical biologist that a process occurring inside a computer was alive. In order to spur discussion on the matter, he considered recruiting a corporate sponsor to offer a cash prize to the person or persons who created the first indisputably living artificial organism. To do this it would have to satisfy a set of criteria established by biologists, preferably biologists who disbelieved that such creatures could ever be computationally created. The premise was exciting, and Langton certainly believed that within his lifetime someone would collect the prize for the organism that fulfilled a-life's Strong Claim. But there was also something about the project that gave him pause.

"I'm of two minds about it," he admitted. "There are ethics that need to be thought through. Suppose in the late forties they'd offered a $10,000 prize for an atom bomb?"

Yes, there was the ultimate danger to consider, a more insidious—yet no less destructive—threat than Los Alamos's previous creation. There was also the question of hubris. In a way, Langton was staring into the same void into which his mythic predecessors had ventured, from the medieval rabbi who summoned the golem, to Victor Frankenstein.

But that was the legacy of legend. Ultimately, that path would wind its way back to vitalism, to superstition. Although he and his colleagues are intrigued—humanly so—by the speculative possibilities of their work, what drives them is not the sort of vision reclaimed from pulp science fiction, but the spirit of methodical inquiry associated with science. It is deeply tied to the urge to understand the universe, particularly the bewitching complexity of biological systems and systems that emulate them.

Langton finally decided that for the immediate future any competitions he organized would reward only small steps toward artificial life, and not the full creation. This, he believed, would help the cause of science. That was the bottom line: Langton was a scientist.

Still, he worried.

"This is not stuff to be taken lightly," he said. "It's not just a $10,000 prize for a computer game that does something. It's *life*."

NOTES AND SOURCES

The main source of information for *Artificial Life* was a series of interviews conducted between April 1989 and December 1991. These were supplemented by books, scientific publications, magazine articles, newspaper accounts, and communications by electronic and hard-copy mail. Generally, unless it is specified that a quotation comes from a written or printed source, or unless the context implies as much, comments within quotation marks are from personal interviews with the author.

The sources who patiently submitted themselves to my questions and interviews include:

David Ackley	Jonathan Connell	Ed Fredkin
Colin Angle	George Cowan	Simon Goss
Richard Bagley	James Crutchfield	William Hamilton
Mark Bedau	Hugo DeGaris	Hyman Hartman
Rodney Brooks	Jean-Louis Deneubourg	Danny Hillis
William Buckley	Gary Drescher	Pauline Hogeweg
Arthur Burks	Doyne Farmer	John Holland
Peter Cariani	Anita Flynn	David Jefferson
Fred Cohen	Walter Fontana	Gerald Joyce
Robert Collins	Stephanie Forrest	Ted Kaehler

Stuart Kauffman	Peter Oppenheimer	Karl Sims
John Koza	Norman Packard	Alvy Ray Smith
Richard Laing	Lynn Parker	Steve Smith
Chris Langton	Mark Pauline	Eugene Spafford
Chris Locke	Steen Rasmussen	Charles Taylor
Pattie Maes	Thomas Ray	Tommaso Toffoli
Norman Margolus	Mitchel Resnick	Michael Travers
Maja Mataric	Craig Reynolds	Paul Viola
David McFarland	Rudy Rucker	Stewart Wilson
Marvin Minsky	John Shoch	Stephen Wolfram
Hans Moravec	Michael Simmons	Larry Yaeger

Artificial life is a new field and has yet to accumulate a literature of its own. However, a-life can reasonably lay claim to a considerable body of work executed in other disciplines, where in retrospect it appears that the authors were addressing relevant subject matters in a spirit akin to that of artificial life studies. Many of these works are listed in the notes below; however, a far broader selection is offered in an extensive bibliography appended to the proceedings of the first artificial life conference. Those proceedings and the sequel, which includes papers generated by the second a-life conference, constitute the best technical primer for the field:

Christopher G. Langton, ed., *Artificial Life,* Santa Fe Institute Studies in the Sciences of Complexity, vol. 6 (Reading, Mass.: Addison-Wesley, 1989). [Hereafter abbreviated as *A-Life I.*]

Christopher G. Langton, Charles Taylor, J. Doyne Farmer, and Steen Rasmussen, eds., *Artificial Life II,* Santa Fe Institute Studies in the Sciences of Complexity, vol. 10 (Reading, Mass.: Addison-Wesley, 1992). [Hereafter abbreviated as *A-Life II.*]

The hundreds of written sources consulted include the following, chosen for direct relevance to passages in *Artificial Life.* In a few cases, I have selected sources for further reading in a subject.

PROLOGUE: *In Silico*

PAGE

1 **"patterns of ones and zeros":** Thomas Pynchon, *Vineland* (Boston: Little, Brown, 1990), pp. 90–91.

3 **PolyWorld:** Larry Yaeger has described his simulation in "Computational Genetics: Physiology, Metabolism, Neural Systems, Learning, Vision, and Behavior; or, PolyWorld: Life in a New Context," unpublished.

5 **"a new class of organisms":** J. Doyne Farmer and Alletta d'A. Belin, "Artificial Life: The Coming Evolution," in *A-Life II*, p. 815.

Eddington: A. S. Eddington, quoted in John D. Barrow and Frank J. Tipler, *The Anthropic Cosmological Principle* (Oxford: Oxford University Press, 1986), p. 613.

7 **Smith:** John Maynard Smith, *The Problems of Biology* (Oxford: Oxford University Press, 1986), p. 7.

Mayr: Ernst Mayr, *The Growth of Biological Thought* (Cambridge: Belknap/ Harvard, 1982), p. 55.

8 **Sagan:** Carl Sagan, "Life," *Encyclopaedia Britannica*, 15th ed., *Macropaedia*, vol. 10, p. 893.

Sober: Elliott Sober, "Learning from Functionalism—Prospects for Strong Artificial Life," in *A-Life II,* p. 763.

9 **carbaquists:** Gerald Feinberg and Robert Shapiro, *Life Beyond Earth: The Intelligent Earthling's Guide to the Universe* (New York: Morrow, 1980), p. 25.

life-as-it-could-be: Christopher G. Langton, "Artificial Life," in *A-Life I*, p. 2.

The Promised Land

PAGE

11 **"promised land":** Stanislaw M. Ulam, *Adventures of a Mathematician* (New York: Scribner, 1976), p. 242.

PAGE

13 **"a sadness":** Ulam, *Adventures,* p. 239.

Von Neumann: Biographical sources about von Neumann include Steven J. Heims, *John von Neumann and Norbert Wiener: From Mathematics to the Technologies of Life and Death* (Cambridge: MIT Press, 1980); Stanislaw M. Ulam, *Adventures,* and "John von Neumann 1903–1957," *Bulletin of the American Mathematical Society* 64 (1958): 1–49; H. H. Goldstine, *The Computer from Pascal to von Neumann* (Princeton: Princeton University Press, 1972); Clay Blair, Jr., "Passing of a Great Mind," *Life,* February 25, 1958; and William Aspray, *John von Neumann and the Origins of Modern Computing* (Cambridge: MIT Press, 1990).

"a perfect instrument": Eugene Wigner, quoted in Heims, *Von Neumann and Wiener,* p. 26.

14 **"I have sometimes wondered":** Hans Bethe, quoted in Blair, "Passing of a Great Mind."

demigod: Goldstine, *Computer,* p. 176.

15 **"I shudder at the thought":** Letter to George Gamow, July 25, 1955, Heims, *Von Neumann and Wiener,* p. 154.

Hixon Symposium: The lecture is reprinted as "General and Logical Theory of Automata," in A. H. Taub, ed., *John von Neumann: Collected Works* (Elmsford, N.Y.: Pergamon, 1963), vol. 5, pp. 288–328.

"hanging on the tail of a kite": "Dr. Gerard" addressed the comment to von Neumann, as transcribed in "General and Logical Theory," p. 320.

16 **"weariness of the body":** Klara von Neumann, in John von Neumann, *The Computer and the Brain* (New Haven: Yale University Press, 1958), p. x.

17 **"reproductive potentialities of the machines":** Letter to Norbert Wiener, Heims, *Von Neumann and Wiener,* pp. 212–13.

PAGE

19 mechanical devices: The best reference to mechanical automata is Alfred Chapius and Edmond Dreoz, *Automata* (Neuchatel: Editions du Griffon, 1958). Sumptuously illustrated, it discusses automata dating from ancient times, with a particularly detailed description of Vaucanson's duck.

"an artificial duck": Chapius and Dreoz, *Automata,* p. 233.

Goethe: Quoted in Chapius and Dreoz, *Automata,* p. 234.

Das freie Wort: Quoted in Chapius and Dreoz, *Automata,* p. 238–39.

20 newspaper account: *Allgemeine bayrische Kronik,* quoted in Chapius and Dreoz, *Automata,* p. 239.

21 Driesch: Horst H. Freyhofer, *The Vitalism of Hans Driesch* (Frankfurt: Peter Lang, 1987). Also, an excellent overview of Driesch's views and vitalism in general is found in the vitalism entry in the *Encyclopedia of Philosophy,* ed. Paul Edward (New York: Macmillan/Free Press, 1967).

"A true doctrine": Hans Driesch, *The History and Theory of Vitalism* (London: Macmillan, 1914), p. 149.

22 Turing machine: A particularly succinct explanation of Turing machines is found in A. K. Dewdney, *The Turing Omnibus* (Rockville, Md.: Computer Science Press, 1989), which also includes technical explanations of other computational exercises central to artificial life.

25 a fellow Hungarian: From Aspray, *John von Neumann.* This book is an excellent source in general for information on von Neumann's early computer experience and automata theories.

28 "the description of this automaton": Von Neumann, "General and Logical Theory," pp. 317–18.

29 "the basic design of every microorganism": Freeman Dyson, *Disturbing the Universe* (New York: Harper & Row, 1979), p. 35.

"aim of von Neumann's reflections": L. S. Penrose, "Self-Reproducing Machines," *Scientific American,* June 1959, p. 105.

PAGE

29 "Possibly such a a system": Walter R. Stahl, "Self-Reproducing Automata," *Perspectives in Biology and Medicine,* Spring 1965, p. 378.

31 Jacobsen: Homer J. Jacobsen, "On Models of Reproduction," *American Scientist,* September 1985, pp. 255–84.

pieces of plywood: The system is described in Penrose, "Self-Reproducing Machines," pp. 105–13.

32 "Artificial Living Plants": Edward F. Moore, "Artificial Living Plants," *Scientific American,* October 1956, pp. 118–225.

33 Dyson: Dyson, *Universe,* pp. 194–204.

"Santa Claus machines": From Robert A. Freitas, Jr., and William P. Gilbreath, eds., *Advanced Automation for Space Missions,* NASA Conference Publication 2255 (Springfield, Va.: National Technical Information Service, 1982), p. 227. [Hereafter abbreviated as *NASA.*] This includes the work of the Self-Replicating Systems Concept Team.

34 "It is safe to predict": Dyson, *Universe,* p. 200.

36 "a fundamentally feasible goal": *NASA,* p. 201. Chapt. 5 in the study, "Replicating Systems Concepts: Self-Replicating Lunar Factory and Demonstration" (pp. 189–335), provides the background, blueprint, and hopes for the project.

39 "Reproductive probes could permit": *NASA,* p. 231.

"It is not too early": *NASA,* p. 240.

40 "we cannot necessarily pull the plug": *NASA,* p. 242.

"we shall have to supply it with goals": *NASA,* p. 242.

41 "a concept of God?" *NASA,* p. 247.

"evolutionary dead end": *NASA,* p. 244.

42 Ulam . . . could recall: Ulam, *Adventures,* p. 32.

43 Von Neumann's cellular model: Von Neumann's most complete description of his automaton is presented in his posthumous *Theory of Self-*

PAGE

Reproducing Automata (Urbana: University of Illinois Press, 1966), edited by Arthur W. Burks. Burks has a more succinct explanation in *Essays on Cellular Automata* (Urbana: University of Illinois Press, 1970), a collection of seminal papers on CAs that he edited.

45 Kemeny: John G. Kemeny, "Man Viewed as a Machine," *Scientific American,* April 1955, pp. 58–68.

Playing by the Rules

PAGE

47 "personoids": Stanislaw Lem, "The Experiment," *New Yorker,* July 24, 1978.

"the computer scientist's Great Work": Rudy Rucker, *CA Lab* (Sausalito, Calif.: Autodesk, 1989), p. 16.

49 Conway: In addition to personal interview, some biographical information was drawn from Gary Taubs, "A Mathematical Madness in Cambridge," *Discover,* August 1984, pp. 41–50.

one journalist: Taubs, "Mathematical Madness," p. 44.

52 Life: The universal computing aspect of Life is described in Elwyn R. Berlekamp, John Horton Conway, and Richard Guy, *Winning Ways for Your Mathematical Plays* (New York: Academic Press, 1982). Also, William Poundstone, *The Recursive Universe* (New York: Morrow, 1985), is an excellent, well-illustrated primer for the game.

56 Gardner: Martin Gardner, "Mathematical Games: The Fantastic Combinations of John Conway's New Solitaire Game 'Life,' " *Scientific American,* October 1970, pp. 112–17. This and other Gardner writings on Life were reprinted in Gardner, *Wheels, Life, and Other Mathematical Amusements* (New York: Freeman, 1983).

58 checkered career: I know of no comprehensive history of CAs. Helpful sources include Necia G. Cooper, "An Historical Perspective: From Turing and von Neumann to the Present," *Los Alamos Science* 9 (Fall 1983): 22–27; Robert Wright, *Three Scientists and Their Gods* (New York: Times

PAGE

Books, 1988); Poundstone, *Recursive Universe;* Ulam, *Adventures;* Rucker, *CA Lab;* Tommaso Toffoli and Norman Margolus, *Cellular Automata Machines* (Cambridge: MIT Press, 1987); and my own article "The Portable Universe," *Whole Earth Review,* Summer 1985, pp. 42–48.

58 one of these caretakers: Tommaso Toffoli, "Cellular Automata Mechanics," master's thesis, University of Michigan, 1977, p. iii.

59 "In like manner, Darwin": C. S. Peirce, *The Philosophical Writings of Peirce* (New York: Dover, 1955), p. 7.

60 Codd: E. F. Codd, *Cellular Automata* (New York: Academic Press, 1968).

61 "What are cellular automata worth saving for?" Toffoli, "Cellular Automata Mechanics," p. iii.

63 Fredkin: In addition to interviews, information about Ed Fredkin was drawn from Wright, *Three Scientists,* and my own *Hackers: Heroes of the Computer Revolution* (New York: Doubleday, 1984).

64 Feynman: Richard Feynman, "Simulating Physics with Computers," *International Journal of Theoretical Physics* 21, nos. 6–7 (1982): 467–88.

66 "One could imagine Timothy Leary": Wright, *Three Scientists,* p. 23.

Wolfram: Of many papers by Stephen Wolfram about CAs and general complexity, the lay reader might best appreciate "Cellular Automata," *Los Alamos Science* 9 (Fall 1983): 2–21; "Cellular Automata as Models of Complexity," *Physica* 10D(1984): 1–35,; and "Computer Software in Science and Mathematics," *Scientific American,* September 1984, pp. 188–203.

75 Packard wrote a program: The snowflake program is described in Wolfram, "Computer Software in Science and Mathematics," as well as in Norman Packard's more technical "Lattice Models for Solidification and Aggregation," in *Proceedings of the First International Symposium for Science on Form,* Tsukuba University (Japan), December 1985.

76 "The motion of a flock of birds": Craig Reynolds, "Flocks, Herds, and Schools: A Distributed Behavioral Model," *Computer Graphics* 21 (July 1987): 25.

PAGE

80 **"One serious application"**: Reynolds, "Flocks, Herds, and Schools," p. 32.

81 **"allelomimetic behavior"**: Jean-Louis Deneubourg and Simon Goss, "Collective Patterns and Decision-Making," *Ethology, Ecology, and Evolution* 1 (1989): 295–311.

Garage-Band Science

PAGE

85 **"The ultimate goal"**: Christopher G. Langton, "Studying Artificial Life with Cellular Automata," *Physica* 22D (1986): 120–49.

87 **Farmer:** In addition to personal interviews, biographical information on Farmer was drawn from Thomas A. Bass, *The Eudaemonic Pie* (Boston: Houghton Mifflin, 1985), including an account of how Farmer and friends used computers and complexity theory to gamble in roulette.

the group called itself a collective: The Santa Cruz Dynamical Systems Collective is vividly described in James Gleick, *Chaos: Making a New Science* (New York: Viking, 1987), pp. 243–72.

88 **"The Last Question"**: Reprinted in Isaac Asimov, *The Asimov Chronicles* (New York: Ace, 1990), vol. 3, pp. 101–16.

91 **"The purpose . . . is to bring together"**: J. Doyne Farmer and Norman H. Packard, "Evolution, Games and Learning: Models for Adaptation in Machines and Nature," in J. D. Farmer, A. Lapedes, N. H. Packard, and B. Wendroff, eds., *Evolution, Games and Learning* (Amsterdam: North-Holland, 1986), p. vii.

"What are the basic principles": Farmer and Packard, "Evolution, Games and Learning," p. viii.

92 **"the primary research instrument of the sciences"**: Heinz Pagels, *The Dreams of Reason* (New York: Simon & Schuster, 1988), p. 13.

"the '60s music scene": Farmer and Packard, "Evolution, Games and Learning," p. viii.

PAGE

99 loops: Langton's most complete description of loops is found in "Self-Reproduction in Cellular Automata," *Physica* 10D (1984): 135–44.

101 "I'm watching it now": Chris Langton, unpublished notebook.

104 vants: Christopher G. Langton, "Studying Artificial Life with Cellular Automata," *Physica* 22D (1986): 120–49.

105 "An ant, viewed as a behaving system": Herbert Simon, *The Sciences of the Artificial* (Cambridge: MIT Press, 1981), p. 64.

"give every appearance of accomplishing": E. O. Wilson, quoted in Langton, "Studying Artificial Life with Cellular Automata," p. 134.

107 "After a paper by Steve Wolfram": Chris Langton, unpublished notebook.

109 "the lambda (λ) parameter": Christopher G. Langton, "Life at the Edge of Chaos," in *A-Life II*, pp. 41–91.

117 A molecular biologist: Gerald Joyce, quoted by James Gleick, "Artificial Life: Can Computers Discern the Soul?" *New York Times*, September 29, 1987, p. C1.

119 "true flocking": Langton, "Artificial Life," in *A-Life I*, p. 33.

God's Heart

PAGE

121 "Many of the problems": J. D. Bernal, *The Origin of Life* (Cleveland, Ohio: World Publishing Co., 1967), p. 173. Bernal's emphasis.

123 Kauffman: The most complete explanation of Kauffman's work is found in Stuart Kauffman, *Origins of Order: Self-Organization and Selection in Evolution* (Oxford: Oxford University Press, 1992). He presents a more succinct version of his ideas in "Antichaos and Adaptation," *Scientific American*, August 1991, pp. 78–85.

origin of life: Some of the information was drawn from Bernal, *Origin of Life;* Robert Shapiro, *Origins: A Skeptic's Guide to the Creation of Life on*

PAGE

Earth (New York, Bantam, 1986); John Horgan, "In the Beginning," *Scientific American,* February 1991, pp. 114–25; Freeman Dyson, *Origins of Life* (Cambridge: Cambridge University Press, 1985); A. G. Cairns-Smith, *Seven Clues to the Origin of Life* (Cambridge: Cambridge University Press, 1985); Gerald F. Joyce, "RNA Evolution and the Origins of Life," *Nature,* March 16, 1989, pp. 217–24; and Francis Crick, *Life Itself* (New York: Simon & Schuster, 1981).

131 Stanley Miller: Miller's experiment has been recounted many times. The original publication was Stanley Miller and Harold Urey, "A Production of Amino Acids Under Possible Primitive Conditions," *Science* 117 (1953): 528–29. In "The First Laboratory Synthesis of Organic Compounds under Primitive Earth Conditions," Miller anecdotally recounts the episode; in Jerzy Neyman, ed., *The Heritage of Copernicus: Theories "Pleasing to the Mind"* (Cambridge: MIT Press, 1974), pp. 228–41.

132 "the single most significant step": Carl Sagan, quoted in Shapiro, *Origins,* p. 98.

"as big as the ocean": *Time,* quoted in Shapiro, *Origins,* p. 99.

"The problem . . . much more difficult": Miller, quoted in Horgan, "In the Beginning," p. 117.

134 Kauffman's theory: Stuart Kauffman, "Autocatalytic Sets of Proteins," *Journal of Theoretical Biology* 119 (1986): 1–24.

"functionally coupled, self-replicating entities": Charles Taylor, " 'Fleshing Out' Artificial Life II," in *A-Life II,* p. 28.

139 "Running equations through a computer": Miller, quoted in Horgan, "In the Beginning," p. 123.

141 "Roman goddess of natural productivity": Steen Rasmussen, Carsten Knudsen, Ramus Feldberg, and Morten Hindsholm, "The Coreworld: Emergence and Evolution of Cooperative Structures in a Computational Chemistry," *Physica* 42D (1990): 111–34.

145 "Aspects of Information, Life Reality, and Physics": Rasmussen later expanded and revised this paper and published it under the same title in *A-Life II*, pp. 767–74.

150 **"The selected molecule":** Debra L. Robertson and Gerald F. Joyce, "Selection in Vitro of an RNA Enzyme That Specifically Cleaves Single-Stranded DNA," *Nature*, March 29, 1990, pp. 467–68.

The Genetic Algorithm

PAGE

153 **"When man wanted to fly":** David Goldberg, "The Genetic Algorithm Approach: Why, How, and What Next?" from Kumpati S. Narendra, ed., *Adaptive and Learning Systems* (New York: Plenum, 1986).

156 **Wiener:** Biographical material on Wiener is found in Heims, *Von Neumann and Wiener*.

"a sympathetic hearing": Wiener, *Cybernetics*, 2nd ed. (Cambridge: MIT Press, 1961), p. 15.

159 **Holland's invention, the genetic algorithm:** Holland gave a complete, and rather technical, description of the GA in *Adaptation in Natural and Artificial Systems* (Ann Arbor: University of Michigan Press, 1975). The friendliest introduction to GAs is David Goldberg, *Genetic Algorithms in Search, Optimization and Machine Learning* (Reading, Mass.: Addison-Wesley, 1990).

"to improve performance": Goldberg, *Genetic Algorithms*, p. 6.

162 **"unnatural selection":** Goldberg, *Genetic Algorithms*, p. 90.

164 **"genetic algorithms . . . have often been attacked":** John Holland and David Goldberg, "Genetic Algorithms and Machine Learning," *Machine Learning* 3 (1988): 95.

168 **"Such efficient logic":** David Jefferson, Robert Collins, Claus Cooper, Michael Dyer, Margot Flowers, Richard Korf, Charles Taylor, and Alan Wang, "Evolution as a Theme in Artificial Life: The Genesys/Tracker System," in *A-Life II*, pp. 571–72.

PAGE

173 **"When I wrote the program I never thought"**: Richard Dawkins, *The Blind Watchmaker* (New York: Norton, 1987), p. 59.

174 **"On my wanderings"**: Dawkins, *Blind Watchmaker*, p. 60.

175 **"If we were, for example, to search"**: Goldberg, "Computer-Aided Pipeline Operation Using Genetic Algorithms and Rule Learning. Part I: Genetic Algorithms in Pipeline Optimization," *Engineering with Computers* 3 (1987): 35–45.

177 **"nucleotide bases found in molecules of DNA"**: John R. Koza, "Genetic Programming: A Paradigm for Genetically Breeding Populations of Computer Programs to Solve Problems," Stanford University Computer Science Department Technical Report STAN-CS-90-1314, June 1990, p. 117. Koza also describes his systems in "Genetic Evolution and Co-Evolution of Computer Programs," in *A-Life II*, pp. 603–30.

181 **Axelrod**: His work with the Prisoner's Dilemma is found in Robert Axelrod, *The Evolution of Cooperation* (New York: Basic Books, 1984), and "The Evolution of Strategies in the Iterated Prisoner's Dilemma," in *Research Notes in Artificial Intelligence* (Los Altos, Calif.: Morgan-Kauffman, 1987).

185 **"Recent developments in Eastern Europe"**: Stephanie Forrest and Gottfried Mayer-Kress, "Genetic Algorithms, Nonlinear Dynamical Systems, and Models of International Security," University of New Mexico Department of Computer Science Technical Report, 1990, p. 18.

Alchemists and Parasites

PAGE

189 **"Progress in physics"**: W. Daniel Hillis, *The Connection Machine* (Cambridge: MIT Press, 1989), p. 142.

193 **AI Winter:** An excellent discussion of artificial life's midlife crisis is offered in Stephen R. Graubard, ed., *The Artificial Intelligence Debate: False Starts, Real Foundations* (Cambridge: MIT Press, 1988). Hillis himself

contributed an essay with a-life implications, "Intelligence as an Emergent Behavior; or, the Songs of Eden," pp. 175–90.

197 "we should doubtless kill an animal": Niels Bohr made this comment in his 1932 "Light and Life" lecture. Quoted in Max Delbrück, *Mind from Matter?* (Palo Alto, Calif.: Blackwell, 1986), p. 236.

199 In this experiment, the measure of a Ramp's fitness: W. Daniel Hillis, "Co-Evolving Parasites Improve Simulated Evolution as an Optimization Procedure," in *A-Life II*, pp. 313–24.

200 sixteen integers in sixty-five exchanges: The history of the sorting network problem is copiously recounted in Donald Knuth, *Sorting and Searching*, Vol. 3, *The Art of Computer Programming* (Reading, Mass.: Addison-Wesley, 1973), pp. 227–29.

201 Red Queen hypothesis: Postulated in L. Van Valen, "A New Evolutionary Law," *Evolutionary Theory* 1 (1973): 1–30.

the presence of parasites might have been integral: William Hamilton, Robert Axelrod, and Reiko Tanese, "Sexual Reproduction as an Adaptation to Resist Parasites (A Review)," *Proceedings of the National Academy of Sciences* 87 (May 1990): 3566–73.

205 he discovered something remarkable: The results are discussed in W. Daniel Hillis, "Punctuated Equilibrium Due to Epistatis in Simulated Populations," unpublished.

211 Sims used a genetic paradigm: Karl Sims, "Artificial Evolution for Computer Graphics," *Computer Graphics* (July 1991): 319–28.

214 "These are powerful methods": Karl Sims, "Interactive Evolution of Dynamical Systems," to be published in *Proceedings of the First European Conference on Artificial Life* (Cambridge: MIT Press, 1992).

219 Tierra: The system is explained in detail in Thomas S. Ray, "An Approach to the Synthesis of Life," in *A-Life II*, pp. 371–408. Ray's work is also described in John Travis, "Digital Darwinism," *Science News*, August 10, 1991, pp. 88–90.

PAGE

226 **"the optimization technique":** Thomas S. Ray, "Evolution and Optimization of Digital Organisms," unpublished, p. 19.

229 **Hubbell:** Stephen P. Hubbell, quoted in Travis, "Digital Darwinism," p. 140.

"the first logical demonstration": Graham Bell, quoted in Malcolm Browne, "Lively Creature Blurs Definition of Life," *New York Times*, August 27, 1991, pp. C1, C8.

230 **This work has three important uses:** Letter from Graham Bell to Murray Gell-Mann, June 17, 1991.

New York Times: Browne, "Lively Creature," p. C8.

*Artificial Flora, Artificial Fauna,
Artificial Ecologies*

PAGE

231 **"It still takes a leap of faith":** Alvy Ray Smith III, "Introduction to and Survey of Polyautomata Theory," in Aristid Lindenmayer and Grzegorz Rozenberg, eds., *Automata, Languages, and Development* (Amsterdam: North-Holland, 1976), p. 405.

234 **L-systems:** Described at length in Aristid Lindenmayer and Przemyslaw Prusinkiewicz, *The Algorithmic Beauty of Plants* (New York: Springer-Verlag, 1990).

235 **ferns:** Pauline Hogeweg and Ben Hesper, "A Model Study on Biomorphological Description," *Pattern Recognition* 6 (1974): 165–97.

237 **"Geometric computation is a path":** Alvy Ray Smith, "Formal Geometric Languages for Natural Phenomena," Pixar Technical Memo 182 (San Rafael, Calif., 1987).

238 **fractal geometry:** As explained in the landmark work: Benoit Mandelbrot, *The Fractal Geometry of Nature* (New York: Freeman, 1977). An account of Mandelbrot's work for the lay reader is found in Gleick's *Chaos*.

PAGE

238 "graftals": Smith explains these in "Plants, Fractals, and Formal Languages," *Computer Graphics* 18 (July 1984): 1–10.

Oppenheimer's work: Peter Oppenheimer, "The Artificial Menagerie," in *A-Life I,* pp. 251–74.

240 embryonic development of an artificial fern: Martin J. M. de Boer, F. David Fracchia, and Przemyslaw Prusinkiewicz, "Analysis and Simulation of the Development of Cellular Layers," in *A-Life II,* pp. 465–84.

243 the following list of rules: John H. Holland, "Emergent Models," in Andrew Scott, ed., *Frontiers of Science* (Oxford: Blackwell, 1990), p. 117. A good description of classifier systems can also be found in Lashon B. Booker, David E. Goldberg, and John H. Holland, "Classifier Systems and Genetic Algorithms," *Artificial Intelligence* 40 (1989): 1–40.

247 an artificial creature in a classifier system: Lashon Booker's GOFER classifier system is described in Jean-Arcady Meyer and Agnes Guillot, "From Animals to Animats: Everything You Wanted to Know about the Simulation of Adaptive Behavior," Ecole Normale Supérieure Technical Report, September 1990.

The creature*: Stewart W. Wilson, "Knowledge Growth in an Artificial Animal," in Narendra, *Adaptive and Learning Systems,* pp. 255–66.

249 "the basic hypothesis of the animat approach": Stewart W. Wilson, "The Animat Path to AI," in Jean-Arcady Meyer and Stewart Wilson, eds., *From Animals to Animats: Proceedings of the First International Conference on the Simulation of Adaptive Behavior* (Cambridge: MIT Press, 1991), p. 16.

251 "What is life?": Mark A. Bedau and Norman H. Packard, "Measurement of Evolutionary Activity, Teleology, and Life," preprint, 1990, pp. 1–2. The paper appeared in final form in *A-Life II,* pp. 431–61.

254 His first experiment: Jefferson's predator-prey experiment is described in detail in Ed Regis, *Great Mambo Chicken and the Transhuman Condition* (Reading, Mass.: Addison-Wesley, 1990), pp. 199–204.

PAGE

256 "Examine the nearby environment": Charles E. Taylor, David R. Jefferson, Scott R. Turner, and Seth R. Goldman, "RAM: Artificial Life for the Exploration of Complex Biological Systems," in *A-Life I*, p. 280.

259 "The total behavioral repertory": Bert Hölldobler and Edward O. Wilson, *The Ants* (Cambridge: Harvard-Belknap, 1990), p. 358.

260 AntFarm: Robert J. Collins and David R. Jefferson, "AntFarm: Towards Simulated Evolution," in *A-Life II*, pp. 579–602.

267 "In the beginning era": David H. Ackley and Michael Littman, "Interactions Between Learning and Evolution," In *A-Life II*, pp. 501–2.

268 "The well-adapted action network": Ackley and Littman, "Interactions," p. 504.

270 a computer simulation of the Baldwin Effect: G. E. Hinton and S. J. Nowlan, "How Learning Can Guide Evolution," *Complex Systems* 1 (1987): 495–502.

"Computers, like microscopes": Ackley and Littman, "Interactions," p. 507.

Real Artificial Life

PAGE

271 "I wish to build": Rodney A. Brooks, "Intelligence Without Representation," unpublished, 1987, p. 7.

273 the glory days of the ninth floor: As recounted in Levy, *Hackers*, pp. 108–28.

278 "subsumption architecture": Explained in Rodney A. Brooks, "A Robust Layered Control System for a Mobile Robot," *IEEE Journal of Robotics and Automation*, March 1986, 14–23.

281 "Insects are not usually thought of as intelligent": Rodney A. Brooks, "Achieving Artificial Intelligence Through Building Robots," MIT AI Memo 899, May 1986. p. 7.

PAGE

282 **"when it hears [the sound]":** Brooks, "Achieving Artificial Intelligence," p. 9.

283 **"the strange richness":** W. Grey Walter, "An Imitation of Life," *Scientific American,* May 1959, p. 42.

284 **"It is quite restless":** Valentino Braitenberg, *Vehicles: Experiments in Synthetic Psychology* (Cambridge: MIT Press, 1986), p. 5.

285 **"Interest arises":** Braitenberg, *Vehicles,* p. 2.

286 **"there is great potential":** Mitchel Resnick, "Children, Computers, and Artificial Life," unpublished, p. 3.

"on a *mechanistic* level": Resnick, "Children, Computers," p. 4.

288 **"This last behavior":** Jonathan Connell, "The Omni Photovore," *Omni,* October 1988, p. 203.

291 **"computational ethology":** According to Michael Travers, "Agar: An Animal Construction Kit" (master's thesis, MIT, November 1988, p. 14), MIT computer scientist David Zeltzer coined the term.

"people and computers": Michael Travers, "Animal Construction Kits," in *A-Life I,* p. 428.

292 **"It's clear":** Travers, "Agar," p. 54.

artificial cockroach: Randall D. Beer describes his homemade insect in *Intelligence as Adapative Behavior: An Experiment in Computational Neuroethology* (San Diego, Calif.: Academic Press, 1990.

295 **Herbert:** The robot is described in detail in Jonathan Connell, "A Colony Architecture for an Artificial Creature," MIT AI Technical Report 1151, August 1989.

297 **Toto:** Described in Maja J. Mataric, "A Distributed Model for Mobile Robot Environment-Learning and Navigation," MIT AI Technical Report 1228, May 1990.

298 **Genghis:** Described in Colin Angle, "Genghis, a Six-Legged Autono-

PAGE

mous Walking Robot," S.B. thesis in electrical engineering and computer science, MIT, March 1989.

301 **"On Mars, gnats could be spread":** Rodney A. Brooks and Anita Flynn, "Fast, Cheap, and Out of Control," MIT AI Memo 1182, December 1989, pp. 11–12.

302 **"robot ecology":** The system is described in Luc Steels, "Cooperation Between Distributed Agents Through Self-Organisation," University of Brussels AI Memo 89-5, June 1989.

304 **a horde of mobile robots:** Rodney A. Brooks, Pattie Maes, Maja J. Mataric, Grinell More, "Lunar Construction Robots," IROS 1990 (IEEE International Workshop on Intelligent Robots and Systems).

The Strong Claim

PAGE

309 **"How dare you sport":** Mary Shelley, *Frankenstein* (New York, Bantam, 1981), p. 83.

312 **David Gerrold:** Noted in Eugene H. Spafford, "Computer Viruses—A Form of Artificial Life?" in *A-Life II*, pp. 727–45.

314 **Here was the way:** As printed in Fred Cohen, *Computer Viruses* (privately published, 1985), p. 83.

316 **the paper summarizing it:** Fred Cohen, "Computer Viruses: Theory and Experiments," *Computers and Security* 6 (1987): 22–35.

317 **Darwin:** Background on Darwin was drawn from A. K. Dewdney, *The Armchair Universe* (New York: Freeman, 1988); Katie Hafner and John Markoff, *Cyberpunk* (New York: Simon & Schuster, 1991); and especially $\aleph_0$, "Darwin," *Software—Practice and Experience* 2 (January–March 1972), pp. 92–96.

319 **Bob Thomas:** Hafner and Markoff, *Cyberpunk*, p. 280.

320 **"It can't be killed":** John Brunner, *The Shockwave Rider* (New York: Ballantine, 1975), pp. 251–52.

PAGE

321 "If one restarted": John F. Shoch and Jon A. Hupp, "The 'Worm' Programs—Early Experience with a Distributed Computation," *Communications of the ACM* 25 (March 1982): 175. The article was originally presented in 1980 as a technical paper.

Core War: A. K. Dewdney's writings on Core War are collected in *The Armchair Universe* (New York: Freeman, 1988).

323 "Some of the possibilities": Dewdney, *Universe,* p. 290.

324 Internet Worm: Many published sources deal with the Morris worm and other computer virus attacks. The best account of the Internet Worm is Hafner and Markoff, *Cyberpunk.* Those wishing a basic primer in computer viruses should look at Lance J. Hoffman, ed., *Rogue Programs: Viruses, Worms, and Trojan Horses* (New York: Van Nostrand Reinhold, 1990). Alan Lundell, *Virus! The Secret World of Computer Invaders That Breed and Destroy* (Chicago: Contemporary Books, 1989), views the phenomenon from the virus-writer's point of view.

325 Brain Virus: Background information on the Brain Virus was drawn from Philip Elmer-DeWitt, "Invasion of the Data Snatchers," *Time,* September 26, 1988, pp. 62–67. A detailed technical analysis is found in Andy Hopkins, "Dissecting the Pakistani Brain Virus," in Richard G. Lefkon, ed., *Safe Computing: Proceedings of the Fourth Annual Computer Virus and Security Conference* (New York: Nationwide Computing Corp., 1991), pp. 608–36. Also helpful was Harold Joseph Highland, "The Brain Virus: Fact and Fantasy," in Hoffman, *Rogue Programs,* pp. 159–64.

326 As of 1989: Eugene H. Spafford, Kathleen A. Heaphy, and David J. Ferbrache, "Further Information on Viruses," in Hoffman, *Rogue Programs,* p. 177.

"Strong Claim": Christopher G. Langton, "Introduction," in *A-Life II,* p. 19.

327 "Within such a system": Andrew Scott, *Pirates of the Cell* (New York: Blackwell, 1985), pp. 73–74.

"satisfies most, and potentially all": Farmer and Belin, "Artificial Life," p. 820.

PAGE

329 **"A virus is expelled"**: W. H. Murray, "The Application of Epidemiology to Computer Viruses," in Harold Joseph Highland, ed., *Computer Virus Handbook* (Oxford: Elsevier Advanced Technology, 1990), pp. 17–18.

330 **"I would also be disappointed"**: Spafford, "Computer Viruses," p. 744.

331 **Lawrence Livermore Laboratory**: John Markoff, "Computer Virus Fight Brings Fear on Risks," *New York Times*, October 7, 1989, p. 61.

"Viruses have two features": Harold Thimbleby, "Turning Viruses to Good Use?" *The Independent*, December 13, 1989.

332 **liveware**: The liveware concept is elucidated in Harold Thimbleby and Ian Witten, "Liveware: A Socially Mediated Mechanism for Managing Distributed Information," unpublished.

333 **"whenever a person wakes up a collector"**: Fred Cohen, "Friendly Contagion," *The Sciences*, September–October 1991, pp. 22–28.

334 **"Similar but considerably more tragic results"**: Spafford, "Computer Viruses," p. 744.

"It involves a threat": Farmer and Belin, "Artificial Life," p. 836.

335 **three laws of robotics**: Isaac Asimov, *I, Robot* (New York: Doubleday, 1950).

336 **"Environmentalists might perhaps regard"**: *NASA*, p. 239.

"Machines, being a form of life": J. P. Wesley, quoted in *NASA*, p. 245.

337 **"There is still something mysterious"**: Roger Penrose, *The Emperor's New Mind* (Oxford: Oxford University Press, 1989), p. 416.

Pattee: Howard H. Pattee, "Simulations, Realizations, and Theories of Life," in *A-Life I*, pp. 63–78.

338 **"biological organisms are autonomous"**: Peter Cariani, "On the

Design of Devices with Emergent Semantic Functions," Ph.D thesis, State University of New York, Binghamton, 1989, p. ix.

339 "Again and again I have heard": Wiener, *Cybernetics,* pp. 175–76.

340 "The day will come": Pagels, *Dreams of Reason,* pp. 330–31.

341 "By the middle of this century": Langton, "Artificial Life," p. 43.

342 "With the advent of artificial life": Farmer and Belin, "Artificial Life," p. 836. Emphasis in original.

343 "To make life itself": J. D. Bernal, *The World, the Flesh, and the Devil,* 2nd ed. (Bloomington: Indiana University Press, 1969), p. 45.

Moravec: Hans Moravec, *Mind Children* (Cambridge: Harvard University Press, 1988), p. 4.

clay-based crystals: Cairns-Smith, *Seven Clues*.

345 "What will these successors be like?" Farmer and Belin, "Artificial Life," p. 836.

346 "What of man's view": *NASA*, p. 247.

ACKNOWLEDGMENTS

Any lay observer attempting to chronicle the beginnings of a new scientific field is at mercy of his or her sources. Fortunately, the men and women of the artificial life movement have been without exception cooperative, gregarious, encouraging, generous—and merciful. (They are listed in the Notes and Sources.) Without their help this book would have been inconceivable. The months I spent with them changed the way I viewed the phenomenon of life, and I hope this book conveys some of that vision.

Chris Langton in particular has been selfless in acting as this outsider's guide. In countless interviews, phone calls, and electronic mailings, he has been consistently illuminating and candid. He would patiently explain and re-explain, disabusing me of wrong-headed notions and generally opening my eyes to the bottom-up, emergent style of artificial life.

I also conducted serial impositions, with similarly generous welcomes, on Rodney Brooks, Doyne Farmer, Danny Hillis, John Holland, David Jefferson, Stuart Kauffman, Chuck Taylor, and Stephen Wolfram. They were more than sources; they were teachers.

Parts or all of the manuscript were read by Brooks, Teresa Carpenter, Farmer, Hillis, Jefferson, Gerald Joyce, Langton, Tom Ray, Taylor, David Weinberg, and Wolfram.

I received help on the illustrations from David Ackley, Randall Beer, Rodney Brooks, Richard Dawkins, Martin de Boer, Rick Friedman, Danny Hillis, Gary Drescher, David Goldberg, John Holland, Chris Langton, Bill Lieberman, *Los Alamos Science* magazine, NASA, Norman Packard, Przemyslaw Prusin-kiewicz, Craig Reynolds, Karl Sims, Stephen Wolfram, and Larry Yaeger. Ronda Butler-Villa of the Sante Fe Institute offered valuable advice on acquiring permissions.

On my travels I benefited from the hospitality of Judy Brown and Henry Shonard, Larry Yaeger and Levi Thomas, Deborah Branscum and Ulf Molin, Susan Kare and Jay Tannenbaum, Deborah Wise and Brook Unger, George Thomas, Erfert and Jay Fenton, Bill Mandel, and Larry Barth. Chris Morgan kindly lent me his cherished copy of *Automata*. New York University's Loeb Library, the New York Public Library, and the Berkshire Atheneum were all invaluable resources.

From the start, Dan Frank has been a perceptive and supportive editor—all a writer could ask for. He was ably assisted by Alan Turkus. Transcription was beautifully performed by Wendy Scheir. My agent, Flip Brophy, was always there when needed, and sometimes just to chat. Most of all, I benefited from Teresa Carpenter's confidence and love.

Finally, I'd like to thank Andrew Max Levy, whose constant lessons in natural emergent behavior provided a rich counterpoint to the workings of artificial life.

ILLUSTRATION CREDITS

Page 79. Craig Reynolds.

Page 100. Chris Langton.

Pages 110–11. Chris Langton, Based on Christopher G. Langton, "Life at the Edge of Chaos," in Christopher G. Langton, Charles Taylor, J. Doyne Farmer, and Steen Rasmussen, eds., *Artificial Life II,* Santa Fe Institute Studies in the Sciences of Complexity, vol. 10 (Reading, Mass.: Addison–Wesley, 1992). [Hereafter *A-Life II*.]

Page 136. Richard Bagley/Doyne Farmer. Reprinted from "Evolution of a Metabolism," in *A-Life II*.

Page 164. David Goldberg. Based on Goldberg, *Genetic Algorithms in Search, Optimization and Machine Learning* (Reading, Mass.: Addison–Wesley, 1990).

Page 166. David Jefferson/Robert Collins/Claus Cooper/Michael Dyer/Margot Flowers/Richard Korf/Charles Taylor/Alan Wang, "Evolution as a Theme in Artificial Life," in *A-life II*.

Page 174. Richard Dawkins. Reprinted from Dawkins, *The Blind Watchmaker* (New York: Norton, 1987).

Page 206. Danny Hillis.

Page 236. Pauline Hogeweg/Ben Hesper. Reprinted from Lindenmayer and Prusinkiewicz, *Algorithmic Beauty of Plants,* by permission of Prusinkiewicz.

Page 245. John Holland.

Page 264. David Ackley/Michael Littman.

Page 294. Randall Beer. Based on Beer, *Intelligence as Adaptive Behavior* (San Diego, Calif.: Academic Press, 1990).

Page 306. Space rover: NASA. Mobot: IS Robotics.

INDEX

Index

Index

Index

Index